VANISHING LANDSCAPES

Vanishing Landscapes

Land and Life in the Tulare Lake Basin

WILLIAM L. PRESTON

University of California Press
Berkeley   Los Angeles   London

University of California Press
Berkeley and Los Angeles, California

University of California Press, Ltd.
London, England

Library of Congress Cataloging in Publication Data

Preston, William L.
  Vanishing landscapes.

  Bibliography
  Includes index.
  1. Tulare Lake region, Calif:—History.   2. Tulare
Lake region, Calif.—Description and travel.   3. Land
settlement—California—Tulare Lake region.   4. Natural
history—California—Tulare Lake region.   5. Agriculture—
California—Tulare Lake region—History.   I. Title.
F868.S173P73   333.73'09794'85   80-6055
ISBN 0-520-04053-8

Printed in the United States of America

1 2 3 4 5 6 7 8 9

CONTENTS

Preface   vii

Introduction   ix

1   The Material Foundation   1

2   The Yokuts: People of the Land   31

3   Invasion, Devastation, and Environmental Disruption,
    1770–1843   47

4   Manifest Destiny: Anglo Appraisal and Occupation,
    1844–1856   61

5   The Formative Era, Part I: Establishing the Modern
    Patterns of Settlement and Land Use, 1857–1871   85

6   The Formative Era, Part II: The Coming of the Railroad
    Brings Agricultural Intensification, 1872–1894   121

7   The Spread and Refinement of the New Order: The Era
    of Small-Farm Prosperity, 1895–1925   164

8   Rural Upheavals and the Rise of Agribusiness,
    1926–1945   190

9   Agribusiness and the Waning Regional Identity,
    1946 to the Present   211

10 Retrospect and Prospect   238

    Appendix I: Native Plants of the Tulare Lake Basin
    with Latin Binomials   245

    Appendix II: Native Animals of the Tulare Lake Basin
    with Latin Binomials   248

    Bibliography   251

    Index   271

PREFACE

My interest in the topographic[1] history of the Tulare Lake Basin stems in part from a childhood inability to visualize the early landscapes of the region as they were depicted in stories and local histories. I tried to remedy the gaps in my imagination by searching for souvenirs of these historical landscapes, often thinking that if enough contemporary evidences of past landscapes were recognized, a much better history of the basin could be written, one grounded in the tangibles of the land.

Childhood efforts to flesh out history evolved into an adult fascination with the region's relic landscapes and a sense of alarm at the continued destruction of native flora and fauna and already-meager cultural remnants. Armed with new histories and with the geographic perspective of landscape study, I now set out to tell an old story in a new way before it is too late to tell it well.

What processes were important in the transformation of this place from a wild oasis expressing the smooth harmonies of nature to a tamed landscape reflecting the rigid conceptions of people? What was the basin like in aboriginal times, when it supported the densest nonagricultural population in North America (Latta 1949, p. 9; Cook 1955a, p. 45; Kroeber 1961, p. 91)? How were the harmonious patterns of the Yokuts land transformed into an unbalanced, but flourishing, agricultural landscape—one greatly altered by human progress and technological domination, yet still with its own unique patterns of settlement and resources?[2] And of the agricultural landscapes of my childhood: have the changes brought by rapid population growth, increased commercialization, and environmental abuse destroyed the land's long-cherished facility for responding compatibly with the attentions of its occupants?

My questions, my fascinations, and my regrets culminate in this effort to examine the processes of land and life which have transformed my favorite place. By reconstructing its nature, its landscapes, and its regional character as they have changed through time, I hope also to provide the reader with a more complete picture than was previously available of the cultural-geographic story of the settlement of California as a whole.

1. The term *topography* is used here as it was by John Leighly in "Some Comments on Contemporary Geographic Method" (Leighly 1937), a usage in which it connotes not only the objective realities of a landscape but also its subjective content.

2. For example, Tulare County is consistently among the top four counties in the nation in terms of the annual value of its agricultural products. Its main rivals include Fresno and Kern counties, its neighbors to the north and the south, respectively.

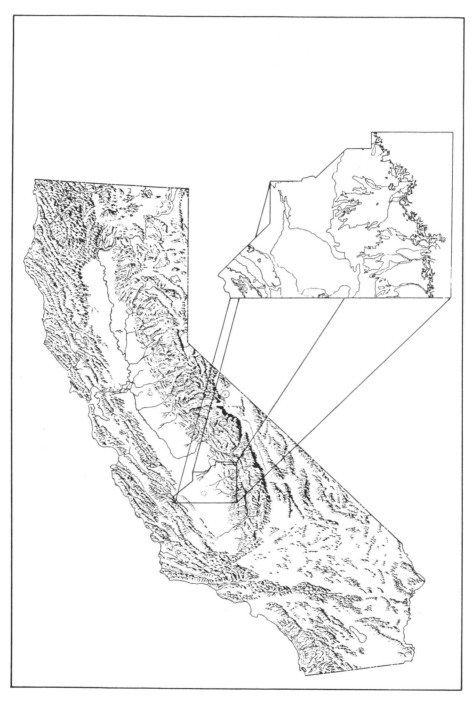

Figure 1. *The Tulare Lake Basin.* Located midway between San Francisco Bay and the Los Angeles Basin, the Tulare Lake Basin possesses a regional identity that has steadily diminished with the demise of Tulare Lake itself and the rise of human-dominated landscapes. (Base map: Beck and Haase 1974.)

INTRODUCTION

Every man's valley can be beautiful beyond the telling, if he lives in sympathy with his environment and heeds the vision of creative writers. (Powell 1948, p. 6)

In the southern San Joaquin Valley of California, midway between San Francisco Bay and the Los Angeles Basin, lies the dwindling remnant of a broad Pleistocene lake. Eastward lie the foothills of the High Sierra; westward, the Coast Range. A century ago Tulare Lake was known as the center of a distinct natural and cultural realm, the Tulare Valley, but the regional identity of the lake basin has steadily diminished with the demise of the lake itself and the rise of human-- dominated landscapes. Once upon a time Tulare Lake and its associated environments were the region's dominant landmarks; now these are subordinate to cultural creations.

The spatial scope of this study will not shrink through time as the regional image has done, but will focus throughout upon the larger Tulare Lake Basin: an area delimited on the north, west, and south by the boundaries of Tulare and Kings counties and on the east by vaguely determined but readily visible limits of cultivation (fig. 1). These boundaries encompassed sufficient natural and cultural homogeneity to prompt their recognition as lines of demarcation even when human minds and physical processes were still unencumbered by administrative influences and controls. Later, for the first half-century of American occupation, the basin was recognized as the core of the Tulare Valley, a region extending from the Kings River to the Tehachapis, which was for many years considered separate from the San Joaquin Valley to the North.

From the very beginning of this account, then, the focus of attention will be the Tulare Lake Basin itself; yet the quest for understanding of processes that affect the basin will at times lead far beyond the confines of the region itself.

In tracing the transformation of the Tulare Lake Basin from a natural to a cultural landscape, this story is fashioned from two perspectives: the ecological and the historical-geographic. The ecological perspective adopted here had its birth in the biological sciences, but its applicability in the social sciences has been widely recognized. In accordance with Julian Steward's model, a series of cultures can be identified, each composed of all the intricate interrelationships inherent in social and subsistence processes at a given time, and each super-imposed in turn upon the Tulare Lake Basin environments (Steward 1955). As the story unfolds, one culture is replaced by a new one (as when a group of interlopers gains regional dominance, or when tech-nologies and livelihoods change rapidly). At times the local culture may be only a microcosm of a much larger cultural world; at times it displays a distinct provincialism. Always, however, the culture changes through time as relationships among people, and between people and their environment, are reoriented in response to local and external pressures and influences.

Cultural anthropologists, including Steward, are traditionally con-cerned with changes in *culture* precipitated by changing relationships between humans and the land. Geographers share this concern but are also interested in the effects of cultural changes *upon the land*. Sub-sistence technology is viewed as a medium through which changes in values, attitudes, and beliefs filter down to and act upon the landscape. From an ecological and historical-geographic perspective, then, this story traces the tangible areal expression of repeated cultural reorienta-tions within the Tulare Lake Basin. It describes the changing character of the land in response to changes in the lives that fashion it.

Drawing on inspiration from Donald Meinig (*The Great Columbia Plain*, 1968; *Southwest: Three Peoples in Geographical Change*, 1971), I will focus upon the evolving *regional character* of the Tulare Lake Basin. The basin may be viewed as a broad stage upon which human actors play—as a whole and coherent region; yet it should not be imagined as a uniform setting. The diverse subregions of the basin have responded differently to natural and cultural processes and in so responding have changed the processes themselves. Thus at intervals I will interrupt the regional story to examine subregional responses in detail.

Although I am primarily concerned with examining the land's sensitivity to changing natural and cultural conditions as expressed in the landscape, I will also consider human sensitivities: the responses, perceptions, and evaluations of travelers and settlers who looked out upon the Tulare Lake Basin at various times during its development. To understand the regional character of past periods, "the land must be perceived through the eyes of its former occupants, from the standpoint of their needs and capacity" (Sauer 1941, p. 362). I have gleaned a retrospective view directly from written accounts (journals, letters, novels) and indirectly by extrapolation from past settlement patterns, local histories, and a variety of maps. I have also integrated passages from creative authors where they fill gaps in observation or eloquently convey a feeling for the geographic expressions of land and life in the basin.

1

The
Material
Foundation

Geological History

The bone of an animal, a shell, a piece of charcoal, or a bit of wood,
brought from the hitherto-unexplored depths of the solid earth, assumes
the character of a monument of the past—a veritable medal of creation.
(Barton 1874).

Thriving environments, some aquatic and some extremely arid,
developed in turn in the Tulare Lake Basin long before human inhabitants arrived. Each prehistoric environment added new materials and
new character to the region, and the physiography and resources of the
basin reflect those "ghost ecosystems." The organization and appearance of human-dominated landscapes likewise reflect parameters and
resources that are products of the geological history of the basin.

Until about 140 million years ago, in the Jurassic period, there was no Tulare Lake Basin—nor even a Great Central Valley—in what is now California. The region constituted only a small portion of a broad, shallow sea floor that received eroded materials from surrounding uplands long since destroyed. The history of the basin begins later, in the Cretaceous period, when a huge batholith of crystalline rock was intruded into the eastern portion of the sea. This batholith was exposed as a mountain range that abutted the fluctuating shoreline well to the west of the present Sierra Nevada.

For ninety million years the spent residues of land and life in these highlands were carried to the western sea by ancient streams, and they settled as a continuous sedimentary pavement on the sea floor. Regional depression and downwarping kept pace with sedimentation, and the sea did not fill with deposits. Much later these materials would be exposed in the Franciscan Formation of the Coast Range, where people could gain access to the fossil and mineral wealth contained in the sediments (Jennings 1953, p. 293). The Sierra batholith and its overlying sediments would likewise yield great quantities of mineral resources (including gold) that would dramatically influence the nature of basin settlement.

About fifty million years ago, in the Eocene epoch, the sequence of erosion and deposition was interrupted. The western edge of the sea floor folded and warped into the geographical forerunner of the Coast Range. These peaks emerged briefly into a world of tropical climate and lush forests and then, yielding to erosion, became once again part of the sea floor west of the Sierra batholith. As subsequent layers of material were deposited upon them, the residues of this and later forest eco-systems metamorphosed into the oils, tars, and gases so valued by basin inhabitants. Marine deposition continued, with occasional interruptions, for the next thirty-seven million years.

By the late Miocene, about thirteen million years ago, the Sierra batholith had been eroded to a low, westward-sloping plain. Renewed uplift of several thousand feet displacement along faults on the eastern side of the batholith steepened the westward tilt of the plain dramatically, creating the Sierra Nevada; the Central Valley lay as a broad coastal plain between the Sierras and the sea (Davis et al. 1959, p. 38). Folding, faulting, and volcanic activity during the next ten million years (until the Pleistocene) isolated the Tulare Lake Basin forever from direct association with marine environments and processes, but fossil reminders of the early marine condition (including brackish fossil water) still remain, encased within twenty-five thousand feet or more of sediments or exposed as surface outcroppings along the western and eastern edges of the basin (fig. 2).

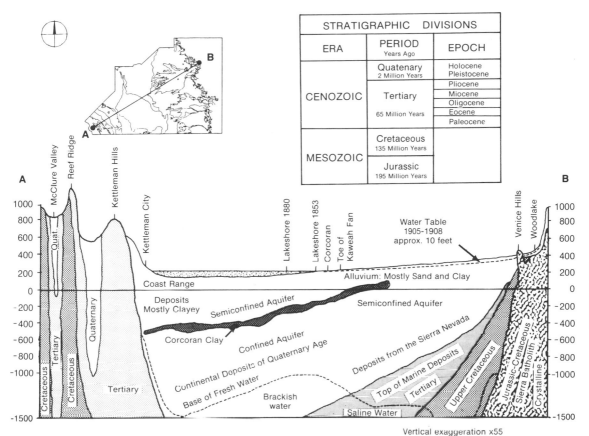

Figure 2. *Geologic and Hydrologic Cross Section of the Tulare Lake Basin.* Between the folded sedimentary rocks of the Kettleman Hills and the Sierra Nevada batholith, thousands of feet of sediments have filled the basin, providing numerous water-bearing layers (*aquifers*) that have been tapped by farmers for irrigation. (Sources: Jennings 1953; Mendenhall 1908; Davis et al. 1959; Lofgren and Klausing 1969; Prokopovich and Bateman 1975; Rodner 1949.)

The birth of the Coast Range during the Pleistocene epoch brought fresher water and terrestrial conditions. Thenceforth the valley trough held great salty bays and a series of brackish or freshwater lakes. Commencing about two million years ago, an especially large and persistent lake filled the southern reaches of the valley. This great-grandfather of Tulare Lake accumulated a peculiar layer of very fine diatomaceous clay sediments (*Corcoran clay*) from 10 to 150 feet thick (Cooper 1968, pp. 147–148). As the regional climate and topography changed, these clays were buried as a distinct lens beneath new materials. Fresh water from rainfall and Sierra runoff became trapped beneath this impervious clay lens, and eventually, when farmers came to settle the basin, the ancient subterranean waters influenced patterns of settlement and livelihood. The abundance of groundwater beneath the basin is due in part to glacial meltwater and pluvial climate during the Pleistocene; glacial advances and retreats in the Sierra Nevada also contributed immense quantities of fine-grained sediments to the basin, altering regional topography and providing the basis for development of rich soils.

As the ancestors of today's rivers brought great quantities of sediment from the mountains, the highlands flanking the basin were carved and shaped into a variety of landforms: hills, alluvial fans, terraces, canyons, and lake basins. These were accentuated as the earth forces responsible for the troughlike setting of the basin were reactivated during the Pleistocene. A major uplift of the Sierra Nevada steepened alluvial fans and terraces on the east side of the basin and accelerated erosional processes there. North of Porterville, Pleistocene erosion completely removed Tertiary sediments, and recent sedimentary layers directly overlie ancient granites and metamorphics; this lack of Tertiary sediments sets the basin apart from other Central Valley regions (Mendenhall, Dole, and Stabler 1916, p. 18). Major folding and faulting also accentuated the Coast Range and transformed its smooth eastern slope—the western flank of the basin—into a series of escarpments, anticlines, and synclines. As a result of these late changes, the Tulare Lake Basin became structurally differentiated from other Great Central Valley environments. Further downwarping produced a topographic basin with interior drainage, a well-defined basin-within-a-valley, its lowest reaches still filled by a great pluvial lake (Davis et al. 1959, p. 29).

The Natural Environment

It was a region of loneliness, emptiness, truth and dignity. It was nature at its proudest, driest, loneliest and loveliest. (Saroyan 1937, p. 36)

By the late Pleistocene, when people first came to the basin, the region's physical structure had become much as it is today: a trough between parallel mountain ranges that trend northwest to southeast. Surface features still changed in response to extremes in temperature and precipitation at the close of the Pleistocene, but soon conditions very similar to contemporary ones prevailed.

The basin's mid-latitude, west coast location places it in a zone of Mediterranean-type climate: rainfall is the most marked index of seasonality. During the summer season, a large and stable subtropical high-pressure cell dominates regional weather patterns, bringing several months of dry weather. Because the Coast Range thwarts direct entry of sea breezes or coastal fog, the basin experiences greater extremes of temperature and drought than adjacent coastal areas. Indeed, an early Franciscan visitor likened the basin in summer to "a huge broiler, where the sun rises, fixing his hot stare on the world, and stares throughout the day" (in Smith 1925), and a century later a basin promoter conceded, "It has the reputation of being a hot place" (Nordhoff 1872, p. 198). At ground level in summertime, northwesterly winds prevail (fig. 3), but they seldom exceed fifteen miles per hour. Summer in the basin is hot, dry, still, and dusty: "Every morning in July the sun streamed pure and white from the mountains, and tumbled in the dust of red gold at evening. There was no variation, no clouds but those like illusionary distant mountains on the horizon, no wind but the clean dry wind which followed the sun. . . . [By late summer] the blue haze was coming into the air, and the sunlight was softer, more golden" (Baker 1931, pp. 82, 190).

Summer leads gradually to fall, a subtle season in the basin, "the period between seasons . . . when the natural forces seemed to hang suspended. There was no rain, there was no wind, there was no growth, no life; the very stubble had no force even to rot. The sun alone moved" (Norris 1903, p. 14).

As the subtropical high-pressure cell weakens and shifts southward, the San Joaquin Valley begins to experience the more varied weather patterns associated with the North Pacific. Cyclonic storms pass through in winter, but most have already spent their fury on the windward slopes of the Coast Range; total winter rainfall on the valley floor rarely exceeds ten inches (figs. 4 and 5). Most rain comes from a few dramatic storms, such as the valley storm described by John Steinbeck in *The Grapes of Wrath*:

> Over the high coast mountains . . . the gray clouds marched in from the ocean. The wind blew fiercely and silently. . . . The clouds came in brokenly, in puffs, in folds, in gray crags; and they piled up together and settled low over the west and then the wind stopped and left the clouds deep and solid. The rain began with gusty showers, pauses and downpours, and then gradually it settled to a single tempo, small drops and a steady beat, rain that was gray to see through, rain that cut midday light to evening. . . . For two days the earth drank the rain, until the earth was full. Then puddles formed, and in the low places little lakes formed. . . . At last the mountains were full, and the hillsides spilled into the streams, built them to freshets, and sent them roaring down the canyons into the valleys. The rain beat on steadily. (Steinbeck 1939, p. 589)

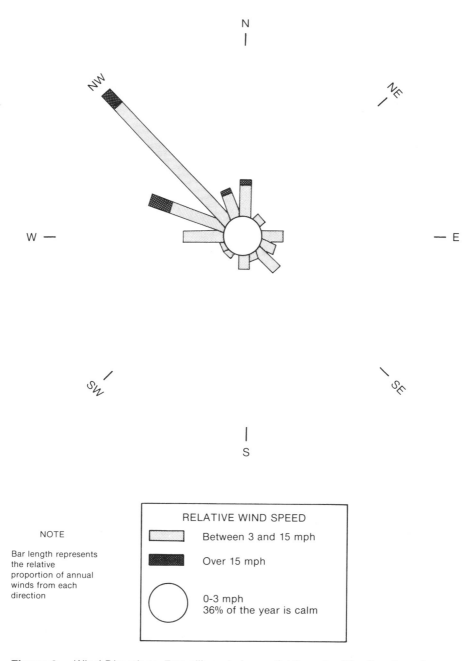

Figure 3.   *Wind Directions*. Prevailing winds parallel the axis of the San Joaquin Valley, blowing from the northwest to the southeast 65 percent of the time, although wind direction frequently reverses in winter. Wind speeds are usually low; the highest velocities occur in April and May, the lowest in November. (Source: U.S. Weather Bureau, Chandler Airport, Fresno.)

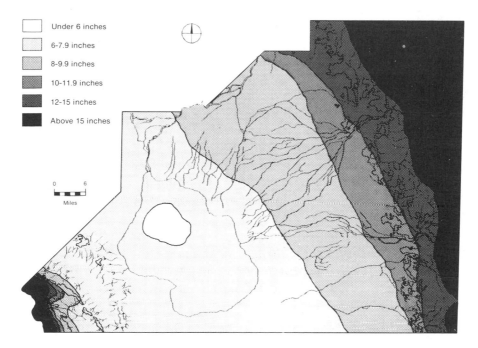

Figure 4.   *Average Annual Precipitation.* Annual rainfall on the floor of the basin varies from less than six inches near the trough to more than fourteen inches near the foothills. In the hills and mountains bordering the basin, average annual rainfall is much greater. (Source: State Department of Water Resources 1958.)

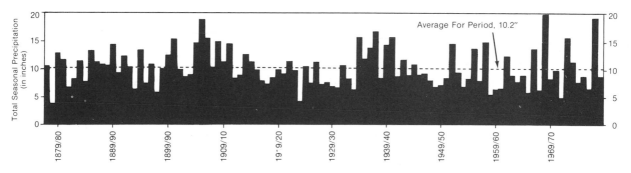

Figure 5.   *Pattern of Precipitation in the Tulare Lake Basin as Exemplified at Visalia for the Period 1877–78 through 1978–79.* Although the average for this period is 10.2 inches per year, actual rainfall varied from about 4 inches in 1879–80 to more than 19 inches in 1968–69. (Sources: U.S. Weather Bureau, Chandler Airport, Fresno; Bookman and Edmonston 1972.)

As storms move eastward, most of their remaining moisture falls on the western slopes of the Sierra Nevada. Mountain rainfall quickly reaches the basin as surface and subsurface runoff, but as much as forty inches of precipitation is stored annually in the Sierra snowpack, to be released to the basin during warmer and drier months. Sierra runoff is indeed far more important than direct precipitation in the basin's hydrologic budget.

In between storms, winter surface winds are usually of low velocities. As in other seasons, most are northwesterly, but warm southeasterlies sometimes occur. Winter temperatures are mild, though often colder than in coastal California; because of the effects of cold-air drainage from surrounding highlands and the rapid radiational cooling permitted by clear skies, freezing temperatures occasionally persist for extended periods on the basin floor. Air drainage and radiational cooling also raise relative humidity, generating ground, or "tule," fogs in low-lying areas. Under extremely stable conditions, a dense layer of fog 200 to 500 feet thick, "a thick, ghostwhite mist" (Austin 1927, p. 150), may blanket the basin continuously for as long as three weeks. Fog is more often a daily affair, dissipating by late morning. Suddenly, sometime in March, it is spring. Days grow longer and warmer, and the basin becomes wetter as Sierra runoff courses down. Then, just as quickly, it is summer again.

Within this general regime, there are important local variations in climate. Average annual rainfall ranges from six inches in the rain shadow of the Coast Range to more than fourteen inches on the low Sierra foothills (fig. 4). Temperature also varies from east to west, usually decreasing with increased elevation toward the Sierra; air drainage and advection further complicate microclimatic patterns (fig. 6a and b). Mean January temperatures in the basin range between 32° and 56°F; mean July temperatures range between 60° and 102°F. Extreme temperatures as low as 20°F in January and well above 105°F in July are common. Prevailing winds parallel the axis of the valley and are of low-to-moderate velocities; spring is the gustiest season, and fall is the calmest. Extremes of precipitation, temperature, and wind are all temporary occurrences within a mild climate: most days are pleasant and clear.

Runoff from Sierra snowmelt and cyclonic storms provides water to the basin's streams, which flow toward Tulare Lake. The interactions of surface runoff and geologic structure have produced a series of distinct surface landforms through the erosion, sorting, deposition, and reworking of sediments. Because of the greater catchment area afforded by the Sierra Nevada, more runoff and alluvium enter from the east than from the west, and the basin is thus asymmetrical in cross section, its

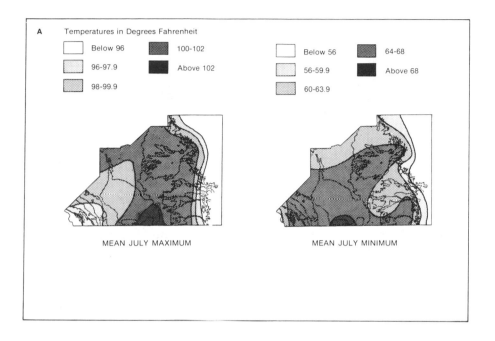

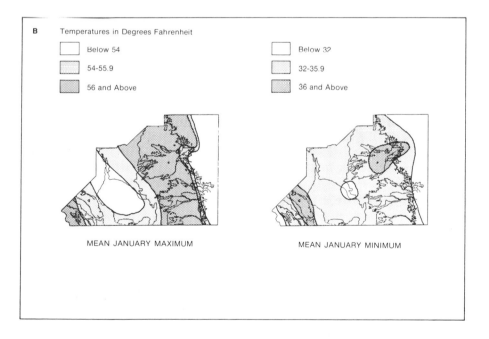

Figure 6a, b.   *Mean Temperatures*. Like rainfall, temperature varies from east to west but usually decreases with elevation. Air drainage and advection further complicate this pattern. Mean maximum temperatures exceed 100 degrees F in most of the basin in July; mean January temperatures drop below freezing only in limited parts of the basin. (Source: U.S. Weather Bureau, Chandler Airport, Fresno.)

lowest elevations close to the western flank (fig. 7). New alluvium is deposited by streams as fans or deltas overlying older valley fill washed down to the basin long ago, except on the upper slopes of the east side, where renewed uplift has caused Sierra streams to cut downward into older deposits. Toward the valley trough, recent alluvium has been deposited more uniformly on top of older fill because no significant rejuvenation or downcutting preceded the current phase of deposition (Holmes and Eckmann 1916, p. 2424), and the basin floor appears quite flat. In contrast to the separate alluvial fans built by the streams of the east side, steep and rather continuous alluvial aprons have been built by the more erratic and torrential runoff from the Coast Range. Old valley fill remains exposed in a few places on the flanks of the Kettleman Hills, but the west side is otherwise overlaid by an almost uniform layer of new alluvium.

The slopes of the Tulare Lake Basin may be divided into four basic landform units, each with its own characteristic soils and terrain. Resid-

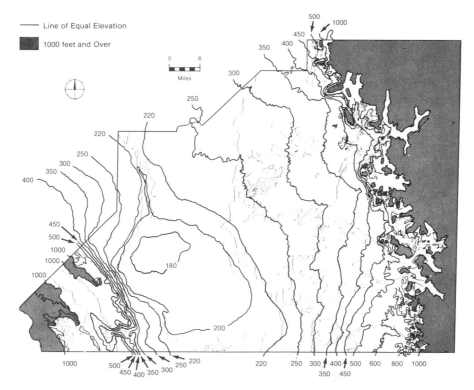

Figure 7. *Elevations.* From the lowest elevations of slightly less than 180 feet in the basin trough, elevation gradually increases to 1,000 feet in the east, where the eastern foothills rise above the alluvium. The basin is asymmetrical in cross section, the steepest slopes being those on the west side. (Source: Davis et al. 1959.)

ual slopes include various outcroppings of weathered, ancient basin and foothill materials and are prominent both along the flanks of the basin and as isolated relief features within the basin proper (fig. 8). Old valley fill, recent alluvium, and lacustrine slopes express depositional processes that have laid down successive layers of sediment within the basin. Old valley fill, a product of ancient deposition, lies as a nearly continuous foundation beneath more recent deposits, and it is also found at the surface where more recent deposition has not occurred (for example, at the margins of the basin and in areas far from streams). Recent alluvium is material that has been deposited along streams since the end of the Pleistocene. Lacustrine deposits occupy the lowest reaches of the basin, areas once covered by Tulare Lake.

As these slopes or surfaces have undergone climatic, biological, and cultural processes through time, their upper layers have been transformed into soils. Because the basin is moderately arid, calcification has been a dominant process in soil development: basin soils are

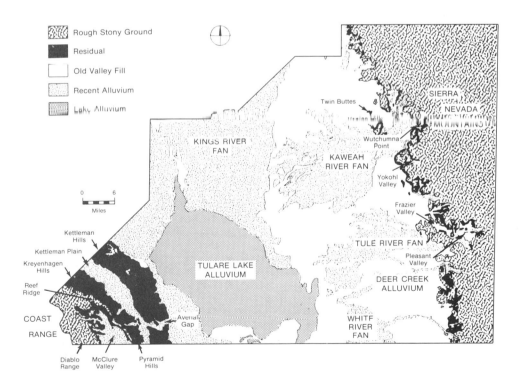

Figure 8. *Physiographic and Soil Provinces.* The surface of the Tulare Lake Basin may be divided into four basic geomorphic units, each with its own characteristic soils and terrain. These units include lake deposits, weathered older alluvium (*old valley fill*), residual materials, and the recent alluvium of alluvial fans and deltas. (Sources: Holmes and Eckmann 1916; Nelson 1917; Storie and Owen 1942.)

relatively deep, and low in organic content (thus somewhat nitrogen deficient) but otherwise well supplied with mineral nutrients. Many basin soils, particularly on the west side, contain salts that can retard plant growth by limiting water transfer if they accumulate in large proportions near the surface (Eaton 1935, pp. 24–25). Two kinds of alkaline compounds, white and black alkali, occur in the basin. Black alkali (highly concentrated sodium carbonate) is more harmful to plants than white alkali; it occurs east of the valley trough but is generally absent to the west because of the neutralizing influence of gypsum (calcium sulfate), which is common in Coast Range alluvium (Holmes and Eckmann 1916, p. 2524). Most plants native to the basin, as well as most introduced species, are unable to tolerate high concentrations of either white or black alkali (Bower and Freeman 1957, pp. 283–284). Prior to cultivation, alkali soils occurred only in poorly drained areas, particularly on lacustrine and low-lying recent alluvial deposits.

Although basin soils vary according to their age, location, and particular history, they may be broadly characterized in terms of their physiographic position. Soils overlying terrace deposits developed from weathered, unconsolidated material laid down by water in the distant past. Some old-valley-fill soils are now being eroded, while others are being buried under new deposits, yet in general they are very deep and fine textured (though in some cases gravelly near streams) and have well-developed profiles. Leaching has promoted the accumulation of lime deposits and the development of clay hardpan two to three feet thick at depths ranging from a few inches to about six feet below the surface. This impermeable hardpan rests upon a deep, permeable substratum. Near the foothills, long oxidation has imparted a reddish cast to old-valley-fill soils, which are thus known as *redlands* (Nougaret and Lapham 1928, p. 19). Deep and fertile, old-valley-fill soils were at first difficult to cultivate in places because of surface pattern of *mima mounds* one to five feet high and ten to over fifty feet across. Mima mounds appear to be a periglacial phenomenon formed under pluvial conditions in the late Pleistocene, and they are most conspicuous near the foothills (Nikiforoff 1941, pp. 38–41; fig. 9a b). In the basin, mima mounds and the intervening depressions are known collectively as *hog wallows*. Another distinctive terrain associated with old valley fill consists of gently undulating sand dunes about ten feet in height located just west of Dinuba. Generally, however, old-valley-fill soils are characterized by nearly level terrain: because they have long been isolated from stream activity, few surface channels or sloughs remain.

On gentle slopes along the eastern flank of the basin, where depositional slopes abut the erosional environments of the foothills, a narrow belt of residual soils has developed. Residual materials merge smoothly with *rough stony ground* (land too steep, rough, or rocky for

A

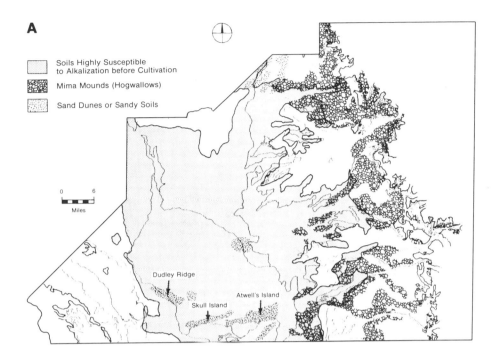

Soils Highly Susceptible
to Alkalization before Cultivation

Mima Mounds (Hogwallows)

Sand Dunes or Sandy Soils

0   6
Miles

Dudley Ridge

Skull Island

Atwell's Island

B

Figure 9. *Distribution of Hog Wallows, Sand Dunes, and Soils Susceptible to Alkalinity, before Farming, 1853.* (a) Most of the lower-lying alluvial soils were actually or potentially alkaline. Hog wallows were common on old valley fill and were most conspicuous near the foothills. Sand dunes were associated with the fluctuating shoreline of Tulare Lake and probably were formed on the southern end of the lake by the prevailing northwesterly winds. Sandy regions in the northeastern basin are ancient wind-borne deposits. (Sources: Storie and Weir 1940; Storie and Owen 1942; Scofield 1967.) (b) Hog-wallow land between Lindcove and Woodlake. (Courtesy of the California State Library.)

cultivation—taken here as the boundary of the basin) above and with alluvial deposits below, except where islandlike hills of resistant residual material protrude through depositional strata. The most prominent residual outcroppings are the Venice Hills (elevation 866 feet) and Twin Buttes (elevation 466 feet) on the east side of the basin north of the Kaweah Delta (fig. 8). In the western basin the Kettleman Hills interrupt the depositional terrain, rising gently as an anticlinal ridge 1,300 feet in elevation. Further west, beyond the Kettleman Plain, lie the Kreyenhagen Hills,[1] Reef Ridge, and the Pyramid Hills, residual outliers of the Coast Range. Because of scant vegetative cover, overgrazing, and greater diastrophic disruption, these western residuals are more severely gullied than their eastern counterparts. Soils that have developed on residual outcroppings are fairly shallow, with bedrock often encountered at depths of less than six feet, and soil profiles are weakly developed although subsoils tend to be more compact (Holmes and Eckmann 1916, pp. 2449, 2462). Residual soils are brown to reddish brown in color (because of protracted weathering), and they tend to retain water well. Gravel and bedrock outcrops remain on residual slopes where rock resistance or local deposition have thwarted weathering processes.

Because alluvial and lacustrine deposits are delivered to the Tulare Lake Basin primarily by streams that flow down from the Sierra Nevada (fig. 10), deposition is regulated by the effects of snowpack storage and melting. A brief discussion of basin stream regimes is thus an important preface to a description of alluvial and lacustrine soils. The regional low-water period usually begins in August, when most Sierra snowpack has melted and no rain has fallen for several months. Stream discharge remains low well into February, although precipitation increases steadily, because much potential runoff is entrapped as snowpack. Peak stream discharge is attained in April, May, and June. This regime affects deposition by all east-side streams, although their respective volumes and landscapes vary.

The perennial Kings River (named *Rio de los Santos Reyes* by Spanish explorers in 1805)[2] brings more surface water and alluvium to the basin than any other stream, accounting for at least half of the alluvial load delivered to the basin each year (fig. 11). The Kings enters

1. The Kreyenhagen Hills were named for the Kreyenhagen brothers, who arrived in the vicinity in the late 1860s to breed cattle.

2. The Kings River—or Rio de los Santos Reyes ("river of the holy kings")—was given its name by a party of Spanish explorers in 1805, according to Padre Munoz, whose diary describes the Moraga expedition of 1806 (Gudde 1965, p. 156). During the initial phase of American occupation it was known as the Wilmilche (Smith in Merriam 1923, pp. 376–377), then as the Lake Fork or River of the Lake (Fremont 1848, pp. 18, 363), but soon it became permanently known as the Kings River.

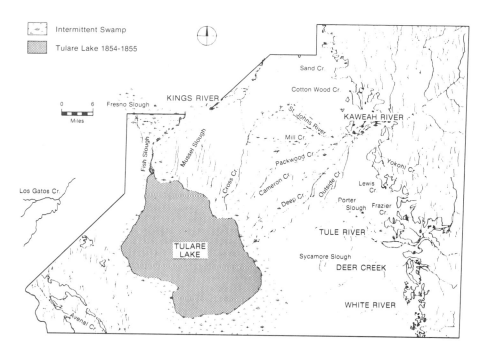

Figure 10. *Surface Hydrology, 1853.* Fed primarily by melting snow in the wetter climes of the Sierra Nevada, basin streams empty into a large, shallow lake. Swamps and swampy sloughs border the lake, especially in spring and early summer.

the Central Valley north of the basin, and in its upper reaches it is incised as deeply as twenty feet into old valley fill. Where it enters the basin, near the town of Kingsburg, the terrain is flat and low lying. The Kings splits into a number of distributaries, debouching its water and alluvium across a broad fan, or *delta*, that slopes about four feet per mile to the west and south.[3] The Kings fan coalesces on the west with Los Gatos Creek fan deposits, forming a ridge at the northern end of the basin that stands at least thirty feet higher than the lake bed. Under normal conditions, this low barrier reinforces the interior drainage of the basin, preventing Tulare Lake waters from entering the San Joaquin River to the north even when the lake surface stands several feet above the level of the upper San Joaquin River. Exceptionally wet years have, however, flooded the basin sufficiently to reverse the flow of Fish Slough and drain Tulare Lake northward via Fresno Slough. Derby, crossing the country in such a year, reported that "the ground between the Lake and the San Joaquin is entirely cut up by small sloughs which

3.   The Kings fan slopes four feet per mile, the Kaweah fan eight feet per mile, and the Tule fan nine feet per mile; the fans of White River and Deer Creek slope twelve feet per mile in their upper reaches.

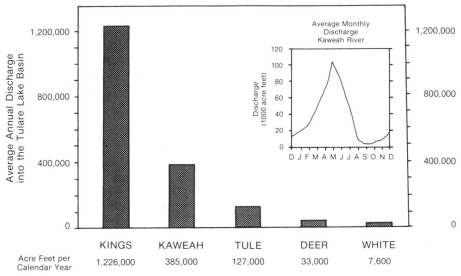

NOTE: One acre foot of water is enough water to cover one acre of land with water one foot deep.

Figure 11. *Average Annual Stream Discharge.* Stream discharge into the basin varies considerably; the flow of the Kings River is twice as large as that of all other basin streams combined. Although their respective volumes differ, the annual regimes of all basin streams are regulated by the effects of snowpack storage and melting. The regional low-water period usually begins in August, and peak discharge begins in March or April. (Source: U.S.D.I. Geological Survey 1966.)

have overflown in every direction, making the country a perfect swamp" (Derby 1852, p. 13).

The Kaweah River (named by early settlers for the Yokuts tribelet that inhabited its upper delta)[4] enters the basin south of the Kings River. Its discharge into the basin is second only to the Kings but less reliable: during dry periods the Kaweah may disappear underground near the apex of its fan. At Wutchumna Point the stream divides into three or more channels incised about five feet into the local terrain. At bends in the larger distributaries, floodwaters have cut "holes" as deep as twenty feet, where water may still stand ten feet deep in late summer. These "holes" were important watering places for wild animals and domestic stock, especially in the early years of settlement. The Kaweah's channels briefly reunite south of the Venice Hills, then divide again into eight or ten shallow channels "which spread out from one another like the ribs of an open fan" (Adams 1855 in Hittell 1911, p. 337)

4. The Kaweah River was given its name by early settlers, after the Gawia, a Yokuts tribelet that inhabited the region close to the apex of its delta. This name quickly replaced earlier appelations: Rio de San Gabriel (Estudillo 1819), Saint Francis River (Derby 1852), and Four Creeks (Blake 1853)—see Gudde 1965, pp. 152–153.

and overflow to form an extensive swamp during the high-water stage. The fertile alluvial deposits of the Kaweah nearly coalesce with the Kings River fan and are crossed by evenly spaced distributaries that proved a valuable irrigation resource for early basin farmers. The Kaweah River fan is better drained than the Kings fan, and, in 1852, Derby found the Kaweah region far more pleasant: "The country, 8 miles in length by 6 in width, . . . is a beautiful, smooth, level plain, covered with clover of different kinds and high grass, and thickly shaded by one continuous grove of oaks of a larger and finer description than I have seen in the country" (Derby 1852, p. 10).

Further southward, the Tule River (named for the rushes that flourished along its banks) enters the basin. It is perennial only above Porterville and rarely flows more than four miles westward across the basin by late summer. Even before irrigation systems diverted water from the lower reaches of the Tule, its porous bed and tree-lined banks soaked up much downstream flow (Cook 1960, p. 252). Because its flow is so irregular, the Tule has deposited a steep fan; its channel is incised nearly eight feet into the headward portions of the fan, but incision rapidly decreases downstream. Lower distributaries and sloughs are barely deep enough to contain ordinary spring runoff, and localized flooding occurs annually. White River[5] and Deer Creek are smaller still. Like the Tule, both are downcutting in their upper reaches, and both are barely perennial even in the foothills. White River and Deer Creek ordinarily disappear underground within ten or twelve miles of their entry into the basin, even during springtime, but occasional floods have carried their waters to Tulare Lake. The fans deposited by these streams are steeper than the Tule River fan. Several additional streams carry water during peak runoff periods but, with the exception of Avenal Creek, deposit little alluvium. Short sloughs on the highland margins of the basin also introduce minor amounts of water and alluvium during storms and floods.

Because recent alluvial soils are young and are annually buried beneath newer materials, their profiles are poorly developed. Weathering and internal modifications have produced only twelve to eighteen inches of light gray to brown, medium-textured soil, and substrata are reached at depths of about six feet. Leaching has in places concentrated lime and heavier materials in the subsoil layers, and subsoils near the valley trough may also contain large amounts of mussel shell (Holmes and Eckmann 1916, p. 2514). The streams of the basin have

---

5. White River was initially known as Moores Creek during the late 1840s; Derby's 1852 map shows it as Gopher Creek. It was eventually rechristened White River either for the whitish rocks upstream or in deference to a local settler (Gudde 1965).

laid down fairly level interfluvial surfaces, broken only by numerous distributaries and short sloughs: level, well watered, and usually well drained, recent alluvial soils have long been chosen as prime farmland.

As the base level for a region of interior drainage, Tulare Lake is the ultimate destination for salts and sediments delivered to the basin by tributary lakes and streams. Lake deposits extend far beyond the recorded shoreline of Tulare Lake; recent lacustrine deposits are quite minor in comparison with those laid down during the Pleistocene. Even in recent times the lake level has fluctuated widely, as much as 28 feet from year to year (Blake 1853, p. 144), and a small increase in depth causes a dramatic increase in the extent of the shallow lake—as seen when Tulare Lake spread over more than 70 square miles following the spring discharge of 1978. At the highest water level on historical record the lake covered about 760 square miles, filling the basin to about the 220-foot-elevation contour and attaining a depth of over 40 feet near the northwestern shore (Thompson 1892, p. 9). At that stage Tulare Lake received inflow from Kern and Buena Vista lakes to the south via Buena Vista Slough and discharged northward into the San Joaquin River. At the other extreme, the lake was known to evaporate completely, even before its water supply was curtailed by agriculturalists (Latta 1949a, p. 275). Estimates from recent lacustrine deposits and from early observations indicate that the average area of the lake over the past several thousand years is probably delimited by the 210-foot-elevation contour.

Lake soils contain greater proportions of clay than alluvial soils, and so they are less well drained. Soils near the margins of the lake are generally light gray in color and have poor water retention. They are lighter in texture than other lake soils and may contain alkali-neutralizing deposits of gypsite (Jennings 1953, p. 292). Deeper in the valley trough, soils are darker in color, heavier, and more water retentive (Retzer 1946, p. 44). Most lake-laid soils are rich in calcium (lime) because of the inclusion of abundant shell framents. Although these soils were at first shunned by basin settlers, their characteristically level terrain and mineral fertility proved suitable for large-scale cultivation once irrigation water became available. Two areas of sand-dune development break the tabletop terrain of the lake plain: Dudley Ridge extends for about three miles along the shore southeast of Kettleman City, and a series of dunes fifteen to twenty-five feet in height, several hundred yards wide, and seven or eight miles long stretches along the southern margin of the lake bed. In times of high water, these dunes stood out as a causeway between Tulare Lake and marshlands to the south. Atwell's Island, Skull Island, and Pelican Island remain as toponyms that testify to this even in times of low water (Elliott 1883,

p. 152). Early Spanish explorers described two lakes when the water was exceptionally high: the Tachi to the north of the sand ridge and the Ton Tachi to the south (Latta 1937).

In addition to surface water, groundwater has been an influential factor in the establishment of natural communities and an important agricultural resource. Three distinct zones of groundwater underlie the Tulare Lake Basin. Nearest to the surface lies a body of unconfined and semiconfined fresh water of recent age, overlying the ancient and impermeable Corcoran-clay lens (fig. 2). Beneath the Corcoran clay, which ranges from 250 to 825 feet below the land surface and is from 25 to 160 feet thick, a body of fresh water is entrapped. Still deeper lies a body of saline fossil water, entrapped above the sediments of ancient seas. The Corcoran-clay lens becomes thicker and deeper westward across the basin, but on the far western flank the clay is absent; here the middle layer of groundwater is unconfined or semiconfined (Davis et al. 1959, pp. 64, 70, 82). Groundwater lies at shallower depths—within eight or ten feet of the land surface prior to irrigation—under recent alluvium on the upper basin slopes, where some natural springs are found as well as under recent alluvium and old valley fill of the valley trough (Mendenhall, Dole, and Stabler 1916, p. 28). Aquifers are recharged by the same sources that supply the basin's surface water: influent streams from the Sierra Nevada. Because downwarped strata underlie the basin to considerable depth, groundwater has little opportunity to flow out of the basin. Capillarity and evaporation deplete groundwater reserves to some extent, but the total volume of fossil and recharged groundwater is so great that these processes have little significance. Pumpage for consumptive and nonconsumptive uses has had a much greater effect upon the regional quality and availability of groundwater, as will be discussed later in more detail.

The Life Layer

There is plentiful game, such as deer, antelope, mule deer, bear, geese, cranes, ducks and many other species of animals, both terrestrial and winged. (Fages 1772 in Bolton 1935, p. 12)

Organic life is intimately related to climate, terrain, soils, and hydrology, and natural communities of the Tulare Lake Basin reflect the regional blend of these elements. Natural vegetation is both a key component of the life layer and an important indicator of landscape change; a reconstruction of the patterns and composition of natural vegetation in the basin is thus an especially important aspect of this study. The ensuing reconstruction depicts natural vegetation of the basin at about the time of European arrival, for earlier written accounts of regional flora are not available. Even at this time, though, vegetation communities revealed a considerable degree of human influence, for aboriginal peoples had wrought great changes in the life layer during their long tenure in the basin.

The flora of the Tulare Lake Basin comprise elements from several kinds of environments. As an early traveler observed, "nature used a lavish palette" (Marsh in Lyman 1931, p. 214). Broad belts of vegetation roughly parallel the north-south contours of precipitation, temperature, and elevation: that is, plant communities change most rapidly along an east-west transect (figs. 12 and 13), and species diversity increases away from the valley trough with increased elevation and precipitation. This general zonation is complicated by patterns of surface- and subsurface-water availability. At the time of European arrival in the basin, perennial grasses, herbs, forbs, and shrubs were the predominant ground cover; even where annuals flourished, they were not numerous except where perennial stands were severely

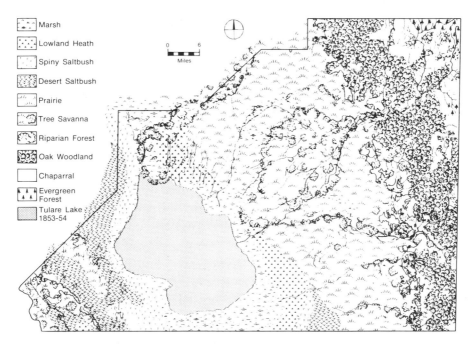

Figure 12. *Vegetation, 1770.* Natural vegetation zones roughly parallel the north-south contours of precipitation, temperature, and elevation. Diversity increases away from the valley trough, although vegetation patterns are complicated by surface- and subsurface-water availability. (Sources: Piemeisel and Lawson 1937; Baumhoff 1963; Scofield 1967; Burcham 1957.)

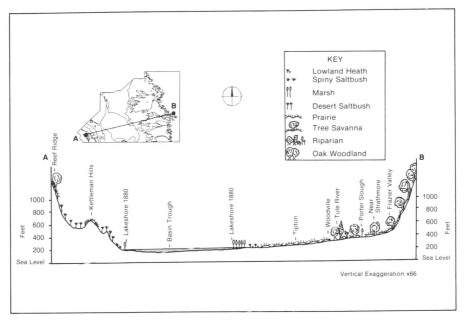

Figure 13. *Hypothetical Cross Section of the Basin's Natural Vegetation, 1770.*
Elevation strongly influences the distribution of vegetation in the hills and mountains, but within the basin the distribution of natural communities can generally be explained in terms of water availability and temperature.

disturbed (Piemeisel and Lawson 1937, p. 23). Trees grew in scattered locations where conditions were favorable, and they were predominantly deciduous. The characteristic natural communities of the basin included tree savanna, riparian forest, marsh, prairie, desert saltbush, spiny saltbush, and lowland heath. I will describe these below in the present tense to set the stage for human occupation of the basin, despite the fact that these communities have been drastically altered since 1770.

The tree savanna of the basin flats and low foothills is an open woodland underlaid by herbaceous ground cover similar to that of the surrounding prairie. The flatland extension of tree savanna is unique to the Tulare Lake Basin: elsewhere, the east side of the Central Valley is bare of trees except along streams (Griffin and Critchfield 1972, p. 36). The basin's savannas probably owe their existence to high ground-water levels beneath the broad alluvial fans of the east-side streams (Piemeisel and Lawson 1937, pp. 6–7). The California white oak (valley oak)[6] is the characteristic savanna tree on the upper slopes of the basin, and in some places the water table is sufficiently high to

6. For Latin binomials for native basin plants, see Appendix I.

support dense stands of white oaks over large areas (Burcham 1957, p. 89), although they more commonly grow in open groves of large trees. On drier or more gravelly soils, the white oak grows in mixed stands with blue oak and interior live oak, which are more common in the foothills. On alluvial fans, especially between the Kaweah distributaries, a continuous forest flourishes from the foothills to the lakeshore. The trees of the Kaweah oak forest are so large and densely clustered that they create a closed canopy in many places: "These trees, like the oak generally in California, are low branched, widespreading, gnarled; they are magnificent in size; many of them must be hundreds of years old; and they are disposed on the plain in most lovely groups, masses, and single specimens" (Nordhoff 1872, p. 198). Early settlers found it difficult to traverse the Kaweah oak forest by wagon.

Oaks give way to other trees near the banks of basin streams. Arizona ash, California sycamore, Oregon ash, walnut, cottonwood, and willow abound, sometimes growing in pure stands (Blake 1853, p. 29). California buckeye, white alder, and California laurel grow along perennial streams, and an array of smaller plants gives the riverbanks a junglelike appearance: tules, nettles, wild hemp, wild blackberries, and wild grape are especially prevalent (Latta 1949a, pp. 118–119). The riparian forests of the Tule, Kings, and White rivers and of Deer Creek stretch like dark green ribbons through the tree savanna, and the riparian forests of the Kaweah spread to the limits of the fan, merging with the tree savanna to create a continuous forest that extends in many places to the shore of Tulare Lake.

Lands subject to seasonal overflow (fig. 10) occur throughout the basin, and marsh species flourish wherever standing water persists. Besides including species peculiar to each surrounding community, the marshland flora includes its own characteristic species such as the common tule,[7] bulrush, cattail spike rush, and sedges (Burcham 1957, pp. 148–149). Most marsh species stay green through the dry season, in marked contrast to the rapid browning of prairie and savanna grasses. Tules (this Aztec term applied by the Spanish to all marshland species [Gudde 1965, p. 329] here denotes only *Scirpus acutus* Muhl.) grow to heights of eight to ten feet along streams and may reach fifteen or twenty feet in height on the lakeshore (Hittell 1866, p. 107). The marsh community was described by Mary Austin in *The Land of Little Rain*:

Last and inevitable resort of the overflow waters is the tulares, great wastes of reeds in sickly, slow streams. The reeds, called tules, are

7. The term *tule* was derived from the Aztec *tullin* or *tollin*, which designated a grouping of plants including the common cattail, bulrushes, and similar plants. The term was used similarly by the Spanish to designate any such marshland plant (Gudde 1965, pp. 329–330).

ghostly pale in winter, in summer deep poisonous-looking green, the
waters thick and brown, the reed beds breaking into dingy pools, clumps
of rotting willows, narrow winding water lanes and sinking paths. The
reeds grow inconceivably thick in places, standing manhigh above the
water; cattle, no, not any fish nor fowl can penetrate them. . . . The
tulares are full of mystery and malaria. (Austin 1903, pp. 240–241)

Grassland communities flourish in the basin wherever annual
rainfall averages eight inches or more. In the eastern basin, as elsewhere in the San Joaquin Valley, prairie grades into tree savanna in the
foothills; the valleyward extension of woodlands on alluvial fans compli-
cates this transition (fig. 12). Perennial bunchgrasses dominate the
prairies and are the dominant ground cover in the tree savanna. The
most important native perennials are purple needlegrass and nodding
needlegrass; associates include bluegrass, California melic, June
grass, foothill needlegrass, bromegrass, and fescue (Piemeisel and
Lawson 1937, pp. 8–10; Munz 1963). Between bunchgrass clumps
grow other perennial and annual herbs. Winter annuals are most
common and include peppergrass and plantain; tarweeds are the
dominant summer annuals (Piemeisel and Lawson 1937, p. 9). Invasive perennials, such as matchweed, are also common. In contrast to
the persistent cover formed by the perennial dominants, annual
grasses form an unstable and highly variable cover. Any disturbance
that increases the space between bunchgrass clumps favors rapid
invasion by annual grasses; for example, the arrival of Spanish livestock initiated rapid replacement of native perennial grasses by native
and European annual grasses (see chap. 3). Species composition
varies annually in accordance with precipitation and the amount of
disturbance (Talbot, Biswell, and Hormay 1939, p. 398). Although
annuals turn green earlier in the spring than perennials do, both are
parched and dry by late spring or early summer.

Seasonal societies of broadleaf herbs and forbs with brightly
colored flowers are a striking element of the prairie landscape in spring
and early summer when their blossoms create "a crazy-quilt of color . . .
with great patches of rose, yellow, scarlet, orange and blue" (Latta
1929, p. 9). More than fifty genera of flowering annuals grow in the
basin prairies, and there are many flowering perennials as well. Early-
blooming perennials include mariposa lily and wild onion; their annual
counterparts include goldfields and fiddle-neck. A regular succession of
floral groupings follows, dominated by California poppy, buttercup,
beardtongue, and tarweed, which provides an outburst of floral bloom in
October (Munz 1963, p. 198). Hog wallow areas on old-valley-fill
prairies hold water during the spring and exhibit a limited but distinctive
variation of the annual flora once the temporary pools evaporate. West
of the lake and at elevations above 800 feet, prairies display another

distinctive flora. In the many washes of the western basin and along intermittent Avenal Creek grow California sagebrush, juniper, wild buckwheat, golden aster, and mule fat; Fremont cottonwoods and California sycamore are found along streams. Prairies and the more drought-tolerant communities of the basin trough overlap to some extent, shifting in response to annual variations in rainfall (Piemeisel and Lawson 1937, p. 11).

The desert saltbush community was described by William Saroyan as "full of every kind of desert plant that ever sprang out of dry hot earth" (Saroyan 1937, p. 36). Drought- and salt-tolerant shrubs thrive on the dry slopes below the prairies of the western and southeastern basin, where annual rainfall averages seven or eight inches. The dominant stand consists of desert saltbush with a spotty intermixture of winter annuals and other herbaceous plants. Peppergrass and plantain are common, but grow less uniformly and to smaller size than on the prairies. Saltbush grows alone toward the valley trough, forming a dense, brushy cover. The seasonal hues of this community are similar to those of the tule swamps: saltbush flowers in spring or early summer and remains green and succulent into the fall, when it stands out against an otherwise parched landscape.

A still more drought- and salt-tolerant community separates desert saltbush from lowland communities on the western and southeastern shores of the lake, where a nearly continuous cover of spiny saltbush flourishes. The alkali-encrusted ground between spiny saltbush shrubs is a poor habitat for annuals, although peppergrass and goldfields appear in places, and the spiny saltbush community rarely overlaps with adjacent communities (Piemeisel and Lawson 1937, p. 13). Although similar in appearance to desert saltbush, spiny saltbush seeds and turns brown in early summer. It requires about seven inches of annual rainfall and grows in the basin only at elevations below 250 feet.

Like the tree savanna, lowland heath reflects the occurrence of a high water table. It flourishes near the lake where seasonal overflow is too brief to support the development of marsh communities. Lowland heath species demand subsurface water, but they are extremely tolerant of dissolved salts and light rainfall, and their distribution varies in accordance with the extent of Tulare Lake and its surrounding swamps. Heath communities generally develop along the edges of basin marshlands, but in times of drought they may colonize the lake bed and adjacent swamplands. Lowland heath also occurs in small patches in the western foothills where seepage is sufficient to support the dominant species, which include seepweed, alkali heath, pickleweed, and salt grass. No annuals exist under undisturbed conditions:

the only break in perennial cover occurs where the alkali crust is too extreme even for the hardy dominants. Each of the main species may form pure stands or may grow in mixed stands with other lowland heath species. Where water is abundant, the lowland heath species—especially pickleweed—form a rank growth several feet high, but in drier locales the plants are smaller and more widely spaced.

People of the Tulare Lake Basin have distinguished the various plant communities primarily in terms of their resource value or of the obstacles they posed to settlement and cultivation, yet all observers have also commented on the dramatic seasonal hues that distinguish certain communities from others. In the sweltering heat of midsummer, perennial bunchgrasses, winter annuals, and drought-tolerant shrubs blend in a parched landscape of dull brownish yellow:

> It was the last half of September and all Tulare County, all the vast reaches of the San Joaquin Valley [were] bone dry, parched and baked and crisped after four months of cloudless weather, when the day seemed always at noon, and the sun blazed white-hot over the valley. . . . The grasses and wild oats, sere and yellow, snapped like glass filaments under foot. . . . Even the lower leaves and branches of the trees were thick with dust. All colour had been burned from the landscape. (Norris 1903, pp. 2, 490)

In contrast, the eastern plains are dotted with green clumps of oaks and crosscut by darker green riparian forests. The Kaweah woodlands stand out boldly from the barren surroundings, a great forest of bluish green. Toward the edge of the lake, the salt grasses are a shimmering silvery gray; the mature tules, like dry cornstalks, hide young green tules below. May Miller described the approach to the lake in the summertime thus: "Finally a blue curve cut into the green and Tulare Lake lay before them. At first it was to Amelie only a part of the September sky, for there was no line between the sky and the water, only mists rising, hiding the distant division" (Miller 1938, p. 363). Across the lake a carpet of pale green saltbush stretches up into the western foothills, then the yellow savanna dappled with a few green oaks reappears.

In autumn the riparian forests are graced with a smattering of yellow and red as deciduous trees and shrubs lose their leaves. With the onset of winter rains "the foothills show a greenness deepening in the gullies" (Austin 1906, p. 20); as the prairies too begin to green, the deciduous oaks and other leafless trees of the savannas and river forests seem suddenly barren in contrast. Out across the plains the placid lake is fringed with bluish brown tules, and on the west the tulares give way to a band of darkened saltbush. The western foothills sport new growth that glows green beneath bare trees and dark green live oaks.

It is the spring color that is most remarkable. The winter greenery explodes briefly into a spectacular quilt of many-hued wildflowers, and light green leaf buds decorate the trees. Such scenes have led several observers to wax poetic: "poppies flow[ed] upon the valley to the dikes of the mountains: the brown earthworks of the Coast Range to the west, the blue white-pointed Sierras halting the flux to the east" (Miller 1938, p. 462); "it seemed that the blood of the whole country burst, after months of restraint, in a brief dark orgasm, an orgasm which was celebrated with the feast of the wildflowers" (Baker 1931, p. 284). The spring spectacle is short-lived, however. With the end of the rains and the growing heat of summer, the landscape begins to fade again to summer hues:

> The spring, which had come so quickly on the heels of the last frost, faded almost as quickly. The south sides of the foothills became spotted with brown, and the spots gradually enlarged until only the shaded north slopes retained the spring green. Where the Indian paintbrushes and the poppies had colored whole fields purple or orange, the rankly growing wild oats mounted until they too turned from green to brown, and then slowly bleached to yellow. Charles saw the spring come and saw it go as if it were something which had happened under his hands, but it moved so swiftly and so smoothly that he felt in no way a part of it. (Baker 1931, p. 57)

And so it goes.

The natural communities of the Tulare Lake Basin include native fauna as well, which have learned to exploit the diverse array of ecological niches offered by basin environments. Of the many species present in the basin, some are too striking and numerous to be ignored in any description, while others are too small or too few to merit more than passing attention. Only those animals that have been important in the geographical history of the basin are noted here; as in the preceding section, the present tense is used as if to set the stage for human occupation of the basin, and the following passage should be read as a description of precontact fauna (ca. A.D. 1700).

Several large herbivores graze on the basin plains, sometimes in great herds. Pronghorn antelope[8] migrate seasonally between the grassy plains and the water holes of the eastern Coast Range or the lightly timbered Sierra foothills (Barker 1955, p. 56). Recalling his visit to the basin, Audubon commented, "We were gratified by the whole

---

8. For Latin binomials for basin animals, see Appendix II.

flock running near us, from which we argued we were in the chosen country of the antelope, the broad tule valley" (Audubon and Bachman 1851, p. 203). Tule elk come to the marshlands in summertime to browse on marsh grasses, venturing much further into the tules than antelope do (Adams in Hittell 1911, p. 331; Manly 1929, p. 302). Seasonal wanderings sometimes carry tule elk up into the foothills as well. Moderate herds of mule deer enter the basin in winter and spring when they leave the high foothills to browse along the lower reaches of the Kings and Kaweah rivers.

Grizzly bears and a few black bears wander among the oak forests and sometimes venture to the lakeshore to raise their young (Grayson 1920, p. 166; Latta 1937). Garcia, a member of Moraga's 1807 expedition to the basin, observed that "bears were everywhere and very dangerous" (Moraga 1807 in Cook 1960, p. 255). The dominant predators are the grey wolf and the ubiquitous valley coyote; Fremont commented that "we saw wolves frequently during the day prowling about after the young antelope" (Fremont 1844 in Jackson and Spence 1970, p. 663). Mountain lions, bobcats, grey fox, kit fox, raccoons, and badgers prowl in small numbers in timbered habitats of the basin (Gifford and Schenck 1926, p. 19; Ingles 1954, p. 117). Smaller creatures are plentiful: William Saroyan characterized the basin as "overrun with prairie dogs, squirrels, horned toads, snakes, and a variety of smaller forms of life" (Saroyan 1937, p. 36). Jackrabbits, Audubon cottontails, ground squirrels, chipmunks, porcupines, skunks, and weasels are especially common. Gophers, rats, mice, shrews, voles, moles, and bats are found in scattered locales, especially in the eastern woodlands (Grayson 1920, p. 106). Water-dwelling mammals include beavers, river otters, and mink; beavers are especially numerous in Tulare Lake, where James "Grizzly" Adams found "beavers' works in every direction" (Hittell 1911, p. 338), and Garcia reported seeing many beavers in all the basin's rivers (Cook 1960, p. 255).

Insects are seasonally significant aspects of basin landscapes and were important in the aboriginal diet. Their presence alarmed William Brewer when he visited the lakeshore in 1861: "The marshy region is unhealthy and infested with mosquitos in incredible numbers and of unparalleled ferocity. The dry plain on each side abounds in tarantulas by the thousands. These are spiders, living in holes, and of a size that must be seen to be appreciated" (Brewer 1861 in Farquhar 1930, p. 203). Gentler insects there are as well: Mary Austin found the lake air "alive with the metallic glint of dragon-flies" (Palmer and Austin 1914, pp. 121–122). Amphibians (frogs and terrapin) and mollusks (fresh water and brackish-water mussels and clams) live in aquatic habitats throughout the basin. Their presence in numerous species and great numbers make these, as well as land snails, significant food resources for aboriginal inhabitants, and cause for comment: "The Tulare Lake clams were several inches deep around the lake where the water was about the right depth. There were more clams there than a person would believe" (Askers in Latta 1937).

Aquatic habitats of the basin range from stagnant backwaters and shallow, tule-choked pools to deep, clear pools and long stretches of flowing water. Seasonal and annual fluctuations within these habitats lend further complexity to regional patterns of wildlife. In Tulare Lake and in the lower courses of streams, fish are abundant: Sacramento perch,[9] Tule perch, Sacramento sucker, and a great variety of minnows (including hitch, thick-tailed chub, Sacramento blackfish, and Sacramento splittail) are common varieties. Sacramento squawfish (an unusually large minnow) and rainbow trout are less numerous. Several anadromous species swim to the Kings River and Tulare Lake in spawning season, water level permitting; these include white sturgeon, steelhead, and Chinook salmon (*Los Tulares* 1978, p. 3; Moyle 1976, p. 114). Audubon found the lower rivers "beautifully clear now, and . . . full of fine-looking fish; the large salmon of these rivers is a very sharky-looking fellow and may be fine eating" (Audubon 1906, p. 185). Although anadromous fishes are only occasional visitors, they come in great numbers and so have served as an important food resource for early basin residents and explorers. A second association of fishes includes those that favor swifter waters, such as the streams of the eastern basin and low foothills. Grayson observed that "all branches of the Kaweah abound with fish" (Grayson 1920, p. 106); most abundant are rainbow trout, prickly sculpin, and several species of minnow (hardhead, California roach, and speckled dace among them). Sacramento squawfish, Sacramento sucker, and Tule perch are also present.

The great diversity of habitats within the basin, its mild climate, and its position along the Pacific flyway bring a diverse array of birds to the region. About 300 species make the basin their seasonal or permanent home. Each species tends to favor a certain kind of habitat, and birds can be roughly classified according to the vegetation communities in which they are most often found. California roadrunner,[10] Costa hummingbird, gilded flicker, and quail are among the many species that favor lowland and desert shrub communities (Grinnell 1915), and birds of prey pass overhead: "the space over this land knew only the presence of hawks, eagles and buzzards" (Saroyan 1937, p. 36).

9. See Appendix II.
10. See Appendix II.

Burrowing owls, California horned larks, western meadowlarks, and western grasshopper sparrows are among the basin grasslands' more common birds, and the grassy savanna is home to turkey vultures, American sparrow hawks, western mourning doves, western kingbirds, and western mockingbirds. The oak woodlands of the foothills and wooded savanna have a greater diversity of birds, the most common species being band-tailed pigeons, screech owls, nuttall woodpeckers, bushtits, and valley quail.

Riparian and aquatic habitats are the richest life zones for basin birds. The narrow riparian zones allow access to the resources of adjacent communities and are favored by long-eared owls, willow woodpeckers, tree swallows, western crows, California yellow warblers, and wood ducks (Grayson 1920, p. 106); belted kingfishers are at home in the slow-moving waters of the delta streams. Marshlands offer a rich and varied habitat, and great blue herons, common egrets, Canadian geese, mallards, marsh hawks, sandhill cranes, and other large birds abound: "We crossed an arm of the lake and landed on a small wooded island, which was a place of birds indeed. There were birds in almost incredible numbers—duck, geese, swans, cranes, curlews, snipes, and various other kinds, in all stages of growth, and eggs by thousands among the grass and tules" (Adams 1854 in Hittell 1911, p. 338). The marshes are also home to innumerable insect catchers, especially redwing blackbirds that "in the spring betake themselves to the reed-fringed marshes in hundreds" (Palmer and Austin 1914, p. 120). Common loons, white pelicans, bald eagles, American osprey, American coots, and California gulls inhabit the shores of Tulare Lake and are joined seasonally by great flocks of migratory waterfowl—cormorants, geese, ducks, pelicans, coots, and others (Cogswell 1977, pp. 20–21). Southern species arrive in early spring, while northern species visit the basin from midsummer through December (Cogswell 1977, p. 26). At dawn and at dusk the lake air is "vocal with the varied cries of coot and mallard and the complaining skirl of the mud-hen, the whistling redwing, the bittern booming from his dingy pool, and all the windy beat of wings" (Palmer and Austin 1914, p. 121), and one need only visit the lakeshore to watch "strange and forlorn fowl drop down" (Austin 1903, p. 242).

Summary: The Natural Setting

The land of the Tulare Lake Basin and the flora and fauna it supports are products of a particular history of geological and ecological development. A complex series of geologic processes created a low-lying basin with interior drainage at the southern end of the Great Central Valley of California. Its location near the western coast of a mid-latitude continent places it in a zone of westerly winds. Climate is further regulated by seasonal shifts of latitudinal pressure systems: summers are warm and dry, while winters are cool and bring a succession of rainstorms. The Coast Range blocks the moderating influences of the Pacific Ocean to a large extent and also catches much of the rain that would otherwise fall into the Tulare Lake Basin. These low mountains amplify the diurnal, seasonal, and annual variations of temperature and precipitation in the basin. The effects of marked seasonality and variability of rainfall are ameliorated by the entrapment and storage of snowfall on the western slopes of the Sierra Nevada and by its summer release to the basin's streams.

Geological history, climate, and hydrology have set the rate and character of processes of landscape formation in the Tulare Lake Basin, of geomorphic sculpting, soil development, and the evolution of plant communities. These, in turn, have influenced the diversity and density of animal populations. Life zones of the basin, like its physiography and climate, change most rapidly along an east-west cross section. Species diversity and the density and stability of natural communities decline from east to west, except along the streams that crosscut simpler life zones and ultimately flow into a large shallow lake whose aquatic habitats are far richer than adjoining terrestrial habitats.

2

The Yokuts: People of the Land

Everything was water except a very small piece of ground. On this were the eagle and the coyote. Then the turtle swam to them. They sent it to dive for the earth at the bottom of the water. The turtle barely succeeded in reaching the bottom and touching it with its foot. When it came up again, all the earth seemed washed out. Coyote looked closely at its nails. At last he found a grain of earth. Then he and the eagle took this and laid it down. From it they made the earth as large as it is. From the earth they also made six men and six women. They sent these out in pairs in different directions and the people separated. After a time the eagle sent the coyote to see what the people were doing. Coyote came back and said: "They are doing something bad. They are eating the earth. One side is already gone." The eagle said: "That is bad. Let us make something for them to eat. Let us send the dove to find something." The dove went out. It found a single grain of meal. The eagle and coyote put this down on the ground. Then the earth became covered with seeds and fruit. Now they told the people to eat these. When the seeds were dry and ripe the people gathered them. Then the people increased and spread all over. But the water is still under the world. ("The Peopling of the World" as told by a Yaudanchi Yokut in Kroeber 1906, pp. 218–219)

The aboriginal peoples of the Tulare Lake Basin knew how their world had come to be. They envisioned themselves as integral parts of that world and recognized the importance of natural balances. They prodded their land into greater production of favored resources but seldom did lasting harm to its life-sustaining capacities. The relationship of the Yokuts to the land was far deeper and more complex than mere subsistence required: life was tied not only economically but also socially and spiritually to the basin and to its natural order. The processes of nature served as continuous reminders of the story of the world, and of the Yokuts' place within it.

The Peopling of the Tulare Lake Basin

As people spilled into the New World across the Bering Straits in ancient times, they applied resource perceptions and subsistence technologies developed in their former homes. Just when the first people arrived in the Tulare Lake Basin is not known. The valley of California probably offered suitable conditions for travel and settlement throughout the prehistoric period of human diffusion into the New World, and one or more of the valley's diverse habitats would almost certainly have proved suitable for the application of any subsistence technology brought by early peoples. Unfortunately, evidence of the first-comers has disappeared along with the ancient environments they exploited. The earliest certain evidence of people in the basin has been found on the western shores of Tulare and nearby Buena Vista lakes (Riddell and Olsen 1969, pp. 121–130) and has been dated at approximately 9000 B.C. (Aikens 1978, p. 135). The first inhabitants were of a very different culture than more recent basin peoples: they were hunters whose artifacts resembled the fluted-point (Clovis-Folsom) tradition prevalent in much of North America at that time. The hunters favored lakeshore locations where large animals congregated; one such place was Dudley Ridge, a higher and drier approach to the lake than was available elsewhere in the swampy surroundings. Bison and other ancient game, including prehistoric horses, probably made use of this ramp.

Settlement by people culturally akin to the Yokuts probably began about 7,000 years ago. The newcomers most likely belonged to the great Hokaltekan language group; their artifacts were much like those of Great Basin peoples but showed certain adjustments to more westerly environments. Though they became increasingly adept at harvesting the foods of the basin, these early gatherers never learned to exploit regional resources as fully as their successors. After Hokaltekan peoples occupied much of western North America, they began to be displaced by new arrivals. In California they were pushed out of the Central Valley as peoples of the expansive Penutian group entered from the north and east (Elsasser 1960, pp. 1–2). Although they, too, were affected by subsequent waves of migration, the Penutians maintained their cultural dominance in the basin. As time passed, they adapted their Great Basin traditions to exploit local resources. Four or five thousand years ago, these forebears of the Yokuts adopted a method of acorn leaching which allowed them to tap a vast new food supply (Aikens 1978, p. 139). This invention helped ensure the stability of their way of life and, together with the intentional setting of fires, figured as a first great step in the extension of technological control over the Tulare Lake Basin.

Diffusion of innovations, linguistic evolution, and the refinement of territorial and subsistence patterns helped differentiate the peoples of the San Joaquin Valley from other Penutians. They began to call themselves *Yokoch* (meaning "people"—Kroeber 1925, p. 488). Gradually the basin Yokuts became further differentiated into regional subcultures although at the time of European contact they still shared enough similarities to be identified as a single culture: the Spanish called them all *Tularenos*, or "people of the tulares." As basin Yokuts interacted with one another and with the varied habitats of the region, their common culture was reinforced by the success of intergroup trade alliances, which demanded a common set of resource perceptions and common management of the regional resource base (Kroeber 1939, p. 2).

Yokuts Subsistence

Their life and customs are those of Nature herself, who with a liberal hand supplies them with wild quadrupeds, fowls, fish, and nourishing seeds, with which they meet their only need. (Bandini 1951, p. 18)

The Yokuts' subsistence technology and the unusual richness of the Tulare Lake Basin permitted the development of one of the highest regional population densities anywhere in aboriginal North America (Cook 1955a, p. 45; Kroeber 1961, p. 91). This was paralleled by complex social patterns approaching the level of tribal organization, which is usually associated with farmers rather than with hunters and gatherers (Bean and King 1974, p. 13), and by cultural elaborations uncommon elsewhere (Applegate 1978, p. 9). High population densities and complex social organization reflected the development of specific cultural institutions that served to enhance the carrying capacity of the land.

The food resources used by the Yokuts were varied, widely distributed, and overwhelmingly abundant in the Tulare Lake Basin. Each natural community offered a distinct set of foods and materials on a seasonal basis, and the Yokuts learned to make use of hundreds of different plants and animals in their diet; they were, indeed, one of the most omnivorous groups on the continent. A few foods were preferred, however, and supplied the bulk of the Yokuts diet: these included acorns, grass seeds, forbs, game, waterfowl, fish, and shellfish. The Yokuts collected these staple foods as they became available and stored surpluses to see them through lean periods, especially early spring. The amount of provisions that could be collected and stored away for winter and spring use must have been a critical factor in adjusting population levels to each locality.

The most important food source was the oak: Fremont judged that the Yokuts "live principally on acorns" (Fremont 1845 in Latta 1949, p. 29). Acorns from the great valley oak were plentiful, but were difficult to hull and less nutritious than other species (Barrett and Gifford 1933, pp. 142–163). Still, a good crop–perhaps 500 pounds per tree–could be expected one year in every three, and at least a partial crop could be collected annually (Wolf 1945, p. 27). Valley oaks grew in the tree savanna and riparian forests, and in the foothills to elevations of 1,500 feet or more, so they were easily accessible as well. Higher in the mountains, at elevations of 3,500 to 6,500 feet, grew the black oak; the Yokuts considered this to be the best and most reliable acorn producer, and their dependence upon it contributed to the ongoing association between basin Yokuts and their foothill neighbors. Yields of 200 to 300 pounds of nuts per tree could be expected in alternate years (Baumhoff 1963, p. 166). The blue oak grew at lower elevations but yielded less and it was relied upon only in emergencies.

Acorns were gathered in the fall and stored whole or as prepared meal. They were made edible by grinding and leaching (to remove the tannic acid they contained), and prepared meal was made into porridge or unleavened bread. Because acorns were easily stored and high in protein and oil, they were a great asset to a largely vegetarian diet; they were essential to the maintenance of dense, semisedentary, nonagricultural populations such as the Yokuts and many of their California neighbors. Wild acorns were not a completely reliable staple, however; Hicks was told by two Paipai informants that "for one reason or another, acorn failure occurs about once every three years, and that it affects all the oaks in a fairly extended area" (Hicks 1963, p. 132; additional evidence of recurrent acorn failure is cited in White 1963, p. 127). In years of local or regional acorn failure, the Yokuts' intimate knowledge of a variety of other foods and their continued option of mobility were their assurance of survival. In addition to acorns, oaks provided bark and wood for medicinal purposes, dyes, and fuel (Balls 1962, pp. 13–14). The nuts of other trees–including buckeye and laurel–were also eaten, especially when acorn production fell short of subsistence needs; buckeyes, like acorns, required leaching.

Techniques for harvesting and preparing grass seeds were highly developed in Yokuts culture and were rapidly applied to weedy grasses introduced by the Spanish, including wild oats (*Avena barbata* Brot. and *A. fatua* L.; Munz 1963, p. 1514). California (and the basin in particular) produces a large amount of seeds, and grass seeds must have been an important protein source, especially in treeless zones near the lake. Fifty to 100 vegetable species were also used by the Yokuts (Kroeber 1961, p. 166). Edible plants were especially varied and abundant near the foothills and along streams, and included clover,[1] peppergrass, fiddle-neck, tansy mustard, filaree, and the roots of many grasses (Balls 1962, pp. 25–27). Marshes and lowland communities supplied iris bulb and tule root, two important sources of flour; cattails, thistle sage, and wild blackberries were gathered in the marshes and along streams (Wester 1975, pp. 21–23; Munz 1963, pp. 1389–1390; Cook 1960, p. 242). Salt grass, important in trade as well as in the local diet, grew plentifully in the lower reaches of the basin. In any given season, some vegetable foods were available, but fresh vegetables were particularly important in the spring and early summer months, when Yokuts acorn supplies were low (Kroeber 1925, p. 479). Even when acorns were plentiful, though, seeds and tubers were probably collected for storage and trade because they kept well without preparation and were good hedges against hunger in return for minimal expenditures of time and energy. Like oaks, these plants served other uses as well, providing dyes, herbs, fuels, and basket materials.

Nearly all native animals figured in the Yokuts' diet: even ground wasps and skunks were relished (Latta 1929, pp. 27–28). Small game was hunted all year long and could be found throughout the basin, but

---

1. Latin binomials of Yokuts food plants not included in Appendix I are as follows: thistle sage (*Salvia carduacea* Benth), clover (*Trifolium* spp. L.), tansy mustard (*Descurainia pinnata* [Walt.] Britton), filaree (*Erodium* spp. L. Her), and iris bulb (*Iris munzii* Foster and *I. douglasiana* Herb.)—Munz 1963.

most abundantly in the timbered habitats at the basin's edge. Waterfowl congregated at the edges of the lake and were hunted or trapped there in great numbers; James "Grizzly" Adams accompanied a band of Tachi Yokuts as they gathered young birds and eggs on an island in the lake and reported finding "birds of various kinds in astonishing plenty" (Hittell 1911, pp. 337–338). Mussels, clams, and terrapin were collected in the lower courses of streams and in the lake, and fresh fish were available in most basin streams. An early American visitor to the basin allowed that, indeed, "the streams being literally filled with the finest quality of fish, . . . these have truly been supplied by nature in as great abundance as could be wished for by any people" (Nugent 1853 in Heizer 1974, p. 12). Smoked or dried fish—not only freshwater species but also salmon and steelhead caught "by the ton" in Tulare Lake and the Kings River—was stored in great quantities as an important Yokuts staple (Baumhoff 1963, p. 169; Askers in Latta 1937). The meat of large game animals was also salted or dried for storage: elk, antelope, and deer were hunted throughout the year as they shifted between basin and foothill habitats. Other large game animals were taken less frequently.

Some basin habitats offered diverse food resources, while others afforded less variety but an abundance of a few staples. Food production was not left to the vagaries of nature nor to the efficiency of the Yokuts' gathering techniques alone, however. Social institutions and values supported the management of food resources and the accumulation of surpluses (Bean 1973, p. xxxvi). The Yokuts actively managed their resources, and in so doing they altered the ecologies of basin habitats as well as their own relationship to the land.

A fundamental tool in resource management was fire. Deliberate burning was practiced by all Yokuts groups, as by aboriginal groups throughout California. The wise application of fire maintained ecological transition zones (ecotones), where flora and fauna were most diverse and abundant, and increased their productivity. By altering the timing of plant growth and maintaining simple stages in ecological succession, fire assisted the spread of preferred food plants; by improving forage for herbivores, fire enhanced the availability of game (Lewis 1973, p. 83; Odum 1971, pp. 151, 220; Leopold 1950, p. 572). Fires were set from midsummer through fall; by releasing nutrients that would otherwise be bound up in slowly decaying plants, fire encouraged grasses and forbs to sprout earlier in the fall and to grow more luxuriantly than they would have under natural conditions. Deliberate burning may also have been practiced in conjunction with game drives, warfare, and communications. In frequently burned areas, oak trees were not harmed; in fact, their accessibility and productivity were usually improved by the removal of underbrush (Lewis 1973, p. 19). Still, Yokuts burning over the centuries must have affected the natural distribution of oaks in the Tulare Lake Basin, and the singular spacing of savanna trees was almost certainly a result of annual firings over centuries (Jepson 1923, p. 39).

It is difficult to say whether the Yokuts intentionally engaged in plant domestication, but it is clear that they applied some of their horticultural knowledge to foster growth of favorite food plants. The Yokuts were very familiar with the habitats and growth characteristics of native plants, and they knew how to care for particular plants to improve growth and productivity; still, "cultivation" probably amounted only to caring for individual plants and small native groves or plots. The abundance of basin food resources and the efficiency of Yokuts gathering techniques may have made food cultivation on a larger scale unnecessary; in any case, taking time off from the very rewarding activities of hunting, fishing, and collecting in order to undertake the time-consuming and risky practice of primitive agriculture would probably have resulted in an initial decline in food production. Still, there is evidence that in some areas plant care may have been carried on to quite a significant extent. For example, a Spanish padre recalled that Yokuts he visited near the southern shore of Tulare Lake in 1805 had "sticks which had been brought for more than eight leagues for the purpose of farming" (Martin 1815 in Cook 1960, p. 244). It is known that Yokuts planted tobacco (Kroeber 1941, pp. 14–15), pruned dead growth from elderberry bushes and grapevines, and transplanted wild plants and seeds to areas where they could be better tended. They may also have sown grass seed. (Bean 1973.) Repeated harvesting of favorite grasses could have fostered the spread of these species by introducing their seeds into disturbed sites, and such selection could have altered the morphologic and distributional characteristics of some grasses. Indirectly, Yokuts manipulation might have weakened the resistance of native grassland communities to invasion by European grasses (Bean and Lawton 1976, p. 44).

Social conventions and relationships also assisted in resource management. Food taboos and totem relationships protected certain animals from overhunting (Kroeber 1971, p. 300; Bean and King 1974, p. 19), and land rights protected especially productive areas from over-exploitation. There is substantial information on record concerning the ownership of oak groves and grass fields by individuals, families, or tribal groups (True 1957, p. 296; Bean 1973, pp. xxxi–xxxii), and the defense of recognized or imagined rights to hunt or gather in a particular area seems to have been a major cause of Yokuts warfare. Bandini observed that the Yokuts "are in the habit of quarreling, particularly over seeds when the trees are bearing fruit, and most of the time these disputes end with a great number of deaths" (Bandini 1951, p. 17). Tribelets convened periodically to assert their group tenure, performing ceremonies to increase the productivity of their domain. It would be difficult to judge what practical returns such ceremonies may have had, beyond the social functions of assembling large numbers of kinfolk and allies, yet these ceremonies emphasize the Yokuts' belief that environmental stewardship was a group concern and their awareness of their collective power of environmental alteration.

Trade associations among basin groups, and between Yokuts and surrounding peoples (from as far away as the Mojave Desert), increased the variety of resources available to each group (Latta 1937). Trade alliances reached across ecological zones and involved considerable exchange in a wide range of goods (fig. 14; Gayton 1946, p.259). Basin trade alliances (and associated ritual and military alli-

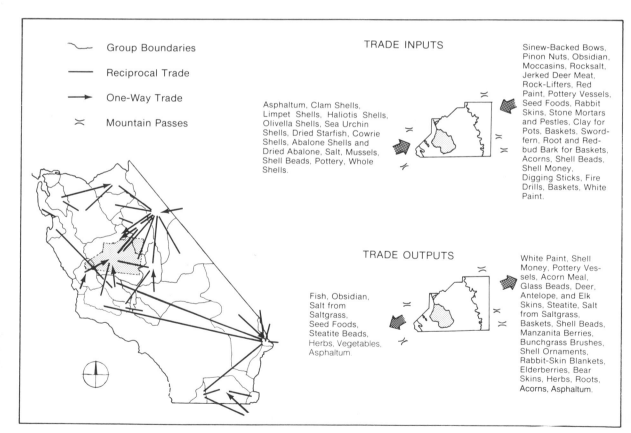

Figure 14.   *Aboriginal Trade Relations Affecting the Tulare Lake Basin, 1770.* Although largely self-sufficient in producing basic foodstuffs, the Yokuts of the basin increased the variety of resources available to them by trading widely with peoples of different habitats. (Source: Davis 1961.)

ances) promoted east-west interchange, reflecting the direction of most rapid environmental change. Trade usually involved simple exchange or purchase of goods, but in some cases hunting, gathering, or fishing rights were exchanged or purchased (Davis 1961, p. 12). By encouraging the redistribution of scarce resources, trade alliances served as buffers against local food shortages. The Yokuts seldom faced famine, but at times when they found themselves unable to maintain their customary lives of plenty, local or distant trade partners could be called upon for assistance. For example, a Chunut woman recalled that "old people told me that once the lake dried up. . . . The creeks dried up too. Many people had to go to their friends at the hills" (in Latta 1949*a*, p. 275).

In addition to foods, trade involved raw materials and artifacts for subsistence, utilitarian, and ceremonial purposes: asphaltum, steatite, magnesite, jasper, pigments, baskets, skins, and blankets were among the goods traded out of the basin (Gifford and Schenck 1926, p. 53). Because of its location between coastal habitats and those of the High Sierra and Great Basin beyond, the Tulare Lake Basin served as a redistribution point for a wide variety of goods and materials (Kroeber 1925, pp. 934–935). The village of Bubal, near present-day Alpaugh, lay astride the dune-ridge causeway across the swamps of the southern lakeshore; the wealth and variety of foreign goods found there suggest that Bubal was not only a cultural center within the basin but an important focus of long-distance trade as well (Gifford and Schenck 1926, p. 113).

Yokuts Population and Settlement

Yokuts demography in the last undisturbed years reflected resource geography, social organization, and subsistence techniques. Although the tribelets shared a common set of resource perceptions and technologies, basin habitats responded differently to their various attentions and activities. Different carrying capacities were partly overcome by technological, social, and economic advances, yet there remained a close correlation between resource zones and population density. The population groupings portrayed on figure 15 were drawn from conservative estimates by Cook (1955*a*) and Baumhoff (1963); the fact that the activities of some groups overlapped in space was taken into consideration. According to these estimates, at least 19,000 Yokuts lived in the basin or visited it seasonally on the eve of European contact.

The highest population densities by far—six to seven people per square mile—occurred in the lush stream-delta and delta-foothill areas

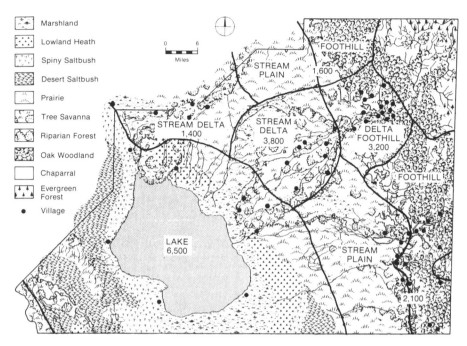

Figure 15. *Yokuts Resource Habitats and Population, 1770.* Although the Yokuts shared a common set of resource perceptions and technologies, the habitats of the basin responded differently to human attentions and thus afforded different carrying capacities. The highest population densities occurred in the lush stream-delta and delta-foothill zones; lower population densities characterized the remainder of the basin, although these densities were still impressive for a nonagricultural people. (Sources: Cook 1955a; Baumhoff 1963; Gayton 1948; Latta 1949a; Kroeber 1925, 1961.)

along the Kings and Kaweah rivers, which offered the full range of Yokuts staples and a broad array of tasty additions to the usual diet; higher delta areas permitted access to foothill resources as well. Lower population densities, two to six people per square mile, characterized the remainder of the basin depending upon the area and the season. The lakeshore offered waterfowl, elk, fish, and many plant foods, and it was more densely settled than the stream plains along the Tule River, White River, and Deer Creek. Still, the stream plains offered acorns, elk, antelope, and small game in abundance, and local population densities were high relative to those achieved by nonfarming aborigines in other parts of North America.

The development of distinct ecological and sociocultural patterns eventually led to the division of Yokuts peoples into separate tribelets that spoke distinct dialects and felt a sense of unity and sovereignty within discrete territories (Kroeber 1925, p. 474). Sixteen tribelets inhabited the Tulare Lake Basin (fig. 16). Around the lakeshore lived

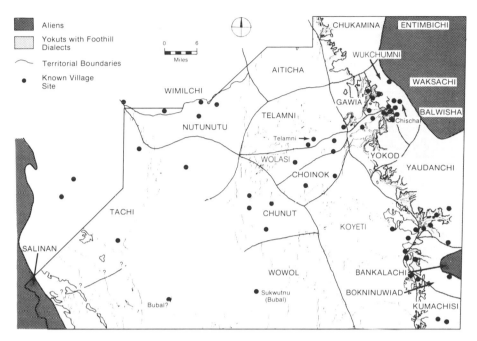

Figure 16. *Known Yokuts Villages, Territories, and Language Areas, 1770.* Tribelet territories and settlement patterns varied in accordance with the carrying capacities of Yokuts habitats. Villages were close together and territories small in the Kaweah Delta, more widely spaced elsewhere. Linguistic barriers rose abruptly between plains and foothill Yokuts and less so between basin Yokuts and other Yokuts groups to the north. (Sources: Gayton 1948; Baumhoff 1963; Kroeber 1925, 1961; Latta 1949*a*; Cook 1955*a*.)

the Wowol, Chunut, and Tachi.[2] Eastward, on the Kings and Kaweah deltas, were the Wimilchi, Nutunutu, Telamni, Wolasi, and Choinok. The Aiticha and Koyeti controlled the adjoining stream plains, and further eastward, in the foothill-delta zone, were the Wukchumni, Gawia, and Yokod. The Chukamina, Yaudanchi, Bokninuwiad, and Kumachisi lived predominantly in the foothills. The spoken dialects of these tribelets were similar and adjacent groups could usually understand one another (Kroeber 1904, p. 170). Linguistic similarities were strongest among plains groups south of the Kings River and extended beyond the southern margin of the basin. Plains and foothill Yokuts spoke very different dialects, probably a reflection of physiographic isolation and of close association between foothill peoples and their non-Yokuts neighbors to the east and west: the Western Mono and Salinan, respectively (Kroeber 1925, p. 487).

2. It is not known which tribe occupied the southwest shore of Tulare Lake. If not occupied by either the Tachi or Wowol, the locality may have supported an unknown tribelet, made extinct by European encroachment (Latta 1937).

Each tribelet was self-governing, independent, and territorially sovereign. The size of tribelet territories varied according to differences in their carrying capacities: territories were smaller in habitats with sufficient local resources to support dense populations than in habitats that required more expansive exploitation. For example, the 1,200 Telamni had a much smaller territory, but a much richer one, than the 800 Koyeti. Stream-delta and delta-foothill tribelets tended to have population densities comparable to that of the Telamni, while smaller populations and larger territories (comparable to those of the Koyeti) characterized foothill tribelets and the Aiticha of the stream plains. The Wowol and the Chunut, of the lakeshore, had large populations (roughly 1,300 people each), but they occupied much larger territories than the equally populous delta tribelets. The largest basin group by far was the Tachi, which numbered about 4,000 people. The Tachi territory extended across several habitats, from the northeastern shore of Tulare Lake to the Coast Range. The Wowol territory was also very large but was less diverse and less productive, which may account for the failure of the Wowol to achieve a population level comparable to that of the Tachi (Cook 1955a).

Most of the territory of each tribelet was visited by hunters throughout the year, but each resource zone was also exploited in turn from a series of villages sited in such a way as to promote convenient access to each important zone of seasonally procurable resources (King 1974, p. 40). Most tribelets had several villages (probably from three to eight), each near a perennial water source and, if possible, near timber as well. With few exceptions (notably among the Tachi), villages were located in ecotones on slightly elevated ground (fig. 17), sites that fostered access to varied resources and protection from normal flooding. Each village controlled a roughly circular territory seasonally endowed with sufficient food resources to sustain the group. In rich habitats such as the Kaweah Delta, settlements might be clustered within a few hours' walk of one another, while in less productive areas, such as the Tachi domain, they might be a day or two apart. In any given season, one, two, or three tribelet villages were occupied; one of these served as the political center for the tribelet. When local resources dwindled or stored staples were exhausted, the population shifted to another set of villages. In rich habitats, certain villages might be inhabited the year around. Bubal, the main Wowol village, maintained a substantial population throughout the year, although the villages of its hinterland were only seasonally occupied (Cook 1955a, p. 42). Bubal's trade functions provided unique access to a wide range of foreign materials and foods and must have compensated for local variations in seasonal resources. In other areas the main villages served as winter residences for most

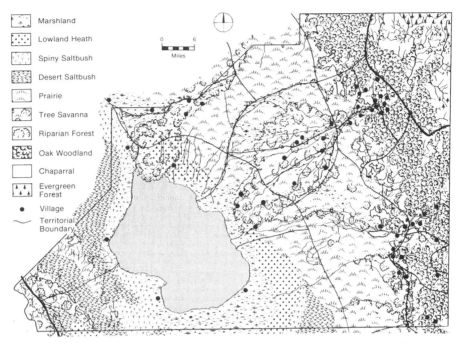

Figure 17. *Vegetation and Yokuts Settlement, 1770.* Although half of the Yokuts villages have not been located, known village sites display a close association between settlement and resource variation. With few exceptions, villages were located at ecotones, which provided a diverse array of resources nearby; convenient access to water was also an important consideration.

tribelet members, but groups would disperse to smaller villages and camps in spring and summer to take advantage of scattered, seasonally available resources. A few elderly people always stayed behind in the main villages (Latta 1949a, p. 99).

Although only a fraction of the precontact Yokuts villages have been located, the number established by each tribelet seems to have correlated loosely with the size of the tribal territory and the productivity of tribelet habitats. The more densely settled tribelets, such as the Gawia and Telamni, had only two to four villages, while tribelets forced to range over larger territories sited more villages: the Yaudanchi, Koyeti, and Tachi each sometimes occupied as many as eight villages in widely scattered locations. Figure 16 depicts known locations of Yokuts villages in the Tulare Lake Basin. It is important to note that half of the known villages have never been located and most were never mapped. Disruption by Europeans led to the abandonment of some villages and resiting of others: Buhal, for example, was probably traditionally located on the western lakeshore but was moved to its mapped location for better protection from Hispano harassment. The principal villages of lake, stream-delta, and delta-foothill tribelets had populations of 1,000 or more inhabitants; Bubal, for instance, had about 1,300. Most other villages were smaller, with between 200 and 800 inhabitants, but even the less populous villages covered substantial areas: the Wukchumni village of Chischa covered the equivalent of eight city blocks (Cook 1955*a*, pp. 43, 47).

Village layout was regulated by tribal law or custom. Yaudanchi houses were aligned in rows and sported brush-covered awnings, while the Wukchumni arranged their villages in the form of a crescent (Cook 1955*a*, p. 47). Most villages had a gaming court of smoothed and tamped earth, a communal sweathouse, and mat-covered granaries and ramadas (Latta 1929, p. 19; Wallace 1978, p. 451). House form varied considerably, despite a general similarity in building materials: a framework of willow poles covered with woven mats of rushes or tules. Permanent housing in lakeshore and Telamni villages consisted of long, wedge-shaped tents up to 300 feet long and built to house a dozen or more families (Latta 1929, p. 31). William Brewer described these dwellings and their inhabitants on a visit to the basin in 1863: "They were hard looking customers. They lived in a long building made of rushes carefully plaited together so as to shed the rain, making a long shed perhaps sixty or eighty feet long" (Brewer 1963 in Farquhar 1930, p. 381). Seasonal housing near the lake consisted of dome-shaped structures about 10 feet in diameter, which could be quickly dismantled and relocated in case of impending flood. Nonlake tribelets built a variety of single-family dwellings of permanent construction, even when intended for only seasonal occupancy (Latta 1929, p. 28).

Each triblet landscape included modified natural communities, a network of trails, and a set of villages, reflecting local relationships between land and life. The Tachi annual round (fig. 18) simply and clearly exemplifies the ways in which natural patterns in time and space were reflected in the landscapes, ceremonial calendars, and subsistence patterns of the Yokuts (Gayton 1946). The Tachi year was divided into three seasons that closely paralleled the annual cycle of plant growth in the basin. The people wintered in Golon, Udjiu, and Walna (villages to the west of Fish Slough) from November through February, their diet based on acorns collected and stored the previous fall, and on small game taken in the grasslands and lowland communities. In late February the Tachi began a series of ceremonies celebrating totemic associations with wildflowers, rattlesnakes, and tanai, a narcotic plant that became available at this time. Members of neighboring groups often attended the closing feast. In May or June, when grass seeds ripened, the Tachi moved eastward to their summer settlements, including Chi and Waiu. The men fished in Tulare Lake and Fish Slough and hunted local game; the women collected seeds

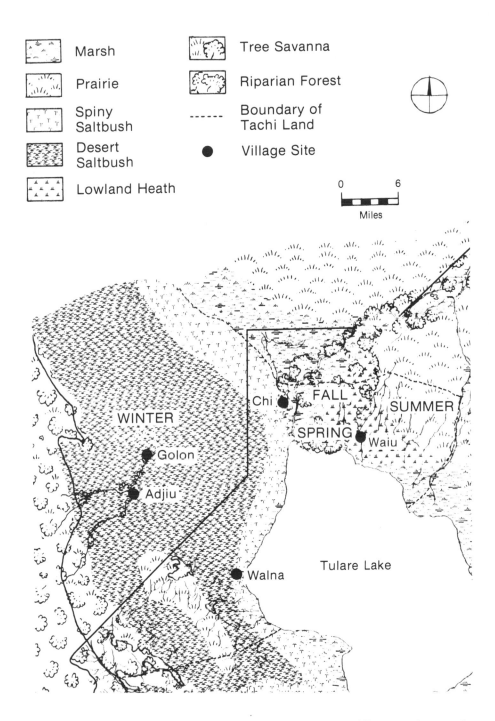

Figure 18. *Tachi Annual Round, 1770.* The Tachi annual round illustrates the ways in which spatial and temporal patterns in nature were reflected in Yokuts landscapes, ceremonial calendars, and subsistence patterns. The Tachi year was divided into three seasons that paralleled the cycles of plant growth in the basin, and Tachi moved from village to village to take advantage of seasonal variations in resources. (Source: Kroeber 1925, p. 480.)

and salt. Camp locations varied, but summer migrations rarely exceeded twenty miles' distance. The Tachi also allowed other tribelets to camp around the lake in summer; sharing of summer territories was a common practice among the Yokuts (Kroeber 1925, p. 480). In September and October the Tachi drifted back across Fish Slough to their principal villages, harvesting acorns along the lower reaches of the Kings River fan. Once they had settled in for the winter, preparations began for the annual mourning ceremony. Guests came from all over the Great Valley to share in special rites, feasting, gaming, and exchanges of ritual gifts and trade goods. Bandini described such a feast, at the end of which the Yokuts sent their guests home with "presents of feathers, pelts, acorns, pine nuts, and other seeds" (Bandini 1951, p. 18). In November the Bear Dance celebrated a new year, the first use of the new acorn crop. Many other activities also reflected changes in the natural environment; for example, trade fairs were scheduled to coincide with periods of high water to facilitate water transport, or with the opening of mountain passes.

Summary

The Penutian forebears of the Yokuts settled the Tulare Lake Basin three or four thousand years ago. The basin offered a wide variety of plant and animal resources, some available on a year-round basis, others only seasonally. As time passed, these peoples altered their technologies, social organization, and their cultural institutions to better suit their new habitats. A distinctive Yokuts value system that supported resource management and the accumulation of surpluses gradually emerged. Not content to glean their living from undisturbed nature, the Yokuts devised ways to make basin habitats more productive and ways to improve their access to favorite resources. Efforts to maintain a high standard of living led to changes in natural evolutionary and ecological processes and the modification of natural communities. Through burning, plant care, and the establishment of boundaries, settlements, and pathways, the Yokuts reorganized the basin's landscapes to satisfy their subsistence needs and cultural desires, and the Tulare Lake Basin came to bear the imprint of Yokuts identity and Yokuts values. Yet the landscapes still expressed the people's intimate and direct identification with the natural parameters of land and life in the Tulare Lake Basin: demography, settlement patterns, subsistence rounds, and ceremonial schedules all revealed an intricate integration of perception, values, technologies, and social organization with the opportunities afforded by basin environments and the constraints imposed by natural patterns and processes.

3

Invasion, Devastation, and Environmental Disruption 1770–1843

> Once, twice, three times or four in many years our fathers tell us travelers go through this valley, the first ones with shining hats and coats of tanned leather. Then men many moons, they say, from their lodge—Hunters Bay—come to the lake with traps. We watch them. They have guns that kill. Our fathers can do nothing. They watch hidden in the tules while the men take our otter and mink. . . . When the otter and mink are gone, the hunters go also. ("Indian Harry" in Miller 1938, pp. 366-367)

A new kind of people, of a different race and seeking different rewards in the Tulare Lake Basin, began to encroach upon Yokuts lands in the late eighteenth century. The strangers came to harvest the basin's resources, as the Yokuts had done, but they had very different ideas of what those resources were and of how to acquire them. They came to exploit the natural bounty quickly and efficiently, not to make the basin their home, and they gave no thought to the balance or harmony of the habitats they plundered. Both directly and indirectly, they inflicted dramatic changes upon the natural and social systems of the basin and of the greater American West as well. In the process of pursuing their assignments and aspirations, however, some of the strangers did make note of the basin's particular characteristics, and they carried their observations and impressions to other regions where people were in search of new lands to settle. The early intruders were important in the appraisal of the basin's suitability for new kinds of settlement and livelihoods and in diffusing images and information concerning the land and people of the Tulare Lake Basin.

First Foreign Visitors

Because we were now in the Plain of the Tulares and because it is a land without trails, the guide and all of us lost our direction and did not know where we were. (Ortega 1815 in Cook 1960, p. 267)

The Spanish entered California around 1770. They had already conquered and colonized lands to the south and had adjusted to many facets of life in the New World, but the prejudices and values upon which their evaluations of new lands and peoples were based had changed little since their arrival in the Western Hemisphere. Spanish explorers usually paid little heed to the Central Valley: their interest lay in establishing missions and pueblos along the California coast, where logistical support could be provided by sea and where rich lands and large native populations were already known to exist. Indeed, the Tulare Lake Basin was still a frontier to the Spanish and their Mexican successors when Anglo-Americans assumed the duties of colonizing California in the 1840s and 1850s.

The first Europeans to see the Tulare Lake Basin were probably deserters from the Spanish armies stationed at coastal missions and pueblos. There is scant written record of these initial contacts, but it is evident that plants, diseases, and customs that had evolved elsewhere were rapidly introduced in the basin and that these introductions were generally disruptive. The arrival of foreign diseases, ideas, plants, and materials often even preceded the arrival of the Spaniards themselves, diffused by contact between Yokuts and their neighbors, bucket-brigade fashion, along established trade routes. Still, the impact of European traits was slight in the basin—as it was throughout the Central Valley—until the 1770s (Cook 1955a, p. 31).

By the turn of the nineteenth century, the Spanish had established themselves thinly around the missions of coastal California, and they began to expand their horizons into the relatively unknown interior (fig. 19). The main incentive for exploration of the Great Valley was the need to restock the dwindling work force at coastal missions, but punitive and political motives also brought the Spanish to the basin. Expeditions were sent to capture renegade soldiers and mission Indians who had sought refuge in the "labyrinth of lakes and tules" (Bolton 1935, p. 12) and to punish any Yokuts who harbored fugitives or stolen Spanish property. The Yokuts had quickly learned to exploit the new "resources" offered by Spanish settlement: cattle and horses, in particular, were recognized as valuable food resources. Political motives for exploration of the basin included the need to fill a territorial vacuum, a vast unnamed region that was beginning to arouse the interest of other nations. The Spanish decided to build a mission in the Tulare Lake Basin, either on the eastern lakeshore or among the oak forests of the Kaweah Delta (Cook 1960, p. 252). Construction would be delayed, but in the interim the Yokuts were to be converted into good Christian workers at coastal missions, where they could be put to work while the basin was explored. This plan did not proceed smoothly, as indicated by Fray Juan Martin's disappointment on leaving the lake-shore in 1805, "without taking with me as many small children as they would give me. Finally I went home, quite disappointed at having lost, because of one villain, such a harvest for Heaven" (in Cook 1960, p. 244).

More detailed exploration began in 1806 under an aggressive program implemented by Gov. Jose Arrillagas, who organized elaborate expeditions to the Central Valley to search for appropriate mission sites. Some expeditions were relatively scientific in their observations, while others did little to aid in the compilation of accurate geographic knowledge, yet all made significant contributions to Spanish opinions about the basin and its people. Early descriptions varied according to the particular area visited and to the season. Most parties entered the basin from the Coast Range during the summer, and even when they later visited the lush eastern deltas, their descriptions remained strongly colored by initial impressions of the basin as a hot, dry wasteland, "a huge broiler" (Smith 1925). Assessments of the region's agricultural potential were bleak: "There is no land fit for sowing crops because everywhere is sand," wrote Martinez in 1816 (in Cook 1960, p. 272). Spanish explorers often noted evidence of soil alkalinity and commonly characterized basin soils as arid, alkaline, and infertile (Cook 1960, p. 252). Soil fertility was generally judged from vegetation cover and the availability of water: only forested and well-watered lands seemed to hold promise.

Whatever the season, the western lakeshore was not viewed with enthusiasm. In 1816, Martinez wrote, "In all our trip we did not see a good tree, nor wood enough to cook a meal, nor a stone, nor even grass

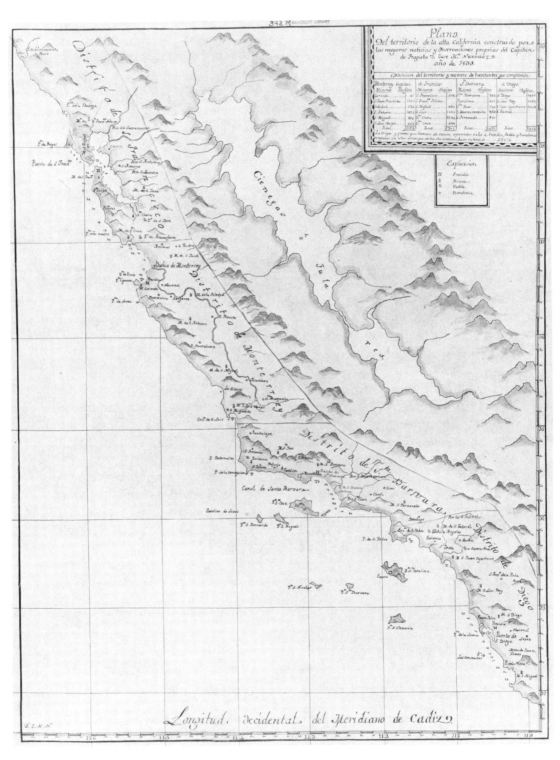

a

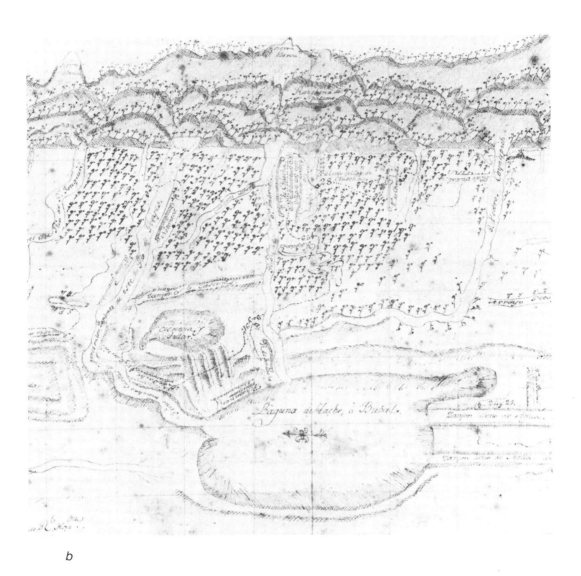

b

Figure 19*a, b.* *"Plano del territorio de la Alta California" by Jose Maria Narvaez, 1830 (portion),* and "Vista de los Tulares. . .y. . .Rancherías de Indios Gentiles y Tierras Reconocidos" by Jose Maria Estudillo, 1819. The Tulare Lake Basin—indeed, the entire San Joaquin Valley—remained a little-known frontier to the Spanish and, later, Mexican settlers of California, whose interests lay primarily in establishing and sustaining a chain of coastal missions and pueblos. Only the threat of foreign encroachment and the need to restock the work force at coastal missions motivated expansion and exploration into the Tulares. (Courtesy of the Bancroft Library, University of California, Berkeley.)

enough for the horses, more than bunch grass, or what grows in the swamps" (in Cook 1960, p. 271). Cabot's 1814 account was no less desolate: "From the time one leaves the coast hills until one reaches the lake it is necessary to carry water and firewood, for there is not a stick in the whole plain. The unhappy Indians start fire with tule roots and other scraps; the water is nasty and salty, so that even the animals dislike it and in places refuse even to touch it" (in Smith 1925). Similar impressions attached to the Kings River fan near the northwestern lakeshore: "In all these lands that I went over there is no timber except a few willows along the banks of the river; neither is there any rock, and they say there is none within twenty leagues distant, which probably is true," wrote Cabot (in Cutter 1950, p. 206); and in 1806 Zalvidea observed, "All the territory covered this morning is alkaline, and with some grass. . . . To the north . . . one can see nothing but bare hills" (in Cook 1960, p. 246).

In contrast, even in the dry season the wooded deltas of the Kaweah and Kings rivers were pleasant, "a delightful contrast to the arid region" (Munoz 1806 in Smith 1925). Bandini noted in 1828 that "the plains that lie between the lake and the great Sierra are undoubtedly the ones that attract attention to these delightful regions. The abundance of pines, live oaks, hazels and other immense trees, together with the pastures and meadows, make an attractive combination" (Bandini 1951, p. 17). The Kings Delta offered "moderately good pasturage, excellent in the river bottoms. All the meadows are well covered with oaks, alder, cottonwood, and willow. The river abounds with beaver and fish" (Munoz 1806 in Cook 1960, p. 252). The Kaweah Delta showed agricultural promise, although the dry season and the permeability of delta soils might hinder cultivation: "The great extent of sand which it has is damaging in its effect, for only at the time of the melting of the snow or in the rainy season does water fill copiously all the stream beds in the oak forest. . . . For this oak forest, which contains about 3,000 souls who want baptism and a mission, is the place most suitable for a mission of all that we have explored. There are fine lands for cultivation and great meadows in many parts of the oak forest which are green all the time" (Munoz 1806 in Cook 1960, p. 252). Long familiar with water-diversion techniques, the Spanish seemed confident that problems of local or seasonal dryness could be overcome. Jose Maria Estudillo, leader of the last organized Spanish search for mission sites in the Tulare Lake Basin, waxed poetic in his praise of the Kaweah Delta: "The land is admirable for its fertility, although rough because of its virginity. With moisture it only invites all to cultivation to give abundant crops of wheat, grains, corn, and all the legumes as long as it is irrigated. And the waters of San Gabriel [the Kaweah] can easily be carried in case of necessity. The pasture remains green and dry the year round" (Estudillo 1819 in Gayton 1936, p. 73). Despite their praise of the eastern deltas, however, the Spanish did not find sufficient incentives for settlement in the Tulare Lake Basin. This may be explained in part by the timing and typical routes of their expeditions (entered in the dry season through the driest part of the basin); in part by the basin's remoteness from the Spanish colonial hearths on the coast; and in part by belated entry and withering colonial drive.

Spanish explorers were also disheartened by the intransigence of the Yokuts, the human resource they had hoped to exploit, and "astonished at their fickleness" (Martinez 1816 in Cook 1960, p. 272). At first they looked kindly on the Tularenos—the people of the *tulares*, the places where the bulrushes grow. The Yokuts, in turn, received the Spanish with "much affection," often presenting the newcomers with gifts (Munoz 1806 and Pico 1815 in Cook 1960, pp. 252, 259). Early encounters were peaceable, and the Spanish left assured that any flaws in Yokuts character could be corrected by a healthy dose of Christian civilization at the missions. In this way, the Spanish would be serving God as well as themselves: "The *pobres infelices* lived like so many brutes in dirt and filth, and were always fighting each other like so many cats and dogs . . . and the people gave us the orphan children, and in this way many of their souls were saved who would otherwise have been lost with the *diablos*" (Olivera 1806 in Cook 1960, pp. 254–255). Until the Yokuts learned to be willing peons, they were to be treated as corvée labor: guided and manipulated, corralled and flogged if necessary. Needless to say, this abuse quickly brought Yokuts resistance and retaliation, and Spanish opinions of the Yokuts grew increasingly negative: the Tularenos were fickle, unreliable thieves, "a republic of Hell and a diabolical union of apostates" (Payeras 1819 in Mitchell 1941, pp. 24–25). Wrote one padre, "The Tulare savages were of a bad disposition and inclined to murder at the word of their wizards or medicine men" (Tapis 1803 in Engelhardt 1912, p. 601). The Spanish quickly abandoned their original goal of Yokuts salvation in favor of applying brute force to prevent the "heathens" from further tormenting the mission padres. In 1819 Payeras wrote, "We, therefore, implore your Honor to send out expeditions in order to recover the Christians, to scour the Tulare country and to make those unruly savages feel the strength of Spanish arms" (in Engelhardt 1912, p. 34). Of a raid on a Wimilchi village, Pico reported in 1826 that "after arriving at the village, the chiefs were able to secure for me, by dark, only those people, heathen and Chinese, who were to be found in the village" (in Cook 1962, p. 183). Coastal Indians were encouraged to raid the basin, and soon the Spanish were making regular retaliatory forays against the Yokuts. Several villages, including Bubal and Telamne, were completely destroyed, and a priest adjudged candidly, "If the other villages are treated in a friendly manner, without giving any indication of our intentions and the first blow is struck, I doubt if there will be any more trouble" (Cabot 1818 in Cook 1960, p. 280).

The increasing hostility of the Yokuts, in combination with the unrest caused by the Mexican Revolution, brought an end to the Spanish dream of establishing a chain of inland missions. The Mexican regime, which assumed control of Alta California in April, 1828, continued to send expeditions into the basin, but these were primarily military in nature. The Mexican government sought to counter Yokuts depredations of the herds at coastal settlements and to recover stolen livestock and renegade Indians, but they found little incentive to evaluate the land for purposes of settlement. Yokuts population was rapidly dwindling and military action could certainly have cleared the way for Mexican settlement, but the dreary scenery along the Los Angeles Trail (fig. 20) did little to arouse enthusiasm for colonization schemes. Still, in order for the Mexican presence in Alta California to be defended against threats of foreign encroachment, the Central Valley had to be settled. The 1840 Law of Colonization, designed to encourage the establishment of cattle ranches in the interior (Becker 1964, p. xxi), did prompt settlement of coastal valleys and of the Sacra-

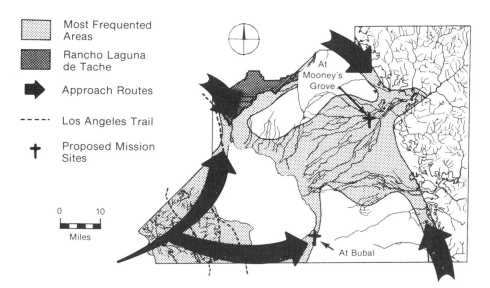

Figure 20.   *Foreign Encroachment, 1770–1843.* Spanish and, later, Mexican priests and soldiers entered Yokuts lands in search of converts and grazing lands; they came, too, to punish what they considered a rebellious and insubordinate population. The most common route into the basin was across the arid lands west of Tulare Lake.

mento Valley to the north, but few Mexican land grants were claimed in the San Joaquin Valley, and only two in the Tulare Lake Basin (both in 1843). One, located between the Kings River and Cross Creek, was never occupied. The other, Manuel Castro's Rancho Laguna de Tache, was situated on the north bank of the Kings River (fig. 20). The Law of Colonization specified that each grant should consist of one league (4,400 acres) of irrigable land, four leagues of land arable with rainfall, and six leagues suitable for grazing (Smith 1939, p. 110). It would have been simple to find several such tracts in the eastern basin, and it is surprising that no more grants were made there. Laguna de Tache lasted several decades but never flourished as ranches elsewhere in California did. Its only building was a bunkhouse near the present site of Laton. Castro's ranch did, however, tie the basin—at least tentatively—into a larger commercial economy and also helped sustain Mexican interest in the region. As the first non-Yokuts attempt to establish a permanent settlement in the basin, Rancho Laguna de Tache also provided a dress rehearsal for subsequent dealings with the Yokuts and their land.

The First American Presence

On my arrival at the Kings River . . . I found a few beaver and elk, deer and antelope in abundance. (Smith 1827 in Merriam 1923, pp. 376–377)

Early Anglo-American arrivals in the basin came in search of furs rather than of native laborers or of agricultural possibilities, but, like the Spanish and the Mexicans before them, American trappers began to tie the basin into the larger economies of California and the United States. They also served as the advance guard of a new group that would soon overwhelm the basin and its people: American pioneers. The arrival of Americans quickly ended the development of Rancho Laguna de Tache and of other Mexican ranchos throughout Alta California; by 1869 the last vestiges of Mexican land grants had been transferred into Anglo hands (Smith 1939, p. 185). Still, despite the brevity of their tenure in the basin, the Hispanos had wrought great changes: Yokuts populations, subsistence, and settlement had been severely disrupted; new flora and fauna, especially European grasses and feral horses and cattle, had been introduced; new place names had been assigned to the features of the basin; and new kinds of boundaries had been delimited there.

Most American fur trappers entered the Tulare Lake Basin from the north. A few Hudson's Bay Company trappers ventured as far south as the basin, but the majority came from the Salt Lake region or New

Mexico. They rapidly hunted the fur-bearing animals of the basin to near-extinction and so never established a permanent fur post there but quickly moved on.[1] Nevertheless, early Anglo visitors did take note of other possible livelihoods afforded by the basin. Perhaps because of their familiarity with Spanish land-use practices, they envisioned the entire Central Valley as a great rangeland. Although they were probably unaware that European grasses (especially wild oats) had already replaced native bunchgrasses on the valley plains, this alteration must have enhanced their appraisal of the region's grazing potential. A few trappers lingered in the basin, with unusual consequences, as lamented by Governor Figueroa:

> Scattering over various regions they identify themselves with the wild natives, following the same kind of life. They live in a wandering fashion with them and in this way become familiar and gain their confidence. From this has come rapidly one positive evil, namely that, influenced by these adventurers, the natives have dedicated themselves with the greatest determination to the stealing of horses from all the missions and towns of this territory. The object is to trade the animals for intoxicating liquors and other frivolities. (in Cook 1962, p. 61)

Peg-Leg Smith lived among the Yokuts as early as 1829, engaging in the capture of wild horses to be sold on the Santa Fe Trail. Smith joined in Yokuts raids upon Mexican coastal settlements, and is credited with teaching the Yokuts the fine art of horse-stealing (Bancroft 1888, p. 278). This exacerbated the Mexican government's problem of maintaining law and order in rural California. In 1833, Governor Figueroa wrote of horse thefts "instigated by the Americans who, under the guise of trappers, insinuate themselves among the wild Indians," and he recommended "to the military commander at San Francisco to send out an expedition every month to those points where it is believed that stolen horses are kept" (Figueroa 1833 in Cook 1962, p. 188).

The Changing Lives of the Yokuts

> What I regret is that so many heathens are dying not only in continuous internal warfare but also from numerous diseases, especially syphilis. (Martin 1805 in Cook 1960, p. 244)

The most immediate and dramatic consequence of foreign visits to the Tulare Lake Basin was the decimation of Yokuts population and the restructuring of Yokuts settlement and livelihood. Yokuts habitats were

---

1. A few beavers survived in secluded spots up to the late 1850s, as noted by James "Grizzly" Adams in 1855 (in Hittell 1911, p. 338).

repeatedly overrun by expeditions and raiding parties. Warfare, massacre, diseases, forced removals, habitat destruction, and anxiety had profound effects upon land and life in the basin, and it would be many decades before pre-contact population levels were again achieved. Foreign contacts were most frequent in the western basin, and direct pressures caused slow eastward migration of the more exposed tribelets. The intransigent Yokuts who remained near the lake relocated entire villages, including Bubal, to more defensible positions (Cook 1955*a*, p. 50; fig. 21). Crowding intensified the already-bitter feuds among Yokuts groups and those between Yokuts and renegades from more rapidly settled parts of California. In at least one instance, a Yokuts chief saw the arrival of a Spanish army as an opportunity to wipe out his neighbors: Pico reported that "this chief offered to supply us with everything and assured us that his village would never oppose the soldiers. On the other hand all his people were ready and willing to give assistance to the troops, if the latter would go and fight the Taches. They offered to go themselves and help drag them out of the tule swamps in the lake because they knew very well where the Taches lived" (Pico 1826 in Cook 1962, p. 184). Intertribal fighting brought many fatalities, but even battle deaths were few in comparison with those from disease, starvation, and exposure. Malaria and cholera epidemics in 1832 and 1833 killed nearly three-fourths of the San Joaquin Valley aborigines (Engelhardt 1912, p. 322), and measles,

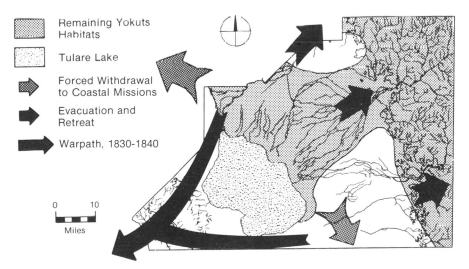

Figure 21.   *Adjustment of the Yokuts to Hispanic Invasion, 1770–1843.* As a consequence of foreign visits to the basin, Yokuts population was dramatically reduced and their remaining settlement patterns and modes of livelihood severely altered. Forced to leave their own territories, some Yokuts groups responded by raiding Mexican settlements to the west.

dysentery, and syphilis were rampant. The Yokuts' stored foods and the tools they needed for hunting and cooking were deliberately destroyed by Spanish, Mexican, and Anglo settlers and soldiers (Cook 1976, p. 286). The vast herds of feral livestock that escaped to this isolated part of California from ranchos and missions grazed so heavily in the basin prairies that native wildlife diminished, and overgrazing permanently altered many basin habitats.

Because of this destruction, the Yokuts faced the twin specters of starvation and exposure. Normal forms of social and economic security were strained to the limits, and local food shortages suddenly became catastrophic. Severe subsistence problems were noted by Ortega as early as 1815 and again by Fray Juan Cabot in 1818; Cabot recorded that the Telamni, whose territory had been noted for its richness, "were almost entirely dispersed and debilitated from starvation" (in Cook 1960, p. 288). Population declined most dramatically in the western basin: by 1822 the lakeshore was nearly uninhabited, and in 1850 the relocated populations of the three lakeshore tribelets were estimated to be about 17 percent of their pre-contact levels (Cook 1955a, pp. 44–45). Death swept through some lakeshore communities so swiftly that bodies were left unburied (Morgan 1914, p. 30). In the foothills, depopulation proceeded more slowly but was equally relentless. By 1850 the Kaweah tribelets were reduced to about one-fourth of their original numbers (Cook 1955a, p. 48), and some eastern tribelets had completely disappeared. Stephen Powers reported in 1848 that "on the White River there are no Indians, nor have there been for many years" (Powers 1877, p. 232).

Hard pressed though they were, the Yokuts did not consent to become pacified wards of the missions: "The experiment of inviting the savages of the Tulare region to come to the missions had been tried. Those who came were instructed and baptized, but by reason of their fickleness and the evil surroundings in their rancherias always with bad results. They would come, not afoot, but on horseback, and on returning to their homes they would drive along horses from the mission herds, slaughter and eat them" (Payeras 1819 in Engelhardt 1912, p. 28). The Yokuts quickly developed an aggressive temperament and a new set of subsistence strategies. Once a predominantly vegetarian people in tune with seasonal variations in local resources, they became a reckless and hard-riding band of horse thieves who preyed upon foreigners' livestock. As early as 1815 an expedition to the Kings River encountered more than 500 dead horses and cattle in Yokuts camps (Picos 1815 in Cook 1960, p. 289),[2] and by the second and third

2. Barker (1955, pp. 41–43) recounts a variety of ingenious methods employed by the Yokuts to capture feral livestock.

decades of the nineteenth century the Yokuts were conducting raids on ranchos and missions a good distance away. Yokuts aggression retarded foreign settlement in some distant regions as well as in the basin itself. Writing of the Salinas Valley in 1846, Edwin Bryant noted: "Few attempts appear to have been made to settle this portion of California. The thefts and hostilities of the Tulare Indians are said to be one of the causes preventing its settlement" (Bryant 1967, p. 371). Some settlements were even abandoned after repeated Yokuts raids (Larkin 1953, p. 306).[3] By 1819 the Yokuts had learned to breed their own livestock and had incorporated cattle into the traditional array of goods at intertribelet trade fairs held on the lakeshore (Smith 1932, p. 19). Past experience later served the Yokuts well in their dealings with Anglo settlers, when they gained a reputation as excellent horse-breakers (Latta 1929, p. 42). Yokuts adaptability and ingenuity were also evident in their rapid integration of introduced grasses into their diet: the Yokuts collected and stored wild oats and prepared them in traditional ways (Kroeber 1961, p. 116). There is also evidence that mission renegades who returned to the basin put their new knowledge of irrigated-cultivation principles into practice along the distributaries of the Kings River, thus becoming the basin's first farmers (Teilman and Shafer 1943, p. 6).

Environmental Alteration

. . . and we found plenty of mustangs, wild horses, in 1807 and afterwards many others with mission brands, and lots of the mission cattle, *muy cimarones*. (Garcia 1807 in Cook 1960, p. 255)

Thousands of feral animals wandered into the Tulare Lake Basin, and vast domestic herds were driven there. Cattle and horses severely disrupted the fragile perennial grasslands, fostering the spread of invasive European annuals, which quickly overwhelmed native prairie associations and soon covered much of the basin. Competition and habitat change also reduced some native grazing animals to the point of local extinction, and increased hunting by the Yokuts accelerated the decline of native fauna. Traditional Yokuts land-use practices, especially burning, also encouraged the spread of European grasses by exacerbating disturbed conditions in native grasslands. By 1833, perennial bunchgrasses had for the most part disappeared, and native wildlife was becoming increasingly scarce (Leonard 1904, p. 183). The very land itself began to change on the west side as once-rounded

3. A description of the planning and execution of these raids by Garner in 1846 can be found in Garner 1970, pp. 160–165.

gulches became steeply banked in response to the effects of exotic plants and animals on drainage patterns (Latta 1937, p. 21).

Although the degree of environmental alteration that resulted from each of these agencies of change during the initial phase of European contact is difficult to measure, their collective impact was tremendous. The composition and distribution of natural communities were altered, and some communities—notably perennial bunchgrass prairies—were almost completely replaced by invasive communities of introduced plants. Natural landscapes gave way to landscapes created directly or indirectly by human agencies. Although the basin was rapidly depopulated, the human imprint upon its landscapes was greater than ever before. This paradox was not apparent to many later settlers, who thought they confronted a wild, natural landscape. Attempts to tame and repopulate the Tulare Lake Basin would have proceeded very differently, however, had the stage not been set by seven decades of modification by Spanish and Mexican soldiers and explorers and Anglo trappers.

Summary

Hispanic peoples began to arrive in the basin after 1770. At first they did little intentionally to change the regional patterns of land and life, but their diseases, their livestock, and their plants, their politics and their values soon began to wield tremendous influence. They thought of the basin only as a remote backwater, an arid frontier populated by untrustworthy savages. It seemed to offer little except pasturage, and even that was poor in some locales. The Kaweah Delta offered some enticement to settlement, but Hispanic power in Alta California began to wane, and the call to settlement went unheeded.

In the late 1820s and early 1830s, another kind of foreigner began to encroach upon the basin: the Anglo-American trapper, the vanguard of Manifest Destiny. Most trappers had only a passing interest in the basin, but they did take note of what they found there. What they found was a region already severely disrupted: a sparsely peopled domain of sick, hungry, and sullen "Diggers" who preyed upon stray cattle. This they reported dutifully, little realizing how different the basin had been only a half-century before.

4

Manifest Destiny: Anglo Appraisal and Occupation 1844–1856

Never was a land so planned for the uses of man, its shielding mountains, its deep alluvial terraces sloping gently to the sun. Men read this occurrence in the hieroglyphics, the glistening waters spilled between the dark patches of the tulares, but years of experience were necessary to read the message aright. (Austin 1927, p. 151)

A new breed of men entered the Tulare Lake Basin in the 1840s: men with a vision, who came to prepare the way for permanent settlement rather than to rob the land of its resources quickly and then just as quickly depart. Long before the Mexican War of 1846, California was recognized as an inevitable extension of American Manifest Destiny; now the time had come to claim it. Settlement was no longer to be a matter of individual families staking out a likely parcel on a poorly known frontier and trying to eke out a living as best they could. The

United States government had undertaken to survey new lands prior to settlement, in order to determine the location of the best farmland and the best sites for railways and towns. The land, it was hoped, could then be occupied quickly and systematically.

Official Surveys

Columns of smoke were visible in the direction of the tule lakes to the southward—probably kindled in the tulares by the Indians as signals that there were strangers in the valley. (Fremont 1844 in Jackson 1970, p. 663)

Government expeditions to the Tulare Lake Basin were led by John C. Fremont in December, 1844; by George H. Derby in May, 1850; and by R. S. Williamson in July and August, 1853. An earlier expedition sponsored by the U.S. Navy entered the Central Valley in 1841. Without actually visiting the region of Tulare Lake, the expedition, led by Charles Wilkes, disseminated information about the basin collected from other—often inaccurate—accounts (Wilkes 1845, 1849). Among the additional unofficial surveys were those conducted by John Audubon in 1848, James Carson and B. J. Farnham in 1850, Col. Andrew Grayson in 1853, and mountaineer James "Grizzly" Adams in 1855. Fremont's report to the U.S. Army instilled particularly favorable ideas about the Tulare Lake Basin in the American mind: Fremont had concluded that at least the Kings River fan was exceptionally well suited for agricultural settlement (fig. 22a). By goldrush times (1849–1850) the American government deemed it necessary to improve transportation and security throughout the Central Valley, which had overnight become a bustling passageway to the Sierra goldfields. Lieutenant Derby was sent to "find a practical route for loaded wagons from the coast to the Kings River" and "to examine the country for a position for a fort to cover passes to the West" against Yokuts raids (Derby 1852, p. 27; fig. 22b). Under the auspices of the Army Corps of Topographical Engineers, Derby thoroughly explored and carefully appraised the basin, concluding that at least certain areas might be suitable for settlement. In the summer of 1853, another party sponsored by the army and led by R. S. Williamson was dispatched to the basin to find a rail route through the Central Valley in conjunction with the proposed Transcontinental Railroad. William Blake, the expedition geologist, wrote in detail about the basin's agricultural potential; like Derby, he was rather gloomy in his overall portrayal of the basin, but he noted a few favorable sites and resources there (Blake 1853; fig. 22c).

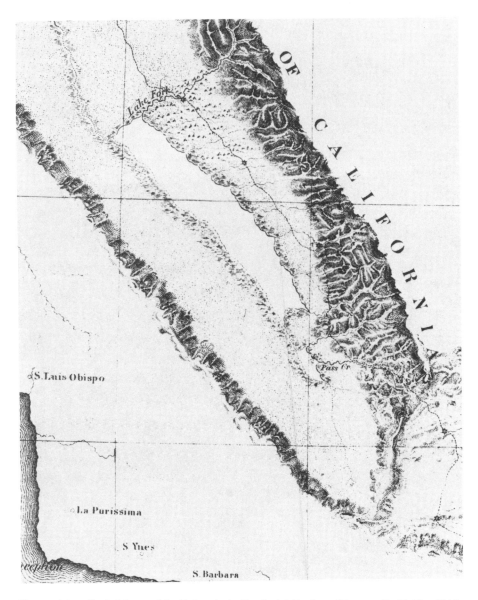

Figure 22. *Early Maps of the Tulare Lake Basin.* (a) Portion of Fremont's 1843–1844 map. One of the first Americans to make an official survey of the Tulare Lake Basin, Fremont helped disseminate initial—but still vague—information concerning the basin's geography and early exploratory routes. (Courtesy of the Bancroft Library, University of California, Berkeley.)

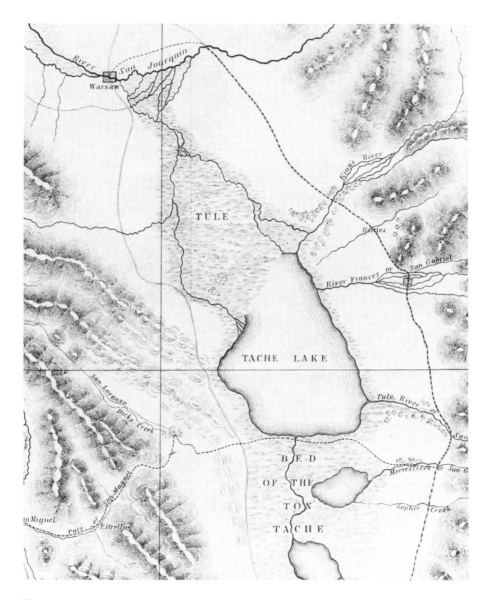

Figure 22*b*. Portion of Derby's 1852 map. Derby's exploration of the Tulare Valley, under the auspices of the Army Corps of Topographical Engineers, was the first thorough and systematic survey of the basin's terrain and settlement potential.

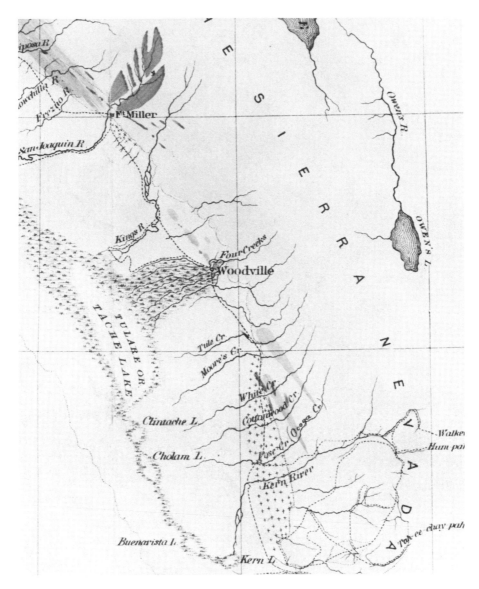

Figure 22*c*. Portion of Blake's 1853 map. The expedition geologist for a Transcontinental Railroad survey, Blake examined the basin's soils, vegetation, and topography in detail, noting the existence of the first American settlement at Woodville [*sic*].

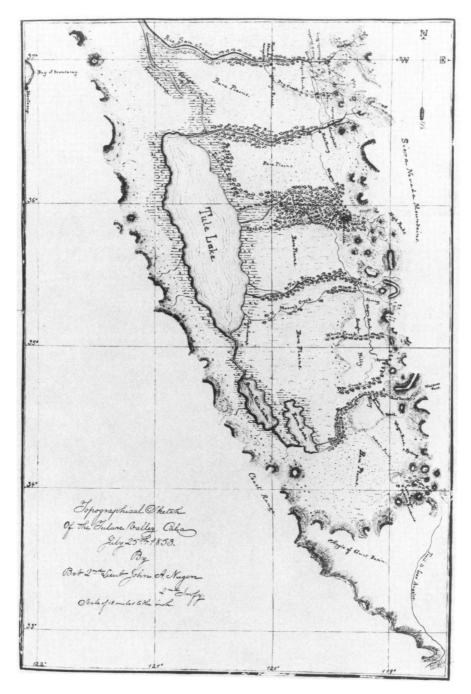

Figure 22*d*. Nugen's 1853 map of the Tulare Valley. Nugen, a military man stationed in the vicinity, paid especial attention to the riparian forests, a striking feature of the otherwise-arid plains.

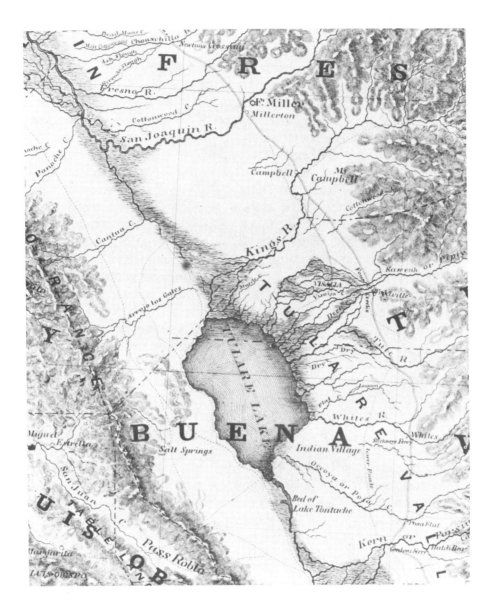

Figure 22e. Portion of Britton and Rey's 1857 map. By 1857 the Basin's topography was well known, and people in other parts of the country were becoming familiar with the Tulare Valley by means of such maps as this.

With the exception of Fremont's winter expedition, most survey parties arrived in the basin during the dry season. Like their Spanish and Mexican predecessors, they concluded from the parched appearance of the countryside that the climate and the general lack of surface water and timber would thwart development of American settlements there:[1] "With the exception of a strip of fertile land upon the rivers emptying into the lake from the east, it is little better than a desert. The soil is generally dry, decomposed and incapable of cultivation, and the vegetation, consisting of artemesias and wild sage, is extremely sparse" (Derby 1852, p. 16). The dry California summers seemed a hindrance, not a boon, to agriculture, and the Great Central Valley's climate was judged to be especially unfavorable: "The climate of this valley is its greatest misfortune. This intense heat poured down so many months upon the submerged prairies, evaporates the water as the time advances, and converts the lakes formed in the wet season into stagnant pools of putrid water, which send out most pestilential exhalations, converting this immense valley into a field of death" (Farnham 1851, p. 328).

American survey parties of this era engaged in the first systematic and scientific survey of basin soils, identifying, classifying, and evaluating them in terms of their physical properties, not simply according to their vegetative cover. For example, Blake wrote of the Kaweah Delta, "The beds of the streams are generally sandy, and the soil near them contains sufficient sand, mingled with the clay, to give it the loose, open character desirable for cultivation" (Blake 1853, p. 27). Blake noted and correctly accounted for the presence of clay and alluvial soils in the basin trough and the coarser texture of surrounding soils (Blake 1853, pp. 190–191). His suggestion that the coarser soils (recent alluvium and old valley fill) would provide a better rail route than the sticky lacustrine soils may have had a profound influence upon the basin's ultimate settlement patterns. Unfortunately, inaccurate appraisals of the basin's soils were still enthusiastically disseminated by some writers—including Farnham, who based his descriptions on hearsay and a brief trip through the Central Valley, describing Tulare Valley soils as "manifestly of volcanic formation, and filled with elements unfriendly to vegetation. On many extensive tracts the muriate of soda covers the ground like frost, and destroys with equal certainty every green thing; while other tracts, larger still, abound in asphaltum, which renders the soil too compact for tillage" (Farnham 1851, p. 327).

1. American appraisals of the basin generally paralleled judgments of the Central Valley as a whole, as examined in Eigenheer's 1976 dissertation, "Early Impressions of Agricultural Resources in the Central Valley of California."

Irrigation and careful scheduling of cropping were suggested as remedies for the adverse effects of dry summers and soil alkalinity. The ease of irrigation in the eastern basin was already evident: "To irrigate the eastern portion it is but necessary to construct dams at the foot of the low hills on the different rivers and lead the water through channels to any portion of the plain desired" (Carson 1852, p. 111). Although some surveyors considered the basin's grasslands infertile and unfit for plow cultivation, others saw the rapid encroachment of European grasses as an indication that pasturage or certain grain crops might flourish there: Carson predicted that "the Tulare Plains will produce, without irrigation, small grain on every foot of them" (Carson 1852, p. 95). Most explorers, however, vowed that grazing was the only proven, suitable, or likely use of the basin prairies or of California in general (Reading 1844; Root 1955, p. 119). The basin's suitability must also have been suggested by the abundance of wild ungulates found there: Audubon reported seeing "a herd of about 1,000 elk" (Audubon 1906, pp. 184–185), and Fremont wrote that he "traveled among multitudinous herds of elk, antelope, and wild horses. Several of the latter, which we killed for food, were found to be very fat" (Fremont 1844 in Nevins and Morgan 1964, p. 17). Carson, with his characteristic enthusiasm, speculated that the basin could, "by introducing on it the herd grass, be converted into the best grazing land in the valley" (Carson 1852, p. 99). The early surveyors also discussed the basin's suitability for human habitation. Valley environments were commonly believed to be unhealthy, as miasmas and exhalations from stagnant marshlands were thought to be the cause of malaria. Addressing this concern, Blake suggested that "it is possible that considerable annoyance will be experienced among settlers from chills and fever; but it might, perhaps, be avoided, to a great degree, by residing on the margin of the adjoining plains, or among the foothills of the mountains. . . . A partial escape would also be thus effected from the great numbers of mosquitos that infest the low ground among the trees" (Blake 1853, p. 27). Although the influence of such common notions upon the basin's early settlement patterns would be hard to gauge— particularly in light of the numerous other considerations involved in the selection of farmland—the early distribution of settlement in the basin would have seemed very reasonable and healthy to Blake.

Early American opinions concerning the various subregions of the basin were remarkably similar to those of the Spanish before them; a hypothetical clockwise tour will illustrate their salient impressions of basin landscapes. Entering from the north, a traveler crossed the Kings River fan, a large tract of fertile land with "broad alluvial bottoms . . . well wooded with several species of oaks" (Fremont 1844 in Nevins and

Morgan 1964, p. 17). After crossing several miles of fertile bottom land, one came to a level plain "intersected here and there with spots of vegetation" (Derby 1852, p. 11); "a rather barren country" (Adams 1855 in Hittell 1911, p. 339), where "a large area of surface is composed almost wholly of clay" (Blake 1853, p. 26). Farther southward lay the Kaweah Delta, and

> here the aspect of the landscape is suddenly changed. Instead of the brown, parched surface . . . to which the eye is accustomed on the surrounding plains, we find the ground hidden from view by a luxuriant growth of grass, and the air fragrant with the perfume of flowers. The sound of flowing brooks, and the notes of the wild birds, greet the ear in strange contrast with the rattling produced by the hot wind as it sweeps over the dried weeds and gravel of the plains. The whole scene is overshadowed by groves of majestic oaks. . . . The soil between the creeks being so well watered and shaded, is naturally of the richest description; as an evidence of which I may mention that I observed poles of willow stuck in the ground by Indians as parts of rabbit traps, which had taken root and sprouted into trees. (Derby 1852, p. 11)

Rich delta landscapes surrounded the traveler as he or she continued on toward the Tule River crossing "rich tracts of arable land, fertile with every description of grass and a fine growth of heavy oak timber in many places" (Derby 1852, p. 10). Williamson noted that "the contrast between this beautifully-green spot and the arid plains on each side is very striking" (Williamson 1853, p. 11). The lushness declined southward across the Tule River fan, and Derby recalled Deer Creek as a sharp divide: southward lay "the most miserable country that I ever beheld. The soil was not only of the most wretched description, dry and powdery and decomposd, but was everywhere burrowed by gophers and a small animal resembling a common house rat. These animals are innumerable, though what they subsist upon I cannot conceive, for there was little or no vegetation" (Derby 1852, pp. 8–9). Turning westward across the southern end of the basin, a traveler crossed "a continuation of the barren sandy desert" (Derby 1852, p. 7), "stretches of alkaline desert, under a sweltering sun, and with mirages mocking us in every direction toward the great Tulare Lake" (Grayson 1920, p. 106). The southern lakeshore was "little more than a very extensive swamp" (Derby 1852, p. 6), and across the swamp lay a still more "miserable barren, sandy desert, with no vegetation but a few straggling artemesias and no inhabitants but attenuated rabbits and gophers" (Derby 1852, p. 15). Such a desert stretched all along the western side of the basin and onto the western foothills, where the ground was "either entirely bare or with a very scanty vegetation of stunted grass and low weeds" (Brewer 1861 in Farquhar 1930, p. 203). Before returning to the Kings River fan, it was necessary to cross the sloughs at the northern end of the lake, but "between these sloughs was miserable in the extreme, and our animals suffered terribly for want of grass" (Derby 1852, p. 16).

As in Spanish times, most favorable comments were reserved for areas where timber and surface water were abundant, especially the upper fans of the Kings and Kaweah rivers and the savannas between the Kaweah River and Deer Creek: "This beautiful plain, covered with luxuriant vegetation, is a fine example of the effect of irrigation, for without these streams it would be a desert . . . and if supplied with water and brought under cultivation would reward the toil of the agriculturalist with rich returns" (Blake 1853, p. 27). The tule marshes inspired the imagination of Carson, who prophesied, "Along the rivers and in the drained tule beds, hemp, flax and tobacco can be raised to an extent and perfection that would stand unparalleled. . . . The tules invite the planter to convert them into rice fields; they can be drained or flooded at pleasure for that purpose" (Carson 1852, p. 95). The prairies might be suitable for grazing, but the flatlands near the lake were "totally unfit for any purpose and can never be settled by anybody but hunters and Indians. We assured the Indians they need not fear squatters, as no white man would ever want their land" (Grayson 1920, p. 106). Despite their reservations concerning the region's settlement potential, American explorers often delighted in the marvelous views they saw from various vantage points around the basin's edge. Before cultivation loosened the soil and made summers dusty, clear air permitted sweeping vistas even in midsummer. From the western foothills, wrote Derby, "with a glass I could distinguish the timber at the north and the tules at the south end of the lake. . . . The peaks of the Sierra Nevada . . . covered with perpetual snow, appeared in close proximity, and rising far above the horizon, seemed as to come down precipitously to the very edge of the water" (Derby 1852, p. 6). And from the Sierra foothills, "there is a magnificent view of the plains of the San Joaquin and Tulares, and of the oak groves of the Four Creeks, spreading out into a wide forest, and uniting on the verge of the horizon with the dark green vegetation of the Tulares . . . and the Coast Mountains may be dimly seen rising above the limits of the far-stretching plains" (Blake 1853, pp. 25, 28).

A Final End to Solitude: First Anglo Settlement

There is no trail but that of wild horses and elk, not a sign of civilization, not the track of a white man to be seen, and sometimes the loneliness and solitude seem unending. (Audubon 1906, p. 185)

The San Joaquin? Why, that's the end of the world. There'll be no settlers there for another generation. (in Lyman 1931, p. 214)

Settlement of the Tulare Lake Basin by Anglo ranchers was hastened by developments elsewhere in California: the gold rush and the ensuing food shortages in California's gold camps and burgeoning cities. From the very beginning, the region was tied into the commercial economy of the state and of the nation. At first it served only as a passageway for people and goods en route to the goldfields of Northern California; but soon vast herds of cattle were brought to the basin to graze, and there was even a brief gold rush in the southeastern foothills.

The first major road to be established through the basin was El Camino Viejo, an inland *carretera* (or cart road) leading from the pueblo of Los Angeles to the Monterey Presidio. This Spanish road crossed the western shore of Tulare Lake and served primarily as an alternate route for travelers who—for reasons of secrecy or banditry—chose to avoid the more heavily traveled El Camino Real, which linked California's missions. Nonetheless, El Camino Viejo (which Americans called "The Old Trace") was an enduring stagecoach and mail route. Because it provided access to the lake plains, it also served as an important local road for west-side cattle ranchers and as a focus of ranch settlement (Latta 1933).

A new route through the Tulare Lake Basin, accessible via Tehachapi or Walker Pass, was the Stockton–Los Angeles Road along the edge of the eastern foothills. It passed through the timbered and well-watered delta lands, which were increasingly the focus of basin settlement, and so was preferable to El Camino Viejo. As east-side stock raising and mining began to prosper, a demand for passage arose where streams crossed the Stockton–Los Angeles Road. Enterprising settlers built ferries across the Kaweah south of the Venice Hills and across the Kings near the foothills and north of Hanford (fig. 23). Some travelers lingered in the vicinity of the ferries to serve the needs of other travelers and of the ranchers who lived in dispersed and isolated dwellings in the lower foothills and near streams. By 1850 a nucleated American settlement had developed near the Kaweah ferry: named Woodsville[2] after its founder, John Wood, it suffered rough beginnings because of Yokuts resentment and competition with other budding towns. Dissatisfaction with the site and situation of Woodsville led several families to strike out in search of a better townsite in the autumn of 1852. They encamped about eight miles west of Woodsville on the north bank of Mill Creek and with the help of local ranchers erected a

---

2. Woodsville is not to be confused with Woodville, a town established eighteen miles to the south at a later time.

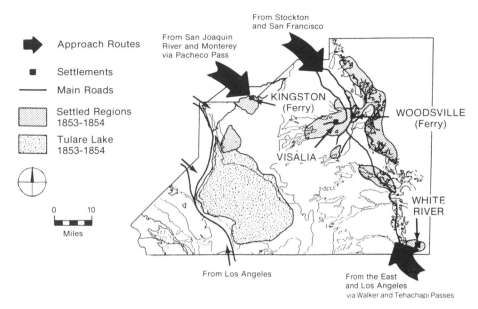

Figure 23. *American Approach Routes and Settlement, 1845–1856.* With American occupation, the focus of attention in the basin shifted to the well-watered east side. Settlement focused upon transport bottlenecks and along the foothill fringe; gold and grazing were the main enticements to settlement, and both drew people to the eastern foothills.

small fort there (fig. 24). This, the nucleus of a new town, they christened Visalia after the Kentucky home of founder Nathan Vise. Because of its central location in an area of rapid settlement, Visalia gained a population of sixty people within a month, quickly surpassing Woodsville (Allen and Avery 1893, p. 229). Once Visalia gained distinction as the seat of newly formed Tulare County in 1853,[3] Woodsville was abandoned (Peterson 1933, p. 123). As Williamson noted, "the delta is fast filling up with American settlers. Already on the second creek is the town of Woodville, which, however, when we passed, contained but one house" (Williamson 1853, pp. 11–12).

Even more important to initial Anglo settlement of the basin than its position astride a route to the gold fields was its function as a stock-raising area. The basin had access to eager markets: the mining towns of the Sierras and the booming cities of Stockton, Sacramento, and San Francisco. Ranching was known to be a successful proposition there; even the dry summers were a boon to grazing because the grass cured naturally to hay (King 1850, p. 35). Feral Spanish and Mexican cattle

3. The Tulare Lake Basin, as the first portion of huge Mariposa County to attract substantial settlement, was the first to be designated as a separate county.

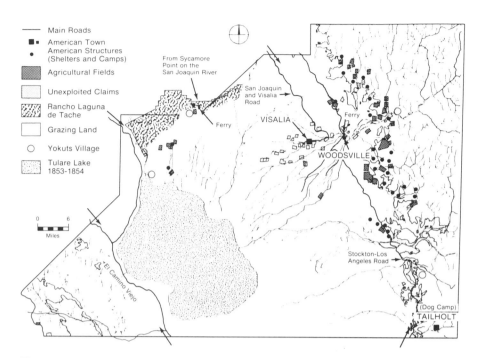

Figure 24.   *Settlement Patterns, 1854.* The early ranching and farming activity was concentrated in the eastern foothills, but by 1854 numerous claims were being staked out along the distributaries of the Kings and Kaweah rivers. (Source: U.S.D.I. General Land Office 1853–1856).

were rounded up and driven to market by basin cowboys, but at first hogs ("tule splitters") were the preferred stock, because they fattened rapidly and could be taken to market either as cured meat or on the hoof. Hogs were taken to the tulares to root in the summertime and driven back to the foothills and oak forests to feed on ripened acorns in the fall (Nordhoff 1872, p. 209). Those that escaped annual roundups menaced Yokuts and Anglo settlers for years to come. The Indian subagent at Visalia reported in 1858 that "most of the acorns gathered by these Indians have been destroyed by the hogs of white men" (Lewis 1858 in Heizer 1974, p. 133). The first American cattle, eastern Durhams and Texas longhorns, were brought to the basin in 1852 and quickly proved more profitable than hogs. Cattle ranching concentrated around Tulare Lake, Visalia, and the Tule River (Mitchell 1976, pp. 34–37), but herds could be run anywhere on the open range. Gradually, however, ranchers began to stake out parcels of the public domain and the Tulare Lake Basin began to pass unofficially into private hands. This trend was supported by the Act to Regulate Rodeos (1851), which held that any unmarked cattle would be considered the property of the owner of the ranch on which they were found.[4] Most of the ranch families lived in wooded areas of the foothills and the upper Tule and Kaweah fans; a few planted crops along the distributaries, but farming was only of minor importance. Food and supplies were freighted in from Stockton, a journey that took seven to fourteen days. The basin's populace in these early years was heavily Southern in heritage: of the 163 American-born settlers in the county in 1852, 95 claimed Southern birth (Peterson 1933, p. 142). The Southern character of the county was somewhat diluted in the course of regional settlement but remained an important aspect of local identity for many years.

The basin again became a pathway for thousands of fortune seekers in 1853; this time they headed southward to a brief gold rush on the Kern River. Soon gold was discovered in the White River area, fulfilling Blake's prediction that it would be found in the vicinity of the Tule River and Deer Creek (Blake 1853, p. 28). A gold camp, Dog Camp, was established in the White River goldfield and eventually grew into the mining town of Tailholt, so called because the miners realized that they had secured only a "tail hold" on the main vein there. By the 1860s the town was known as White River. Though the basin did not prove to be a major gold-producing region, there were still several gold miners listed in the 1860 census. Meanwhile, Visalia thrived as a business and supply center serving ranchers, lumbermen, and passing miners. Soon 1,200 or 1,500 discouraged miners had returned from the gold districts, as Barton recollected, and they "embarked in different callings, such as hog raising, farming, and lumbering. Not a few turbulent spirits—such as gamblers, politicians, and pick-pockets—accompanied this influx. All these different callings left their mark upon the character of the new settlement; some of them for good, some calculated to leave a stain upon the pages of our history" (Barton 1874). Nevertheless, whatever their particular character flaws may have been, these men had come to make their homes in Tulare County. At last cultivation of the basin's lands was undertaken in earnest by a large and energetic population accustomed to gambling on nature and, more importantly, familiar with the techniques of water diversion developed in conjunction with hydraulic mining. As early as 1854 an irrigation project was begun near Visalia, the first such project in the entire San Joaquin Valley and the first step in a new episode of environmental alteration that would ensure the spread of settlement throughout the basin (State

4. In response to the Rodeo Act, annual rodeos were established at several locations in the basin, including Mooney's Grove, Bravo Lake, Elk Bayou, Visalia, Cross Creek, Kings River, and the lakeshore (Latta 1937). These were typical western rodeos, involving competitions, exhibitions, and a great deal of drinking.

of California Engineer 1880, p. 37). Land-use patterns at this time, though, still clearly reflected early judgments concerning the "natural" fitness and limitations of basin lands: cattle grazed on the lake plains, cultivation was confined to alluvial fans and deltas, and settlement was concentrated along streams in the lower foothills and at natural bottlenecks in transportation (fig. 24).

The Original Federal Survey, 1853–1855

Edwin told Amelie she must imagine boundaries where there were none and draw a square for themselves to ensure a precise return. But Amelie could see no hope of geometry imposed upon this great expanse of dried grasses, and laughed even as Edwin spoke of men's papers and plans. They could mean nothing in this vast valley forever set apart between barriers only the lost or foolhardy would cross. (Miller 1938, p. 382)

However ridiculous geometrical division of the empty grasslands might seem, the basin had entered the United States as part of the public domain, and so a rectangular survey would be imposed. The Public Land Survey was held by federal officials to be the first step in effective control of new lands. It facilitated the speedy transfer of land into private hands, so that individual farmers could begin to conquer and improve well-defined parcels of the environment. Parcels arbitrarily designated by lines on paper were thenceforth treated as inviolable and equivalent environments themselves. The framework for the survey of the Central Valley began with the establishment of the Mount Diablo Base Line and Meridian in 1851. With the exception of the Laguna de Tache grant, some foothill and lake-bed regions, and lands experiencing seasonal overflow, most of the basin was surveyed and subdivided by 1855 (fig. 25) into townships of thirty-six mile-square sections. Seasonally overflowed lands were deemed unfit for cultivation and were turned over to the state of California as entire townships of Swamp and Overflowed Lands, which the state was to dispose of in such a way as to promote reclamation (U.S.D.I. General Land Office 1855, p. 18).

In the course of the initial survey, the basin's resources were evaluated more thoroughly and systematically than ever before. Deputy surveyors were instructed to record the agricultural potential of each parcel, as determined through examination of the land surface, soil, vegetation, and water supply (U.S.D.I. General Land Office 1855, pp. 16–18). However scientific this survey was intended to be, though, judgments of agricultural potential were once again based primarily upon the quality and abundance of natural vegetation, and thus the

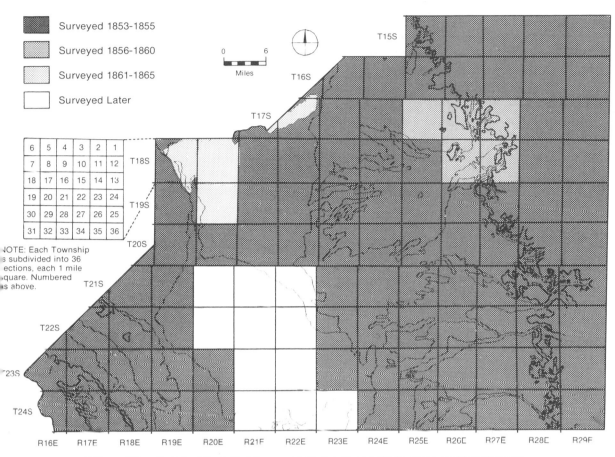

Figure 25. *Dates of the Initial Survey of Federal Land*. To facilitate rapid settlement, the federal government imposed a rectangular survey: each township was subdivided into thirty-six sections, each one mile square (640 acres). The last part of the basin to be surveyed was the reclaimed lake bed. (Source: U.S.D.I. General Land Office 1853–1856.)

federal classification of basin land proceeded in much the same way as had earlier Spanish, Mexican, and American evaluations (Eigenheer 1976, pp. 159–160). Timbered areas were judged to have first-rate soils, while grassland soils were designated as second or third rate, depending upon alkalinity and the apparent health and thickness of grass cover. The similarities of successive land classifications are apparent in the sample townships illustrated in figure 26. Although parcel classifications help quantify surveyors' impressions, they cannot be taken as consistent and accurate appraisals of preagricultural land quality. The ratings were made by different individuals working at different seasons over the course of several years. Annual and seasonal variations certainly influenced assessment of vegetation cover and water supply, and they may also have affected the objectivity of the surveyors themselves. Townships inaccessible during the period of survey either because of flooding or because of the presence of Tulare Lake waters were classified as Swamp and Overflowed Lands, and their entry in the surveyors' record was incomplete or delayed. Given these weaknesses in the evaluation process, the ratings roughly agree with unofficial evaluations and spontaneous observations made prior to the survey by a variety of individuals.

New alluvial soils, timbered and free of alkali, were assigned relatively high ratings (e.g., T18S R25E, T23S R27E, T20S R24E, and T18S R21E, fig. 26). The surprisingly poor showing of T22S R25E may

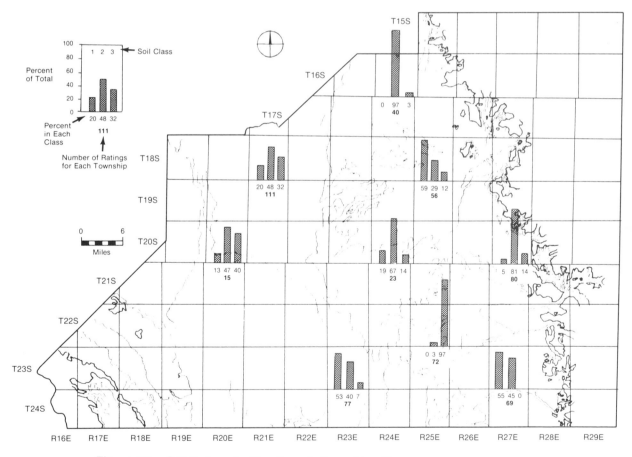

Figure 26. *Soil Ratings for Nine Sample Townships.* The government surveyors evaluated the agricultural potential of the surveyed land, assigning a rating to each parcel. Although ratings were based primarily upon the quality and abundance of natural vegetation, they constituted the first systematic evaluation of the basin's resources. (Source: U.S.D.I. General Land Office 1853–1856.)

be attributed to local alkalinity and to the broken and sandy surface associated with abandoned channels near Sycamore Slough. Townships comprised primarily of old-valley-fill soils, which supported grasslands but rarely showed evidence of strong alkalinity, were judged to include a large proportion of second-rate soils (e.g., T16S R24E, T20S R27E, and T23S R27E); hog wallows were evidently considered neither evidence of low fertility nor major obstacles to cultivation. Variations in the grading of soils in T20S R20E and T23S R23E may be attributed to the belated entry as well as to incomplete recording of classifications within them: by the late 1870s, heavy soils near the valley trough were recognized as suitable for grain production despite their scant vegetation. The surveyors who participated in the original survey typically proposed stock raising as the most profitable use of the basin as a whole and of the San Joaquin Valley in general. Arable lands were thought to lie primarily in timbered areas and on the moist eastern fringe (U.S.D.I. General Land Office 1853–1856; State of California Surveyor General 1854, 1855). Although it was ventured that grasslands might be suitable for limited cultivation (for example, that the high water table might permit the cultivation of winter wheat or barley south of Hanford), such optimism was considered premature.

The effects of the original survey were dramatic and immediately evident, and the concept of land as a commodity was quickly and indelibly imprinted upon the landscapes of the basin. Inherent in this concept was the judgment of land in quantitative terms. The survey fostered psychological and economic frameworks that favored uniformity over diversity, large parcels over small ones. The concept of a balanced farm composed of a variety of kinds of land—such as had been advanced in the Mexican Law of Colonization—was discarded outright, never again to influence regional patterns of land ownership. Settlers hoped to acquire large tracts of level and uniformly excellent land. The luckiest arrivals did so; those who did not, and their successors, would thenceforth strive to impose comparable uniformity upon their own holdings, reforming the natural terrain and native soils to fit the land uses they intended to pursue. The concept of developing a variety of small-scale uses on each farm, uses designed to suit each kind of land, was rejected as inefficient, backward, and uneconomical. The seeds of California agribusiness had been planted.

From the time of the original survey, then, land in the Tulare Lake Basin was a commodity: land ownership allowed speculation in real estate and in the world commodity market. Farmers were increasingly oblivious to local limitations upon land use, and cropping patterns grew more diverse and flexible with rising confidence in technology. Diversity and flexibility in land use proceeded at the expense of, rather than in harmony with, the natural diversity of basin environments. In some ways this would not be fully apparent in the culture and landscapes of the basin for another hundred years, because farmers only gradually acquired the technological means to effect a full separation from natural controls. Nevertheless, the federal survey assumed an initial and continued dominion of people over the environment, and settlers not only respected this concept but demanded its preservation. Property lines became more important by far than the natural processes and patterns that crossed them. Farmers considered themselves part of the life layer only within the confines of their own personal property, and even there their identification with the land—as its owner—was weak and increasingly transitory. Simple identification of units of land on paper also made possible the easy acquisition of property by people who had never been in the vicinity of the basin: the feasibility of land speculation, the concept of improvements or subdivision aimed at future profit, and the gambler mentality of farmers were enhanced and perpetuated, as was the local dominance of the market economy that fueled them.

The Final Reduction of the Yokuts

> After the bloodshed is done we come back to the lake of our fathers. But there is no longer food as there was in the beginning. The antelope and deer are frightened away and the herds no longer come to our waters. We dare not hunt too far, lest the stockmen think we are thieving. The fish are caught with hooks and carried away in barrels, not swimming into out willow traps as we need them. The White men trample our blackberry patches, not caring if the stems that bear fruit are all broken. The ducks fly from the guns and though they come to our traps, they are fewer. Another year with no acorns, our people are too lean to hunt, and the children are starving. ("Indian Harry" in Miller 1938, p. 368)

The relationship between American settlers and Yokuts followed a course similar to that of the earlier relationship between Hispanos and Yokuts. At first, when contact amounted only to brief and occasional encounters between Yankee travelers and resident Yokuts, American impressions of the natives were relatively favorable. Derby described them as "well built athletic men," and noted that "nothing could exceed the kindness and hospitality with which they treated us" (Derby 1852, p. 11). Fremont found them "dark skinned, but handsome and intelligent" (Fremont 1844 in Latta 1949a, p. 29). Such appreciation was short-lived, however. The Yankees had come to occupy and, above all, to control the basin.

Like new settlers everywhere, the Americans arrived in the basin with a well-formulated mental set, but, unlike the Hispanos, they did not include a place for the Yokuts in their social or economic orders. As agricultural settlement extended over the basin, the Yokuts were left to fend for themselves; American social and economic opportunities were off limits to them. As the remaining Yokuts habitats were taken over by swarms of settlers (fig. 27), social friction and outright conflict ensued, setting the stage for the complete separation of the Yokuts from their native land. A necessary precondition for this removal was general acceptance of the notion that the Yokuts were a hindrance to the inevitable and proper development of the basin. This attitude was evident as early as 1846: "As there is little doubt but that the Tulare Valley will be the first place pitched upon by emigrants for settling, we may reasonably hope that the outrages which for so many years have been committed almost with impunity, will in the course of a few months, come to an end" (Garner 1970, p. 172). The mere chance that any land might go undeveloped because of the presence of savages was intolerable (Rawls 1975, p. 433), and within a few years the Yokuts fell to the lowest possible level of esteem in the minds of American settlers. They were odious "Diggers," "wild beasts of the field in human shape," and "thieving, treacherous and bloodthirsty" as well (Carson 1852, pp. 89, 13). Action, either removal or extermination, was demanded by irate settlers who petitioned the Indian subagent at Fort Miller (near Fresno):

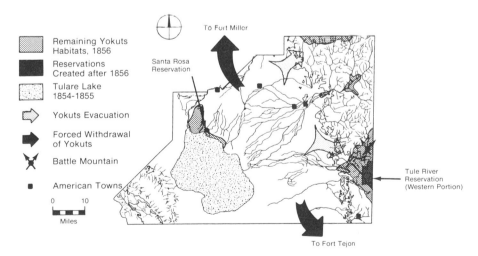

Figure 27. *Final Reduction of the Yokuts, 1850s.* The few surviving Yokuts were forced to abandon their old habitats completely and either take up residence on reservations or else retreat to marginal lands that were of little value to American settlers.

"The presence of these Indians in a region so densely populated by whites whose exclusive business is stock-raising is prejudicial to their interests in many ways. These Indians and a community of stock-growing people cannot inhabit the same country. . . . This is the last time their peaceable removal will be attempted and . . . should they return they will surely be harshly dealt with" (letter to Lewis 1858 in Heizer 1974, p. 130).

Important as removal or outright extermination were in the reduction of the Yokuts, disease and habitat destruction were the primary agents of their demise. As a soldier wrote to his commander at Fort Miller in 1853: "I find that a great number of them fall victim yearly to the fever, ague or other fevers so prevalent during the summer and fall months, their mode of living being no guarantee against disease" (letter to Wright 1853 in Heizer 1974, p. 12). By 1853 only one or two thousand Yokuts lived in the basin (Heizer 1974, p. 22), primarily in the foothills, on the eastern lakeshore, and among the timber on the upper Kaweah fan. These survivors had to contend with direct and indirect destruction of their food supplies, the second major cause of Yokuts reduction. Food caches were vandalized by settlers and livestock, and Yokuts habitats were destroyed indirectly by long-term environmental change. Domestic and feral livestock also competed with the Yokuts for the basin's acorns, roots, and grass seeds in an ecological struggle recognized as early as 1856: "Their spring and summer food such as clover, wild lettuce, serrino, grass roots and various other kinds of vegetables . . . have this season, and will hereafter be, consumed by cattle, horses, and hogs before maturity. The acorns, the most important and most available breadstuff, . . . are consumed by the hogs of the whites" (Lewis 1856 in Heizer 1974, p. 254).

As their traditional subsistence methods became increasingly futile, the Yokuts turned more and more to preying upon the domestic livestock of settlers: "The wild Indians give us some trouble. They come down from the tulares, steal our horses and drive them into the mountains where they kill and eat them. They prefer horse flesh to the finest beeves" (Garner 1970, p. 200). The inevitable consequence of this adaptation—the expropriation of American property—was warfare: "Times are squally here. The Indians have broke out on the Four Creeks, and driven off a great many cattle. They have stolen three or four hundred head of horses from Santa Barbara, and carried them up into the mountains on Tule River. The miners on Kern River have quit work and forted up. There have been two fights on Four Creeks, and the Americans were whipped both times" (Bright 1856). Several battles and massacres occurred between 1844 and 1856, culminating in the last great act of Yokuts defiance at Battle Mountain in 1856 (fig. 27).

In 1857, the final vestiges of Yokuts relationships to the land were preserved in the establishment of a reservation located three miles east of Porterville. This site proved too close for the settlers' comfort, however, and in 1876 the reservation was relocated to its present site ten miles up the south Tule River on 42,500 acres withdrawn from public sale in 1873. Nearly 1,200 people from various aboriginal groups were taken to the Tule River reservation as wards of the federal government (Robinson 1955, p. 13). A few Yokuts managed to stay outside the reservation, in the foothills or among the tules, where they "were almost universally employed by settlers in various callings—in guiding the plow through the primeval sward, in fencing new fields, in depositing the seed in the earth, or in guarding the increase of herds" (Barton 1874). Nonetheless, most were eventually rounded up and taken to the small Santa Rosa reservation near Lemoore. By 1905 there were only 154 Yokuts in the basin. Their culture and their intimate relationship to the land were gone forever. Population fluctuated somewhat thereafter but never again reached substantial proportions: in 1960 only 325 Yokuts lived on the Tule River reservation (Curtis 1907–1930, vol. 14, p. 153; State of California Advisory Commission on Indian Affairs 1966, pp. 81–82). Their only lasting legacy in the basin consists of transliterated toponyms (Kaweah, Yokohl, Wutchumna, Tache), low midden mounds near the vanished lakeshore, game fields, and small artifacts (mortars and pestles, arrow points) that are discovered from time to time as fragile reminders to present inhabitants that other people lived in the Tulare Lake Basin long before the coming of the whites.

Environmental Alteration

The appearance of the landscape changes with the changing civilization. . . . The wild, the romantic, the beautiful yield to the shock of pioneer civilization. Forests are felled, and lowing herds soon give to the broad plain the appearance of a desert waste. . . . The stock beat down the undergrowth, and enabled the streams to deepen their own channels, whereby the swamps were reclaimed into dry land, almost in defiance of the efforts of man. (Barton 1874)

Ideas, technologies, and life-forms introduced from elsewhere continued to transform basin landscapes during the early years of American settlement. Natural communities were disrupted by growing numbers of livestock and feral animals, and by accidental introductions of exotic plants. European annual grasses continued to spread vigorously at the expense of native bunchgrasses, and seeing how these foreign grasses flourished, settlers began to contemplate the large-scale introduction of field grains (Reading 1844). Native wildlife was further diminished by hunting, habitat destruction, and competition with domestic species for the available forage. The new settlers quickly undertook the forceful transformation of the physical landscape as well. Water was diverted, trees felled, fields plowed and fenced, roads built, and towns established. All of this took place on a localized scale during this early period, but the impact was significant: in the process of forceful American expansion, the Yokuts landscapes—like the Yokuts themselves—were swiftly and almost completely removed. The very nature of American attitudes toward their land was, indeed, something the Yokuts could barely fathom.

Summary

Intelligent Indians tell of a company of two or three white men who came through here, perhaps as early as 1845. In each of [their camps] they cut down a tree. The cutting of these trees filled the Indians with more consternation and horror than any phenomena they have been privileged to witness before or since. The word was sent from tribe to tribe that a large coyote, with white eyes and long, red hair covering its face, had destroyed two trees by force—a work thought to be impossible with man. (Barton 1874)

The years from 1844 to 1856 were most important as a transition between two very different ways of life in the Tulare Lake Basin: the termination of a balanced relationship between land and people, and the introduction of a new relationship based upon forceful control of the land by people. American settlement of the basin was spurred by developments elsewhere in California, especially the rising demand for food occasioned by the gold rush and the rapid urbanization of the San Francisco Bay Area and the Sacramento–San Joaquin Delta. Settlement was also regulated by outside controls, especially the framework of settlement and property relations implemented by the federal government for the orderly colonization of the American West. This, perhaps, was the most dramatic change during the initial era of American settlement: the Tulare Lake Basin (like the state of California as a whole) was transformed from an isolated and self-sufficient world unto itself into a small part of a very large world, a place in which people depended upon outside connections for their very subsistence.

5

The Formative Era,
Part I: Establishing
The Modern Patterns
of Settlement
and Land Use
1857–1871

This country is so remote from the main centres of population that probably the chief occupation of residents here must be the breeding of cattle and sheep. (Hittell 1866, p. 158)

In the 1850s and early 1860s, the Tulare Lake Basin remained a vast, dry pasture in practice as well as in the minds of visitors and settlers. The dry grassland environment, the geographical isolation, and a conservative outlook combined to retard agricultural diversification even when the rest of California began to boom in the years after the gold rush. In 1857 only 2,700 of the county's 105,600 acres of arable land were planted to crops, the majority of this along the Kaweah distributaries. Cattle, sheep, hides, leather, and wool were shipped out of the basin in exchange for currency, food, and dry goods. The cattle economy and ranching lifestyle flourished until the mid-1860s, when changing cultural and environmental conditions brought about substantial reorientations.

Stock Culture: Gamblers and Pikes

South of the San Joaquin cattle have been up until now supreme, and their owners—who were not and are not always owners of the soil, but often mere squatters—have assumed all the power and airs of lords of the country. (Nordhoff 1872, pp. 196–197)

California's phenomenal population growth, especially the rapid growth of its cities, sustained a rising demand for meat and crops long after the gold camps disbanded. Much of the grazing land of the state was soon converted to cropland, but cultural and environmental conditions in the basin supported the continuation of ranching. There were great expanses of open range and suitable forage, plenty of livestock, and an eager market. Ingrained prejudices also protected the low labor requirements of stock raising: many of the ranchers were former miners who gambled on the natural fertility of the basin just as they had gambled on striking it rich in the mines. They simply bought some animals, set them out to pasture, and waited. If, at the time of the annual rodeo, they found their herds had increased—why, the gamble had been a success. They raised no feed, provided few shelters, drilled few wells, and built no fences, and they claimed huge tracts of land as ranches: John Sutherland's alone covered 14,000 acres on the south side of the Kings River (Smith 1932, p 47). Despite rampant plant and animal introductions which greatly changed its natural communities, the basin's landscapes remained nongeometrical and natural in appearance.

The emergence of the Tulare Lake Basin as stock country was evident in the federal census of 1860: Tulare County far surpassed Fresno County, its only San Joaquin Valley competitor, in population as well as in stock numbers and agricultural production (table 1). The Kern River Basin and the Owens Valley, still part of Tulare County at this time, were sparsely settled and sparsely grazed until the late 1860s, when they emerged as new focuses of stock culture and (like Fresno and Tulare counties before them) claimed new political identities of their own. Thereafter, the Tulare Lake Basin and Tulare County were roughly coextensive until Kings County was created in 1893 (fig. 28),

TABLE 1

Selected Statistics of Tulare and Fresno Counties, 1860

	Tulare County	Fresno County
Number of inhabitants	4,638	4,605
Number of farms	469	85
Improved acres	20,313	3,770
Bushels of wheat and barley	69,507	26,975
Value of orchard and garden products	$6,405	$1,250
Value of animals slaughtered	$75,995	$1,650
Number of range cattle	37,379	10,444
Number of sheep and swine	49,067	36,777

SOURCE: U.S.D.I. Census Office 1864, Vol. III.

although Tulare County has continued to include a sparsely settled expanse of foothills and the High Sierras.[1]

As the reputation of Tulare County spread, cattlemen from such Southern states as Missouri, Arkansas, Tennessee, and Texas streamed into the southern San Joaquin, to the Visalia region in particular.[2] Of the 3,300 non-Indians in the county by 1860, half were Southern born, and three-fourths of these were male (Hittell 1866, p. 462; Nordhoff 1872, p. 195). These so-called Pikes (after Pike County, Missouri) shared a strong distaste for farming and a hearty dislike of racial minorities. They also had distinctive tastes in food and housing, as well as strong political beliefs: so strong were their Southern loyalties that the federal government felt compelled to maintain military facilities at Fort Babbot (Visalia) during the Civil War (Rush 1964, p. 130), "for this town [Visalia] has long been the Mecca of the Pike. His cattle wandered over a million of acres hereabout; his will was law; his vacqueros were the ministers of his will and his voice was public opinion" (Nordhoff

1. The sparsely-settled eastern portion of Tulare County is not here considered as part of the Tulare Lake Basin, but because only a tiny fraction of it is suitable for settlement or cultivation, its inclusion in census statistics does not significantly affect figures. That is, Tulare County statistics generally derive from the characteristics of the Tulare Lake Basin itself. Note also that Tulare County, and later Kings County, statistics do not include the northwestern corner of Kings County until this area was ceded by Fresno County in 1909.

2. A saddle-manufacturing industry was engendered in Visalia as an outgrowth of the area's stock-raising emphasis. Known as the Visalia saddle, the product had a low horn, skirt, and other design features that proved more comfortable than traditional saddles for both rider and horse; this basin innovation diffused widely throughout the American West (Mitchell 1976, pp. 45–48).

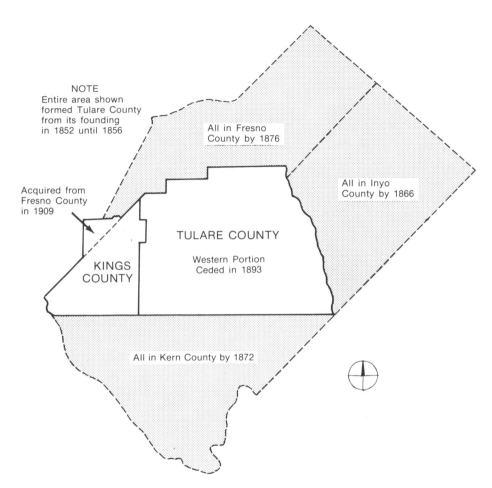

Figure 28. *Political Boundaries of Tulare and Kings Counties.* Tulare County was formed from part of Mariposa County in 1852, and its area was reduced steadily from 1856 onward. Areas subsequently included in Inyo, Kern, and Fresno counties are shown on the map by broken lines. Kings County was formed from the western portion of Tulare County in 1893 and attained its present boundaries in 1909, when it annexed part of Fresno County. (Source: Coy 1973.)

1872, p. 195). This populace had a marked effect upon the basin's towns, which served as "mere feeders to the mines, the cattle ranches, the sheep country. They had the manners of the frontier and the decaying, tawdry vices that filtered down from San Francisco, sluiced out by intermittent spasms of reform. They were wide open, . . . a very cesspool of the iniquities driven to a last stand by the influx of home-seekers" (Palmer and Austin 1914, pp. 136–137). The prejudices, perceptions, and traditions of the Pikes lingered in the basin long after stock raising had declined in importance, and the stock raiser's heritage of expansive holdings and boom-or-bust enterprises remained indelibly etched in the character and landscapes of the Tulare Lake Basin.

In the early 1860s the arrogant cowboy character[3] of the basin began to crumble in the face of climatic fluctuations, the effects of careless land use, and the encroachment of new technologies, economies, and ideas. These forces brought sharp reorientations in land use and the development of a new regional character that persisted into the twentieth century. Ranchers had been encouraged by a healthy market to increase their herds without regard for the capacity of the rangelands or the quality of the stock, and large numbers of cattle starved to death during the droughts of the late 1850s and 1860s. A Mussel Slough woman vividly recalled life on the lakeshore during such a year:

> The country was nothing but a dry, barren desert with bands of wild roving cattle that would come out of the timber along the river in the morning and go out to the lake to feed. Where the water of the lake had receded a little grass would spring up and they would get a little feed. The poor things were almost starved . . . so we could not blame them for eating the hay we had stacked for our horses. The settlers all dug ditches for fences to keep them out but without much effect. (in Brown 1941, p. 82)

The real upheaval of the basin's livestock economy, however, came in response to the floods of 1861 and 1862, when thousands of cattle drowned. Before recovery could be made, drought struck again, followed by another severe flood in 1867–1868. In both floods the rising waters spilled far beyond the official limits of Swamp and Overflowed Lands.

These natural calamities initiated a slow transition to pasture management and stock improvement (Burcham 1957, pp. 253–262), but when the floodwaters subsided, farmers found it easier than before to secure good lands around the distributaries of the Kings, Kaweah, and Tule rivers. Some ranchers had left the basin forever; indeed, Tulare County's population actually declined from 4,638 in 1860 to 4,533 in 1870 (U.S.D.I. Census Office 1864, 1872). Recovery was effected, not by a return of the ranchers, but by immigration of new farmers. Shortly after the 1868 flood it was discovered that soils that supported good stands of introduced pasture grasses would also grow wheat and barley, and soon an influx of hopeful homesteaders arrived. This first

---

3. In a trip through the basin in 1855, Ingraham Kip (first Protestant Episcopal bishop of California) described it as a lawless country, "infested with Californian and Mexican, whose trade is robbery, and who will often down a traveller for the sake of the horse on which he is mounted" (Kip 1892, pp. 30–31).

revival was short-lived: many of these immigrants left the basin during the three succeeding years of drought for places where, "as they said, 'it rained sometimes.' Multitudes went to Oregon" (Cone 1876, p. 102). Nevertheless, grain cultivation in the basin was encouraged by a strong demand for flour in California and around the world, and farming soon became a strong competitor for Tulare County grasslands.

The transition from ranching to farming did not go smoothly at first, for competition overlapped into social spheres. Ranchers chided the newcomers as "sky farmers" or "sandlappers"; the former term referred to their dependence upon the basin's unreliable rainfall, while the latter likened them to a local bird that scratched in the dry sand for food. Conflicts between farmers and the dwindling ranks of ranchers were largely resolved by passage of the so-called No Fence Law (Act of February 4, 1874), which reversed the stipulations of the Trespass Act. This act, popularly known as the Fence Law, had permitted ranchers to let their herds roam freely over the open range, for farmers could sue for damages to their crops only if their fields were fenced. Since fencing was prohibitively expensive in treeless regions of the basin prior to the invention of barbed wire (in 1874), this law effectively discouraged the expansion of cropping. The No Fence Law enabled farmers to confiscate stray cattle and to sue ranchers for damage to their crops, regardless of whether their fields were fenced (Ludeke 1980). The arrival of the basin's first rail line, in 1871, also hastened the demise of the free range and helped ensure the security and profitability of farming in the Tulare Lake Basin. As Nordhoff noted at the time,

> The railroad is really a great civilizer. It not only quiets the Indians—it drives off the Pikes. . . . The Pikes, poor and rich, are panic-struck. They are getting ready to leave the country before the railroad shall utterly ruin it. And they are wise. Their empire is gone. . . . They are selling out cheap, and emigrating by scores to Arizona, and if you were here now you might buy town lots and farms at very moderate prices, from men who "don't mean to live near no railroad, not if they know it." (Nordhoff 1872, p. 196)

Cattle ranching withdrew from recent alluvial lands, but with new breeds of cattle (which replaced the longhorns still common as late as 1872) and more intensive management, stock ponds, and irrigated pastures, it remained a significant land use in the basin.

Many cattle ranchers turned to sheep raising in the hope that sheep might be better able to subsist during dry years than cattle. Despite low wool prices after the Civil War, stock raisers rapidly built up their flocks, and soon Tulare County was the leading sheep-raising county in California.[4] The flocks were led to mountain pastures in the Sierras and coast range during the dry summer and driven back to the prairies in winter. This scheme made good use of the available forage and kept sheep raising viable despite the protracted drought of 1877−1879. Transhumance remained an important economic pattern in the basin until Sequoia National Park, established in 1890, barred sheep from its mountain meadows. Eventually the sheep industry was regulated by the same competition that had affected cattle and swine ranching before: sheep were relegated to marginal lands[5] and to areas remote from lines of transportation. As farming expanded over the moist delta lands, stock raising retreated toward the valley trough and onto the dry grasslands of old valley fill. In the 1880s the basin's sheep industry focused on the White River−Deer Creek area, but as grain replaced pasturage and was in turn replaced by diversified cropping, sheep raising was pushed to the basin trough and arid western foothills (Mitchell 1976, p. 92). By 1900 Lemoore was the nation's primary shipping point for wool. Stock raisers retreated from some areas even before homesteaders had arrived, and the relatively dense ranch settlement of such places as the Yokohl and Frazier valleys was never replaced by farm settlement of comparable density. Remnants of the cattle era survived in the landscape, however, with "low, formless houses with purlieus of pomegranate and pampas grass and black figs, and the high, stockaded, acrid-smelling corrals to mask the receding waves of the cattle industry. On the Sierra side the guttered mesas, the hoofworn foothills advertise the devastation of the wandering flocks" (Palmer and Austin 1914, pp. 130−131).

Early Agricultural Diversification

The Truth is, that much of this great valley is so fit for a garden that it is wasteful to use it for a cattle or sheep range, or for field crop. Wherever the farmer can have water for irrigation, the careful culture of small tracts will pay, for many years to come, extraordinary profits. (Nordhoff 1872, p. 200)

4. Sheepherders came to the basin from other lands as well, as Mary Austin noted with some distress: "In the sixties there appeared little, long armed French and Basques, with hungry hordes of sheep at their heels, pasturing in the public lands" (Palmer and Austin 1914, p. 131).

5. *Marginal lands* is a subjective designation and its application herein changes through time. In any given era covered by this study it is used to denote lands that were at the time considered unfit for the prevailing crop(s) or activities. During this early period, it applies to all land except recent alluvium.

As stock culture declined in the 1860s, the Tulare Lake Basin proved to be one of the most attractive agricultural frontiers of California. Its virtues were touted far and wide: "Here are lands for all, a fertile soil, a delightful climate, and everything the heart of man can desire. Timber and water are abundant, and the woods provide for thousands of swine. Every description of grain, fruit and vegetables can be raised in profusion. Thousands of acres of swamp land await reclamation to become equal in fertility to the Delta of the Nile" (Fabian 1869, p. 23). The remarkable agricultural capabilities of the well-watered, level alluvial lands were quickly demonstrated, and an established settlement network promised to ease the colonization process. Gold, grazing lands, and the lake had lost their power to attract immigrants to the basin; now the quality of the basin's soil was touted. Like gold and the natural grasslands, soil became a speculative commodity, real estate, a medium to be used in satisfying commercial markets and personal ambitions. And farming became a business venture: "Farmers who have the means to buy a house and maintain themselves one year have a sure thing if they will enter into more varied culture than only wheat" (Bowles 1869, p. 444).

Land legislation promoted easy access to the public domain, and settlers and speculators rushed in to claim farmland and townsites. Land values rose rapidly as booster campaigns spread information (and misinformation) about the basin's potential for agricultural success and town growth. The California State Agricultural Society, founded in 1854, printed promising accounts in its *Transactions*, and the San Joaquin Valley Agricultural Society was organized in 1860 expressly for the purpose of advertising the virtues of the region's eight counties. The expectations of early settlers were colored, however, by familiarity with the regions they had recently departed: "In Missouri the land had been green and rolling, with a slope down to the river and a rise of cornfield or woodland, . . . but here, as on the ocean, were only two surfaces—there, water and sky; here, land and sky" (Miller 1938, p. 384). The flatness of this touted paradise, and its dryness, shocked and disappointed many newcomers and became overriding images of the place. To immigrants from lands where abundant timber was a sure sign of fertility, the basin's general lack of trees seemed a "grand obstacle in the way of agricultural improvement" (Dana 1861, p. 305). The grasslands, especially the dry prairies on old valley fill, were still thought fit only for grazing (Eigenheer 1976, p. 385), and until 1868 the wooded distributaries of the Kings, Kaweah, and Tule fans remained the focuses of settlement and cultivation. Characterizations such as this were commonly applied to soils of the valley trough and on the wide interfluves between distributaries: "From the bend of the San Joaquin

River, southward, a district 60 miles wide by 150 long, most of the soil is a barren sand, in many places covered with an alkaline efflorescence" (Hittell 1866, p. 157). J. D. Whitney, the official state geologist, condemned the soil between the Kings River and the Kaweah Delta as "crisp with alkali and salt, as if it had been frozen while saturated with water" (Whitney 1865, p. 367). The lands south of the Tule River evoked a similar description: "The road this day was through a desolate waste—I should call it a desert—a house at Deer Creek and another at White River were the only habitations. The soil was barren and, this dry year, almost destitute of vegetation" (Brewer 1863 in Farquhar 1930, p. 381). In the 1860s there was a new interest in scientific explanation of natural phenomena, and soil fertility was usually explained in terms of climate: the dry atmosphere of the basin must hinder the decomposition of wood and grasses, which under moister conditions enriched the soil (Hittell 1866, p. 11). If this was the case, then clearly only the moister soils of the basin would have agricultural potential. Once again the Kaweah Delta emerged as the most attractive part of the basin, "a large tract of fertile land with abundant moisture" (Hittell 1866, p. 158).

Those engaged in agricultural experimentation began to focus upon improving their understanding of the diversity of soil characteristics, the extent of particular soil types, and the crops best suited to each. In a new wave of optimism, it was suggested that even alkali lands—long thought fit only for grazing—might be made to grow "bulbous, tuberous and leguminous plants, such as potatoes, turnips, carrots, beets, parsnips, beans, peas, vetches and clovers" (Thompson 1857, p. 147). The vast tule lands, so long condemned as loathsome malarial swamps, were reappraised as well. This new awareness of the diverse potential of lands once considered marginally suited to settlement was directly related to settlers' new-found confidence in reclamation. Tobacco, rice, wheat, cotton, and grapes were suggested as likely crops for reclaimed lands (Fabian 1869, p. 25; Hittell 1866, p. 181; Cronise 1868, pp. 324–328). One man speculated that, if drained, the lake bed might be planted to vineyards, while another suggested that grapes might be grown with success on dry terraces near the foothills (Hyatt 1867, p. 48). Another premature suggestion was to plant the tule lands to cotton, although it was cautioned that "its cultivation can never be extensive. The cotton states have three times as much rain as California, and I presume that only our moistest lands could produce a good crop of it" (Hittell 1866, p. 181).

Few new suggestions were actually implemented on a commercial scale in the basin during this period, for, as Nordhoff observed, "the old settlers have but little energy for such new pursuits, and in general, where they do not keep cattle, they content themselves with wheat, barley, and other field crops, and do not plant trees" (Nordhoff 1872, p. 200). The fact that innovative land uses were suggested at all, however, reflects a new sense of the diverse potential of the basin. A great deal of small-scale experimentation with new crops was under way in California in the 1860s, encouraged by a State Bounty Act (1862) that offered premiums for the cultivation of a wide variety of crops. Many experimental plots of new crops were planted on the Kaweah Delta, often with very successful results. By 1867, fully 9,000 of the basin's 14,000 arable acres were planted to crops other than grain or else left fallow (Chapman and Gordon 1867). The basin stayed ahead of adjacent areas during the 1860s despite rapid settlement of the San Joaquin Valley as a whole, and by 1870 Tulare County boasted 35,000 improved cropland acres to Fresno County's 24,500 and Kern County's meager 9,000 (U.S.D.I. Census Office 1872, Vol. II). Still, overall, innovation stopped far short of the basin's potential:

> When one compares the possibilities of this region with what he finds actually accomplished, he is always disappointed. The orange grows near and in Visalia; the olive would flourish there; of the English walnut there are some good trees, and in the foothills all these and the almond would do well, even better, I think, than about Los Angeles; for in the foothills they have scarcely a touch of frost. But there are not more than six bearing orange trees, nor a dozen olives within twenty miles of Visalia, and the culture of these profitable fruits is scarcely known. (Nordhoff 1872, p. 200)

Whatever promises were made concerning the profitability of diversification, wheat and barley remained the most easily grown and marketed cash crops. Grain grew on delta bottomlands with unquestioned success. The absence of trees made clearing unnecessary, while the dry season controlled plant diseases and prevented interruptions in summer growth. Farmers could even postpone harvests in the basin without fear of sudden storms, and they could store grain in the open until wagons came to take it to port (Silver 1868, pp. 177–178). Grain quickly became the major crop of the Tulare Lake Basin and, in fact, of the whole Central Valley as well. The expansion of grain farming stalled temporarily at the edge of new alluvial lands, but timid experiments with dryland grain farming on old valley fill soon dispelled old fears that lack of timber meant infertility. The farming frontier spilled out across the plains as continued immigration, a good market for grain, and (in 1872) the coming of the railroad fueled the advance of settlement. Visions of wheat's future in the basin grew still more grandiose when the adobe soils of reclaimed marshlands proved to be adaptable to grain production (Fabian 1869, p. 27). Already the basin landscape of the 1870s could be foretold: "wall-to-wall wheat."

In the spirit of renewed expansion of settlement and renewed concentration on cereal grains, farmers abandoned their interest in exploring the region's varied agricultural potential. Land was again assessed sheerly in terms of amount, rather than kind: wheat grew well on most soils, and profitable grain farming required large-scale operations. Transportation access was one of the few remaining qualitative concerns. Wheat barons replaced cattle barons after only a brief flurry of small-farm diversity. Both achieved success through the exploitation of the basin's grasslands; both ignored the potential selectivity inherent in the land and so intensified the region's vulnerability to the whims of nature. Moreover wheat farmers, like the cattle ranchers before them, placed their hopes on short-term gain rather than on long-term prosperity:

> The farming is, for the most part, slip-shod and disgraceful. In the whole San Joaquin Valley, from Stockton to the Tejon Pass, I have not seen a dozen well-kept farms, and yet I have traveled slowly and kept my eyes open. It should be said that the Valley has hitherto attracted but little attention from farmers with capital . . . and it must be added that a great many people have quietly got rich in it by the most slip-shod farming. You would be surprised to see how much wealth is in the hands of farmers and grazers about a place like Visalia—and what poor use they make of it. (Nordhoff 1872, p. 228)

Slipshod methods and short-term gambles were by no means inexcusable, however, for there were a great many risks involved in basin farming in the early years. Pioneer settlers had to cope with the depredations of wild animals upon their livestock and their crops, as well as with malaria and other frustrations. To settlers from the humid East, the unfamiliar and unpredictable climate proved especially vexing. Traditional folk wisdom and hallowed rituals were unsatisfactory: nearly all customary agricultural practices had to be adapted in some way before they were useful in this new clime, and even careful adaptation did not always ensure success. Protracted drought could deny farmers their crops even if they employed the most modern and scientific methods of dryland cultivation. Following the severe drought of 1862–1864, basin farmers decided to assert control over at least one aspect of their environment: surface water. In this they were assisted by the great wealth of hydraulic technology and engineering confidence that remained as a legacy of the gold rush. The first agricultural diversions of water in the basin were made near Visalia and on the upper Tule River in the mid-1850s (Grunsky 1898a, b; fig. 29). Irrigation systems were gradually implemented with success along the Kings River, Deer Creek, and even Sand Creek (Browne 1869 p. 206). So well arranged in relation to early settlement, many natural distributaries and sloughs were straightened or deepened and integrated into irri-

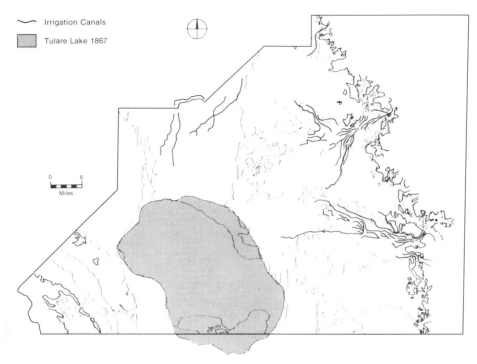

Figure 29. *Irrigation Canals, 1871*. The first agricultural diversions of water in the basin were made near Visalia and on the upper Tule River in the mid-1850s. So well arranged were they in relation to early settlement that many natural distributaries and sloughs were integrated into irrigation systems. (Sources: Grunsky 1898*a*, 1898*b*; Hall 1886.)

gation systems: among these were Outside, Deep, and Mill creeks on the Kaweah, upper Mussel Slough on the Kings, and Porter and Callisan's sloughs on the Tule. Other potential sources of irrigation water, including groundwater, were not tapped at this time, although it was noted that "lying as it does between two great mountain ranges, there is no reason to doubt that flowing wells can be got" (Nordhoff 1872, p. 201).

Drought was not the only incentive for the development of irrigation. Diversification, intensification, and land speculation also required such improvements. The earliest systems reflected the subsistence needs of isolated stock raisers, but by the early 1860s irrigation was seen as a tool for increasing crop yields. As large-scale grain farming became preeminent, small farmers needed either to ensure high yields of grain or to diversify their production. Both options demanded irrigation, and early irrigation projects were most often joint efforts of many small farmers. Large landholders did not generally invest in irrigation until the 1870s and 1880s, in part because of their reliance upon economies of scale. Their hesitance may also have stemmed from observation of the early irrigation systems used by their small-farm neighbors: some systems were poorly adapted to local conditions, most were extremely wasteful of water,[6] and not all were particularly successful in raising yields. Ultimately, though, farmers large and small recognized the speculative value of watering arid lands. Irrigation development proceeded apace as confidence in the future settlement potential of the basin grew and individual ties to the land loosened. By 1871 irrigation was a significant feature of Tulare County agriculture, especially on the Tule and Kaweah river fans. By 1899 the basin dominated the southern San Joaquin Valley in irrigated acreage (table 2), and the development and refinement of irrigation systems has continued ever since.

Building Homes and Empires: Claiming the Public Domain

> The railroad which is shortly to run through this country will cause an influx of thousands of settlers, who will here make for themselves the most delightful homes in the world. To Tulare County the immigrant in search of land can direct his steps with the surety of meeting with what he wants. (Fabian 1869, p. 23)

The rate and character of basin settlement were heavily influenced by land-alienation policies administered by the federal and state governments. The grid laid down on initial survey provided a uniform

6. Conservation of irrigation water was not undertaken in earnest until the 1880s and 1890s, when the price of water rose and the allotment per acre diminished (Grunsky 1898*a*, 1898*b*).

TABLE 2

Progress of Irrigation in the Southern San Joaquin Valley, 1890–1899

Acres irrigated	1890[1]	1899
Tulare Lake Basin	168,455	179,648
Kings County		92,794
Tulare County	168,455	86,854
Fresno County	105,665	283,737
Kern County	154,549	112,533

SOURCES: U.S.D.I. Census Office 1896, Vol. V; 1901, Vol. V.

[1]Earlier statistics of irrigation not available.

matrix for rapid implementation of policies that, like the survey system itself, largely ignored differences in land quality. An individual could select and claim a parcel of land from a map that showed no sign of the environmental diversity of the basin. An artificial system now structured human relationships to the land, and farmers, rather than attempting to devise a system to accord with nature, learned to adjust nature to suit the system. In the long run, the orderly mechanisms of transferring land from public domain to private interests proved not only successful in disposing of federal lands but also profoundly important in shaping the basin's landscapes. The interplay among land-alienation policies, physical geography, and cultural factors during the initial phase of American farm settlement was decisive in the development of the regional landscapes of the Tulare Lake Basin.

When California was admitted to the Union, the Tulare Lake Basin became federal property subject to the policies of the U.S. General Land Office. Most of these policies were applied throughout the American West, although large tracts of California's coastal valley lands were subject to different treatment because they had already been granted to individuals by the Spanish and Mexican governments of Alta California. The goals of the federal government with regard to pioneer settlement were three: (1) to settle the land as quickly as possible by transferring the public domain into private hands, (2) to provide for internal improvements, and (3) to establish a local framework for education. The land policies that guided settlement of the basin closely reflected these goals.

To induce rapid settlement, direct purchase of land at $1.25 per acre was made possible immediately following the initial survey. Unlimited amounts of land anywhere in the basin could be purchased outright, provided they had not formerly been claimed. Various forms of scrip were also appropriated by legislative acts designed to stimulate settlement. The most important of these, the Military Bounty Act of 1847 (amended in 1855), gave a bounty of 160 acres (one quarter section) to any soldier who had served fourteen days or more in any American conflict since the Revolution or to his heirs. Preemption, as outlined in the Pre-Emption Act of 1841, was also possible in California from 1853 on. Designed to ensure the transfer of land to settlers rather than to speculators, preemption provisions gave preferential rights to purchase up to 160 acres at $1.25 per acre to people who occupied the land prior to survey or who were willing to reside upon and improve the land. Direct purchase (cash entry), military scrip, and preemption were especially popular means of acquiring basin land in the first decade after the gold rush. The Homestead Act (1862) was, like the Pre-Emption Act, designed to ensure the transfer of the public domain directly to farmers.

Up to 160 acres could be acquired free of charge by any person who fulfilled the residence term stipulated in the act.

Internal improvements were encouraged by the provisions of the Improvement Act (1841), the Swamp and Overflowed Lands Act (1850), the Timber Culture Bill (1873), and the Desert Lands Act (1877). The Improvement Act entitled the state to select parcels of at least 320 acres in any location previously surveyed but left unclaimed. Unlimited numbers of parcels could be purchased for $1.25 per acre. The Swamp and Overflowed Lands Act specified that most land classified as "S & O" land by the initial survey be deeded over to the state. Until 1855 the purchase of S & O land from the state was limited to 320 acres per person at $1.25 per acre, the proceeds to be used for state-sponsored reclamation. The Timber Culture Bill allowed a settler to claim 160 acres if, after ten years, he or she had planted 40 of those acres to trees; in 1878 the stipulations were reduced to 10 acres of trees in eight years. The Desert Lands Act allowed a settler to purchase 640 acres at $1.25 per acre if he or she reclaimed at least 80 acres by irrigation within three years. These last two acts were applied toward the acquisition of only a small number of basin acres.

To encourage prompt construction of railroads, tremendous tracts of land were granted directly to railroad companies. Revenues from the sale of these lands were to defray construction costs (Act of July 1, 1862, amended in 1864). Twenty sections (12,800 acres) could be claimed for each mile of track built: the odd-numbered sections within twenty miles on each side of the tracks. The companies also received rights-of-way 400 feet wide, necessary depot sites, and assorted additional privileges. Revenue for public schools was provided by grants of land to the state, which was in turn to use the proceeds for the construction of common schools, a state university, and public buildings. The Act of March 3, 1853, reserved sections 16 and 36 in each township for common schools; in 1866 the state was empowered to select "in lieu" lands (also known as "indemnity lands") of equivalent acreage in the unreserved public domain for any school sections that had been preempted. Additional lands were granted to the state under the Morrill Act (1862) for the purpose of establishing "colleges for the benefit of agriculture and the mechanical arts" (Robinson 1948; Dana and Kruger 1958).

The first step in securing title to a portion of the public domain was selection of a parcel and registration (entry) at the local land office in Visalia. Land entries (initial patent applications) for both state and federal lands in the basin were filed at Visalia. Initial entry brought provisional title to the selected land: the applicant still needed to fulfill any stipulated requirements of the act that pertained to his or her claim.

At the end of the specified time (usually a period of years), if the patent holder could prove that the required improvements had been completed or could make a living from the parcel or sell it for a profit, the final patent (full title) was granted. If the patent holder could not "prove up," title reverted to the federal government or to the state of California. Full title could be secured immediately only by cash entry, although even in this case the deed to a piece of property might be denied for years pending the adjudication of prior claims.

The methods of acquiring land in the Tulare Lake Basin were many and diverse, but so were the problems associated with them. An average homesteader might encounter problems pertaining to title security in addition to the numerous pitfalls inherent in "proving up." The absence of a good land-classification guide exacerbated settlers' problems, as did ill-informed officials, lax administration, blatant fraud, and the rapid reduction of the public domain by land speculators. These problems thwarted settlers' attempts to claim and hold viable parcels of land and thereby enhanced the opportunities of a few individuals to accumulate vast holdings in the Tulare Lake Basin.

Settlers who purchased or preempted land from the federal government during the 1850s frequently found that their titles were hard to defend. Before entries could be made, the exact boundaries of adjacent claims had to be determined; overlapping claims and scant records posed serious problems in cases where presurvey claims and Mexican land grants were involved. The resolution of title conflicts delayed the opening of some very desirable areas, including the Kaweah Delta, for many years. The entry process in the basin as a whole was delayed until 1856, and claims associated with Castro's Laguna de Tache grant were not officially defined until 1866; the title of Lemantour to his Mexican grant south of the Kings River was eventually denied (Bowman 1958; U.S.D.I. General Land Office, patent bk. J-5, index 1). Disagreements between state and federal authorities as to the limits of S & O lands made it equally difficult to secure final patent to state lands. Not a single parcel of S & O land had been patented in 1863, thirteen years after these lands were deeded over to the state (State of California Surveyor General 1863, p. 5). Because of these problems, most basin farming in the 1850s and 1860s took place on lands of questionable title, which may help explain the failure of many basin farmers of the era to invest substantial energy in improving their land.

Wonderful claims had been made for the efficacy of federal land policies in assuring "homes for the homeless" (Nordhoff 1872, p. 197): "Land monopoly is entirely prevented. You may buy six hundred and forty acres from the railroad company, but you cannot buy a single acre from the Government unless you settle on it and improve it for a year;

and the country thus withheld from general sale is, in fact, dedicated to the use of small farmers, for no man can acquire a great body of land lying together and no one man wants two or three alternate sections" (Nordhoff 1872, p. 197). Instead of encouraging the development of small farms, however, in practice the federal land policies tended to favor large holdings used for purposes other than homesteading. In the rush to dispose of its lands, the state of California altered some provisions to expedite sales. Especially significant was the 1859 decision to double the purchase limit of S & O lands to 640 acres. In 1866 the county gained control of the remaining S & O lands and in 1868 dropped all acreage limitations. Fees were reduced to the point where some lands were given free on proof of reclamation work, and actual verification of such work was seldom sought (Barton 1874; Brown 1941, pp. 101–102). Liberal policies and lax enforcement promoted the acquisition of vast holdings by speculators, who removed tremendous tracts of land from the public domain and drove land prices out of the range of most small farmers. As early as 1869, Charles Reed of the California State Agricultural Society observed that because of "the accumulation of our lands in the hands of corporations and wealthy individuals for speculative purposes . . . lands which but 2 years ago could have been bought off the government of the State for from $1 to $1.25 per acre, cannot now be bought for less than $10 to $15 per acre" (California State Agricultural Society 1869, pp. 161–162).

Near the lakeshore and on the Kaweah Delta, great tracts of S & O lands were acquired by individual speculators. One entry in 1869 transferred 1,600 acres in T17S R24E to Riddell Speer, and 3,044 acres in T18S R23 and 24E were bought by W. R. Owen in 1866 alone (U.S.D.I. General Land Office, patent bk. E, p. 101; patent bk. F, pp. 16, 19, 21). Although the Swamp and Overflowed Lands Act satisfied the state's desire to dispose of its lands quickly, the intended revenues never materialized. Few attempts were made to reclaim S & O lands purchased for speculation, and the rapid transfer of these lands into private hands prevented the state from profiting from the gradual rise in property values which occurred in the course of regional settlement. Instead, the financial returns were realized by a few private interests. Lands selected by the state under the Morrill Act were also hastily disposed of via the sale of college scrip. As figure 30a illustrates, the lands available for scrip acquisition were not limited in terms of their physical endowments. Huge tracts in some of the most fertile parts of the basin, where water and timber were plentiful, were acquired through scrip application. The heaviest use of college scrip entry was in T18S R21E (the Mussel Slough country) and in T20S R24E, where some scrip selections became the foundations of wheat empires. Large scrip selections were also made elsewhere but on a more sporadic basis: for example, in 1861 and 1862 S. J. Packwood acquired 1,324 acres in T21S R27E, and H. L. Hutchinson claimed 640 acres in T16S R25E through college scrip application (U.S.D.I. General Land Office, patent bk. E-11, p. 135, 365−368). After several years of almost unlimited empire building by a few individuals, including the famous western land barons Miller and Lux, in 1868 Congress limited college scrip entry to three sections (1,920 acres) in any one township (Gates 1961, pp. 104−109).

Rapid reduction of the public domain was also accomplished through use of military scrip, an almost perfect mechanism for claiming land anywhere in the basin at prices well below the $1.25 per acre minimum set by Congress. Not only could military scrip be applied to any surveyed land, but it was also legally negotiable for cash. Former soldiers and their heirs had little difficulty in selling scrip, and speculators were particularly eager to buy it. E. Johnson, an active Tulare County settler, amassed sufficient scrip to file for more than 972 acres of Kaweah Delta land in T20S R24E in 1860; this scrip had originally been issued to six different men for their respective services in the Mexican War (two men), the Florida War, the Northeastern Frontier Disturbance, the Black Hawk War, and the California Indian War (U.S.D.I. General Land Office, patent bk. H, pp. 543−545, 547−549). Such transactions were the rule: less than 2 percent of military bounty entries were made by the actual grantees or their immediate kin. Scrip entries by bona fide soldiers or their heirs do, however, reveal something of the geographical origins of early settlers. Land on the Kaweah Delta was claimed by direct application of scrip earned for participation in the Cayuse and Rogue River wars (Oregon), the Mexican War, the California War, the Texas Volunteers (Civil War), the Black Hawk War (Wisconsin) and even the War of 1812 (U.S.D.I. General Land Office, patent books A−Z). Military scrip, like college scrip, was applied most heavily for land on the Kaweah and Tule river fans, especially in the lush areas comprising T18S R24E and T19S R25E (fig. 30b).

The public domain was reduced dramatically in a single stroke by a grant to the Southern Pacific Railroad on December 12, 1874 (U.S.D.I. General Land Office, patent bk. E, pp. 157−198), of alternate sections along the proposed route. Even "in lieu" land selection showed little concern for timber, water, or soil quality (fig. 30c). Under the terms of the grant, the Southern Pacific was to dispose of this land in some fashion within three years after completion of the line, so in theory the lands would be withheld from settlement only briefly. To acquire land from the railroad, however, a settler had to pay inflated prices and to comply with various stipulations in the deed of sale. Because of these

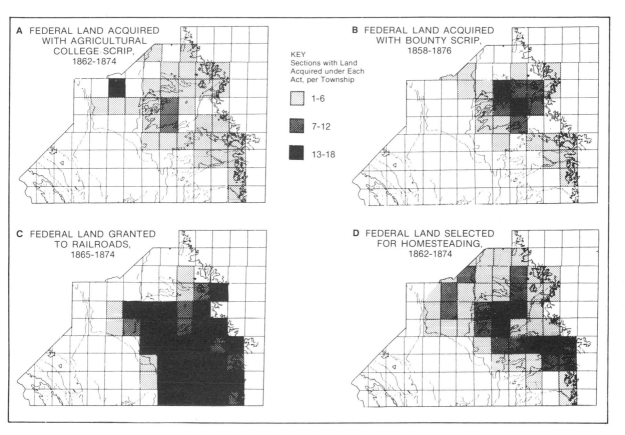

Figure 30. *Lands Claimed under Various Government Acts.* The federal government provided a variety of methods by which individuals could claim or purchase federal land. Maps *a*, *b*, *c*, and *d* illustrate the patterns of claims and purchases, reflecting the availability of land and its apparent desirability for settlement, although in some cases (particularly in the case of grants to the Southern Pacific) land acquisition proceeded without attention to the varied quality of the land. (Source: Eigenheer 1976.)

drawbacks, railroad sections tended to remain vacant even in areas where other lands were settled eagerly.

The Homestead Act, designed to foster the survival of yeoman farmers, was an important means of acquiring basin land but was severely restricted in its application. A homesteader could select only surveyed land that had not been claimed or granted by other means and could claim no more than 160 acres (amended later to 320, then 640 acres). In many parts of the basin, even a full section was not a viable economic unit in the 1860s and 1870s, for successful dryland wheat farming demanded much larger holdings as well as expensive machinery that most small farmers could not afford. The only practical homestead selections were well-watered alluvial lands, where acreage limitations could be offset by such intensive practices as irrigated gardening. For a brief time even the poorest homesteader could acquire a parcel of prime basin land, but scrip holders and others who were under no acreage limitations soon claimed most of the region's best farmland. Patterns of homestead selection reflect the acreage limitations imposed by the Homestead Act: old-valley-fill soils with little timber or water were rarely selected, and once the most fertile recent alluvial lands were claimed, homestead entry largely ceased (fig. 30*d*).

Despite the variety of methods by which land could be acquired, no single means played a more important role in the settlement of the basin than direct purchase of land from the federal government or the state. Cash entry was limited only by the availability of unclaimed land and the wealth of the purchaser. As early as 1867, 37 percent of the land selected in the basin was purchased directly (Chapman and Gordon 1867); and as a means of amassing vast holdings, cash entry proved exceedingly effective. A few individuals recognized the agricultural potential of the basin in the 1860s and quickly purchased great tracts in full-section blocks both east and west of the valley trough (fig. 31*a*). William Chapman bought more than 24,300 acres in a tier of townships (T24S R17-20E) in the southwestern corner of the basin in 1869 alone (U.S.D.I. General Land Office, patent bk. E, pp. 198, 212–215). This was but a fraction of the 170,000 acres he eventually owned in this area and nearby (U.S.D.I. General Land Office, tract entry indexes). In the northeastern corner of the basin, J. Williams and S. Haas purchased several thousand acres in 1867–1869 (U.S.D.I. General Land Office, patent bk. E, pp. 157–89, 218–221); their purchases largely account for the full-section pattern of landholdings in these parts (fig. 31*a*).

The failure of land-alienation policies to satisfy some of the settlement ideals advanced by the federal government—especially the expressed desire for the transfer of the public domain into the hands of small farmers—did not detract from the overwhelming success of these policies in promoting rapid settlement. By one means or another, most basin land had been transferred into private hands by 1874 (fig. 31*b*), but land-office transactions continued for several decades as the dying lake exposed more land and as marginal lands to the south and west became more attractive in light of technological innovations, economic reorientations, and regional population growth.

Because land entries are the earliest quantitative record of settlers' perceptions of land quality, they are very useful in the analysis of initial settlement. Initial entries reveal clear patterns of environmental evaluation, patterns that changed as settlers became more familiar with the basin's lands and as technological innovations made possible the cultivation of once-marginal lands. Prior to 1867 the lands selected for

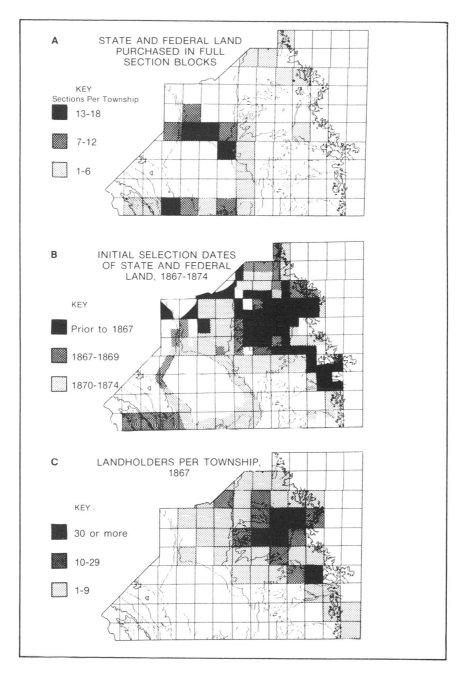

Figure 31. *Patterns and Progression of Settlement.* As illustrated by map *a*, actual settlement did not always proceed with the transfer of the public domain into private hands; full-section blocks selected for speculative purposes remained vacant for many years in some areas. Maps *b* and *c* reveal an overwhelming early preference for settlement of lands on the Kaweah, Tule, and Kings river fans; little land in these areas was left open to speculators (cf. map *a*). (Sources: Eigenheer 1976; Chapman and Gordon 1867.)

settlement were primarily in the timbered and well-watered Kaweah Delta region. This corresponds rather well with the soil ratings recorded by the initial survey (fig. 26), although three townships on old valley fill (T16S R24E, T20S R27E, and T23S R27E) were avoided by early settlers despite their good soil ratings. As figures 31c and 32a illustrate, farms on the Kaweah Delta were typically small and closely clustered, especially near Visalia in T18S R25E, becoming larger and more scattered away from this locale. This pattern endured well into the twentieth century. From 1867 to 1869 the farming frontier expanded out to the edges of the grasslands. Most delta lands had been claimed, but grasslands were gradually found to be well suited to farming. The rather large number of entries filed for marshlands in the Kaweah area (fig. 31b) suggests that reassessment had found these lands more favorable as well. Expanding awareness of the potential of still-unclaimed basin lands exploded in a rush to occupy marshlands and grasslands between 1870 and 1874. The focus of settlement shifted from the Kaweah Delta to the Kings Delta. Large grassland tracts south of the Tule remainded sparsely settled, however, in part because of the tremendous railroad selections in that area (fig. 30c) and in part because of the distance from established towns of the northern basin. Between 1867 and 1876, direct purchase, scrip, S & O entries, and massive grants to the Southern Pacific Railroad were the primary means by which land was removed from the public domain; after 1876, homestead- and desert-land entries became more common as a result of improved irrigation techniques and increased acceptance of intensive land-use practices (cf. T22S R25E and T20S R27E). Sales of S & O lands remained important as Tulare Lake yielded more and more land to settlement (e.g., T21S R22E and T23S R23E; fig. 31b).

The various modes of land alienation also influenced the distribution of farmsteads in the Tulare Lake Basin. As one would expect, farmsteads were most closely clustered on homesteaded land, particularly on the fertile Kings and Kaweah Deltas (e.g., T18S R21E and T18S R25E in fig. 32a). Less concentrated settlement would be expected in areas where lands were acquired under the terms of acts that permitted larger holdings, especially since such tracts were often left unimproved by speculators or were used as huge wheat or cattle ranches. T21S R22E illustrates the lower concentration of farmsteads in a typical area acquired primarily by scrip application and S & O entry (fig. 32b). Once settlement expanded onto the grasslands, after 1867, school lands (sections 16 and 36) and railroad lands (odd-numbered sections) were often purchased by adjacent homesteaders to enlarge their holdings, and dwellings remained widely scattered. Because of increased mechanization and other economic considerations, as well as the relaxation of government restrictions on acreage, later arrivals also tended to acquire larger parcels; later settlement thus did not tend to fill gaps in farmstead distribution. Especially striking distributions of farmsteads resulted from the checkerboard pattern of railroad lands. For several years, the odd-numbered sections were withheld from settlement, and only even-numbered sections were claimed; farms were thus dispersed in small clusters of four or less. When railroad lands finally became available, the initial pattern persisted as settlers bought up adjacent properties from the railroad. This pattern is apparent in such areas as T22S R25E (fig. 32b). Increased urbanism and the growing scale of basin farming also generally precluded the development of clustered patterns of farm settlement on lands held for speculation.

Land-selection records do not fully represent the landholding patterns established during the period of initial settlement. Only productive lands or those with especially favorable locations were retained through the acquisition of final patent in accordance with government requirements. Less valuable claims were generally canceled or abandoned. Once firmly transferred, land could be sold, subdivided, or merged to form larger holdings according to the whims of private interests and the designs of speculators. Patterns of initial parcel size and arrangement tended to persist despite changing economic conditions, technologies, and cultural perceptions (fig. 33a, b), but more and more the initial boundaries showed up only in vestigial forms, as roads or fencelines within larger properties.

In the rush to dispose of its lands, the state facilitated the acquisition of large holdings. As competing small farmers learned to their dismay, the extensive practices employed in the basin were in the long run profitable only on large holdings; distance to markets also favored economies of scale. Between 1860 and 1870 the number of farms in Tulare County actually declined from 426 to 377, as small holders conceded defeat; and average farm size increased from 154 to 235 acres (U.S.D.I. Census Office 1864, Vol. III; 1872, Vol. III). Besides driving out many ranchers, regional drought hastened the inevitable process of small-farm abandonment and the expansion of larger holdings. Still, in 1870 the average Tulare County farm was significantly smaller than the average California farm—at 482 acres, the latter was more than twice as large (U.S.D.I. Census Office 1872, Vol. III)—and Tulare County had more farms than adjacent Fresno or Kern counties. Though farm size increased after the construction of rail lines through the basin, a substantial number of small farms survived. Tulare County's overwhelming head start in rural settlement and the responsiveness of its alluvial lands to cultivation enhanced the success of its

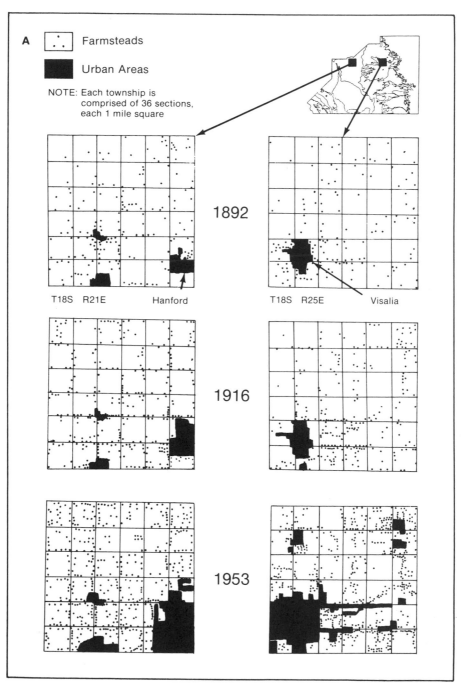

Figure 32. *Land Alienation and Farmstead Dispersal.* The various methods of land alienation influenced the distribution of farmsteads. Lands selected in small parcels under the provisions of the Homestead Act or by cash entry (a) show dense clustering of farmsteads; this was particularly apparent in the vicinities of Hanford and Visalia. Lands available more cheaply and in larger blocks (e.g., railroad land grants and Swamp and

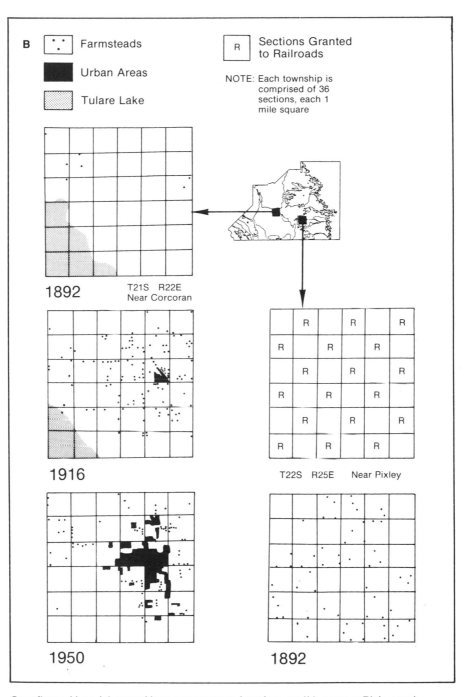

B Farmsteads

Urban Areas

Tulare Lake

R Sections Granted to Railroads

NOTE: Each township is comprised of 36 sections, each 1 mile square

1892   T21S R22E
Near Corcoran

1916

T22S R25E   Near Pixley

1950

1892

Overflowed Lands) reveal less concentrated settlement (*b*), as near Pixley and Corcoran. Settlement patterns in T22S R25E indicate that the granting of land to railroads delayed, rather than accelerated, their settlement. (Sources: Thompson 1892; Holmes and Eckmann 1916; U.S.D.I. Geological Survey, 7.5′ and 15′ series; U.S.D.I. Bureau of Land Management.)

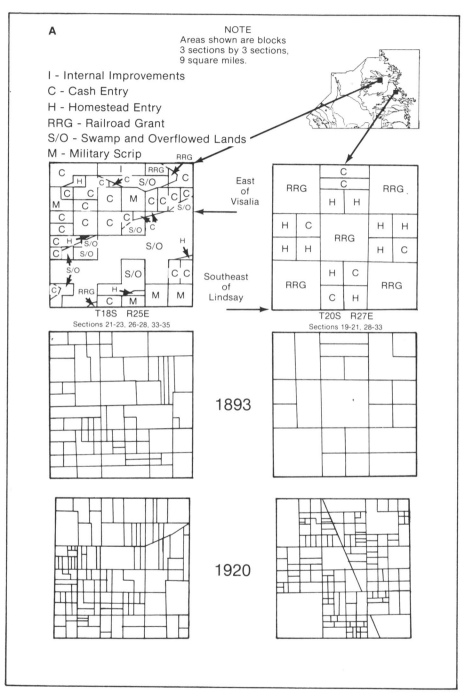

Figure 33*a, b.* *Disposition of Federal Lands and Subsequent Subdivision.* Patterns of initial parcel size and arrangement tended to persist despite changes in economic conditions, technologies, and cultural evaluations. The ways in which land was initially acquired by individuals in these sample areas are reflected many years later in the size

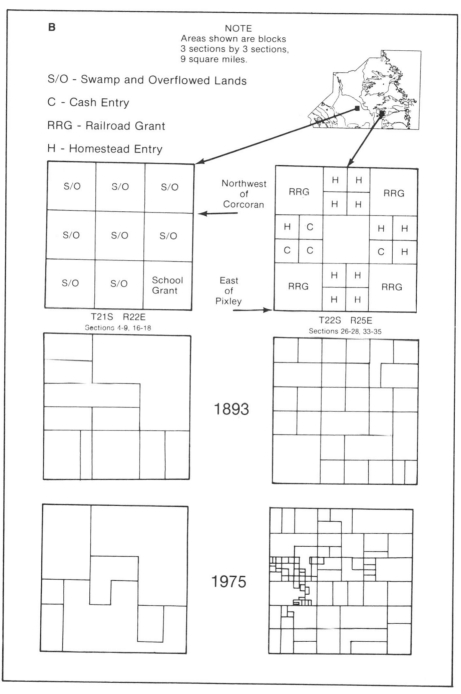

and arrangement of individual parcels. (Sources: U.S.D.I. General Land Office Final Patent Maps; Thompson 1892; Moyo 1920; Corcoran Irrigation District, Pixley Irrigation District.)

small farms, and average farm size has remained small relative to that of adjacent San Joaquin Valley counties. The enduring legacy of land-alienation policies is still remarkably apparent in the basin, however, in that parcel size is clearly a local phenomenon: districts taken up under different land acts at different times have retained their cadastral distinctiveness (fig. 34).

Communications and Town Development

They have to go to Stockton with four-horse wagons each summer and bring back a year's supplies. But they have plenty of everything—all they need. They live like lords. (Miller 1938, pp. 302–303)

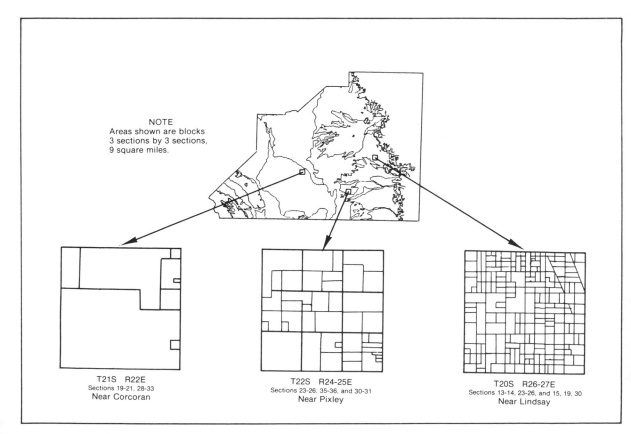

NOTE
Areas shown are blocks
3 sections by 3 sections,
9 square miles.

T21S R22E
Sections 19-21, 28-33
Near Corcoran

T22S R24-25E
Sections 23-26, 35-36, and 30-31
Near Pixley

T20S R26-27E
Sections 13-14, 23-26, and 15, 19, 30
Near Lindsay

Figure 34. *Subregional Parcel Size, 1975.* The enduring legacy of land-alienation policies is still remarkably apparent in the basin. Districts taken up at different times, under different acts, have retained their cadastral distinctiveness. (Sources: Corcoran Irrigation District; Pixley Irrigation District; Lindmore Irrigation District.)

Until 1858, communications were direct and dependable only on a local basis. Attachment to the rest of the nation and to the world beyond was through the ports of San Francisco and Los Angeles. Within California, land routes led in and out of the basin (fig. 35). The Stockton-Los Angeles Road was by far the best route for long journeys and connected with several roads into the foothills and onto the basin plains; the most important side road led to Whitmore's ferry, a crossing on the Kings River south of Laton. Known first as Kings River Station, then as Kingston, this locale became an important commercial and communications portal of the basin. Steamers landed passengers and freight

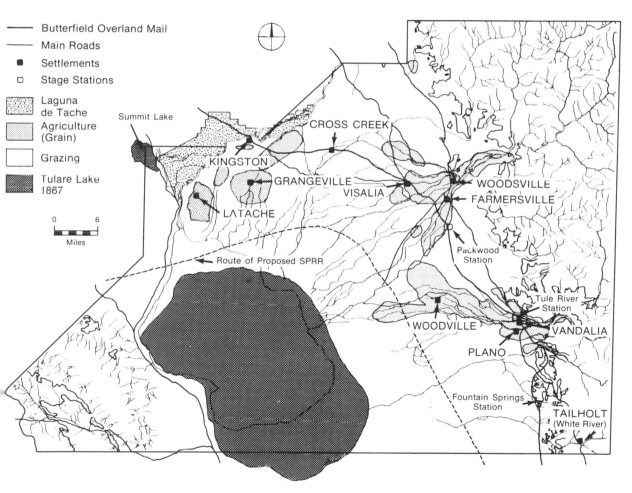

Figure 35. *Prerailroad Settlement Patterns.* Prior to the arrival of railroads, settlement was centered on the alluvial fans and linked by the major north-south roads. Agriculture (primarily grain cultivation) gradually replaced grazing on the upper fans of the Kings, Kaweah, and Tule rivers. (Source: Chapman and Gordon 1867.)

near the junction of Fresno Slough and the San Joaquin River, whence wagons completed the overland passage to Visalia by way of Kingston. It was in Kingston that many settlers caught their first glimpse of the basin: "As a typical station town Kingston had a number of dwellings, a general store and post office, a blacksmith-shop and saloon, and a large livery stable. All were frame buildings erected on substantial stone and brick foundations" (Conkling and Conkling 1947, pp. 288–289).

The White River gold rush of 1853 demanded faster and more reliable communications, and for a short time the basin was linked by stage service to Los Angeles. In September 1858 the basin was integrated into a unified national communications network: operating largely on the money and prestige of the Wells Fargo Company, the Butterfield Overland Mail established semi-weekly service to Visalia and Kingston. The stage route entered the valley at Tehachapi Pass, followed the Stockton-Los Angeles Road to Visalia, diverged there from the main road to follow the highest available ground to Kingston, and then continued on to San Francisco. A second stage service through the basin was established by the Stockton, Albuquerque and Kansas City Mail. Their stage entered the basin from the north and traveled along the Stockton-Los Angeles Road, making scheduled stops at Visalia. Telegraph connections were established for military and political considerations during the Civil War. However unsubstantial these early communications links may seem in light of later developments, their impact on the basin was dramatic. Geographic information diffused more widely and more rapidly than ever before to potential immigrants, and soon the basin was a well-known region and a popular destination. The early routeways also affected the distribution and concentration of population within the basin by bringing new areas to the attention of settlers, lands beyond the perimeters of the heavily settled Kaweah Delta. The road was particularly important in spreading settlement westward onto promising lands heretofore neglected. Wherever the stage line crossed sloughs or streams, stations were built: Fountain Springs, Tule River, Packwood, Visalia, Cross Creek, and Kingston (fig. 35). All of these served as nuclei for town growth, although Fountain Springs, Packwood, Cross Creek, and Kingston never became substantial towns.

As in the rest of California, settlement of the Tulare Lake Basin was basically urban. From the very beginning of the American era, immigrants were attracted to the Golden State by the promise of commercial gain, and this incentive tied settlement closely to the services and opportunities afforded by towns, which often preceded substantial rural settlement. In this way the pattern of California's settlement more closely resembled that of older states in the East than its contemporaries along the Mississippi Valley (Pomeroy 1965, p. 84). Before the inauguration of regular transcontinental stage service in 1858, Visalia, Venice (founded one mile north of the abandoned site of Woodsville in 1857) and Tailholt—White River were the only nucleated settlements in the basin. Visalia was still locally dominant—indeed, it had become the largest town between Stockton and Los Angeles. An early visitor noted, "This place is quite a flourishing and entertaining town. They are improving very fast. Many brick buildings are going up" (Putnam 1857–1860). In the mid-1850s a small settlement developed where the Kingston road traversed Cross Creek, about four miles south of present-day Traver. The founding of Cross Creek as a rough-and-tumble cow town came about because of its situation at a transport bottleneck; the town owed its survival to a small hinterland, a post office, and an Overland Mail station.

These first towns—Visalia, Woodsville, Tailholt, Kingston, and Cross Creek—were essentially local responses to locally perceived needs and opportunities, generated in close association with productive hinterlands, as were the newer communities of Latache, Plano-Vandalia, Grangeville, Woodville (not to be confused with Woodsville), and Farmersville, all established before the coming of the railroad. In contrast, towns founded after the lines were completed were more often products of promotion and speculation. Their sites reflected the development of new routeways and associated facilities and were selected by small-time local speculators as places where towns would likely prosper, sites with promising situations. Still, productive hinterlands were the only assurance of survival. Kingston survived the Civil War despite the discontinuation of stage service because it served as a commercial and service center for the Kings Delta and the lakeshore. The combined businesses of transport and stock raising kept Cross Creek alive, and transport and mining kept Tailholt on the map. Fountain Springs and Packwood, on the other hand, perished quickly, for they were never able to compete with the central place functions performed by Tailholt or Visalia, respectively. The Tule River station grew into a substantial town called Porterville: like Farmersville, Plano, and Woodville, it continued to prosper long after Kingston, Cross Creek, Venice, Tailholt, Latache, and Grangeville had declined in the face of spatial and economic reorientations brought about by the railroad. With the addition of stage service. Visalia was able to steal all of the minor functions once performed in Woodsville and Venice, and so the basin's oldest town perished also.

The first buildings in Tulare County were hardly impressive, usually constructed of adobe or rough-cut timber. Newcomers were less inclined to invest in permanent homes than to cash in on future prosperity, and they sank their money into empty lots and "paper townsites." A preference for investing in land rather than in buildings often characterized the basin, but never again as intensely as during the livestock era, when one visitor remarked that "the absence of barns and the small dwelling houses strike the stranger's eye. But, more than all, there is an apparent want of comfort, which . . . is greatly heightened by the absence of shade trees. Intent on making money, few plant trees for shade or ornament" (Cronise 1868, p. 385). According to another, "there is a great deal of wealth in the immediate vicinity of Visalia, but it is chiefly in the hands of the cattle-owners, who are, everybody tells me, the least civilized part of the community. . . . Men worth from $40,000 to $60,000 sometimes live in shanties and, aside from a peach-orchard, have no sign of thrift or forethought about their places" (Nordhoff 1872, p. 200). Rural dwellings and town homes were generally simple and small, often reflecting the architectural traditions of settlers' home regions. Slightly altered versions of the Appalachian dogtrot house were common in this era of the Pikes (Jackson 1972, p. 187): "There are Pikes with property, and Pikes without. When he has a farm, you may know it by a house with a room on each side, and a broad open passage in the middle, . . . and if you go in, you shall find that they cook by an open fire, and that bacon, and stringy greens, and corn pone are the fare" (Nordhoff 1872, p. 196). The attitudes and resources of settlers in the 1850s and 1860s seldom allowed for much creative flexibility in house design; embellishment was limited not only by the notion that much housing would be temporary but also by a lack of materials: "Here, along this River of the Kings so many different kinds of men were trying to conquer, only one sort of house was possible, limited to the lumber hauled on one wagon" (Miller 1938, p. 413).

Even when railroad connections brought an increased sense of permanency and enhanced access to materials, houses remained small. The Tulare Lake Basin was a cultural backwater, a place to make money, not a place to spend it. The socially ambitious continued for many years to build their mansions in San Francisco, Stockton and Sacramento and to visit Tulare County only when business demanded their presence. In this respect Visalia's landscapes were unique in the basin: as county seat, it attracted people committed to enduring interests in the basin. This commitment was supported by Visalia's location in an especially fertile area brought under cultivation at an early date. Homesteaders had been unusually numerous and successful in Visalia's hinterland, and the inertia of early settlement combined with the benefits of a good site enabled the town to remain dominant and to prosper throughout the 1850s and 1860s. By the time of the Civil War it served an area more than 200 miles across and a resident population of 1500:

> As you approach it, you find the land well fenced, the houses so near each other as to betoken what here are called small farms. . . . A prosperous, well established community. (Nordhoff 1872, p. 203)

> Being centrally situated and the only town in the County of any size, it enjoys an active trade, which is every year expanding as the country around it fills up with settlers. Besides its public schools, it has a well conducted and flourishing seminary, a handsome courthouse, several halls, churches, and other public edifices, many fireproof stores, and a large number of tasty cottages and mansions, nearly all occupying large lots planted with trees, vines and flowers. (Cronise 1868, p. 328).

Such a concentrated and populous settlement had last existed in the basin at the Yokuts village of Bubal nearly sixty years before—and indeed Visalia was reminiscent of Bubal in that its residential functions were clearly subordinate to its role in regional commerce: by the 1860s Visalia supported eleven mercantile stores, eight saloons, two hotels, and many supply and processing establishments (Smith 1939, pp. 369–370).

Environmental Alteration

Agricultural alteration of the Tulare Lake Basin increased dramatically in the 1850s, 1860s, and early 1870s. Unmanaged grazing not only altered patterns of natural vegetation but profoundly changed the productive capabilities of certain lands, for overgrazing led to severe soil compaction and accelerated erosion. The change from cattle to sheep was particularly detrimental to fragile basin communities: "They ate into the roots of the lush grass and left the quick rains to cut the soil. The wool in the hand was always worth the next season's feed to the sheep-herder" (Palmer and Austin 1914, p. 131). Through habitat alteration, domestic livestock also crowded native fauna off the basin plains. The disappearance of native animals accelerated as farmers colonized the basin, for wildlife was seen as a direct threat to crops and herds and was actively exterminated: "The antelope lives in the open plain and in the desert. The valley of the San Joaquin was once full of great herds of them, but they, like other large game, have become rare now" (Hittell 1866, p. 319). Antelope and elk were completely dispatched by 1870 (McCullough 1969, p. 24), and soon few game animals frequented the basin at all.

As Tulare County settlers devoted more of their energies to cultivation, they induced further changes in regional patterns of vegetation. The exotic oats introduced by the Spanish were themselves succeeded by filaree as the dominant grass cover (Burcham 1957, pp. 191–194). Where grazing had already limited the rejuvenation of woodlands, farmers—in quest of fuel, building materials, and cleared land—rapidly reduced the extent of basin timber (Cronise 1868). Neither did the detrimental effects upon soil quality end with the transition to farming. Dryland grain cultivation, without crop rotation or fallowing, damaged soil quality to an extent that alarmed observers as early as 1868:

> We are now "running upon wheat" in California. Crop after crop of it is being raised, in opposition to the law which requires rotation, while in addition to this excessive drought upon the life of the land, we are doing nothing whatever to restore to the soil the element of which even judicious cultivation despoils it. Poverty as hopeless as that of the Sahara must inevitably overtake a county that is thus willfully given over to vandal cultivation. (Magee 1868, p. 329).

Magee suggested land reform as a solution to soil deterioration in the belief that small farmers would "live better and preserve the quality of the soil at the same time" (Magee 1868, p. 337). Early warnings of the deleterious effects of dryland monoculture went unheeded, however, for at first the consequences of soil depletion were not dramatically evident.

The most striking modification of the Tulare Lake Basin during the period between 1857 and 1871 was the reordering of its natural landscapes into cultural landscapes of geometrical forms. The smooth ecotones of nature were replaced by sharp edges and angles: fields, fences, farmsteads, town plats, and roads marked the land off into a new series of zones and territories. The elements of the life layer could not spread freely across this new geometrical fretwork, and they were actively replaced with a new, agricultural life layer. Native flora were cleared away and replaced with crops in rectangular fields; native animals were killed and replaced by tame livestock; standing water was drained, and flowing water was rechanneled into geometrically arranged canals. Human dominance was for the first time loudly proclaimed by the landscapes of the Tulare Lake Basin.

Summary

Whereas the 1840s and early 1850s served only as a watershed between two extensive occupancies—that of the Yokuts and Hispanos

California rancheria des Indiens d'hooks, sur les bords d la rivière de la plume

Plate 1. *Yokuts Village.* With a foreground of mima mounds, this sketch of a Yokuts village by F. Wikersheim typifies the modest accommodations of the basin's early dwellers. (Courtesy of the Bancroft Library, University of California, Berkeley.)

Plate 2. *Early Ranch Dwelling.* The first American dwellings in the basin were small and frequently served only as seasonal residences of cattle raisers. This building on the Kaweah Delta east of Visalia illustrates the simple construction common in the region prior to the arrival of the railroad. (Courtesy of the Tulare County Chamber of Commerce.)

Plate 3. *Town of Kingston, 1860.*
Founded at the site of a ferry on the
Kings River, Kingston served as a
gateway for the basin's first American
settlers. Drawn to such transport
bottlenecks, entrepreneurs founded
American settlements at Kingston,
Woodsville, and White River. (Courtesy of the Tulare County Library.)

Plate 4. *Visalia's Main Street, 1863.* Initially settled by homesteaders, Visalia soon became a rough-and-tumble cattle
town. The only sizable settlement between Stockton and Los
Angeles, it served a huge hinterland and continued to prosper
despite competition from neighboring towns. (Courtesy of the
Tulare County Library.)

Plate 5. *President Harrison at Tulare, 1891.* The coming of the railroad rapidly destroyed the basin's traditional isolation and radically altered the nature of the region's settlement and economic structure. (Courtesy of the California State Library.)

Plate 6. *Main Street of Dinuba, Late 1880s.* Towns created and sponsored by the railroads arose overnight, but the fortunes of these towns were often disrupted by fire and economic depressions. (Courtesy of David Martzen Studio, Dinuba.)

Plate 7. *Town Residence in Hanford, 1883.* Railroad lots were small and residences in railroad towns often modest. Many parcels were bought only for speculatory purposes. (Source: Elliott 1883. Courtesy of California History Books, Fresno.)

. TOWN RESIDENCE OF JAMES MANASSE. HANFORD. TULARE CO. CAL.

Plate 8. *Grain Terminal at Cross Creek, 1884.* At harvest time, long lines of wagons waited to off-load grain for railroad shipment to world markets. In 1884 over 90 percent of the basin's cropland was planted to wheat. (Courtesy of the Tulare County Library.)

Plate 9. *Grain Harvester, 1903.* Early farm machines were cumbersome and unwieldy, but they were a great boon to agriculture in the basin, where the labor supply in the early years was sparse. This picture was taken near Terra Bella. (Courtesy of the Tulare County Museum.)

ARTESIAN WELL.

NORTH END OF TULARE LAKE, AT MOUTH OF KING'S RIVER. LAST VOYAGE OF THE "WATER WITCH". STUMPS OF SUBMERGED FOREST.

Plate 10. *View of Tulare Lake from the Northeastern Shore.* Residents soon learned to tap artesian wells and to divert the basin's streams, which brought an eventual end to Tulare Lake. (Source: Elliott 1883. Courtesy of California History Books, Fresno.)

OWNER OF BARON GWYNNE, 13th, AND BADEN CHERRY.   SCENE ON HAMILTON-DALE RANCH, T. J. DALE, PROPRIETOR.   12 MILES EAST OF BUENA VISALIA, TULARE CO., CAL.

Plate 11a, b. *Homesteads near Visalia and near Hanford, 1892.* As grain farming was displaced by intensive farms based on smaller units and irrigation, the basin took on a more settled appearance. The greater permanence of farmers' attachment to the land was reflected in the planting of orchards and exotic ornamentals and in increased attention to architectural fads. (Source: Thompson, 1892.)

RESIDENCE AND RANCH OF WM. J. NEWPORT, HANFORD, TULARE CO. CAL.

Plate 12a, b. *The Foothill Fringe near Porterville, circa 1925.* The rapid expansion of citrus cultivation into the Thermal Belt with the introduction of pump irrigation transformed pasture lands into densely settled orchard districts dotted with tank houses and palm trees. (Courtesy of the Tulare County Chamber of Commerce.)

Plate 13. *The Advent of the Automobile Age.* (*a*) So popular was automobile transportation in the basin that by the late 1920s the Visalia Electric Railroad discontinued passenger service and burned its coaches (outside Woodlake); (*b*) auto travel also increased the concentration of businesses in the larger basin towns, such as Dinuba (shown here in the late 1940s—compare with plate 6). (Courtesy of the Tulare County Chamber of Commerce.)

Plate 14. *Cotton Pickers, 1930s.* Cheap and abundant labor supply was a boon to intensive farming in the basin. Successive waves of Chinese, Japanese, Filipinos, Mexicans, blacks, and Midwesterners ("Okies") came in search of farm wages. Those who remained diversified and enriched the ethnic character of the basin. (Courtesy of the Tulare County Chamber of Commerce.)

Plate 15. *Cotton Strike at Corcoran, 1933.* Strife and occasional violence between growers or processors and migrant laborers have always been a feature of basin agriculture, but such problems were especially prevalent during the Great Depression years. (Courtesy of the Bancroft Library, University of California, Berkeley.)

Plate 16. *Cotton Picker of the Post-war Era.* After 1945, mechanization became increasingly important in basin agriculture. Developments in power farming, irrigation, and chemistry ensured the total agricultural transformation of the region. (Courtesy of the California Department of Water Resources.)

Plate 17. *Friant-Kern Canal near Porterville.* Completed in 1949 as part of the Central Valley Project, this canal was used for the first importation of water into the basin. The damming of the Kaweah and Tule rivers also augmented the irrigation resources of the east side, and intensive farming expanded despite a rapid decline of the ground water table. (Courtesy of the California Department of Water Resources.)

Plate 18. *The California Aqueduct South of Kettleman City.* Completion of this portion of the California Water Plan in 1969–1971 brought agricultural intensification to the west side and so tamed the basin's last agricultural frontier. (Courtesy of the California Department of Water Resources.)

Plate 19. *Corporate Equipment Yard near Corcoran.* Since World War II, land consolidation and the growth of corporate farms have supplanted an older identity based upon small farms and personal attachment to the land. (Photo by the author.)

Plate 20. *Basin Landscapes.*

(a) Northeastward from Kettleman City, where Interstate 5, the California Aqueduct, and large holdings give the landscape strong angularity;

(b) field crops and corporate landscapes at Corcoran;

Plate 20. *Basin Landscapes.* (continued)

(c) irrigated orchards along the Friant Kern Canal southwest of Porterville;

(d) new construction and population growth change the face of old basin communities and landscapes (near Porterville). (Courtesy of Caltrans, State of California Department of Water Resources, and U.S. Department of the Interior.)

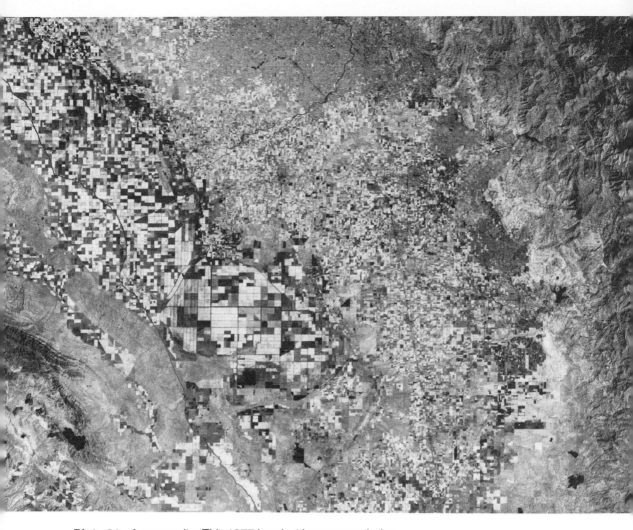

Plate 21. A composite: This 1977 Landsat image reveals the cumulative impact of several centuries of human occupation on the landscapes of the Tulare Lake Basin.

Plate 22. *Vanishing Landscapes* (near Tulare).

of old and that of the new American trappers and ranchers—the years between 1857 and 1871 brought the introduction of nearly all of the processes and general modes of organization of land and life that would ultimately direct the intensive settlement of the basin by American farmers and townspeople. Landscapes and land uses were subjected to regulation by external forces, especially market conditions. To enhance the responsiveness of their land to external demands, farmers applied ever-increasing amounts of technology and extended their direct control over more and more aspects of the environment. Inevitably, the environment changed as settlers freed themselves from its original constraints, and soon there were new problems with which to cope. For the time being, however, basin farmers were confident of their abilities, and their optimism was rewarded: the Tulare Lake Basin emerged as the leading agricultural region of California's Great Central Valley.

As innovation proceeded on recent alluvial lands, new crops and land uses pushed grain and grazing out onto old-valley-fill or lacustrine soils. As successive land uses expanded outward from the Kaweah Delta—the hearth of agricultural innovation in the basin—most of the region was occupied. In the process of expansion, however, basic differences among the diverse subregions of the basin persisted: they were, indeed, cemented to some extent by the differential effects of land-alienation policies. Outside regulation by government was exceedingly important in establishing the framework for settlement. Though government policies were based upon the democratic ideal of equal access (or, at least, fair competition) and were designed to ignore environmental variation, however, this blind democracy actually fostered spatial variations in land use and inequality of landholdings in the basin.

Settlers' relationships to the land were increasingly commercial and transitory. Property values and productivity overshadowed any sentimental concerns that might hinder the rearrangement of land, water, and vegetation: environmental transformations aimed ideally at quick profit. In the prevailing culture of the basin a farm was selected, not as a permanent home, but as a likely short-term investment or, perhaps, a likely spot on which to build a commercial empire. The built environment reflected this attitude: it was generally simple, even rustic, except in commercial centers where an air of permanence might pay off. Even the development of towns was increasingly a product of outside forces: they sprang up along communications routes set by national companies, and although their survival still depended upon local productivity, such productivity depended to a large degree upon the efficiency and success of surrounding farms. In this way the towns themselves did indirectly reveal the effects of externally formulated land policies.

Thus in the 1850s and 1860s the Tulare Lake Basin was suddenly and forever swept up in large-scale extraregional processes. Isolation ended almost before it could be noticed, and a new group of settlers worked enthusiastically to live up to new standards of profit, efficiency, and human dominion over the land—standards that new linkages afforded and future linkages would demand.

6

The Formative Era, Part II: The Coming of the Railroad Brings Agricultural Intensification 1872–1894

The great rich valley which has so long lain asleep, given up to horses and cattle, is waking up. (Nordhoff 1872, p. 183)

As had happened elsewhere in the American West, the construction of a railroad initiated a new pattern of settlement in the Tulare Lake Basin. The cultural and physical attributes of the basin were further homogenized, for the railroad brought improved access to world commodity markets: bonanza wheat farms spread across the basin. The railroad destroyed any remaining vestiges of regional isolation, bringing in its wake even greater control by the national economy and culture. Land uses changed rapidly in response to changing market conditions, technological innovations, and rising property values, and change was accompanied by renewed experimentation and renewed concern for the diversity of basin environments. The more prosperous the basin

121

became, the more it resembled other farming districts of California. As time went on, the built environment became more and more standardized; where early lines of communication ·had reflected natural obstacles and the regional contours of nature, the lines of the railroad, laid down on paper in faraway offices, were straight and unyielding. Some earlier patterns of land use and settlement did persist, however, despite dramatic reorientations brought by the railroad. Certain subregional contrasts were even intensified by the competition engendered by regional growth and by full entry into the world market economy.

The Southern Pacific Railroad Comes to the Basin

The strategies of the railroad in the Tulare Lake Basin embodied the ideas and designs of the Big Four: Collis P. Huntington, Leland Stanford, Charles Crocker, and Mark Hopkins. These men had created the Central Pacific Railroad and rapidly gained control of the Southern Pacific; both railroads, by the late 1860s, sought routes through the basin as part of their California networks. The Southern Pacific's plans were formulated well before the merger with the Central Pacific, but the initial laying of tracks in Tulare County was under the direction of the Big Four (Daggett 1922, pp. 439–440).

The specific route of the railroad was determined by engineering considerations, land-grant requirements, local aid, and the desire to ensure monopoly control. R. S. Williamson, leader of the Transcontinental Railroad survey of the basin in 1853, had proposed a route parallel to the Stockton–Los Angeles Road and close to the eastern foothills (Blake 1853, p. 36), but technological and agricultural developments soon made this proposal obsolete. In January, 1867, a different proposal by the Southern Pacific—a more westerly route reflecting new settlement away from the foothills as well as the availability of land for railroad acquisition on the basin plains (fig. 35)—gained congressional approval. The potential for town promotion was also an important consideration. Most railroad townsites were surveyed before the line was built, and so the facility of townsite acquisition controlled the final route selection. The absence of urban centers north of the basin permitted an efficient, straight route southward from Stockton to Tulare County and subsequent promotions of Modesto, Merced, and Fresno— but Visalia, with nearly 1,000 residents by 1870, was an established town to be reckoned with. Its citizens wanted the tracks routed through their town but were unwilling to pay the exorbitant bribes the Southern Pacific demanded. Finding insufficient incentives to justify the costly detour, the Big Four chose to continue on the established trajectory that passed west of Visalia and to maximize their returns by building a proprietary town nearby. The initial site chosen was on Packwood Creek, six miles southwest of Visalia, but as necessary acreage was not secured there, a new site nine miles southwest of Visalia was selected. Midway between the northern and southern county lines, midway between the lake and the foothills, this site for Tulare City seemed ideal. Land purchases began in July, 1872, and continued until 1,600 contiguous acres had been bought.

Railroad construction proceeded into the basin from the north in June, 1872, and it continued southward through the proposed junction with the Central Pacific at Goshen, pausing temporarily at Tipton (fig. 36). The tracks reached Delano (in Kern County) by August, 1874, and by September, 1876, the line through Tehachapi Pass to Los Angeles was complete (Daggett 1922, p. 126). Feeder lines shot out quickly. In August 1874 Visalia was connected to the trunk line at Goshen (*Tulare County Times* 1874) by an independent line that came under Southern Pacific control in 1899, and in 1876 the Southern Pacific built another branch line westward from Goshen to serve the rich Mussel Slough country north of Tulare Lake (*Visalia Weekly Delta* 1876). This line eventually terminated near Coalinga. Years later, in response to the threat of a competing line in the vicinity, track was laid from Mendota south to Armona (1891), and in the first decade of the twentieth century a spur was built from the main line to Stratford.

Town promotion was an integral part of railroad building in the American West, and a visitor found the Tulare Lake Basin no exception: "She perceived the strange crop beneath and all around them that the dry plain was bearing. Stakes, square small pine stakes, set regularly in a great fallow garden patch where there was no sign of seed sprouting—the markers for what was to come. . . . The men who had put these stakes here were children playing mumblety-peg. This will be the town . . . the railroad has decided" (Miller 1938, p. 423). Loading and water stations were sited at five- to seven-mile intervals along the tracks, and, to maximize their returns, the Big Four decreed that at least one major town be founded near the center of each county along the route. Tulare City was to be the dominant town of Tulare County, and the Big Four hoped their town could steal the role of county seat from Visalia. Because deeds to town lots could not be passed on to buyers until the line was complete, land granted to the Southern Pacific was not convenient for townsites; major towns such as Tulare and Hanford were platted near, but not on, granted land. Purchasing land from private parties was an easy matter, because the railroad was seen as a great boon to settlement and regional development (Smith 1976, p. 357). The

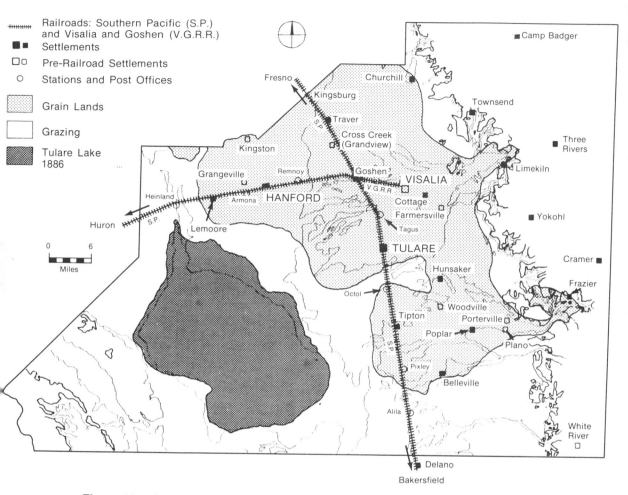

Figure 36. *Settlement Patterns, 1884*. The railroad reshaped settlement structure in the basin, creating important towns, such as Tulare and Hanford, which dramatically reduced Visalia's dominance of the region. Grain farming expanded rapidly onto lands once thought fit only for grazing.

political and economic power of the Southern Pacific was widely recognized: the railroad could found a town in the middle of nowhere, build it, settle its hinterland, and nurture it until settlement gained momentum, at which point settlers would be called upon to repay their debt by paying high rates for rail service. Promotional techniques included the establishment of rail offices, arrangement of lot sales, reduced immigration rates, donation of land for public buildings and industries, construction of hotels, and, of course, political pressure.

Nearly all Central Valley railroad towns shared a set of common features: centrality, accessibility from railroad land grants, and a uniform plat (see Smith 1976). Smooth transfer of lots was ensured by the adoption of a uniform plat, a rectangular grid aligned with the tracks rather than with the cardinal directions. Blocks were 400 feet by 320 feet, divided into thirty-two lots, and had axial alleys 20 feet wide. Residential streets were 80 feet wide, and major commercial arteries were 100 feet across. Uniformity was carried through to the naming of streets: alphabetical names (A Street through Z Street) and California county names were preferred (Smith 1976, p. 190; fig. 37a, b). By the 1880s the responsibilities of town platting and promotion had been passed on to a Southern Pacific subsidiary, the Pacific Improvement Company, which retained the Southern Pacific plat. In contrast, independent towns such as Visalia (fig. 38) had more varied plats, usually aligned with the grid of the government survey. The original railroad plats also contrasted with subsequent additions to railroad towns, for adjacent landowners who subdivided their property as the towns grew rarely adopted the railroad plat or alignment. A special hybrid street pattern—the Central Valley railroad town—was the result.

Standardized railroad towns developed during the early years of the Southern Pacific in Tulare County included Tulare (1872), Goshen (1876, Egyptian for "best of the land"), Hanford (1877, for the Southern Pacific auditor), Lemoore (1877, for a local settler), Tipton (1884, for Tipton, England), Traver (1884, for an early developer), and Alila (1885, "land of the flowers," renamed Earlimart in 1909 to advertise the early ripening of its crops). Independent interests developed a town around the Pixley station (named for the editor of the *San Francisco Argonaut*) in 1886. Another private attempt to promote a town at Hardwick station failed, as did a small town platted just north of Armona station; Armona (coined from Ramona) was resurveyed and promoted by the Pacific Improvement Company in 1891 as a junction town, but the standard plat had to be altered to accommodate property lines remaining from the original plat (Gudde 1965). Townsites were not platted at such stations as Quail, Heinlein, Remnoy, and Octol, which served only as crossroads and loading platforms (Southern Pacific Company 1888).

Several of the railroad towns grew rapidly—especially Tulare, which by 1876 boasted extensive railroad facilities, a general store, a drugstore, a hardware store, two blacksmiths, two carpentry shops, a wheelwright, a lumberyard, and a flour mill (Crofutt 1879, p. 230; Central Pacific Railroad Company 1876). Wrote one observer: "The company's shops and grounds at this place . . . are surrounded with rows of beautiful trees, chief of which is the 'bluegum' [eucalyptus]. These trees, from a distance, give the place more the appearance of grounds surrounding some palatial residence, than where several hundred men are employed manipulating iron" (Crofutt 1879, p. 230). The success of railroad towns promoted in the 1880s was even more

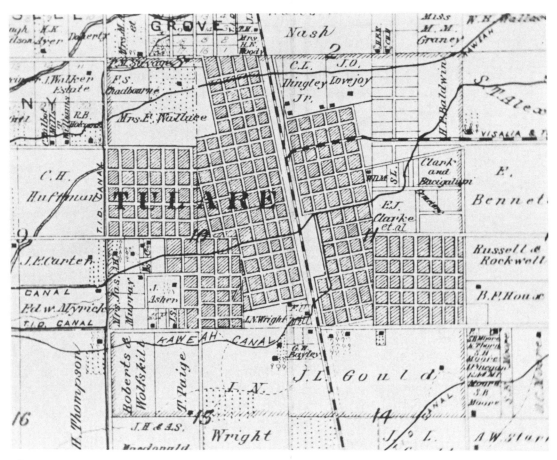

a

Figure 37*a, b. Plats of Two Railroad Towns.* Tulare (*a*) and Hanford (*b*) were established and promoted by the Southern Pacific Railroad: their plats were aligned parallel to the tracks. Such alignments often contrasted with subsequent additions to railroad towns. (Source: Thompson 1892.)

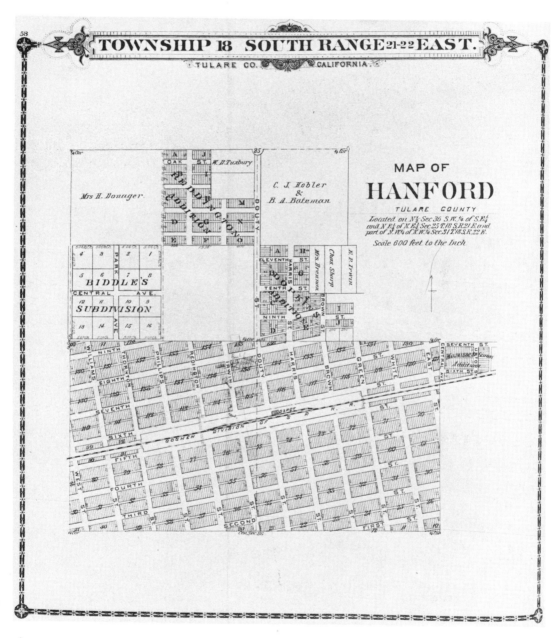

b

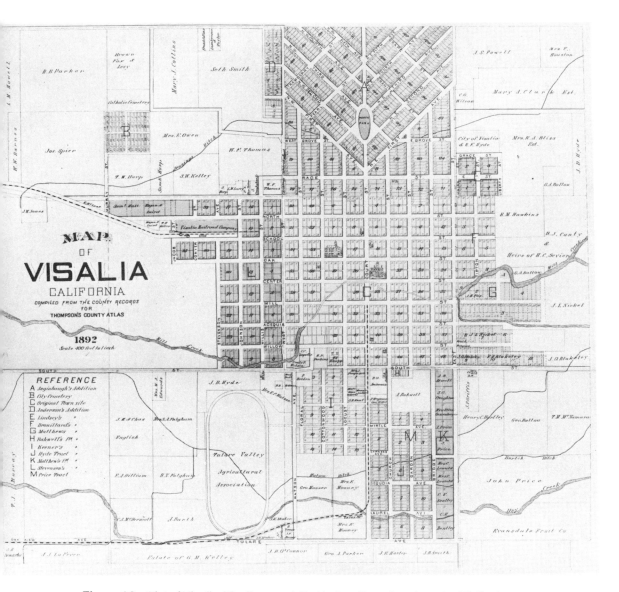

Figure 38. *Plat of Visalia*. Visalia was platted before the railroad reached it. Such independent towns generally had more varied plats than railroad towns, and their streets were usually aligned with the cardinal directions of government survey lines rather than with the tracks. (Source: Thompson 1892.)

spectacular: sixty days after Traver lots were first offered for sale, the town had post and express offices, a railroad station, a drugstore, an implement store, two general stores, two lumberyards, two hotels, two barbershops, two livery stables, three saloons, and a Chinatown (Smith 1939, p. 385). Chinatowns, in fact, developed in many California towns because railroad workers recruited from China remained when the track laying was completed; in this way the railroad had a marked effect upon the composition of the basin's population.[1]

The railroad also had a profound effect upon earlier towns. By the 1870s, settlement on the Kings, Kaweah, and Tule fans had generated local supply and service centers: Latache and Grangeville on the Kings fan, Farmersville on the Kaweah fan, Plano and Woodville near the Tule River (fig. 36). Plano, Farmersville, and Woodville were sufficiently distant from railroad towns to survive as small settlements, but Latache, Grangeville, Kingston, and Grandview–Cross Creek were quickly drained of their populace and functions by railroad towns. A Grangeville resident lamented that "towns are springing up around us like magic, and Grangeville, in her desire for something new, is daily walking off to Hanford and Lemoore, and ere long Grangeville, that great powerful city . . . will be remembered among the things that were" (Carrie 1877 in Brown 1941, p. 48). As a contemporary observed, "The locomotive is a great centralizer. It kills little businesses and builds great ones" (George 1868, p. 303). Even Visalia was vulnerable: some of its citizens and a few businesses relocated in Tulare, which quickly rose to regional dominance, although Visalia was able to retain the county seat.

The effects of railroad promotion were not always dependable, however, even where the Big Four made efforts to support the growth of large towns. Although Tulare City's population reached 2,697 by 1890, in 1891, when the railroad shops and roundhouse were moved to Bakersfield, many businesses and houses were moved south as well (Centennial Home Tour Committee 1972; Mitchell 1976, p. 143): "Two hundred families moved out in mass and an equal number followed them within a year. The town was dead; business was at a standstill; vacant houses stared gloomily out onto the empty streets. There was no hope for the future. Ten years later the houses were still being moved away to other towns and on to farms for dwellings" (Gist 1952, p. 81). Twenty years of railroad nurture had not been sufficient to generate self-sustaining growth. Goshen and Tipton also declined when their railroad facilities were transferred to other localities in 1873 and 1874, respectively (*Visalia Weekly News* 1873; *Kern County Weekly Courier* 1874). Despite such local setbacks, the influences of improved access, railroad promotion, and regional agricultural potential caused regional settlement to proceed rapidly. Between 1870 and 1880, the county's population climbed 149 percent (from 4,533 to 11,281), and it rose an additional 118 percent (to 24,574) by 1890 (U.S.D.I. Census Office 1072; 1883; 1896: Vol. I).

1. Chinatowns disappeared when the basin's Chinese population was driven out of the area by force in the 1890s.

The Wheat Boom and the Rise of Bonanza Wheat Farms

The railroad and barbed wire fencing brought an end to the open range. Property values soared, and land uses were geared more and more directly to market conditions. The basin's landscapes began to lose their regional identity, becoming "merely part of an enormous whole, a unit in the vast agglomeration of wheat land the whole world round, feeling the effects of causes thousands of miles distant—a drought in the prairies of Dakota, a rain in the plains of India, a frost on the Russian steppes, a hot wind on the llanos of the Argentine" (Norris 1903, p. 54). The wheat boom began earlier in other parts of California. Experimental shipments of wheat from San Francisco to New York, Australia, and Great Britain in the late 1850s found an eager market for the hard, dry, white grain of the Central Valley (Paul 1958, pp. 392–398), and by 1860 more than half of the state's wheat crop was unloaded in Great Britain alone (U.S.D.I. Census Office 1864, Vol. III, p. 10). California was the premier wheat state in the Union by the mid-1870's, and it continued to rank first or second until the 1890s, when competition and local diversification changed the emphasis of California agriculture.

The Tulare Lake Basin proved very well suited to grain farming, and by the time it joined in the wheat boom, a market for its grain was well established. The railroad facilitated marketing and settlement, and new technologies and attitudes supported the development of huge bonanza wheat farms. Many obstacles to successful grain cultivation had been overcome before the railroad era. The fertility of the basin plains and the suitability of its climate for agriculture had been demonstrated. It seemed, in fact, to be a "natural" wheat region, with level terrain, easily plowed soils, dry summers, and abundant spring runoff. Minor inconveniences such as hog-wallow terrain were ignored, for the early machinery was light and maneuverable, and remaining obstacles were challenged by innovative techniques and ever-increasing mechanization. Local innovations in farm equipment and dryland-cultivation techniques diffused widely through the American West and, indeed, the world.

Grain farming had begun to emerge in the basin even before the railroad era. It was neither capital intensive nor technologically complicated: settlers of limited means could take up wheat farming with a few horses or oxen, a plow, some seed, and a likely parcel of land. Suitable land was still plentiful, although land prices were rising fast: "There are many thousands of acres in Tulare County which can be rented for a price equivalent to one quarter of the crop, by men who have teams and tools to put in wheat, and land can be bought on credit also, by men who have capital enough to put in their crops" (Nordhoff 1882, p. 156). Squatting was also an option, especially on railroad land, which was often opened to settlement with promises of preferential treatment before the company had secured full title. Settlers assumed that when their land came up for sale they would be charged low government prices, but land values rose quickly, in part because of their improvements. When the time came to sell, the Southern Pacific demanded payment at inflated prices. This, in combination with discriminatory rate structures and other injustices, brought substantial popular resentment to bear against the Southern Pacific in the 1870s. Conflicts culminated in May, 1880, in the bloody Mussel Slough incident, an outright battle between settlers and the railroad which underlined the role of monopolies in California and prompted Frank Norris to write *The Octopus* (1903), a muckraking expose of the Southern Pacific's illicit dealings in which Norris likened the railroad to an octopus with "tentacles of steel clutching into the soil" (Norris 1903, p. 51).

No matter who owned the land or how large the farm was, success was measured in tons of wheat harvested; its "volume was the index of failure or success, of riches or poverty" (Norris 1903, p. 61). The railroad had brought new capital, higher land taxes, and improved equipment. Huge mechanized grain operations were increasingly practical and increasingly necessary, and it became still easier for large landholders—settlers or speculators—to get rich. Mechanized farming was especially successful in the basin, and it benefited from the research activities of the Department of Agriculture. Gang plows, scrapers, combination seeder-harrows, and twine-knotters for binding grain were enthusiastically adopted, and by the late 1880s massive steam combines pulled by three dozen draft animals were plying the land. Awesome in appearance, these machines were difficult to maneuver; land along meanders and sloughs was not cropped, remaining as refuges instead for wild plants and animals (Gist 1974, p. 88). In 1886 an enterprising settler harnessed steam as a locomotive force for huge combines and plows, the forerunners of the self-propelled tractors that would soon reshape the basin's land. Another local invention was the hog-wallow leveler, which introduced a new and important facet in farmers' relationships to their land: terrain modification. The relationship of people to the land was sealed. It was a relationship of force, "Force that made the wheat grow, Force that garnered it from the soil to give place to the succeeding crop" (Norris 1903, p. 634).

Wheat farming prospered in the basin through the 1880s. Production focused on three adjoining districts: Traver, Mussel Slough, and Tulare (Smith 1939, p. 246). The geographical pattern of grain production was reflected in the spread of large farms over these grassland regions and in Traver's rise as the chief regional shipping center for wheat; by the 1880s it was the premier grain-shipping point in California. The number of farms in the basin increased nearly sixfold between 1870 and 1880, and average farm size increased markedly (table 3). The proportion of basin farms larger than 500 acres also rose dramatically. As Nordhoff observed, "although the farms here are in general of 640 acres or less, there are not wanting some of those immense estates for which California is famous" (Nordhoff 1882, p. 95). Large they were: many bonanza wheat farms comprised 10,000 acres or more, and in certain districts 10,000 acres represented an average farm: the land from Tulare to the Sierra foothills was farmed by only five or six landholders (Smith 1939, pp. 170, 246). "As far as one could see," wrote Frank Norris, "to the north, to the east, to the south, and to the west, was all one holding, a principality ruled with iron and steam, bullied into a yield" (Norris 1903, p. 60). As Nordhoff commented after visiting many basin farms of this era, "Farmers in this country make two mistakes not uncommon to American farmers, but less excusable here than elsewhere. They try to own too much land, and they are content with shabby houses" (Nordhoff 1872, p. 145). Farmsteads were sometimes showplaces of the finest in contemporary architecture and landscaping, but far more often they were rather rude shanties set out amidst the vast wheat fields: "There is no vegetable garden, there are no trees, there is absolutely nothing to make life endurable or pleasant" (Nordhoff 1872, p. 187).

Hired labor was an integral part of bonanza-wheat-farm operations, and plenty of able-bodied workers were arriving in the basin in hopes of securing land or employment: "Fences and houses can be built by contract. . . . Men make it their business to do this; and at the

TABLE 3

Proportion of Farms by Size Category, Tulare County, 1860–1890

Farm Size	1860	1870	1880	1890
Under 10 acres	9%	1%	2%	1%
10–49 acres	48	46	8	12
50–99 acres	19	25	19	10
100–499 acres	22	27	60	60
500–999 acres	2	1	5	9
1,000 or more acres	0	0	6	8
Number (all sizes)	469	377	1,125	2,193

SOURCES: U.S.D.I. Census Office 1864; 1872; 1883; 1896, Agriculture, State and County Reports.

nearest turn the intending settler can always have all his necessary "improvements" done by contract, even to ploughing his land and putting in his first crop" (Nordhoff 1882, pp. 111–112). After the initial surge of railroad building, many thousands of Chinese men released from railroad employment found work in the Central Valley, and by 1890 there were 954 Chinese residents of Tulare County (U.S.D.I. Census Office 1896, Vol. I). Some worked as field hands, others as peddlers. Writing in 1888, Thompson and Warren noted that "there must be nearly a hundred Chinese vegetable wagons running in the county, for no neighborhood is without one. [Yet] so strong is the feeling against Chinese that many would prefer to patronize white gardeners at higher rates rather than contribute to the support of Chinamen" (Thompson and Warren 1888, pp. 115–116). Even though their contribution to regional development was immense, all too often the Chinese were scorned by American settlers. The economic depression of the 1890s brought several forced deportations of Chinese from the basin, but already a move toward smaller holdings had reduced the farm employment available to them: "The Chinaman still fills an important place in California country life, but the white man ousts him wherever he comes into competition with him for the best places, and this is going on so steadily that it is absurd to cry out against the Chinese nowadays. The small farmers, the 160 and the 40 acre men, have no use for Chinese" (Nordhoff 1882, p. 168). Despite the declining demand for hired labor toward the end of the wheat-boom era, a new regional relationship between landed and landless residents had been cemented in lasting regional attitudes and values. This relationship would endure a succession of changes in crops and in the ethnic background of the agricultural work force; in fact, it would, in time, become a primary feature of the basin.

Regional concentration on wheat and barley during the bonanza grain era helped formulate another enduring aspect of basin agriculture: specialization. So specialized were the endeavors of basin farmers that they relied upon outsiders to supply their everyday needs: "There are farmers who own several thousand acres, and who do not raise even a potato for their own families. Wheat, wheat, wheat is their only crop and for this everything else is neglected. Their families live on canned fruits and vegetables; all their supplies are bought in the nearest town, of the groceryman" (Nordhoff 1872, p. 131). Each crop had its own particular repertory of techniques and machinery, as well as its own marketing procedures. A successful farmer needed a thorough knowledge of all aspects of production; he was a businessman, a producer of a given commodity: "Crops were reckoned in dollars, and the land was valued by principal plus interest, and crops were bought and sold before they were planted. Then crop failure, drought, and flood were no longer little deaths within life, but simple losses of money. . . . They were no longer farmers at all, but little shopkeepers of crops, little manufacturers who must sell before they can make" (Steinbeck 1939, p. 316). They depended upon urban markets and long-distant processors, shippers, and financiers. They were committed to mass production and mechanization no less than producers of steel or cloth would be, and if they were not vigilant and worldly wise, their profits would be whittled away by "the grain merchants, the hucksters, the middlemen, the shippers, the railroad men, the sack makers, the law makers, the assessors, and the tax collectors, who manage to hold the agricultural classes in a condition of servitude unparalleled in a free country" (Browne 1873, p. 301).

Still, like farmers the world over, bonanza wheat farmers were vulnerable to unpredictable changes in the weather, which could jeopardize not just their profits but their economic survival. The wheat farmers, like the basin stockraisers before them, were gamblers as well as businessmen, "the turning point of profit or loss being a light shower at the critical time or the occurrence of a norther for a day or two" (Hilgard, Jones, and Furnas 1882, p. 14). "In a good season they sell their wheat for a large sum," commented Nordhoff, "and either buy more land or spend the money on high living; and when a dry year comes they fall into debt, . . . and when the next dry year comes it brings the sheriff" (Nordhoff 1872, p. 131). As a Grangeville farmer wrote to John Muir, "for the last ten years we have played at farming as at cards, speculating and gambling, scouring over thousand-acre lots with mustangs and gangplows, and putting in crop after crop" (in Muir 1874). The aim was to play out the soil and then move on to something new. More attention was given to increasing the amount of land in cultivation than to perpetuating its fertility. Insufficient fertilization and fallowing caused rapid soil depletion in the grain districts: "When, at last, the land, worn out, would refuse to yield, they would invest their money in something else. By then, they would all have made fortunes. They did not care. 'After us, the deluge' " (Norris 1903, pp. 298–299). On the drier lands west of the Kings River, such gambling ended almost as quickly as it had begun. In 1899 Orlando Barton lamented:

The plains are given up to desolation. Eight or ten years ago large crops of wheat were raised on this land, which was all located, and farmhouses built on nearly every quarter section. . . . But not a spear of anything green grows on the place this year. . . . The houses of former inhabitants are empty, the doors swing open or shut with the wind. Drifting sand is piled to the top of many fences. The windmills, with their broken arms, swing idly in the breeze. Like a veritable city of the dead, vacant residences on every side greet the traveler by horse team as he pursues his weary way across these seemingly endless plains. (In Latta 1949b, p. 263)

Even in the rich Mussel Slough country around Hanford the soils began to show the effects of careless use; a visitor to the area observed that, "at the time of my visit, dead spots were appearing in the magnificent grain fields at the time when the grain was but a few inches high" (Hilgard, Jones, and Furnas 1882, p. 45).

The gamblers eventually learned to take better care of their land, to make longer-term investments of capital and energy. As land uses intensified, technological innovations shifted the risks increasingly from "controllable" nature to the capricious outside market. Gambling and specialization, however, remained salient aspects of bonanza wheat farming and of basin farming in general from the railroad era to the present. The zenith of bonanza wheat farms came in 1884, when more than 90 percent of the basin's cropland was planted to wheat (Hardy 1929, pp. 221–222; U.S.D.I. Census Office 1883, Vol. III). The 1880s and 1890s brought new lands into competition with California—the Pacific Northwest, India, Australia, Argentina, Canada, the Great Plains, the Ukraine—and as the world supply of wheat and barley rose, grain profits plummeted, reaching their low point in 1894 (Saunders 1960, pp. 40–43). Basin farmers began to turn to intensive cultivation of other, more profitable crops. Fruits, vegetables, and dairy products found good markets, and improvements in agricultural and transportation technology made their production increasingly lucrative. Regional intensification raised land values, necessitating greater returns per acre than before, and thus supported further intensification. As the agricultural frontier expanded, grain (like ranching before it) was pushed from recent alluvial lands by more gainful land uses, and stock raising was in turn pushed farther towards the margins of the basin. This shift was reflected in the rise of Terra Bella, in the sparsely settled southeastern basin, as the leading grain shipping point of the basin by the turn of the century (Smith 1939, p. 246). Huge grain ranches persisted, especially on reclaimed land in the lake bed, where the world's largest grain farm was located in 1903 (Tulare County Planning Department 1975, p. 8). Grain also persisted as a companion crop on the deltas, where it was irrigated and grown in rotation with other crops. The success of this innovation was commended to John Muir by a Mussel Slough settler: "Look at that broom corn, dense and impenetrable as canebreak, with panicles enough to sweep the State; and that Indian corn, grown after wheat, with ears so high you cannot reach them; and at these level sheets of alfalfa, mowed heaven knows how often" (Muir 1874).

Irrigation and Agricultural Involution

Irriguous [*sic*] revivals are breaking out all over the glad plains, and wildcat farming is dead. (Muir 1874)

With the coming of the railroad, land appraisal in the Tulare Lake Basin changed: good lands were any tracts along the route that could be made to grow grain. New towns, strung out along the line, provided new opportunities for investment. Land development was guided by two imperial forces: grain culture and its steel support, the railroad, bound in a symbiotic relationship based upon monopoly and fueled by conservatism. Although these forces dominated the basin through the 1880s, however, other forces began to redefine land quality and to free settlement from the spatial and economic constraints imposed by the designs of the Big Four, and the most powerful of these forces was irrigation. Changing market conditions, rising taxes, and environmental degradation weakened the grip of grain culture on the basin; diversification and intensification (supported by irrigation) emerged as new trends in the modification of regional landscapes. The railroad, in turn, quickly seized the new opportunities afforded by regional development and again became a force to be reckoned with.

In the early 1870s, irrigation was recognized as a method by which farmers could gain more control over their domain and, at the same time, vastly increase the value of their property. Muir remarked that land prices in the Mussel Slough country increased about fourfold with the construction of an irrigation ditch (Muir 1874) and the potential value of canals as transportation arteries was also noted (Cone 1876, p. 108). Experiments with intensive cultivation of new crops proved successful, and it was quickly apparent that the returns from a set of irrigated companion crops (orchards, grains, alfalfa) would be far greater than from dryland grain alone. Higher land taxes and higher costs encouraged the rapid development of large-scale irrigation systems, which profoundly affected the basin's landscapes as well as its political geography.

The construction of large-scale irrigation systems in the basin was not difficult. Because terrain was generally level, the costs of canal construction and field preparation were low, and when farmers most needed water—in spring and early summer—the streams were full. Initial difficulties were primarily legal in nature, for the development of water legislation in California was guided by two conflicting legal traditions: the principle of prior appropriation as observed during the gold rush, and the doctrine of riparian rights derived from the ancient traditions of English common law. Riparian rights restricted the use of water to landowners along a stream. Others were prohibited from using the stream's water if use would diminish its volume or quality. Because it precluded access to water for purposes of irrigation, this doctrine was incompatible with agricultural development in the arid West. In the early years of California settlement, riparian rights were upheld, although miners and early irrigators tried to circumvent them by ranking water rights in terms of the date and amount of each claim—that is, by respecting prior appropriation. A foothold on a stream could usually be gained in this way, and water could then be channeled to distant properties without regard for the rights of downstream users. Rights of prior appropriation were sanctioned by the state in 1862, when ditch and canal companies were granted the right to condemn private land for right-of-way purposes. The concept of prior appropriation was often challenged by large landholders, who invoked riparian rights to thwart cooperative efforts of small farmers whose lands lacked stream frontage, and irrigation was long restricted to a local scale reflected in short canals and large expanses without irrigation.

This ongoing controversy culminated in passage of the Wright Irrigation Act of 1887. Common law had viewed ownership of water and land as separate; the Wright Act provided for the ownership of water and land as a unit. It prescribed the formation of irrigation districts composed of local landowners and empowered to obtain water through condemnation of existing riparian rights. The Wright Act (as revised in 1897) served as a foundation for further legislative measures that removed the remaining legal obstacles to irrigation; the Reclamation Act of 1902 and the doctrine of "most beneficial use" were among the most important of these measures (Miller 1973, pp. 9–42). Water, in theory, became available to all landowners and all properties. The influence of government sanction, guidance, or restriction on land use and settlement in the basin was again evident; here, as elsewhere in the American West, it would be difficult to underrate the role of government fiat in landscape evolution. The role of government continued to expand as more and more people—and more conflicting processes and interests—vied for rights to use the basin's resources and to alter its landscapes.

The first cooperative efforts to divert Central Valley streams on a large scale took place in the basin and were organized as mutual companies. Each member purchased company stock proportional to the amount of land he or she intended to irrigate, and the accumulated revenue was used for construction expenses; additional levies were assessed for operating expenses. Important early cooperative projects included the Lower Kings River Ditch (Lemoore Canal) and the Peoples Ditch, both completed in 1872 on the Kings Delta, and the Last Chance

Ditch (1873). The Wutchumna Canal Company was organized in 1872 to divert water from the apex of the Kaweah fan; an earlier Kaweah-fan irrigation project had been the Consolidated Peoples Ditch, constructed in 1864 (Grunsky 1898a, 1898b; fig. 39). Private corporations also financed the construction of irrigation systems in conjunction with land-development and colonization schemes, for irrigation greatly enhanced the attractiveness of basin lands to immigrants who had been warned to "be sure of water—whatever else you lack, see to it that you have this *sine qua non*. With it you can raise almost anything that grows on the face of the earth; without it crops will be uncertain and failure frequent" (Cone 1876, p. 173).

　　Irrigation development accelerated with the formation of irrigation districts after passage of the Wright Act. The first districts in Tulare County were the Alta Irrigation District on the Kings Delta and the Tulare Irrigation District on the Kaweah Delta. By 1894 there were six irrigation districts in the basin, comprising 500 miles of main canals and 800,000 acres of agricultural land (Higgins 1895, p. 240). New districts continued to be formed into the twentieth century until irrigation water

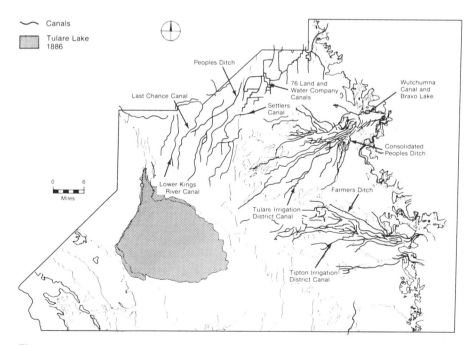

Figure 39. *Irrigation Canals, 1892.* Large-scale diversions of the Kings, Kaweah, and Tule rivers by cooperative water companies had begun. With the development of major canals, artificial irrigation of the Kings River fan surpassed the early predominance of irrigation in the Kaweah and Tule river regions. (Thompson 1892; Grunsky 1898a, 1898b; Hall 1886.)

became available to most basin farmers (fig. 40). The resources and appeal of these irrigation districts were limited by their fragmented distribution and their loose confederation or outright competition. Each district furthered its own interests, protecting its own access to a dwindling water supply, with the result that initial development of the basin's water resources proceeded in an uncoordinated and rather wasteful manner. Somewhat aghast after a survey of Tulare Valley irrigation projects, the state engineer reported in 1880 that "with one or two notable exceptions, all the irrigation that has been effected so far has been done with little or no system, and with a lavish waste of water that could never be permitted in any well regulated plan for the irrigation of districts now under cultivation" (State of California Engineer 1880, p. 123). Denied water for development, areas adjacent to irrigated tracts often remained under such extensive uses as dryland grain or grazing. Within the districts, new settlers were "obliged to buy not only land but water, as if the first-comers had taken possession of the clouds" (Muir 1874). In the late 1880s and 1890s water companies even advertised for settlers and then "played the part of Providence in making farming possible" (Austin 1932, p. 199). Such activities changed the patterns of basin settlement and irrigation, for watering the land was no longer possible only along streams and short canals. A patchwork of noncontiguous developments spread across the basin: settlers and speculators, armed with the power of eminent domain, carried water across dry lands and created geometrical oases far from streams.

Between 1872 and 1894 the expansion of irrigation in the basin was accomplished largely by diversion of the Kings, Kaweah, and Tule rivers and of Deer Creek. Their distributaries were canalized and ditches were constructed to carry their water farther toward the shrinking lake. With the exception of the '76 Canal and a few short ditches near Sand Creek, most irrigation networks were confined to recent alluvial lands, for as late as 1900 surface water supplied 90 percent of the basin's irrigation water (Zimrick 1976, p. 18). In the late 1800s, some observers suggested the development of storage ponds and reservoirs and the importation of surface water from adjacent regions, noting that the basin's waters had been spread nearly to their limits (Nordhoff 1882, p. 142; Strahorn, Holmes, and Mann 1908, p. 1329; California State Agricultural Society 1875, pp. 429–431). Tulare Lake supplied irrigation water for a few farms, but the steady decline in the quantity and quality of its water precluded consideration of the lake as a significant water resource.

Control of surface water helped to stabilize basin agriculture, but farmers were still not assured of adequate water. Drought could sharply reduce irrigation supplies, and areas located outside of irrigation

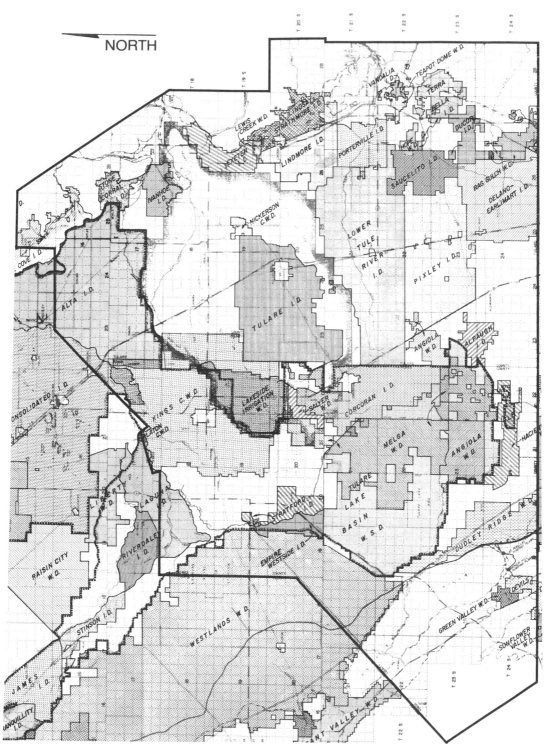

Figure 40. *Major Water Agencies of the Basin Today*. Irrigation development accelerated with the formation of irrigation districts after the passage of the Wright Act, eventually yielding a complex mosaic of water districts and companies covering the entire basin. (Source: State of California Department of Water Resources 1978.)

districts or away from streams were generally unable to obtain irrigation water at all. To increase their own control of the situation, farmers near the valley trough on old valley fill began to tap underground aquifers. The nature of subsurface strata—made of "pure alluvial soil without any rock or gravel"—was seen as a particular regional advantage because it made early well drilling relatively simple (Cone 1876, p. 107). Once again, technological advances, including refined well-drilling techniques developed in the goldfields, were eagerly adopted. Steam-powered drill rigs and pumps appeared in the late 1870s, taking their place beside muscle-powered drills and wind-driven pumps already present for domestic purposes. Wells drilled through the Corcoran clay lens produced flowing water at the surface without pumping, and the drilling of new artesian wells spread a patchwork of irrigated acreage and diversified farming far beyond the reach of surface systems onto old valley fill and recent alluvium near the valley trough (fig. 41). Artesian flow diminished by 1885, and by 1900 many former artesian wells had to be pumped because overdraughts had weakened hydro-static pressure (Mendenhall 1908, p. 36). The adoption of wind-,

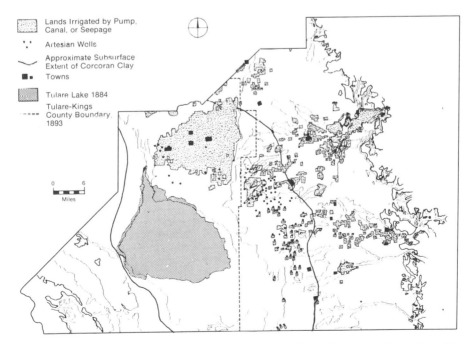

Figure 41. *Irrigated Land, 1886.* The major growth of irrigation on the Kings River fan stimulated rapid development of this area, bringing a westward shift of settlement away from the Kaweah fan. Westward expansion was also assisted by the drilling of artesian wells that tapped aquifers beneath the Corcoran-clay formation. (Sources: Mendenhall, Dole, and Stabler 1916; Hall 1886.)

steam-, and gas-powered pumps sustained the expansion made by artesian irrigation, and by the 1890s power pumps were also used to drill wells on the upper terraces of the basin. Accessible groundwater had been discovered beneath the redlands, and these areas proved well suited to orchards and vineyards. The first pump irrigation of terrace lands in the Cental Valley occurred in the region between Exeter and Lindsay, which was transformed into a densely settled orchard district long before canal irrigation was available there. As Mary Austin observed, "wherever along the belt the rivers fail, the pumps take up the work; strenuous little Davids contending against the Goliaths of drought. They can be heard chugging away like the active pulse of the vineyards, completing the ribbon of greenness that spans from ridge to ridge of the down-plunging hills" (Palmer and Austin 1914, p. 136). Even after surface water became available to these areas, pump irrigation remained more widely practiced in Tulare County than anywhere else in the Central Valley (Mendenhall, Dole, and Stabler 1916, p. 283).

Patterns of land use and settlement changed greatly with the advent of widespread irrigation and agricultural intensification. The early dominance of the Kaweah Delta as a hearth of settlement and innovation was rapidly eroded by developments on the Kings Delta, especially in the Mussel Slough district. Here surface water was readily available, and furrows or checks were not needed: "The soil became thoroughly saturated for a distance of 200 yards or more on either side of the branch ditches, making it wholly unnecessary to overflow the fields" (Muir 1874). Wells were actually drilled to lower the water table to combat alkalization (Grunsky 1898*b*, p. 35). So rapid was the turn to irrigated, diversified cropping in this densely settled district that the area quickly outpaced the Kaweah Delta in production. By 1879 there were 61,200 acres irrigated by the Kings River, the majority located within the basin proper. Only 22,000 acres were irrigated by the Kaweah and only about 4,500 by the Tule (State of California Engineer 1880, pp. 4, 59–60). By 1886 most of the Kings fan was contiguously irrigated, while elsewhere in the basin irrigation was still confined to isolated locales. Dense settlement and agricultural prosperity on the Kings Delta led to the development of a political identity separate from that of the Kaweah Delta: in March, 1893, Kings County was formed, its seat of government at Hanford. Once the new county obtained some additional land from Fresno County in 1909, Kings and Tulare counties together included all of the Tulare Lake Basin (Menefee and Dodge 1913, p. 17).

The Tulare Lake Basin lost but quickly regained its regional lead in irrigation (table 4), and the general patterns of expansion established between 1872 and 1894 continued. Irrigated acreage expanded southward from the Kings River, filling gaps along the Kaweah and Tule

TABLE 4

Acres Irrigated, Southern San Joaquin Valley, by County, 1890–1930

	1890	1900	1910	1920	1930
Lake Basin	168,455	179,648	456,653	586,530	680,077
Tulare County	168,455	86,854	265,404	398,662	410,083
Kings County		92,974	190,949	187,868	269,994
Fresno County	105,665	283,737	402,318	547,587	533,992
Kern County	154,549	112,533	190,034	223,593	180,106

SOURCES: U.S.D.I. Census Office 1896; 1901, Vol. V; U.S.D.C. Bureau of the Census 1913; 1922, Vol. III; 1932, Agriculture, Vol. II.

deltas. Lacustrine deposits were reclaimed and irrigated, and even the White River region came under both canal and well irrigation. On old valley fill, irrigation spread south from Dinuba to engulf the land around Traver but stopped short north of Cottonwood Creek, a clear demarcation that persisted for many years (fig. 42). The node of irrigated terrace land between Lindsay and Exeter expanded southward to the Tule River.

In the first decade of the twentieth century, irrigation was limited more by organizational and environmental restrictions than by lack of

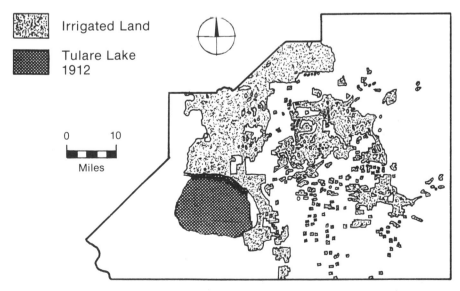

Irrigated Land

Tulare Lake 1912

0   10

Miles

Figure 42. *Irrigated Land, 1912.* The expansion of surface irrigation systems continued on the alluvial fans and on old valley fill along the Kings River. Wells account for the growth of irrigation on terraces of old valley fill and on the old lacustrine deposits. (Source: U.S.D.A. Office of Experiment Stations 1912.)

water. The development of areas far from streams was retarded, of course, except where a high water table existed—yet, in addition, some areas where water was readily available did not respond well to irrigation. For example, irrigators in the Traver area encountered severe problems with alkalization. Land uses reflected gaps in irrigation: dryland grain, grazing, and pasturage still predominated there, whereas orchards, vineyards, and dairying were beginning to replace these uses in irrigated areas. The most rapid extension of irrigation in the second decade of this century was on the lake bed and eastern deltas (fig. 43). By this time the lake covered only two townships, its dry margins irrigated by the same distributaries that had once maintained it. Further to the north, the old marshlands along Fish Slough were also lined by canals. The frontiers of irrigation had reached the limits of recent alluvium on the east side with development of new irrigation districts and ditch companies; expansion had been supported by a favorable market for dairy products and row crops. Some water was channeled into the basin from the south to irrigate newly occupied lands south of the lake, but the amount of imported water was small. Expansion of irrigated acreage continued until, by 1930, the hydrologic resources of the basin could be spread no further: new sources of water would be needed if the spread of intensive land uses was to continue.

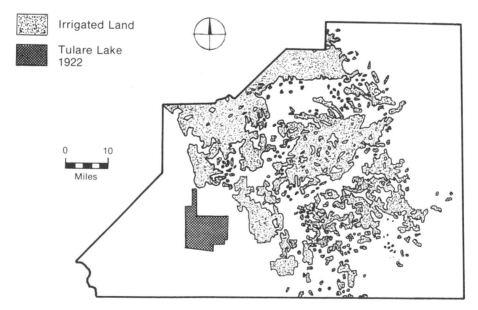

Figure 43. *Irrigated Land, 1922.* Almost all of the new alluvial soils of the eastern basin were irrigated by 1922, but old-valley-fill and alkaline lake soils were still not entirely irrigated. (Source: State of California Department of Public Works 1922.)

The Substance and Effects of Diversity

It is this diversity, this constantly recurring charm of novelty and undeveloped possibilities, that casts a spell over all those who have once experienced it, and are not governed merely by the desire for gain, but also by that of home-making. (Hilgard, Jones, and Furnas 1882, p. 11)

The rising profitability of intensive agriculture in the basin led to a great deal of experimental cropping. The basin's markets rewarded diversified endeavors as never before, and new developments in transportation, processing, and refrigeration expanded the market for basin fruits and dairy products to global proportions. The development of diversified land uses in the basin resembled earlier patterns of agricultural innovation there: new developments originated on the recent alluvial lands of the east side and spread outward onto old valley fill, lacustrine soils, and, finally, onto residual soils. Technological advances and changing attitudes toward farming and toward the land helped farmers adjust to local disadvantages such as water scarcity, hardpan, and frost. The government also provided assistance under the auspices of the Hatch Experiment Station Act of 1887, which provided for the establishment and support of an agricultural experiment station in the basin to help farmers broaden their options and make the best use of the available resources.

The first move toward commercial production of new kinds of crops occurred in the Mussel Slough district, where irrigated corn and alfalfa were made companions to wheat in the early 1870s (Grunsky 1898b, p. 89). Farmers here soon boasted that "the yield of all kinds of crops is marvelous. . . . Five crops of alfalfa a year is common, and vegetables—well, we will never tell you—the yield is immense" (Crofutt 1879, p. 229). By 1885, commercial plantings of grapes, apricots, and peaches had been made on the Kings fan, and soon orchards were planted in other irrigated regions as well. In the 1890s, small acreages of evergreen fruits (lemons, oranges, and olives) were grown with irrigation at higher elevations where frosts were less severe; evergreen fruits were a minor proportion of the basin's orchard acreage until about 1910. The planting of orchards and vineyards reflected a new attitude on the part of farmers: a stronger commitment to the basin as a permanent home, a greater interest in the care and conservation of their land. As Gist noted, "therein lies the element of permanence, for those who have possessed the land, have tilled it and passed it on undamaged to another generation in an unbroken family heritage" (Gist 1952, p. 210). The basin's lands were finally being domesticated, not just mined of their fertility through the application of brute force. Speculation and blind faith in technology still supported reckless land use on the part of some farmers, but no longer was the land's long-term agricultural capacity as severely jeopardized by short-term gambling as it had been in the past. Thompson and Warren celebrated this transition: "As the great herds of cattle have gone, and the great herds of sheep are going, so the great wheat ranches will go, and in their place we shall have 'sandlappers,' no end of gentle, industrious, intelligent 'sandlappers' (Thompson and Warren 1888, p. 63).

Another outgrowth of diversification was the gradual emergence of distinctive agricultural regions within the basin. The Mussel Slough region became known as the Lucerne district, a reference to its concentrated dairying and large expanses of irrigated alfalfa; the Four Creeks country of the lower Kaweah Delta became noted for alfalfa, dairying, irrigated grains, and deciduous orchards. The Tipton-Pixley region to the south was characterized by dryland grain and grazing (Crofutt 1879, p. 230), and in the Corcoran area west of the Southern Pacific tracks, grain, dairying, and sugar beets were the primary land uses. In the southeastern corner of the basin, irrigated alfalfa and cereal grains were the primary crops until citrus orchards became common north of Porterville (Mendenhall 1908, p. 20). The Alta district around Dinuba emerged as a densely settled region of evergreen and deciduous orchards and vineyards. The Lone Tree district (near Lemoore), the Lakeside district (south of Hanford), and the Cross Creek district (near the juncture of Cross Creek and Tulare Lake) gained identities as new regions of irrigated grain and alfalfa farming. West of the basin trough and between the irrigated tracts, pastures and dryland grain still prevailed. In these areas beyond the reach of irrigation systems, diversified endeavors were slow to develop. James Wright, a settler in the Kettleman Hills, recalled that "the only neighbors we had were desert squirrels or chipmunks, rattlesnakes, antelope, coyotes, horned toads, lizards, north winds, and sandstorms" (in Latta 1949b, p. 338). These agricultural regions reflected the reemergence of concern with the quality of the land. Varied agricultural patterns were established in response to regional variations in climate, terrain, hydrology, and soil characteristics, but also reflected the varied patterns of historical settlement and innovation.

Expanded settlement and rising productivity brought a demand for new lines of communication. In response to the spread of orchards along the eastern flank of the basin and to the threat of a competing line in the area, the Southern Pacific built a second trunk line parallel to the original tracks. Completed in 1888, it ran from Fresno to Famosa (in Kern County) and nearly duplicated the route of the old Stockton–Los Angeles Road (fig. 44). Stations were established at Dinuba, Monson,

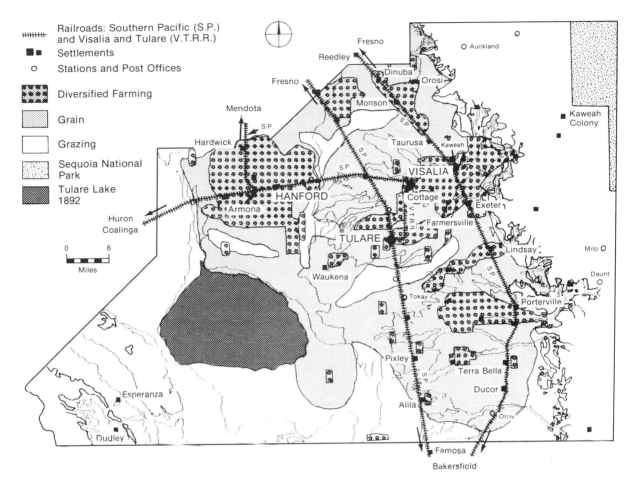

Figure 44. *Settlement Patterns, 1894.* Diversified farming displaced grain farming just as grain had displaced grazing in an earlier era. The irrigated lands of the Kings River were largely planted to diversified crops, and the focus of new settlement had shifted back to the east side along the new parallel line of the Southern Pacific.

Taurusa, Kaweah Station (on the Saint Johns River), Exeter, Lindsay, Porterville, Plano, Terra Bella, and Orris. Once again the stations were sited without concern for terrain, soils, or prior settlement; instead, the uniform occupation of space perceived as offering uniform opportunities was favored. In contrast to the first line, however, the new rails were routed through an existing town, Porterville. A later line connected Visalia and Tulare. The Pacific Improvement Company again appropriated certain stations as nuclei for town development, and platted standard railroad towns at Dinuba (1888, derivation of its name uncertain), Monson (1888, for Monson, Maine), Exeter (1889, for Exeter, England), and Lindsay (1889, the maiden name of Hutchinson's wife)—see figure 45. At Porterville (1888) and Plano (1889), the company established standard plats adjacent to the existing towns, which were drained of their functions and populations by promotion of the new sites (Smith 1976, pp. 315–320). Subdivisions at Taurusa and Orris were unsuccessful, as was Terra Bella (which was resurveyed and privately developed in 1908; Mitchell 1976, p. 138).

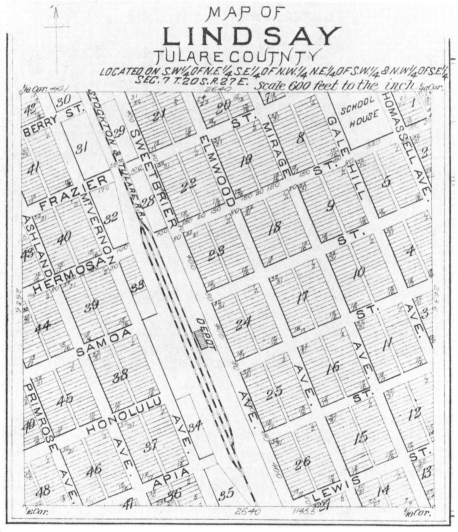

Figure 45. *Town Plat of Lindsay.* The Southern Pacific Railroad established towns along its new eastern line, employing the standard railroad plat and alignment as at Lindsay. At Plano and Porterville, the Southern Pacific platted new towns adjacent to the existing settlements, which were quickly drained of their populations and businesses. (Source: Thompson 1892.)

Substantial towns founded independently on the eastern flank of the basin during this period included Poplar (1880), Ducor (1888, coined from Dutch Corners), Orosi (1888, for "land of gold") and Lemon Cove (1894, for its early lemon groves). Small settlements or shipping centers developed at Hunsaker, Bellville, Townsend, Cramer, Limekiln, Tagus, Yokohl, Frazier, Camp Badger, Cottage, Tokay, Aukland, and Milo (figs. 36 and 37). In addition, three new communities developed on the margins of the basin to serve the needs of tourists and those engaged in ranching, mining, and lumbering in the foothills: Three Rivers (1879) and Springville (1889) flourished, but the Kaweah Cooperative Colony (a commune founded in 1885) disbanded in the early 1890s. Only three new towns were platted west of the tracks during this period: Waukena (1886, a corruption of Joaquin) was the center of a successful agricultural colony west of Tulare. To the west of the lake two tiny villages, Dudley and Esperanza, were founded. Dudley was located in McClure Valley (later named Sunflower Valley) in the Devils Den Region. Esperanza (Spanish for "land of hope") was a futile attempt to relocate the Socialist colony previously attempted on the Kaweah River (Latta 1949b, p. 335). Both villages were short-lived. The success of railroad towns, which were vigorously promoted, retarded the growth of the larger independent towns but did not destroy them. The railroad's efforts to promote east-side towns had more dramatic repercussions upon the old railroad towns along the original tracks: for example, Dinuba quickly replaced Traver as the principal town of the northeastern basin.

A new kind of settlement venture—the agricultural colony—arose as an outgrowth of railroad access and intensified farming in the basin. Large landholders and speculators began to subdivide tracts as large as 5,000 acres into small, ten- to forty-acre farms. They installed irrigation systems and advertised for settlers, often platting a central town as well (Thompson 1892). In many cases these subdivisions were settled by groups of people who had immigrated to the basin together, and the advantages of this kind of community were widely advertised: "A neighborhood grows up at once; a certain and rapid enhancement in the value of the land purchased is recurred; schools, churches, post and express offices, stores, good roads. . . and all the other conveniences of life enjoyed in older communities are created far earlier than is possible where one settler is located at a time and the growth of population is slow and precarious" (California Immigrant Union 1875, p. 63). Many agricultural colonies were established in the Central Valley between 1870 and 1920. Thompson's *Official Historical Atlas Map of Tulare County* (1892) listed thirty-nine colonies and an additional twenty-five subdivisions (primarily agricultural ones). Land subdivision was motivated by speculation and encouraged by a new level of regional development. With the advent of diversified farming and rail transportation, a well-managed small farm could provide a good living for a family; on the other hand, intensification of production on a very large farm was quite impractical, so subdivision offered greater returns for large landholders: "As soon as proprietors become convinced of the necessity and practicality of the change in methods of cultivation. . . experience will teach them that it will be more profitable for them to divide up their estates into farms of convenient size, and either sell them or let them to good tenants, on long leases, than to undertake the management of ranches of such enormous magnitude, under the improved system of husbandry" (Hilgard, Jones, and Furnas 1882, p. 77). The maps of Lucerne Colony, Traver Colony, and Level Orchard Land Colony depict typical basin colonies (fig. 46). Access to water was the primary consideration, because a dense net of rural roads assured transportation even to areas far from the tracks.

Some agricultural colonies failed to endure because of locational disadvantages or bad management, yet others flourished. The most successful colonies served as foundations for the development of substantial communities such as were soon found around Dinuba and Waukena: densely settled, well-irrigated districts with closely spaced farmsteads. As such they represented an entirely new phenomenon in basin settlement. Often, though, the colony parcels were purchased by adjacent homesteaders or by speculators and so were never developed as independent farms. Average farm size in the Tulare Lake Basin, indeed, continued to increase until about 1900 because grain farming and grazing continued to expand and speculators continued to amass tremendous acreages (table 5). In the long run, too, ten- to

TABLE 5
Characteristics of Farms and Farm Production, 1870–1900

	1870	1880	1890	1900
Number of farms	377	1,125	2,193	3,144
Average acreage	235	364	423	460
Cropland acreage	88,644	409,838	928,677	1,447,232
% improved	40	79	63	56
% irrigated			18	12
% in wheat	61	91	30	12
Number of range cattle	34,074	32,989	49,037	59,219
Value of orchard products	$11,500	$27,335	n.a.	$1,371,678

SOURCES: U.S.D.I. Census Office 1872; 1883; 1896; 1901, California: Reports by County.

A

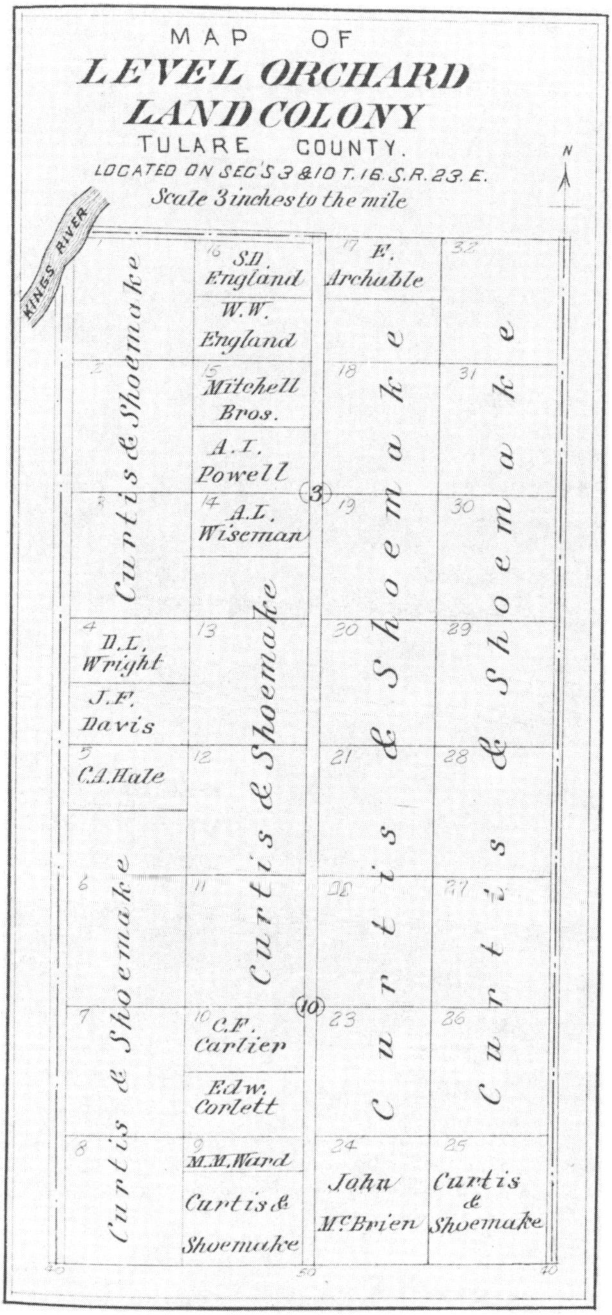

MAP   OF
LEVEL ORCHARD
LAND COLONY
TULARE   COUNTY.
LOCATED ON SEC'S 3 &10 T. 16. S.R. 23. E.
Scale 3 inches to the mile

Figure 46. (*a, b, c,***)** *Typical Agricultural Colonies of the 1880s and 1890s.* Numerous agricultural colonies were established as an outgrowth of railroad access and expanded irrigation facilities. Speculators often divided large tracts into ten- to forty-acre farms, provided irrigation water, and advertised far and wide for settlers. (Source: Thompson 1892.)

(*a*) Map of Level Orchard Land colony on the Kings River. In this case, it appears that a number of the parcels intended for individual purchase were instead bought up by yet another speculative concern.

B

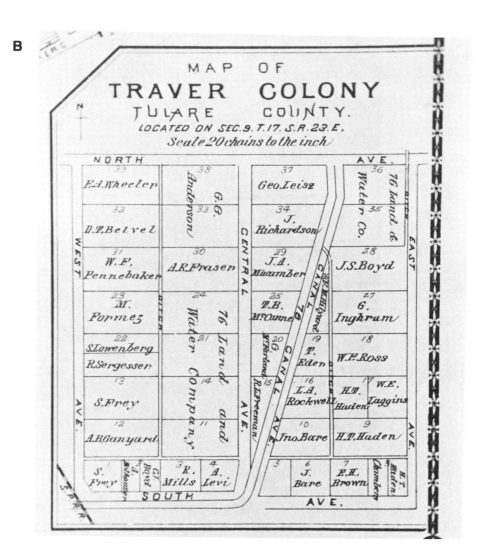

(*b*) Map of Traver Colony. Provided with railroad access and an elaborate irrigation system, Traver seemed certain to thrive, and the colony grew very rapidly. Unfortunately, poor irrigation practices on alkali-prone soils rendered the area's fields uncultivable after a few years.

(*c*) Map of Lucerne colony. Located on the rich alluvial lands of the Mussel Slough country—the heart of agricultural intensification in the 1880s and 1890s—the Lucerne colony offered settlers an opportunity to engage in dairying or the cultivation of small orchards.

forty-acre farms proved to be too small, and many colony parcels were consolidated or abandoned. Agricultural colonies gradually disbanded in the twentieth century, and today the remaining vestiges of these settlements are difficult to discern except where they were especially successful.

Environmental Observations and Boosterism

> It is now autumn, but their fields are full of Spring. The generous soil seems unwilling to rest, and continues to pour forth its benefactions more lavishly than the most sanguine could anticipate. (Muir 1874)

Rapid agricultural settlement and the expansion of irrigation systems and diversified cropping produced dramatic changes in the basin's landscapes, and these changes, in turn, were evident in the perceptions and comments of residents and travelers. The basin no longer seemed to be a vast and isolated wilderness. The herds of wild animals and the broad expanses of native vegetation were gone, yet the cultural landscapes of most parts of the basin were not yet sufficiently impressive to offset the overriding images of flatness and monotony. Instead of offering "picturesque scenery like the prairies of the west, it is a vast undulating plain or dead level, with an occasional tree or park of oaks to diversify the general monotony" (Elliott 1883, p. 97). Still, the success of new farming ventures in certain parts of the basin commanded interest and attention. The valley trough and the regions west and south of the Tule River were least appealing in this respect (Hilgard, Jones, and Furnas 1882, p. 28). Sparsely treed and barely settled, they seemed barren: "To the right, left and front, sheep abound, but not a tree or shrub" wrote Crofutt of the Tipton area (Crofutt 1879, p. 230), and the state engineer reported that "all south of Tulare Lake and a large portion north of the lake, on the west side of the great basin, may be classified as non-irrigable land, not only on account of the absence of sufficient water supply, but by reason of the general unfitness of the soil for cultivation by irrigation" (State of California Engineer 1880, p. 28). For the first time, specific types of terrain (such as hog wallows) and soils (such as redlands) were described and analyzed without reference to their natural vegetation cover, although regional appraisals were still grounded in observations of soil fertility and climate as these related to the potential for agricultural settlement.

For the most part, agricultural appraisal of the basin was overwhelmingly positive during the railroad era. East of Tulare Lake the land seemed to be a uniform medium, "nearly all adapted to tillage, with or without irrigation" (Elliott 1883, p. 97), and easily plowed and seeded: "There is no tough sod to be broken a year before using," wrote Botsford. "There are no stones to be removed from the ground—one may travel a day's journey in the broad valley without seeing one half the size of one's fist; there is no brush to be cleared from the land at great expense" (Botsford and Hammond 1885, p. 49). Though some of the most favorable evaluations were advanced by people who had a vested interest in regional development, the whole period was characterized by pervasive optimism. General fertility of a specific parcel of land was judged empirically, in terms of its response to cultivation and the experiments of farmers and settlers. The fecundity of the basin was noted by such observations as this: "It is the custom to make fences of sticks of willow, sycamore, or cottonwood, cut to the length of eight feet, and stuck into the ground in December. These strike root at once, and grow so rapidly that in the second year the farmer cuts his firewood from these living fences" (Nordhoff 1882, p. 102). In contrast to Hispanic judgments of soil quality, which were generally deduced from natural vegetation, empirical observations attributed fertility to the entire basin rather than just to its recent alluvial soils. Better understanding of the basin's climate brought more positive evaluations as well. The low summer humidity was touted as a boon to farmers, who could "work in the harvest fields in the warmest weather, exposed to the sun's heat, without being inconvenienced thereby, and without fear of suffering a sun-stroke" (Botsford and Hammond 1885, p. 7). The long dry season now seemed not only eminently healthful but ideal for cotton cultivation and raisin drying as well. Promoters promised that any remaining problems posed by seasonal drought could be solved by irrigation anywhere east of the basin trough, and that even after expenditures for irrigation, the costs of cotton production would be lower than in the South (Powell 1874, p. 39; Cone 1876, p. 170; California State Agricultural Society 1875, pp. 322–324).

Sporadic experimentation in Tulare County and adjacent regions encouraged the development of new land uses, as did the growing awareness that environmental damage was resulting from the careless practices of extensive grain farming:

> The raising of wheat is not always profitable, while there are many successful men in the business. Yet land capable of raising Adriatic figs, Zante currants, French prunes, Malaga raisins, Bahia oranges, Sicily lemons, citrons, limes, dates and olives, and our own incomparable peaches, apricots, nectarines, pears, quinces, plums, pomegranates, apples, English and native walnuts, chestnuts, pecans and almonds, in a climate surpassing that of Italy, is too valuable for the cultivation of simple cereals. (Kitchener and Baker 1884, p. 3)

With new confidence in their ability to make even formerly marginal lands productive, and elated by the success of crop experimentation, observers in the 1870s and 1880s no longer asked *whether* a given tract of land might be made to grow crops but rather *which* crops might grow best there. The desert was beginning to seem like an oasis. Soils were evaluated in terms of their adaptability to irrigation rather than their relative fertility (Cone 1876, p. 113); even alkali soils were viewed with new optimism by boosters of the basin: "All soils contain alkali. If they did not, they would be perfectly barren. As nothing will grow in a manure heap, so nothing will grow where the alkali is too strong. We have too much of a good thing in some places, and that is all there is to it" (Elliott 1883, p. 98). Old-valley-fill and residual soils, recently thought fit only for grazing, now seemed ideally suited to grains, wine grapes, lemons, and oranges. As widespread experimentation with tree crops and ornamental trees continued, farmers were consistently rewarded. Only the most heavily hog-wallowed areas were dismissed as totally unsuitable for cultivation. The preference for timbered alluvial soils weakened as their limitations became apparent: delta soils were too rich for profitable grain farming, for the grain grew so tall that it lodged before maturity (Eigenheer 1976, p. 300). The savannas, in contrast, seemed ideally suited to wheat and barley, the scattered trees "protecting the grain from too intense heat of the summer sun and turning the balance in its favor in severe drought" (Hilgard, Jones, and Furnas 1882, p. 18). And as reclamation of marshlands continued they, too, seemed suited to more diverse crops: "It is safe to calculate upon at least one-third more produce from these reclaimed lake lands than from the best valley lands" (Cone 1876, pp. 112–113). It began to appear that something profitable would indeed flourish on each and every kind of soil in the basin.

Advertisement of the virtues of the Tulare Lake Basin accelerated in response to developments in communication, irrigation, and diversified cropping. The promotional outlets of the railroad and semipublic organizations such as the California Immigrants Union eagerly joined in promoting settlement of the basin. Cone's 1876 *Two Years in California*; Hilgard, Jones, and Furnas's 1882 *Report on the Climatic Features and the Agricultural Practices and Needs of the Arid Regions of the Pacific Slope*; Nordhoff's 1872 *California for Health, Pleasure and Residence*; Fremont's 1887 *Memoirs of My Life*; and Crofutt's 1879 *New Overland Tourist and Pacific Coast Guide* also praised the basin and were widely read. Most outstanding was the new conclusion that much of the basin was suited to small-farm settlement: "Two crops a year from irrigated land will make less land necessary to the farmer, who can do as much with eighty acres as with one hundred and sixty elsewhere" (Nordhoff

1872, p. 129). Irrigated farms of 40, 80, or 160 acres of orchards, vineyards, or field crops had proved to be quite profitable, and subdivisions and agricultural colonies had made small farms once again available to people of limited means. The agricultural frontier involuted back upon the irrigated lands of the eastern fans rather than surging ahead onto the dry margins of the basin. At last the Tulare Lake Basin was advertised, not as a place to strike it rich, but as a fine environment for homemaking and community building:

> To the person who desires a pleasant and comfortable home on a large or small farm or in town, the 76 Land and Water Company's lands and the new town of Traver offer every inducement. Traver is the center of a prosperous farming region, and as the large canal, supplying an abundance of water, insures success in all agricultural pursuits, there is no risk in the purchase of land. There is always a market for all the products raised, and the shipping facilities for transporting the same are excellent. (Kitchener and Baker 1884, p. 17)

The most significant change in environmental awareness after the construction of the railroad through the basin was a sudden recognition of people's role in changing the face of the land. Concern went beyond the recognition that a human landscape was emerging: cause-and-effect relationships between human practices and environmental degradation were recognized. Such observations helped people identify problems and formulate more conservative agricultural practices, and strengthened the conviction of settlers that the land could be altered still further. The natural vegetation had by this time been widely destroyed. Majestic oaks and riparian timber belts were the sole pre-agricultural remnants, and even they were disappearing: "The oaks are old and ragged, many are fast decaying, and when gone, the country will be nearly bare, as there are few young trees growing up to take their place" (Crofutt 1879, p. 230). Farmers undertook to clear away the remaining trees from their properties; "Everyone regretted the necessity of having to cut the oak forest, but progress or economics or common sense would allow no other way out. Land values in the valley had increased and proportionately so had the taxes on the land . . . so of necessity the owners had to clear the land and make it suitable for farming" (Gist 1974, p. 143). The need for retaining some kind of timber in the basin, "not only for firewood but for the general purposes of civilized life," was clear (Hilgard, Jones, and Furnas 1882, p. 18).[2]

2. The environmental influences of trees were not always judged correctly, however, as this quote by Nordhoff suggests. "I suspect that the oak groves make Visalia hotter in summer than the more open plain surrounding it. It has the reputation of being a hot place" (Nordhoff 1872, p. 198).

Pampas grass, pitahaya, palm, maple, catalpa, locust, and pomegranate were introduced for shade or ornamentation, and several species of foreign and domestic trees were suggested as possible commercial timber species for the dry plains: eucalyptus, China tree, European oak, and local cottonwood were among these. Gradually introduced tree species began to change the appearance of the basin's urban and rural landscapes.

Alterations produced in the course of irrigation became topics of extensive concern and controversy. Nordhoff believed that irrigation was increasing the frequency of hard frosts and that it was thus harmful in some ways (Nordhoff 1882, p. 152). Irrigation was also blamed for the ill health of people in low-lying areas where surplus waters collected: Flynn cautioned that "we have not to go far to see the evil effect of too much irrigation with defective drainage. A dense growth of weeds on the land and enervating malaria are the sure followers of bad drainage" (Flynn 1890, p. 35). On the other hand, diversion of water "removed the cause of the fevers" in formerly damp areas (Nordhoff 1872, p. 198). Irrigation also altered the soil, and not always for the better: "The irrigation water . . . has brought with it, from the depths, all the supply of alkali salts that before had gradually been washed beyond the reach of ordinary rainfall by an occasional wet season" (Hilgard, Jones, and Furnas 1882, p. 44). Continued well drilling was suggested as a remedy: this could lower the water table sufficiently to offset alkalization, and the dissolved or suspended solids removed by crops could still be restored to the soil by application of waters withdrawn from underground (Hilgard, Jones, and Furnas 1882, pp. 25–28, 44). Another solution might be grazing, for manure should neutralize the soil sufficiently for plant growth (Elliott 1883, p. 98). At a larger scale, the contraction of Tulare Lake and the increased salinity of its waters were no mystery. Stream diversion was recognized as the cause, and observers knew that continued irrigation would lead to the welcome disappearance of the lake. By this time Tulare Lake was no longer seen as an interesting curiosity nor as a fine place to hunt or fish: instead, it seemed merely an unsightly impediment to progress, "the one natural feature of the county that our conscience will not let us praise. . . . It is devoid of a single element of beauty and its uses are few. . . . It is a great, unsightly mud-hole" (Thompson and Warren 1888, p. 66). Positive effects of irrigation were evident in the landscape as well: "The Mussel Slough Country, in Tulare County, over which I rode in 1872, when a sheep-owner told me it was too barren even to run sheep without risk, has in six years assumed the appearance of an old-settled and rich farming country in the east . . . with shade trees thirty and forty feet high along the roads, and apples, pears, plums, prunes and vines in bearing" (Nordhoff 1882, pp. 150, 140). It must have seemed that if irrigation expansion continued, the entire basin would soon be transformed into a vast garden; yet, for the time being, its landscapes still evoked images of dryland grain and dust, "infinite, flat, cheerless, heat-ridden, unrolling like a gigantic scroll toward the faint shimmer of the distant horizons, with here and there an isolated live oak to break the sombre monotony" (Norris 1903, p. 30).

In the fall, after the wheat stubble had been burned and the skies had cleared, the land still seemed vast and almost uninhabited. The landscapes of the wheat-boom era were much like those of the basin prairies in Yokuts times. As the grain germinated, "the winter brownness of the ground was overlaid with a little shimmer of green," then "the earth disappeared under great banks and fields of resplendent colour" (Norris 1903, p. 369). As the dry season progressed, the grain changed from "a vast silent ocean, shimmering a pallid green," to "a dirty yellow stubble, the ground—parched, cracked and dry—a cheerless brown" (Norris 1903, pp. 386-387, 448).

The coming of the railroad, however, had brought important changes in basin landscapes. Where silence had once been an important image, now "the sweetness was gone from the evening, the sense of peace, of security and placid contentment was stricken from the landscape [as the train roared through], filling the night with the terrific clamour of its iron hoofs" (Norris 1928, pp. 49–50). The railroad also brought improved access to building materials and architectural innovations, and town and farmstead landscapes began to take on an increasingly substantial appearance: "No pine cabins—white houses, white picket fences, white barns and outhouses. Prosperous" (Miller 1938, p. 623). Still, houses remained small: the small lots of the railroad plat, the limited budgets of laborers and small farmers, the external orientation of speculators and prosperous farmers, and the mild regional climate conspired to keep them that way. Irrigation and permanent plantings—orchards, vineyards, and ornamental trees—were "an anchor that would enhance the attachment of settlers to their land" (Miller 1938, p. 396). Settled attitudes and more consistent contact with the outside world brought national architectural fads to the basin as well. The residents of the Mussel Slough district were among the first in the region to erect stylish Victorian homes, and John Muir noted that as the country became irrigated, "cheerless shanties sifted through and through with dry winds, are being displaced by true homes embowered in trees and lovingly bordered with flowers; and contentment, which in California is perhaps the very rarest of the virtues, is now beginning to take root" (Muir 1874). As irrigation and intensive farming spread eastward to break as a wave against the Sierra foothills, so did the settled, domesticated appearance of the countryside. The proud new farmsteads were depicted in sketches made for Thompson's 1892 *Official Historical Atlas Map of Tulare County*.

Environmental Alteration

But the plains of Tulare are fast passing away. Irrigation is making gardens, orchards, vineyards, and wide fields of fragrant alfalfa, of the parched wastes, and soon no one will think of applying the term 'plain' to any portion of the great and fertile valley of Tulare, green all the year round, and teeming with life and thrift. (Thompson and Warren 1888, p. 67)

Many significant modifications of the environment brought by the railroad involved the built landscape. The basin was rapidly seeded with new towns, many of them part of settlement schemes formulated elsewhere and applied with little attention to local factors of site or situation. The importance of town siting and promotion became clear as time passed, as the new settlements grew outward over the land and the activities of their citizens came to influence every aspect of basin life. By 1890, settlement had resulted in an overall population density equal to that achieved by the Yokuts. Yokuts population, however, had increased mostly through cultural adaptation to the environment, whereas American expansion was based upon conquest of the natural environment. Settlement proceeded not as an outgrowth of the discovery of the basin's natural capabilities, but as a product of settlers' tireless efforts to divorce their lives and their livelihoods from natural processes and controls. Rail lines and irrigation canals helped to free settlement from natural patterns, just as domesticated plants and animals and a commercial economy had freed American settlers from many natural constraints on subsistence. As the basin's population grew, its native flora and fauna were further altered by the introduction of new plants and animals from different lands. Water was confined and channeled to nourish the new life layer, and even gravity was reversed when water was pumped up from underground aquifers for irrigation. In their desire to maintain control and neat order, farmers and developers applied more force to the land—force powered at first by muscle and later by wind, steam, electricity, and gasoline. Reclamation of marshlands and hog-wallowed areas proceeded swiftly, and more and more land was brought under cultivation. The commercial productivity of the basin rose rapidly, and in turn it grew as a market for the products and ideas of other regions.

The alterations of the environment that occurred during this period, however, were by no means entirely beneficial. Several adverse effects of the massive diversion and reapplication of water were already noticeable: the extent of Tulare Lake and its surrounding marshlands were radically altered, and the lake's salinity increased greatly. As late as 1882 the lake's waters had been "copious with fish" (Hilgard, Jones, and Furnas 1882, p. 52), harvested commercially in large quantities, but by the winter of 1888−89 the lake fish had begun to die off (Lapham and Heileman 1901, p. 454). The lake was soon too saline for many species and it supported almost none by 1900. One commercial activity—irrigation—had ruined another—commercial fishing.

Another undesirable effect of irrigation was increased soil alkalinity caused by a rising water table. Where groundwater had once been fifteen to eighteen feet below the land surface on the Kings Delta, for example, it rose to within two to eight feet of the surface with irrigation (Lapham and Heileman 1901, p. 467). The high water table thwarted leaching, and the widespread practice of seepage irrigation (as opposed to flood irrigation) further concentrated salts in topsoil layers as the water evaporated rather than ensuring that salts were flushed out. The Traver and Mussel Slough regions experienced particularly severe problems with alkalization, an important factor in the decline and virtual abandonment of once-prosperous Traver in the early 1890s (Lufkin 1952; *Tulare Advance Register* 1931). Similar problems developed on the recent alluvial soils of Deer Creek and the Tule River (Grunsky 1898a, pp. 74−75), but the Kaweah Delta experienced little rise in groundwater and hence little alkalization (Grunsky 1898b, p. 38). Conversely, the drilling of wells lowered the water table under old valley fill in the redlands adjacent to the foothills of the Sierra Nevada, and increasingly powerful pumps were needed to sustain irrigation there. The tapping of the aquifer below the Corcoran clay also resulted in a noticeable decline in artesian flow as early as 1885 (Mendenhall 1908, p. 36).

Summary

The construction of a Southern Pacific Railroad line through the basin led to reorientations in land use and settlement. At first the availability of transportation encouraged wheat cultivation, a land use that was spread across the basin with little regard for variations in soil type or other qualitative phenomena. The prevailing cultural condition of the cattle era persisted in the large scale of operations, in the gambler

mentality of farmers, in rampant speculation, and in exploitative attitudes toward the environment. Less and less land was available to
newcomers, and established settlers abused the land as they bullied it
into ever-greater yields of wheat and barley. After 1884, however, rising
land taxes and environmental backlash helped encourage a change
from monoculture to diversified endeavors. More intensive land uses,
supported by more intensive control of the basin's hydrologic resources,
and crop diversification promoted by local variations in climate and soil
began to spread outward from the delta hearths of innovation. The
effects of this new order were evident in the landscapes and social
order of the basin. Many large farms were subdivided and sold, so that
more land was made available to newcomers and established farmers
alike. The distribution of irrigation systems and the various methods by
which they were implemented became important determinants of
settlement and productivity.

With increasing diversification came changes in the attitudes and
perceptions that had flourished since the cattle era. The varied natural
character of the basin's lands was once again important in land-use
decisions and agricultural assessments, and a permanent attachment
to the land began to develop, reflected in increasing numbers of permanent cultural features on the landscape and the rise of chauvinistic
attitudes, to wit:

> This great valley is not as widely and favorably known as its territorial
> extent and productive capacity warrant. It has too long been confounded
> with the San Joaquin Valley, [but] Tulare Valley is better watered, better
> timbered, and has a more universally level surface than the San
> Joaquin. . . . Irrigation is more generally employed, and a greater pro-
> ductive capacity is thereby developed, and a larger degree of material
> prosperity enjoyed. All Tulareans should co-operate in giving the name
> of their great valley a wide and honorable notoriety, leaving the inhabi-
> tants of the San Joaquin to look out for the name and fortune of their
> portion of the state. (Thompson and Warren 1888, p. 13)

The patterns of land use that had begun to take hold by the end of
the railroad era proved remarkably flexible and contributed to the
success of further agricultural and urban settlement of the basin.
Although diversification reflected closer awareness of local environmental variations, however, such variations were not accepted with
resignation. Farmers undertook to eliminate environmental restrictions
on land use by heavy applications of technology, supported by a per-
vading attitude of dominance over nature together with a pervasive
optimism. Technological attitudes and developments complemented
the older agricultural traditions of the Tulare Lake Basin: commercial-

ism, large-scale landholding, rampant speculation, and reliance upon hired labor.

The agricultural developments and the basic settlement patterns established during the formative years—1857 to 1894—set the mold for subsequent evolution of the Tulare Lake Basin. Both local innovations and economic, social, and technological developments outside the basin were to herald further expansion and refinement of the regional patterns of agricultural production and settlement, but the general outlines of the prevailing processes had been established.

7

The Spread and Refinement of the New Order: The Era of Small Farm Prosperity 1895–1925

This is a day of changing conditions in the farming region. The period of great land holdings is passing away, the days of speculation in wheat farming are gone; the mistakes of fruit planting have been outgrown, and we are beyond the stage of costly experiment; the importance of irrigation is clearly seen for large areas. It is a time of development. The foundations of a great industrial empire are being laid, and a young and vigorous civilization firmly established. But much of the land is still thinly populated. It is so vast that it can only be occupied by degrees. (Wells 1908, p. 5)

A prosperous new era of growth and opportunity characterized the nation during the first decades of the new century, as the national economy recovered from the slump of 1894. Nowhere was this recovery more rapid or more dramatic than in agriculture. Widening markets, high prices, new technologies, and an accumulation of competence all brought new faith in agriculture as a way of life. The Tulare Lake Basin was primed and ready to respond to the new prosperity, and the occupational patterns and specialized techniques that had developed in prior decades spread rapidly across the basin's lands. As these patterns matured, regional patterns of agricultural specialization began to merge with patterns elsewhere in the American West, yet the basin still retained a distinctive setting, a distinctive regional character, and a series of unique regional landscapes.

Transportation and Settlement

There is not now and apparently never will be any question about splendid markets for all that the San Joaquin Valley produces or will produce as settlement and development increase. (Heermans 1915)

Lively markets for basin products, the continued expansion of agricultural settlement, and settlers' dissatisfaction with the policies and practices of the Southern Pacific supported a flurry of railroad construction in California. Competing lines were not blessed with government subsidies, as the Southern Pacific had been, and so they built their tracks where commercial opportunities were most promising. The local populace, eager to support alternatives to the Southern Pacific, influenced route selection by pledges of depot sites, rights-of-way, and terminal facilities, and by stock subscription (Daggett 1922, p. 329). The expansion of the agricultural frontier toward the valley trough prompted construction of the San Joaquin Valley Railway, "The Peoples Road," from Stockton to Bakersfield in 1898 (fig. 47). Feeder lines included a branch through Tulare to Visalia. The new line was immediately purchased by the Atchison, Topeka and Santa Fe Railroad, but continued to offer some relief to local shippers from the high rates charged by the Southern Pacific. The new line also stimulated settlement, although the Atchison, Topeka and Santa Fe did not undertake to found communities or plat townsites; agricultural colonies or independent towns developed near depots or shipping platforms. Among the more successful of these were Angiola (1897, for the founder's wife), Alpaugh (1906, for its founder), and Allensworth (1909, a black agricultural colony named for its founder). Alpaugh originated as a colony on Atwell's Island, the site of the Yokuts trade center, Bubal, and grew quickly in response to the wheat boom on the eastern lakeshore despite its location several miles from the railroad. Corcoran (1905, for an Atchison, Topeka and Santa Fe civil engineer), Stratford (1907, for a local rancher) and Waukena (resubdivided in 1908), flour-

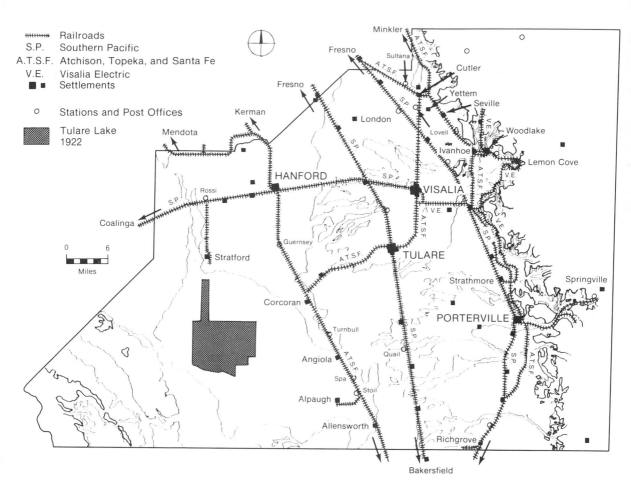

Figure 47. *Railroads and Settlements, 1925.* New lines built by the Atchison, Topeka, and Santa Fe and the Visalia Electric railroads filled in the rail network of the Tulare Lake Basin, providing competitive rates for produce and efficient passenger service to most localities.

ished as well; additional attempts at town building (Guernsey, Stoil, Spa, Blanco, Turnbull, and others) failed.

The pace and density of community development and town growth on the west side of the basin fell far short of developments on the east side. This can be attributed to the persistence of extensive wheat farming in the valley trough and to the greater commercial opportunities afforded by diversification on the east side. Other drawbacks in the western basin included large parcel size (because much of the land had been taken up as S & O land), generally inferior soils, and limited supplies of water for domestic use or irrigation: as a Lemoore man commented drolly, "There was always two certain things about water on the West Side. There was certain to be very little of it and that little was certain to be little, if any, short of poison" (in Latta 1949*b*, p. 32). As the west-side communities wrestled with these problems, new developments helped sustain them and promised a better future: artesian wells in the Alpaugh area, which produced large amounts of natural gas, were brought into commercial production by 1920, and oil deposits were found to underlie portions of the western basin. As the remaining vast, unsubdivided tracts of land on the west side began to attract the attention of farm corporations, west-side settlements gradually came to serve as company towns of sorts: Corcoran, for example, functioned largely as a cotton-ginning center for surrounding company farms.

Agricultural intensification and population growth continued to focus on the east side. The eastern rail network grew denser as regional and national lines were added. Among these was the Visalia Electric Railway, in operation from 1905 to 1924. Although its existence was brief, the Visalia Electric provided frequent passenger and freight service between towns and rural areas of the Kaweah Delta and helped stimulate the expansion of permanent cropping by providing efficient and inexpensive transportation of fruit to main-line stations. It also promoted the recreational development of Lemon Cove and Three Rivers. Unfortunately, the company's profits declined rapidly with the advent of automobile transportation, and the line became one of the first electric interurban railways in the nation to go out of business. Another flurry of town building accompanied agricultural and transportation developments in the eastern basin. Cutler (1897, for its founder), Sultana (1897, for the raisin grape), Strathmore (1900, Scottish for "broad valley"), Yettem (Armenian for "paradise"), Terra Bella (resubdivided in 1908), Richgrove (1909, for its oranges), Woodlake (1910, for nearby Bravo Lake), Ivanhoe (1912, after the novel), and Seville (1913, for the citrus region in Spain) were successful new towns of this era (fig. 47). Their plats varied, but all adhered to a grid pattern, usually aligned with the cardinal directions. Although rail companies joined in promotion of independent towns along the tracks, these generally remained subordinate to older railroad towns nearby—yet they survived, a testimony to the rapid population growth and widespread commercial opportunities that accompanied the expansion of diversified, intensive farming.

Few towns were founded in the Tulare Lake Basin after 1910. By that time a dense pattern of settlements had already been established, and the improvement of rural roads after the introduction of the automobile expanded the hinterlands of existing towns and dramatically altered their form. The pattern of rural roads (fig. 48) reflected the varied density of rural settlement as well as the persistence of patterns estab-

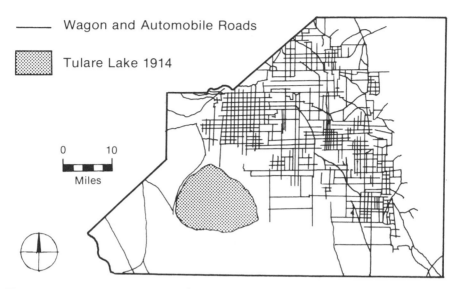

Figure 48. *Wagon and Automobile Roads, 1914.* The pattern of rural roads reflected the varied density of rural settlement as well as the persistence of patterns established by the federal survey and by land-alienation policies. (Source: Judge 1914.)

lished by the federal survey and by land-alienation policies. Diagonal routes, which cut across properties, were bothersome and were gradually abandoned in favor of section-line roads. Only those diagonal roads that paralleled the railroad persisted; some of these were subsequently adopted as routes for state and federal highways and so remain to the present. As late as 1914 the trip by automobile between Fresno and Bakersfield required a day's travel "on rotten roads—hardly a decent mile between the two towns. A neglected, sandy trail, with occasional broken-up oiled stretches. Towns along the way were little, lonely, sandy places, unattractive and poorly improved—not a mile free from unmerciful jolting" (Murphy 1915, p. 364). Yet by 1915 a graded highway ran through Tulare County to Los Angeles, and by 1917 there were nearly as many miles of graded and paved roads in the basin as in the Los Angeles region (Tulare County Planning Department 1975, p. 10).

As irrigation canals and rail lines had freed the basin's inhabitants from the spatial constraints of great distance from water and from markets, the automobile freed them from the spatial constraints of great distance from the railroad. Since the founding of the first truck-freight company in the basin in 1920, farmers in every part of the region have been assured of rapid transportation of their crops to market. So successful were automobiles in serving the transport needs of the basin that no new rail lines were built there after 1925, and some existing lines were even abandoned: the Octopus was beginning to wither. New roads and faster transportation brought most parts of the basin within easy reach of the goods and services of one or more towns, and promoted the centralization of processing and commercial facilities in a few of the larger towns; many of the smaller towns survived only as bedroom communities. The impact of the automobile on basin landscapes was enormous: pavement and signs spread through town and country, large spaces were turned over to service stations and parking, land uses within towns readjusted to the opportunities and constraints introduced by automobile-borne shoppers, and isolated farmsteads began to fall into disrepair as farmers became commuters.

The Conditions and Determinants of Small-Farm Prosperity

> The cattle king and the grain monarch have yielded their scepters to the small producer, and the land has become a land for the many. (Heermans 1915)

> Prosperity throbbed riotously from end to end of the San Joaquin. (Gist 1952, p. 198)

The first quarter of the new century brought accelerated growth, steady expansion of markets, improved transportation, vast permanent plantings, inexpensive power for irrigation, and widespread and incessant advertisement of basin lands, towns, and products. All of these processes and innovations strengthened trends that had evolved in preceding decades. Farming had never been more lucrative: urbanization and industrial growth in Europe and America brought an expanding market for agricultural commodities, and prices for farm products of all types actually rose faster than prices for other commodities. Farm prices rose more than 89 percent from 1899 to 1910 (Shideler 1957, pp. 5, 19), and jumped another 140 percent with the eruption of hostilities in Europe at the beginning of World War I. Farmers in the Tulare Lake Basin and elsewhere responded by eagerly adopting technologies and ideas that had been only sparingly applied in prior decades, and farm productivity and efficiency rose dramatically. The experience garnered from decades of trial and error in diversified farming ensured success with a variety of crops, and new agricultural science and educational services were offered by county extension offices established in accordance with the Smith Lever Act of 1914. The use of farm machinery increased tremendously because of labor shortages and high prices for farm produce during the First World War, and "power farming" allowed even greater farm efficiency after the war.

In most American agricultural areas, productive lands were almost all farmed by this era, but much of the basin was still a frontier. It offered valuable opportunities for new farmers, fertile land open for settlement, and established towns and transportation services that had proved themselves successful in the past. Renewed faith in agriculture as a respectable occupation and as an avenue to middle-class well-being brought a new influx of settlers to the basin: "Soil hungry people seeing the rich returns of the fertile valley lands, although knowing nothing of crops or the difference between good and valueless land, sought out anything that looked like earth and put their life savings into it. High prices made it possible for them to get by for a time, but a day of reckoning was at hand" (Gist 1952, p. 198). This new wave of optimism transformed the basin into a land of opportunity and small farms. The average size of basin farms fell rapidly between 1900 and 1925; as early as 1908 a visitor observed that "there is a decided tendency toward small farms" (Strahorn, Holmes, and Mann 1908, p. 1309). A family could make a living on a small parcel, especially if they grew fruit, and fully 61 percent of the basin's farms in 1925 comprised forty-nine acres or less; only 28 percent had been so small in 1900 (table 6). It seemed that the regional relationship between people and the land had become more democratic than in days past, that soon independent and carefully husbanded family farms might prevail. This new trend was celebrated by one observer in 1915: "Small farms are rapidly becoming a feature of Tulare County; many families are not only making a good

TABLE 6

Proportion of Farms by Size Category, 1900–1925

	1900	1910	1925
Number of farms, all sizes	3,144	5,858	9,465
Under 10 acres	4%	5%	6%
10–49 acres	24	42	55
50–99 acres	13	17	18
100–499 acres	42	28	17
500–999 acres	9	4	2
1,000 acres or more	8	4	2
Average acres per farm	460	242	159

SOURCES: U.S.D.I. Census Office 1901, Vol. V; U.S.D.C. Bureau of the Census 1913, Vol. VI; 1927.

NOTE: Later such tables include statistics on the proportion of land in farms of each size category, but this information was not available until 1925.

living, but are each year adding to their bank account, from the returns of a twenty-acre orchard, vineyard or alfalfa field" (Miot 1915, p. 9).

Despite the new prosperity of family farms, the ecology of farming in Kings and Tulare Counties was still regulated and disrupted by speculation and the principles of commerce: "Farming is a business here, and is conducted on better business principles than in many sections of the country. The farmers are learning to think in terms of interest on their investment and labor income and to study the problems of farm management" (Morse 1915, p. 34). Although this period of small-farm prosperity encouraged the wise management of farmland in order to maximize yields on limited acreages, many careless and wasteful practices persisted on large farms as a legacy of the cattle and wheat eras: "Land and such waters as are utilized have cost little heretofore in the San Joaquin Valley, and things that cost little are lightly valued, no matter what their intrinsic worth. This spirit is fostered by the immense holdings of some of the larger companies. Few of these companies practice intensive cultivation, though their lands are among the best in the valley" (Mendenhall, Dole, and Stabler 1916, p. 33). Although farm tenancy was rising, the proportion of basin farms operated by tenants remained relatively low: 15 percent in 1910, 12 percent in 1925 (U.S.D.C. Bureau of the Census 1927). Farms planted to permanent crops (orchards and vineyards) were rarely rented or leased; tenants were most numerous in grain and alfalfa districts west and south of the orchard districts (Morse 1915, p. 32). The landscapes of orchard districts reflected the residents' more stable attachment to their land in "avenues lined with palm or other ornamental trees and country homes surrounded by handsome lawns" (Menefee and Dodge 1913, p. 172). The owner of such an estate was recalled as follows: "He liked the country. . . . He knew each peak in the line of rugged mountains, not by name but by long familiarity; and he knew each tree on his place, its weakness and its strength. He never thought of selling out and leaving his ranch" (Baker 1931, p. 157). As time went on, however, some orchards were left to managers by owners who lived far from the basin (Morse 1915, p. 32–33), and the proportion of manager-operated farms in Tulare County rose steadily (table 7). Manager-operated farms, in turn, included a disproportionately large share of the basin's land. The spirit, as well as the land-use practices and plantings, of speculators and absentee farmers thwarted the development of settled landscapes in the basin and hindered its transformation into a settled and stable community.

The retention of large tracts of land by nonresident speculators also encouraged inflation of land prices. Speculation and inflation attracted a veritable army of realtors to east side towns and cities. "It is

TABLE 7

Type of Farm Operation, 1900–1925

Farm operator	Tulare County			Kings County		
	1900	1910	1925	1900	1910	1925
Tenant						
% of farms	25	12	11	26	21	17
% of land	n.a.	12	12	n.a.	27	23
Manager						
% of farms	3	6	9	5	3	4
% of land	n.a.	12	14	n.a.	19	14
Owner						
% of farms	72	82	80	70	76	80
% of land	n.a.	76	74	n.a.	54	63

SOURCES: U.S.D.I. Census Office 1901, Vol. V; U.S.D.C. Bureau of the Census 1913, Vol. VI; 1927.

doubtful if any rural section elsewhere supports as many real-estate agents to the square mile," reported one visitor. "There are literally dozens of them operating in Tulare County or with Tulare County lands" (Morse 1915, p. 17). Frequent sales and constant promotion drove land prices far above the actual income-producing value of the land, as many optimistic but uninitiated first-timers would later learn to their dismay: "Beyond Tulare we again came into a sandy, desert-looking country and were astonished to see billboards in one of the little towns offering 'bargains in land at one hundred and thirty-five dollars per acre'—when to all appearances the country was as barren and unpromising as the Sahara" (Murphy 1915, p. 365). Small farmers and first-time investors were forced to buy their land on time, and by 1925 fully half of the basin's farms were mortgaged (U.S.D.C. Bureau of the Census, 1927, p. 3); yet, although mortgage indebtedness was a source of worry, the value of farmland was growing rapidly, and investment in land seemed a secure venture. Speculation, absentee ownership, and inflated land prices had detrimental social and environmental implications: the more money spent on land, the less was available to be spent on homes and community facilities or on caring for the land; and the higher prices rose, the more temptation there was to sell. "This is not necessarily bad, but may become so. The whole situation is forced, and the effects upon community stability are unfortunate," observed a representative of the Presbyterian Church sent to survey social conditions in the basin (Morse 1915, p. 18). He added,

The rapid increase of population had not been altogether by permanent acquisition. . . . There has been continually a considerable shifting, particularly noticeable in some sections. A rapidly growing community, a community of diverse racial elements, might be expected to show many marks of instability. Add to this a large influx of population at certain seasons of the year, made up in part of itinerant workers, in part of property owners having their permanent residence elsewhere, and in part of tourists, and you have a situation which could make the acquisition of community stability a slow and difficult process. (Morse 1915, p. 37)

Rising land prices and rampant speculation contributed to the creation of a rural proletariat: landless people who, like their landlords and employers, were not permanently committed to the basin. Although farm prices rose steadily, farm operators felt unable to pass profits along to seasonal employees, and farm labor wages remained paltry. Foreigners and recent immigrants were recruited to work on basin ranches; the ethnicity of the agricultural work force changed through time according to changes in American immigration policy and in political and economic conditions abroad (table 8). The original Chinese workers were replaced by Japanese, Mexican, Portuguese, Filipino, Black, and Armenian arrivals; from about 1910 onward (except during the Great Depression) Mexicans were increasingly numerous. Unfortunately, the growth of Mexican population in the basin is hard to document: the mobility of farm workers made it difficult for census representatives to find them, and in addition the census classification of Mexicans and Chicanos has changed frequently. Some farm workers, notably the Portuguese near Hanford and the Armenians of Yettem, managed to gain a foothold in the basin and to establish permanent and stable communities of their own (Smith 1939, pp. 412−413). Others, finding themselves supplanted by cheaper recent immigrants, left the basin to seek factory jobs elsewhere in California or to start farms of their own in sections where land prices were less inflated. Some even returned to their native lands or were forcibly repatriated. Still, the abundant supply of farm laborers kept wages low, and even small farmers could afford to hire migrant crews. Although farm workers were vital to the success of intensive farming, their lives were a sorry plight. They made their homes "in shacks and temporary structures of almost every sort. Made-over freight cars, one-room houses, structures ultimately destined to be pump-houses, house wagons, buildings half-frame, half tent-cloth" (Morse 1915, p. 37). The shifting lives of fruit workers were characterized in this analogy: "Up and down this empire belt proceed two great companies, the herds of 'fruit-hands' and the

TABLE 8

Ethnic Composition of the Tulare Lake Basin Population, 1890–1970

Year	Total Population	Native White	Foreign-Born White	Foreign-Born White Groups[1] ≥ 2% of Total	Other Races	Other-Race Groups ≥ 0.5% of Total (In Order of Predominance)
1890	24,574	84%	11%	None	5%	Chinese, Black, American Indian
1900	28,245	86	10	None	5	Chinese, American Indian, Mexican, Black
1910	51,670	83	13	Portuguese, Mexican	4	Japanese, Chinese, Black
1920	81,062	81	15	Mexican, Portuguese	5	Japanese, Chinese, Black
1930	102,827	82[2]	13	Portuguese	5	Japanese, Black, Chinese
1940	142,320	88	8	Portuguese	4	Japanese, Black
1950	196,032	90	6	None	4	Black, Japanese
1960	218,357	90	5	None	5	Black, Filipino, Japanese
1970	252,932	n.a.	n.a.	Not available[3]	7	Black, Filipino, Indian, Japanese

SOURCES: U.S.D.I. Census Office 1896; 1901, Vol. I; U.S.D.C. Bureau of the Census 1913, Vol. II; 1922; 1932, Vol. III; 1942; 1952a; 1961a; 1973.

[1] Northern Europeans, Canadians, and Australians are excluded because they were not important in the agricultural work force.

[2] This figure includes 10% Mexicans—classed as White from 1900 census onward.

[3] Census notes that 26% of the total regional population is classified as Spanish language or surname.

army of bees following its successive wave of fruit and bloom. Gangs of pruners, pickers, and packers are shifted and shunted as the crop demands. Interesting economic experiments transact themselves under the worried producers' eye, alien race contending with alien race" (Austin 1927, p. 157).

Increasingly dependent upon migrant labor, vulnerable to market fluctuations and the vagaries of weather, and ruled by wholesalers and processors who dictated amount and time of harvest, growers banded together in cooperative associations such as the California Fruit Exchange (organized in 1895 and later known as Sunkist). These associations undertook to regulate harvest procedures and marketing, to maintain quality standards, to regulate production, and to reduce growers' costs—including the cost of hired labor. The success of growers' collusion was proudly advertised in promotional pamphlets of the time: "California farmers themselves largely determine the prices at which their products sell . . . instead of letting somebody else do that job for them. . . . This is the obvious result of the organization of coopera- tive associations large enough to dominate the industries whose products they handle" (Hodges and Wickson 1923, p. 16). Soon every commercial crop of the basin was produced, processed, and marketed under the auspices of one or more grower organizations. The impact of cooperatives was immediately evident in the landscape: huge can- neries, packinghouses, and storage facilities were built in towns along the tracks, and rural placards proclaimed growers' affiliations. In time the large organizations became involved in every aspect of basin agriculture, from landholding to transportation. Caught up in a great web of cooperative or corporate control, small farmers had to deal with a complex set of regulations and constraints; in return they were assured of protection against the threats of organized labor, market price fluctuations, and rising production costs.

Farm Organization

Every farming part of the county can show people who make more than a living from 20 acres—and even less—in fruit, grapes, or alfalfa. (Levick 1912, p. 16)

The same conditions that transformed farming in the Tulare Lake Basin during these years also affected other regions of the American West where diversified farming was dependent upon irrigation. The rural transformations of the Los Angeles Basin, the Salinas Valley, the Imperial and Coachella valleys, and the Tulare Lake Basin during the first decades of this century were unprecedented in American agricultural history. In some ways the individual identities of these regions were lost in the process of their transformation: they emerged as Western Specialty Crop Regions (cf. Taylor 1952), sharing generally similar patterns of settlement, population, and economics, and similar problems. Agricultural settlement in these regions was essentially urban in nature: more than two-thirds of their populations lived in towns and cities, and their tastes, customs, and spending habits were distinctly urban as well. Here, in these diversified oases where a tremendous variety of crops was grown, the farmers bought all their food in grocery stores and spent much of their time on paper work. They adopted the business techniques of their urban counterparts, and the work force from which they hired was urban as well—urban, that is, but poor—for one of the most important traits shared by these new oases in the arid West was their dependence upon the labor of diverse groups of migratory workers who would flee to the state's cities when their labor was no longer needed. The communities of these regions were characterized by extreme social inequalities that tore at their social fabric more each year. Still, the landscapes of the several western specialty crop regions developed differently, in accordance with variations in their respective environments and settlement histories.

By the 1920s, three kinds of intensive farm operations had emerged in the Tulare Lake Basin which found their rough counterparts in other irrigated western regions as well: orchards, general farms (where field crops or row crops predominated),[1] and dairy farms. The landscape and organization of each farm type reflected a distinctive set of environmental, technological, and economic considerations as well as externally imposed commercial or governmental regulations.

The development of orchards began with the first plantings of tree crops in the early 1860s, but not until about 1900 were deciduous fruits and nuts, evergreen fruits, and grapes widely cultivated as commercial crops (table 9). Orchards and vineyards expanded rapidly as urbanization in California and innovations in transportation and processing caused the market for fruits and nuts to grow. High summer temperatures, abundant spring runoff, and the absence of soil-borne diseases and harmful pests enhanced the basin's suitability for tree crops (Webber 1948, p. 533), but each crop had its own particular requirements and sensitivities. Evergreen fruits (citrus and olives), more sensitive to cold spells than to soil deficiencies, were most successful in the eastern "thermal belt," a zone above 350 feet elevation where

---

1. Although this is not the standard definition of a general farm, it is the clearest descendant of "true" general farms seen in the Tulare Lake Basin.

TABLE 9

Expansion of Orchard Production, 1890–1920

	1890	1900	1910	1920
Value of orchard products ($ million)	n.a.	1.4	3.3	25.4
Selected measures of production				
Peaches (thousands of bushels)	136	1,412	1,518	2,190
Grapes (tons)	4,500	42,874	93,236	n.a.
Oranges (bearing trees)	21	197,907	801,175	2,568,744
Lemons (bearing trees)	4	45,767	41,069	187,642
Walnuts (bearing trees)	n.a.	141	1,966	6,635

SOURCES: U.S.D.I. Census Office 1896, Vol. V; 1901, Vol. VI; U.S.D.C. Bureau of the Census 1913; 1922, Vol. VI.

slopes promoted cool-air drainage, resulting in relatively warm winter temperatures. Tulare County's thermal belt—wider and warmer than elsewhere along the Sierra foothills—invited extensive citrus and olive plantings. Only alkaline or very poorly drained soils proved unsuitable for evergreen orchards; where temperature and water conditions were favorable, the profitability of fruit cultivation even justified expenditures for soil improvement. Grapes, more frost tolerant, also flourished on a wide range of soils, although they could tolerate only slight concentrations of alkali (Holmes and Eckmann 1916, p. 2422); both table grapes and limited varieties of wine grapes were found to grow well in the basin. More closely resembling native trees in their growth requirements, deciduous fruit and nut trees proved adaptable to most basin climates; only prunes and apples produced poorly (Retzer 1946, p. 27). Peaches, pears, figs, apricots, plums, pomegranates, walnuts, and almonds fared well on well-drained and alkali-free alluvial slopes of the eastern basin; pears proved suited to some soils too alkaline for other tree crops (Lapham and Heileman 1901, p. 478).

An array of innovations helped orchardists overcome the limitations imposed by the basin's climate, hydrology, and still-isolated location. The cool winter nights common even in the thermal belt demanded some means of heating evergreen orchards; early wood-, coal-, and tar-burning heaters were replaced by oil-burning smudge pots about 1915, and wind machines were introduced after 1920 (Coit 1927, pp. 250–269). The expansion of commercial orchards onto the upper basin slopes also depended upon pump irrigation, and the introduction of inexpensive electric pumps in about 1900 was a boon to orchardists. The development of iced railcars, then refrigerated railcars, allowed basin fruit to be shipped to distant markets without great risks of spoilage and helped basin orchardists compete successfully with their counterparts in less remote regions. Refrigerated lockers, introduced in the 1920s, facilitated price regulation and alleviated peak-season labor shortages in packinghouses (Anderson 1953, pp. 188–189). The introduction of refrigerated ship holds and the opening of the Panama Canal expanded the market for basin fruits to global proportions.

Early orchards were small, seldom comprising more than ten acres, but gradually expanded to an average of sixty acres. Trees were planted in grid patterns, vines in east-west rows to promote raisin drying. Palms were often planted along boundaries for decoration, and small numbers of unusual fruit trees were sometimes included for experimental purposes. It was common to grow mustard or other native weeds in orchards during the rainy season and to plow them under in spring to enrich the soil (Storie and Owen 1942, p. 11). Orchardists needed only a small inventory of equipment, although a great deal of hired labor was required for pruning, thinning, harvest, and packing. Since equipment was minimal, farmsteads were simple:[2] a house, a pump house, an equipment shed, a barn and corral for work stock were the only necessities (Zimrick 1976, p. 113; Cook 1913, p. 31). Farmsteads were located on the uphill side of the property to be near the irrigation wells, and they were often quite attractive:

> Against the white house trellises wound with rose branches were spilling clusters of midsummer bloom, above the yard the great round ferny-leaved chinaberry tree and delicate light-spattered locust arched greenness overhead. Beyond the dark square of the tank house was more green—soft mist green of the willows clouding along the ditch, flat green of alfalfa pasture, lighter green of cottonwoods near the barn, shadowy green of almond orchard and deep green of vineyard. (Miller 1944, p. 39)

Fruit was hand picked, treated (sprayed, gassed, washed, and waxed), packed in boxes, and loaded onto wagons or trucks for hauling to the railroad. The timing of harvest varied with each fruit, and laborers were needed intermittently from early spring through late fall or even into winter:

> With the ripening of the olives the migratory fruit pickers begin to come into the valley. The fruit tramps . . . would come into the San Joaquin Valley in the fall to pick the Navel oranges; they would move on into Southern California for the winter oranges; they would come back into the San Joaquin Valley for the spring Valencias; and then, pausing

---

2. A great deal of information about farm organization and farm landscapes in this and later eras was drawn from Steven Zimrick's 1976 dissertation, "The Changing Organization of Agriculture in the Southern San Joaquin Valley, California."

perhaps to chop cotton, they would drift up above Sacramento for the peaches, and they might go on up into Oregon to work in the apples before they came back into the San Joaquin. (Baker 1931, p. 191)

As more kinds of tree crops were introduced, the demand for laborers began to stabilize somewhat, although long intervals between employment have continued to characterize the lives of fruit workers to the present.

Permanent plantings in the orchard districts brought a striking departure from the bleak summer landscapes of grain and grazing. The dark hues of the citrus orchards were as outstanding as the marshland tules and savanna oaks of former times: "With relief one hails the beginning of a strip, dark green, scalloping the foothills—the citrus belt" (Austin 1927, p. 156). Vineyards were still more distinctive, "forests of stakes and wires supporting the brilliantly green runners of the vines" (Baker 1931, p. 61). By early fall,

the air was bronzed and clear. . . . The vineyards . . . looked like the rough surface of a green lake. The olive trees were gray, severe trees intimate with the soil; the orange trees were pompous and green; above the orchards there were the tops of umbrella trees and tank houses. (Baker 1931, p. 265)

A blue haze settled on the alfalfa fields and the rattle of mowing machines sounded. There arose the scent of hay, the strong smell of sulfur from the drying yards where the peaches yellowed in the sun, the smell of raisins in the vineyard rows. (Mainwaring 1932, p. 45)

As winter set in,

frost colored the peach leaves, burned the grape leaves brown, threw them to the dusty earth. (Mainwaring 1932, p. 35)

The vineyards were lined with naked stumps. . . . Something sad about the fields in winter. (Bezzerides 1938, p. 68)

The grass in the groves was turning green, but the country was still brown. . . . There was a black, powdery frost on the ground some mornings. In the next month there would be fog and they might not see the sun for weeks. The shade trees were bare, and the houses over the country were pitiful, flimsy-looking structures without the massive layers of foliage. (Baker 1931, p. 270)

Winter, however, did not last too long; soon it would be spring, another brief season in the basin:

Valleys in which the fruit blossoms were fragrant and pink and white waters in a shallow sea. Then the first tondrils of the grapes, swelling from the gnarled vines, cascaded down to cover the trunks. . . . And then the leaves broke out on the trees and the petals dropped from the fruit trees and carpeted the earth pink and white. (Steinbeck 1939, p. 473)

Thus the spring passed and summer was on, coming into the valley passionately. The white blanket on the hills was drawn about their tops, the foothills became brown. Heat waves moved among the vines as the sun poured its rays unmercifully on the plain. (Mainwaring 1932, p. 34)

Specialized dairy farms developed in the basin at about the same time as distinctive orchard operations, and for many of the same reasons. At first dairying was part of mixed farming, one of several activities conducted experimentally at a small scale on each farm. Irrigated alfalfa and pasturage were good companion crops to wheat and orchards, requiring little attention and enriching the soil. There were district creameries in Visalia, Tulare, and the Tule River region by the 1860s, but for the next fifty years dairying remained a sideline (Mitchell 1976, pp. 84–85; Small 1926, pp. 323–324). As technological developments and refinements in transportation and marketing encouraged the emergence of full-scale dairies, their association with other land uses weakened (table 10). Like orchards, dairies were supported by regional diversification of farming in general and by enhanced access to water and reliable transportation, local and statewide population growth, and the favorable regional environment. The expansion of dairying was not restricted by stringent environmental controls: alfalfa grew very well in the basin, producing seven or eight annual cuttings between April and October (Martin and Leonard 1949, pp. 677–679). It flourished on a wide range of recent alluvial and old-valley-fill soils, and even on alkali soils with sufficient irrigation. Other feed and forage crops such as sorghum, milo, and native salt grass usually grew well on soils too poor for alfalfa.

TABLE 10

Dairy Farms and Products, 1900 and 1925

	1900	1925
Farms reporting dairy products	2,267	5,532
As percent of all farms	73	58
Number of cows two years and older	10,748	49,540
Average cows per farm	5	9
Average milk production per dairy farm (gal.)	1,734	6,014
Total value of all dairy products ($)	245,130	5,281,479
Average value per dairy farm ($)	108	955

SOURCES: U.S.D.I. Census Office 1901, Vol. V; U.S.D.C. Bureau of the Census 1927.

In addition to developments in transportation, refrigeration, mechanization, and marketing—which encouraged both orchardists and dairy farmers—there were several innovations during this period that were specifically important to dairy operators. The centrifugal cream separator, introduced in 1885, was a great boon because the basin's hot summers prevented separation by cooling. Because dairying began as a sideline activity, profits depended upon maintaining low labor requirements; such labor-saving devices as mechanical cream separators and milking machines (introduced in the early 1920s) were eagerly adopted (Peterson 1939, pp. 356–362) and encouraged the development of full-time dairy farms. By the late 1890s the basin was dotted with small dairies, each with perhaps a dozen cows and six acres of irrigated pasture or alfalfa. Cultivation requirements were light because alfalfa could be cropped continuously for five or six years after planting. After milking machines became available, even a family dairy with only one or two hired milkers could keep many cows. Dairy farmsteads included a residence, a large barn, wooden corrals and fences, a pump house, sheds, and irrigated fields of pasturage and feed. Grapes and fruit were commonly grown as well, to provide additional income (Zimrick 1976, p. 50), and dairy landscapes still varied according to the kinds of auxiliary activities conducted there.

Lands suitable for dairying were found throughout the irrigated portions of the basin, but the primary dairy regions developed in the vicinity of Hanford, Visalia, and Tulare and between Tipton and Porterville. By 1910 cooperative and independent creameries were established in Traver, Dinuba, Poplar, Tipton, Woodville, Porterville, Visalia, and Tulare. At first milk was delivered to creameries by wagon, but truck transport prevailed after the First World War. Milk and creamery products were taken to markets in the Los Angeles region by train until refrigerated trucks became available in the late 1920s (Tinley 1936, p. 12). Although the basin had a Dairy Union by 1886, cooperative regulation of quality and prices did not begin until 1903, when the Tulare County Co-Operative Creamery was founded. The Tulare County Cow Testing Association was established in 1911, and numerous other dairy associations were organized thereafter, at first mostly on a local scale (Zimrick 1976, pp. 224–227).

The third type of farm to develop in the basin during this period, the general farm, should not be thought of as a typical American mixed farm. With its emphasis on field crops rather than dairying or orchards, it simply developed more directly than the other two types from the more generalized farms of earlier periods of basin settlement. It was on general farms that traditional basin practices and attitudes persisted most clearly. Corn, sorghum, sugar beets, vegetables, and other field crops were cultivated as companions to grain and deciduous fruits in the 1880s and 1890s; most were grown as annuals and were planted in rows and furrows to permit clean cultivation. Field crops demanded more labor than either orchards or alfalfa cultivation, and so general farms emerged more slowly than orchard and dairy operations from the less-demanding diversified farms or wheat ranches. In fact, it was only after the introduction of cotton in about 1922 that general farms began to flourish. Experimental plots of cotton had been planted in the 1870s and 1880s near Visalia, and later in the Tule River region, but harvest-labor shortages and other problems prevented its large-scale cultivation (Camp 1921, p. 3). New varieties revived experimentation in the 1910s, but again the high costs of production and the high labor requirements made competition with established cotton-belt areas uneconomical (Cook 1925, p. 335). In the 1920s a new variety of cotton, an influx of agricultural laborers, and a rising worldwide demand for cotton combined to promote the rise of mixed farms in the basin. Acala cotton, a Mexican variety introduced in the basin by the U.S. Department of Agriculture in 1915, was a medium-staple cotton well suited to the basin's soils and high summer temperatures.

The Tulare Lake Basin quickly became an important cotton producer. Its high spring and summer temperatures ensured early germination and rapid growth, while light precipitation and low humidity retarded weed growth and the ravages of such pests as the boll weevil and bollworm. Irrigation, required throughout the growing season, increased costs but promoted good yields, and the dry fall weather facilitated harvest and open storage (Gregor 1962a, pp. 394–397; Doyle 1942, p. 355). Like alfalfa, cotton proved tolerant of a wide range of temperatures and a variety of soil types. The best cotton soils in the basin were recent alluvium and old valley fill, but cotton could tolerate moderate alkalinity as well (Raney and Cooper 1968, pp. 88–91). Egyptian (feed) corn, milo (sorghum), sugar beets, rice, small grains, and alfalfa were grown in rotation with cotton. Row crops were cultivated deeper than small grains and required heavier irrigation; although this entailed more labor, investments were rewarded in the long run by reduced salt accumulation (Lapham and Heileman 1901, pp. 465–466).

Foreign and domestic cotton demand continued to rise after the war, while the prices of various orchard crops began to decline as a result of overproduction. Many farmers replaced orchards with cotton fields in the 1920s, especially in the Mussel Slough area. Unlike perishable fruits, cotton could be stored indefinitely and withheld from market until prices were high. As an annual crop, cotton was also well suited to market regulation: when prices were low, acreage could quickly be shifted to other commodities, and when high prices were forecast, a cotton crop could be planted quickly. Rising irrigation costs also encouraged cotton cultivation, which required less water than alfalfa and gave greater financial returns per acre. The introduction of tractors and tractor-mounted implements in the 1920s was also a boon to cotton cultivation, allowing one or two individuals to plant, cultivate, and mow large tracts of row crops (Wik 1967, p. 361). Cotton acreage in the basin rose from 937 acres in 1920 to 13,390 acres in 1925, and to 90,184 acres by 1930 (U.S.D.C. Bureau of the Census 1922, 1932). Initially restricted to the east side, cotton cultivation followed the expansion of irrigation systems westward across the basin.

Distinctive general-farm landscapes began to emerge after 1920 as cotton fields became more and more evident. Most general farms were small: two-thirds covered less than 100 acres and 40 percent less than 50 acres (Zimrick 1976, p. 164). General farms grew quickly, however, and by 1930 the average cotton-growing farm comprised 183 acres (U.S.D.C. Bureau of the Census 1932). Early general farmsteads consisted of a house, a barn, "the tank house, the windmill, the China-berry tree and the ditch as always" (Miller 1944, p. 226), and sometimes corrals or fenced pastures for work stock—though these were torn down as animal labor was replaced by machines. Tractor- or truck-towed trailers hauled cotton to the gins, usually a distance of less than ten miles, after harvest by hand. Early gins included cooperative, independent, and corporate facilities, but the latter assumed increasing importance as time went on. Ginned, baled cotton was sent by rail to North American markets or by sea via the ports of Los Angeles, Oakland, or San Francisco to the especially active Asian markets.

Town-and-Country Regions of the Basin

As if its waters had some special virtue, wherever a river is poured out upon the plain some particular crop is favored. (Austin 1927, p. 156)

As cropping patterns became more closely adapted to local soil types and climatic variations (more closely adapted, indeed, than they would ever again be in the basin), the emergence of distinctive crop regions within the area became still more evident (fig. 49). Lands skirting the eastern foothills on residual and old-valley-fill soils were rapidly converted from wheat fields to permanent plantings: "Where there had been barren fields were orchards and vineyards, row on row to the foot of the mountains" (Mainwaring 1932, p. 44). The orchard zone seldom extended more than ten miles into the basin from the foothill fringe, and remained interspersed with dryland grain fields throughout the first

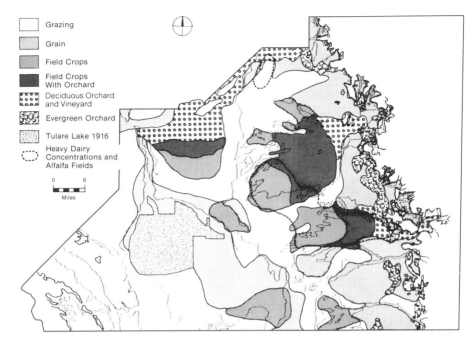

Figure 49. *Land Use, 1916*. Out of the small zones of crop specialization which had developed in the nineteenth century emerged broad specialty regions that closely reflected local soil types and climatic variations. Grain and grazing were pushed even farther toward the periphery of the basin.

quarter of the twentieth century (Morse 1915, p. 12). Deciduous orchards began to replace evergreen ones near the western edge of this belt. The densely irrigated and well-drained upper fans of the major streams were planted to a variety of crops—including deciduous fruits, alfalfa, grain, and row crops—and the lower Kaweah Delta and Tule River fan supported many dairies as well. Intensive farming spread rapidly onto lacustrine soils around Alpaugh and onto recent alluvial soils around Corcoran, both relatively alkali free despite their low-lying positions. Between the deltas and along their bases, broad belts of alkali soils with scant irrigation resources were relegated to use as pasturage or planted to alfalfa or dryland grain. Large grain regions also remained northeast of the Kaweah Delta and near Deer Creek, and new grain areas developed on the reclaimed lakebed near Stratford and west of Corcoran. Between the grain fields and the orchards, row crops replaced grain and pasture. Grazing had greatly diminished in the basin but still prevailed west of the valley trough and in the eastern foothills, where the cultural landscape was still insignificant: "On the west of the Kings River the land lies as the Creator left it, save for solitary roads winding between grey sage brush and pale blue lakes that vanish to the sky as the wanderer draws nearer. Beyond this grey desert the near Coast Range lies in a series of brown humps, a train of kneeling camels brought to rest" (Miller 1944, p. 44). Cattle were also grazed where local concentrations of alkali were heavy or where irrigation systems were still poorly developed.

A familiar sequence of land-use changes continued as grain and grazing were pushed still further toward the edges of the basin by the expansion of intensive farming on the deltas and upper terraces. With this succession came more settled landscapes: more homes and schools, better roads, more trees and shrubs and orchards, more stores, churches, packinghouses. As rural landscapes matured, the relationships between towns and their respective hinterlands grew stronger. A series of town-and-country regions began to emerge, each with a main town, subordinate villages, and a distinct zone of associated farms. In the northeastern basin, Dinuba served as the central town of a raisin belt; oranges were widely grown near Orosi, and south and west of Dinuba lay a section devoted to dairying. Throughout this region farms tended to be small and prosperous: "This entire district is a checkerboard of orchards and vineyards. These, all in small tracts, well-kept and generally well-provided with comfortable country homes, present a picture both beautiful and impressive of assured prosperity" (Menefee and Dodge 1913, p. 170). Southward, the Exeter, Lindsay, Strathmore, and Porterville regions stretched along the edge of the foothills, covered with "orange groves and yet again orange groves, one practically continuous stretch. Not even a fence divides them. The chain of foothills is their background, but it is a rampart up which they climb and into whose recesses all along the way they cluster. No canals or ditches here, no alfalfa, no green mats of saltgrass pasture, no oaks or cottonwoods. Parched and dry, hard and barren-looking, is the soil in the places unset to orchard" (Menefee and Dodge 1913, p. 172). Porterville also drew business from foothill cattlemen and claimed to be the "largest initial beef-shipping point in the State" (Morse 1915, p. 24). The foothill settlements of Three Rivers and Springville served districts noted for their "apples of fine quality, and grazing" (Menefee and Dodge 1913, p. 172), but were probably more noted as resorts. South of the Tule River on the basin plains, the towns served hinterlands where dryland grain still prevailed: "Ducor and Terra Bella are stations serving a wheat region. Between White River and Deer Creek the rolling lands have been wholly devoted to grain. But a change is at hand" (Wells 1908, p. 58). Indeed, just seven years later it was advertised that in this area, "large farms are being rapidly broken up into smaller tracts, and orange, olive and deciduous fruit orchards, vineyards and alfalfa fields are everywhere appearing" (Ducor Chamber of Commerce 1915, p. 1). To the west, Tipton, Pixley, and Alila-Earlimart were "shipping stations for wool, sheep, cattle and grain. Earlimart is an ambitious colony project where rapid growth is promised due to settlement in small tracts" (Wells 1908, p. 53). Poplar, Woodville, and Tulare served "a rapidly growing dairy and alfalfa industry" (Morse 1915, p. 12), and in their hinterlands "alfalfa fields adjoin, making vast meadows. . . . Fruit growing, frequently in colony tracts, remains a feature however, and vineyards of considerable acreage are noted" (Menefee and Dodge 1913, p. 171).

Northward, on the Kaweah Delta, was Visalia. Long recognized as perhaps the most fertile area of the basin, the delta flourished, a "rich diversified farming, fruit, and dairying section producing all general farm products such as hay, grain, corn, pumpkins, Egyptian corn, sugar beets, as well as peaches, pears and prunes . . . and the summer's heat, striking this fallow, moisture-soaked loam causes such a riotous growth of all kinds that a general unkempt appearance is presented. Orchard alternates with woodlot and saltgrass pasture with cornfield and dairy farm" (Menefee and Dodge 1913, pp. 170–171). Visalia itself was, by this era, a city

> "of no mean order," full of civic pride, well paved and clean. The public buildings are good, and there are various packinghouses and manufacturing industries. . . . In addition to the usual mills, foundries, machine shops, et cetera, of a flourishing town . . . there are dried and green fruit packinghouses and large canneries employing much help. (Wells 1908, pp. 49–51)

Similarly, on the Kings Delta, Hanford, Lemoore, and Armona were surrounded by prosperous orchards and vineyards: "no part of the valley shows more prosperous farmers than this," wrote one visitor. "The streets of Hanford are well shaded and the whole place attractive by reason of vines and palms, and a variety of ornamental trees. An opera-house, a free library, good hotels, schools and churches, a creamery, packinghouses, condensed-milk cannery, fruit cannery and winery, and solid business blocks attest the prosperity of this young town" (Wells 1908, p. 68). Fringing the lacustrine soils south of Hanford were Corcoran, Angiola, and Alpaugh, embedded in "a great alfalfa belt, not only supplying its dairies with feed, but furnishing enormous quantities of hay for shipment. Great grain fields there are producing extraordinary yields" (Menefee and Dodge 1913, p. 171). The far western basin was still very sparsely settled and used primarily for sheep raising.

Environmental Alteration

The east of the San Joaquin Valley has been made exact by man's will and man's geometry. Precise angles of irrigation canals cut vineyards and orchards of nectarine, peach, almond, apricot and fig into water-bound green triangles, rectangles, and squares. Straight roads make no deviation for white ranch houses set under individual plantings of walnut, umbrella and Lombardy poplar, for the county roads east of the Kings river are laid out in exact section lines and in themselves draw a sur-veyors plat. (Miller 1944, p. 44)

The most dramatic modification of the basin during the first quarter of this century was the spread of intensive farming and the more settled landscapes associated with it. Remnants of Tulare Lake suddenly stood in the way of expansion; "never much more than a shallow morass" (Murphy 1915, p. 365), it now seemed "a catch basin whose water is valueless" (Mendenhall, Dole, and Stabler 1916, p. 96). The basin's first official reclamation district was formed in 1890, but full-scale reclamation efforts did not begin until after 1905. There were twenty-five reclamation districts in the basin by 1930, thirty-five by 1940, each delimited by dikes and levees (Retzer 1946, p. 79). Comprising virtually all of the land below the 200-foot elevation contour, these districts brought dramatically new landscapes to the basin trough. Although there were still substantial risks involved in settlement, reclaimed districts quickly attracted droves of settlers who hoped to try their hand at grain farming on the rich virgin land: "as the waters vanished, speculators and settlers stampeded to Kings County, and Lake-landers were as numerous as in mining fields" (Menefee and Dodge 1913, p. 201). Reclamation abruptly terminated the lake's traditional role as a habitat for migratory fowl, yet the lake—like the Yokuts who once dwelt along its shores—would not entirely disappear despite the wholesale efforts of settlers to vanquish it. As with the Yokuts, confinement seemed the only solution: the thirty-six square miles of T22S R20E were designated for lake impoundment, and overflow was allowed to remain there to evaporate.

The spread of intensified farming and settled townscapes continued, and the process that fueled this advance—irrigation—continued to lower the basin's water table, especially under old valley fill (Grunsky 1898b, p. 37) and to tear away at the remaining vestiges of natural vegetation along streams where it had thus far survived (Holmes and Eckmann 1916, pp. 2504–2513). The less intensive cultural landscapes were transformed into new, more intensive cultural landscapes, more densely settled and more permanently and carefully cropped. In some districts, though, notably Traver, past modification had already damaged the land's ability to respond well to cultivation; here there was some reversion to simpler cultural landscapes. Traver farmers, for example, found that cultivation without flood irrigation quickly brought salts to the surface and rendered soils useless; similar problems with careless or ill-advised irrigation practices occurred elsewhere (fig. 50). The cultural landscape also began to deteriorate in northern Kings County, where field crops were sown in place of the orchards which had been damaged by alkalization and frosts.

Summary

The years between 1895 and 1925 were very unusual ones in the history of basin farming, similar only to the brief spell of small-farm diversity that occurred between the decline of cattle culture and the rise of bonanza wheat farms in the mid-1860s. The basin's farmers enjoyed an increasingly intimate relationship with the land: experimentation flourished on small farms, especially on the delta lands, and more and more people had a chance to try their hand at basin farming, to develop

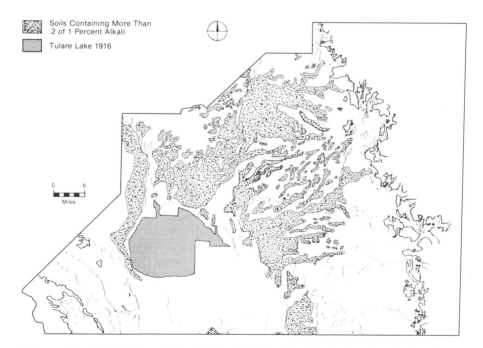

Soils Containing More Than
.2 of 1 Percent Alkali

Tulare Lake 1916

0   6
Miles

Figure 50. *Distribution of Alkali Soils, 1916.* South of Hanford and on the dry plains (as near Traver), irrigation increased the area and extent of highly alkaline soils. (Sources: Nelson 1917; Holmes and Eckmann 1916.)

a more permanent attachment to the land. As intensification and experimentation spread outward from the well-settled recent alluvial lands along the Kings and Kaweah rivers, new cropping patterns emerged, reflecting regional variations in soils, climate, and settlement history. The basin's towns began to take on new roles as service and supply centers for distinct farming regions, and the specializations of their respective hinterlands became apparent in town landscapes as well.

In contrast to their predecessors in the 1860s, however, the farmers of the basin in the early twentieth century dealt with more complex landscapes, with dense settlement and transportation networks, and with a variety of new agricultural technologies. A trend toward specialization was gaining momentum—not regional specialization, as in the wheat era, but local or individual specialization, heavily reliant upon connections with the global market economy and upon the labor of transient crews of farm workers. Until about 1925 the effects of these trends were favorable: the basin's lands were ever more verdant, more rewarding as a medium for livelihood or speculation. Prosperity spread across the basin: "Whatever a man wanted he could now have for his own. Caution was a word unknown. Why not gamble? The man who dared to gamble was repaid a thousand times. Every day success and abundant returns were taken as a matter of course" (Gist 1952, p. 197). But progress advanced on weak foundations, and soon the bubble would have to burst. After 1925 the basin's landscapes would once again revert to an older pattern: larger farms and fewer people in intimate contact with the land, less experimentation and fewer opportunities for people to rise in the established social or economic orders. Profits gained from farming, concentrated in the hands of fewer and fewer people, would cease to flow into the creation of proud towns and farmsteads, and would once again be drained away from the basin as the people who gained the most from regional farming invested their money in new opportunities elsewhere.

8

Rural Upheavals and the Rise of Agribusiness 1926–1945

Farming here is not farming as easterners know it; most of the ranches are food factories, with superintendents and foremen, administrative headquarters and machine sheds. Even the owners of small ranches usually concentrate on a single crop; and they must send to the store if they want as much as one egg. In addition to the permanent employees the valley uses a great deal of seasonal labor that forms a constant problem. The migratory worker . . .lives apart from other residents, occasionally in barracks behind the fields & orchards, more often in crude shelters of his own devising along the river bottoms. Because there are too many who want to work, the migrant cannot command an adequate return for his labor. The inhabitants of the towns do not know him and his family and local governments feel no responsibility for him. No one knows how to help him with his problems and no one knows how to get along without his help. (W.P.A., Federal Writers' Project 1939, pp. 440–441)

During the first quarter of the twentieth century, regional diversi-fication and small-farm prosperity were supported by a vigorous economy, cheap irrigation water, thriving towns, firm faith in tech-nology, steady population growth, and the intermittent assistance of small crews of migrant workers. New pressures and changes, both local and national in scale, began to alter the conditions of basin farming after the First World War. The high commodity prices that had sup-ported the golden era of American small-farm prosperity collapsed; the purchasing power of foreign markets declined sharply; overproduction and high operating expenses forced American agriculture into a crisis situation even before the Great Depression of the 1930s (Shideler 1957, p. 284). In the basin, the expansion of rural settlement slowed abruptly, and the nature of farming was greatly altered. Farmers lost confidence in agriculture as an occupation as their very survival became tied to the strength of the government. With caution and uncertainty replacing ambition and optimism, basin farmers and farm corporations petitioned the government for broader application of protective tariffs and crop supports; this new economic nationalism would pervade the basin's agriculture for decades to come. The net effect of these new trends was to foster the reemergence of old patterns: larger farms, less cropping stability, fewer people farming the land, and a growing degree of social stratification and environmental degradation.

Environmental, Social, and Economic Stresses

The population of the Tulare Lake Basin continued to grow, rising 76 percent between 1920 and 1940; the proportions of urban and rural population remained relatively stable (table 11). Town development

TABLE 11

Growth of Regional Population, 1920–1940

Year	Total Population	Percent of Increase	Total Urban	Urban: Rural
1920	81,062	57	25,253	31:69
1930	102,827	27	35,332	34:66
1940	142,320	38	43,737	31:69

SOURCES: U.S.D.C. Bureau of the Census 1922, Vol. III; 1932, Population, Vol. III; 1942, Population, Vol. II.

finally commenced in the sparsely inhabited western basin—not as an outgrowth of developments in transportation or agriculture, but because of a new stimulant: "Here on this dry west side of the valley we have a reservoir of something more precious than snow, only it is under, not on top of the ground. Some day, where we see only sheep camps and Kettleman's ranch will be derricks, one of the greatest oil fields in the world" (in Miller 1944, p. 163). In the middle and late 1920s, petroleum and natural gas were discovered in fossiliferous sandstone strata under the Kettleman Dome and the plains to the east of it. Commercial production began in 1928 and provided sufficient employment to sustain two new towns: Kettleman City (1929, after an early rancher) and Avenal (1929, Spanish for oat field; named by the Standard Oil Company, which quickly obtained title to vast tracts of land which had been granted to the railroads in the area). At first, "the towns' unpainted shacks seemed from a distance, a heap of brown cigar boxes flung out on the desert" (Miller 1944, p. 44), but as time passed they took on a more respectable appearance. Other fields were soon brought into production in the Pyramid Hills, Dudley Ridge, and Alpaugh-Hanford areas (fig. 51),[1] and additional mineral resources of the west side (chromite, fuller's earth, gypsum, and quicksilver) were developed as well, giving western Kings County a much-needed economic boost as well as an entirely new kind of identity and image: "Kettleman Hills [is] an oilfield of outstanding richness, where crude oil comes from the ground as gasoline, and natural gas wells of great depth are tapped for the needs of industry" (Drury 1935, p. 397).

As in previous eras, however, the growth of basin population reflected rising agricultural productivity, now supported and directed by different conditions than before. Until the late 1940s the basin's irrigation needs were met entirely by the development of local water resources. At first the expansion of intensive farming was supported by development of surface-water resources, and water was cheap and plentiful. The late 1920s and early 1930s brought dramatic price increases as demand rapidly outpaced the supply of irrigation water, and a severe drought in the mid-1920s also encouraged basin farmers to turn to the development of groundwater resources. The capacity of pumped wells trebled by 1929, until well production amounted to about twelve times the volume of summer stream discharge from the Sierra Nevada into the basin (Meigs 1939, p. 266). Groundwater levels dropped, especially under old valley fill on the east side, because

---

1. Discoveries of oil and gas fields were made in Tulare County also, including a small oil field south of Porterville in the vicinity of Terra Bella and a sizable gas field (Trico) southwest of Allensworth.

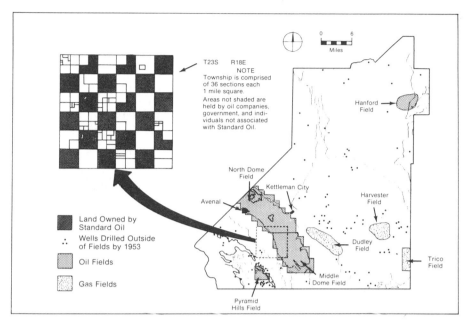

Figure 51. *West Side Oil and Gas Lands.* Development of oil and gas resources in the 1920s spurred new growth and development on the west side. Kettleman City and Avenal were developed as oil centers; exploration and drilling continued into the 1950s. (Source: Jennings 1953.)

irrigation withdrawals quickly exceeded recharge capacity (fig. 52). For example, the water table below the Tulare Irrigation District (on recent alluvium) fell from a 1922 level of 22.3 feet below the surface to 49.7 feet below the surface in 1946 (Rodner 1949, p. 145; fig. 53). Groundwater dropped beyond the technological and financial reach of many basin farmers, and rising irrigation costs—combined with drought, low farm prices, and worldwide depression—led to the abandonment of more than 20,000 acres of farmland in the upper San Joaquin Valley in the late 1930s (Meigs 1939, p. 266). But new irrigation technology promised better days: watering the San Joaquin Valley with runoff from moister parts of the state. The California Water Plan was approved in 1933, and construction commenced in 1938, under the auspices of the U.S. Bureau of Reclamation. The Friant-Kern Canal, across the eastern basin, was finally completed in 1950, by which time basin agriculture had settled solidly into new patterns involving a far larger scale of operations than had prevailed since the end of the bonanza wheat era (Cooper 1968, p. 149; Eilsen 1947, pp. 22–25).

The conversion from dryland wheat to irrigated, intensive farming was a critical step not only in the development of basin land use

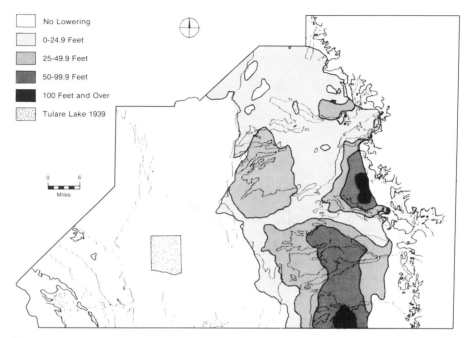

Figure 52.   *Groundwater Lowering, 1921–1939.* As a result of severe drought in the mid-1920s, the basin's farmers turned increasingly to groundwater pumping. Pumpage soon greatly exceeded the basin's natural recharge capacity, and water levels dropped—especially under areas heavily reliant upon well irrigation, such as the old-valley-fill terraces near Lindsay. (Source: U.S.D.I. Bureau of Reclamation 1939.)

patterns but also in the establishment of new social arrangements. Cultivation, harvest, and processing of irrigated crops such as fruit and cotton relied upon an abundant supply of cheap seasonal labor. To sustain the high profits enjoyed during the First World War, farmers and processors joined in increasingly efficient control over agricultural employment and wages. The San Joaquin Labor Bureau, founded in 1926, helped basin farmers exploit new pools of cheap labor and supported the establishment of low wage standards. Basin farmers and townspeople regarded the new laborers recruited from Mexico and the Philippines as racially inferior and met their efforts to establish permanent homes in the basin with hostility and sometimes with violence. Unable to create stable lives for themselves, the workers came to the basin when they were called and set up housekeeping in squatter settlements or in barracks provided by the growers. When local work was over, they left to follow the harvest northward, then southward again, wintering in flophouses or squatter settlements in Stockton, Sacramento, or Los Angeles or on ranches in the Imperial and Coachella valleys. As intensification proceeded, more and more

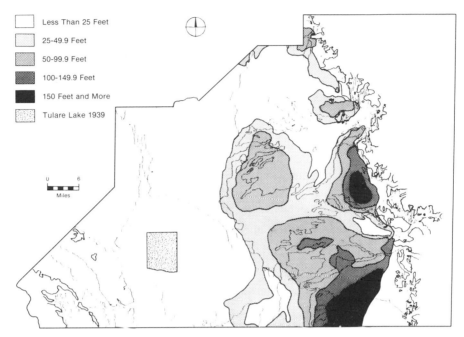

Less Than 25 Feet

25-49.9 Feet

50-99.9 Feet

100-149.9 Feet

150 Feet and More

Tulare Lake 1939

Miles

Figure 53. *Depth to Groundwater, 1939.* Severe depletion of groundwater resources dramatically lowered the water table under much of the basin. In some cases the water table fell beyond the technological and financial reach of many farmers, forcing them to abandon their farmland. (Source: U.S.D.I. Bureau of Reclamation 1939.)

migrant workers were needed, and more arrived every year. Their growing numbers alarmed basin residents, who considered the squalor of migrant life a result of the low character of farm workers and viewed squatter settlements as a public-health problem rather than as a social or moral issue. Public outcries led to mass evictions, and tensions were aggravated by inflammatory editorials in basin newspapers, which alluded to the poor character and Communist allegiance of farm workers and bemoaned the dire economic straits in which growers found themselves (McWilliams 1939).[2]

Then came the Great Depression. Farm wages fell to an all-time low, despite the fact that agricultural production continued to rise. Growers continued to advertise for more laborers long after the ranks of the unemployed had reached alarming proportions, and the conditions of migrant life deteriorated further. Finally, farm workers—like the growers before them—were forced to organize. The Industrial Workers of the World had failed to unite Central Valley farm workers after the

2. The social and spatial development of migrant labor in California is discussed in vivid detail in Carey McWilliams' 1939 expose, *Factories in the Field.*

First World War, but depression conditions deteriorated to the point where local unions began to develop. In 1933 a wave of agricultural strikes swept California, and Corcoran gin workers initiated a violent valley-wide cotton strike. The strikers gained few benefits from such actions, but growers were inspired to reimplement an old strategy that had proved effective in keeping wages low: the recruitment of new workers of different races and nationalities to replace the dissatisfied work force on hand. The newcomers would be disorganized and easily manipulated, and the troublemakers could be deported if necessary. Southern blacks were among those recruited to pick basin cotton; they came in small numbers at first, and took up residence in segregated sections of towns and rural settlements (McWilliams 1939, pp. 220–224). Continued labor agitation led to the formation of the Associated Farmers of California, which first convened in Fresno in 1934, its stated aim "to muster a show of force when required" (McWilliams 1939, p. 233). The influence of this and other grower organizations was strong in rural areas:

> California's rural regions were unaccustomed to field labor strikes. Their populations were . . . neither large nor diverse enough to supply counter-vailing or neutral groups to moderate tempers and defuse conflict situations. The pattern of response to agricultural strife . . . was characterized by near-unanimity of support for the growers and an easily-manipulated willingness to justify the resort to violence. During the San Joaquin strike, for example, the Visalia *Times-Delta* commented favorably on a rumor that the Ku Klux Klan was planning a resurgence in the Valley. (Stein 1973, pp. 225–226)

The arrival of yet another group of migrants exacerbated the uneasy situation. Thousands of Dust Bowl migrants streamed into the San Joaquin Valley in the mid-1930s, fleeing drought, depression, and mechanization "back home." In search of the widely advertised opportunities awaiting newcomers in the Golden State, about 110,000 "Okies" from Oklahoma, Arkansas, Texas, and Missouri took up residence in the valley during this period (McWilliams 1942, p. 32). To some extent, jobs were available to them, because the forced repatriation of Mexican nationals during the depression and the rapid expansion of cotton cultivation in southern California had left basin farmers anxious to secure a dependable work force (Stein 1973, p. 41). Many farmers encouraged the influx of migrants, who would harvest the increasingly profitable crops for meager wages, for the more workers on hand, the more cotton could be harvested and the more could be safely planted the next year. The ranks of farm workers swelled until there were from three to ten workers available for every job in valley agriculture (Stein 1973, p. 77), and their growing numbers strained the resources of local agencies to the limit. Unlike the Mexicans, Japanese, and Filipinos before them—who fled to large cities or returned to their homelands when social tensions or unemployment mounted—the Okies came as families in search of permanent homes. They were white Anglo-Saxon Protestants, Americans of long standing, and were determined to avoid permanent interstate wandering. Although they eagerly attempted to establish themselves as members of their adopted communities, they found that there were few permanent jobs available; unable to leave, much less to buy farms of their own, they purchased lots in cheap subdivisions or shacktowns if they could, or lived in labor camps built by growers or by the government, or simply camped along ditch banks. The efforts of the Okies to join basin society were still met with hostility as the decade drew to a close, and when the Second World War began many left the basin to work in war-related industries in coastal California cities. Ironically, an acute agricultural labor shortage developed with their departure, and the importation of Mexican *braceros* was resumed under state auspices. Bracero contracts stipulated that workers must return to Mexico at the end of the harvest season, and it seemed to some that the problems created by a seasonal demand for large numbers of farm workers had thus been solved. The legacy of depression-era migrants was already clear, however: their presence had sustained a drive toward agricultural intensification and specialization and had helped large operations persist and grow, and their settlements had cemented a social segregation of space that would remain a salient aspect of the region's human geography.

From the 1920s through the early 1940s, Hanford, Visalia, and Tulare each had about 8,000 residents. The slow growth of basin towns when the agricultural work force was growing so rapidly indicates the extent to which farm workers were excluded from urban life. The basin's population rose 38 percent between 1930 and 1940, but rural settlements grew much faster than towns (table 12), their growth directly

TABLE 12

Differential Increase of Population, 1920–1940

	1920	1930	Increase	1940	Increase
Total population	81,062	102,827	27%	143,320	38%
Rural population	55,809	67,495	21	98,583	46
Urban population	25,253	35,332	40	43,737	24

SOURCES: U.S.D.C. Bureau of the Census 1922, Vol. III; 1932, Population, Vol. III; 1942, Population, Vol. II.

proportional to local increases in cotton planting: Earlimart emerged as an Okie town, and Little Oklahomas developed on the fringes of Farmersville and many other rural towns. The larger rural towns had small department and grocery stores, seed and equipment outlets, movie houses and soda fountains, and tree-lined streets flanked by the small frame houses of local farmers and other long-term residents. The structure and substance of these towns made it impossible for them to absorb large numbers of poverty-stricken migrant families, and towns-people complained that they were unable to provide for the schooling of so many children. Where the newcomers did manage to find housing or house lots, they brought social stratification, chronic unemployment, and poverty, and they quickly developed "an extraordinary facility for making themselves inconspicuous. . . . They are forced by circum-stances to be inconspicuous. . . . They do not congregate in the center of town, they linger about the outskirts. They make their purchases, such as they are, not in the downtown shopping districts, but in the cheaper roadside stores. Many communities throughout the coun-try . . . are often wholly unaware of the presence in their midst of several thousand migrants" (McWilliams 1942, pp. 6–7).

By 1939, 60 percent of the Okie families were still living in the California county in which they had initially taken up residence (Mc-Williams 1942, pp. 32–33). The typical migrant settlement consisted of a cluster of small, makeshift houses,

> located on the banks of a river, near an irrigation ditch or on a side road where a spring of water is available. From a distance it looks like a city dump, and well it may, for the city dumps are the sources for the material from which it is built. You can see a litter of dirty rags and scrap iron, of houses built of weeds, of flattened cans or paper. It is only on close approach that it can be seen that these are homes. (Steinbeck 1938, p. 6)

As Okie settlements matured, their landscapes took on a more sub-stantial appearance:

> They say you can go into a big Okie settlement . . . and you can judge by a man's place to the very month how long he's been there. . . . If he is living in a tent or trailer, he's been there less than six months. If a family is in a garage on the back of a lot, they've been here more than six months. If the garage now houses the car, and the family is in a two-room shack in the front of the lot, they've been here more than a year. And if the house has expanded and living is fairly decent, they've been here for more than two years. (Pyle in Stein 1973, p. 52)

In addition, there were new settlement forms created by some of the larger growers: "hidden by the gentle, scarcely-perceptible swell of the plain in the heart of the ranch are the clusters of administration buildings on a miniature main street with a gay little garden. Beyond lie the separate labor camps for American, Mexican, Filipino and Japanese workers" (W.P.A., Federal Writers' Project 1939, p. 67). A few of the largest fruit ranches took on the appearance and functions of company towns; the growers, like their hired laborers, participated only marginally in the growth and development of basin communities.

Rural Changes and the Growth of Large Farms

By 1926, fluctuating prices, increasingly expensive irrigation water, migrant-labor unrest, rising land taxes, and the growing profitability of machine-harvested field crops had tipped the scales in favor of large farms once again. Despite fluctuating economic conditions, speculation and a commercial orientation had been salient characteristics of basin agriculture from the beginning: "No matter how clever, how loving a man might be with earth and growing things, he could not survive if he were not also a good shopkeeper" (Steinbeck 1939, p. 316). After 1925, the better "shopkeepers" tended to be those with enough capital to invest in equipment and the financial backing to undertake substantial risks. The ability to change crops quickly to take advantage of a shifting market was the key to successful field cropping, but as mechanization increased, such flexibility became increasingly expensive. Special machinery was needed for each kind of crop, and this made flexibility costly. Wealthy farmers could afford to invest in a varied inventory of new and more efficient machinery, and through mechanized cultivation of large holdings they could also achieve economies of scale, bringing lower production costs, shipping rates, interest rates, and so on.

Small farmers had to maximize their returns by intensive cultivation of a particular high-value crop, investing in the specialized machinery it required. High yields per acre could sustain a family farm and meet the land taxes, but small farmers remained extremely vulnerable to the financial disasters wrought by droughts, freezes, cost increases, and falling prices. In earlier eras, small farmers had an important advantage: they became involved in irrigation projects early and held the lion's share of irrigated land. Large-farm irrigation increased dramatically during the 1920s, however, and as the water table dropped it was the large farmers who could afford high water prices and the powerful pumps needed to reach deeper and deeper pools of groundwater. With secure access to irrigation water and an abundant labor supply, they, too, could grow labor-intensive irrigated crops such as oranges, peaches, grapes, and cotton, and they could grow these on a large scale. Economies of scale also enabled them to bear the additional expenses imposed by government regulation and rising taxes. Only by banding together in cooperative associations or by affiliating with corporate producers could small farmers hope to achieve the advantages that came so readily to large farmers, and co-ops and marketing associations flourished.

Changing agronomic conditions were clearly reflected in regional patterns of land tenure. Until 1925, the number of farms in the basin rose steadily, but between 1925 and 1945 the number declined by about 10 percent, from 9,465 to 8,505—that is, about 960 farmers went out of business (U.S.D.C. Bureau of the Census 1927, 1946). Average farm size grew from 159 acres in 1925 to 213 acres in 1945; Kings County farms were still the larger, but average farm size in Tulare County was rising rapidly (table 13). Nearly 60 percent of the basin's farmland was held in farms of 1,000 acres or more by 1945; only 31 percent was in farms smaller than 500 acres, despite the fact that 94 percent of basin farms were 500 acres or less in size. John Steinbeck lamented that "as time went on, the businessmen had the farms, and the farms grew larger, there were fewer of them. And all the time the farms grew larger and the owners fewer. And there were pitifully few farmers on the land any more" (Steinbeck 1939, p. 316). Farm ownership and operation reveal still more about basin farming: for example,

TABLE 13

Farms by Size Category and Landholding by Farm Size, 1925 and 1945

	Kings County		Tulare County		Lake Basin	
	1925	1945	1925	1945	1925	1945
Farms (all sizes)	2,359	2,119	7,106	6,386	9,465	8,505
Under 100 acres						
Farms	75%	70%	80%	75%	79%	73%
Farmland	14	10	19	12	17	11
100–499 acres						
Farms	20	24	16	19	17	21
Farmland	19	19	22	20	21	20
500–999 acres						
Farms	2	2.5	2	3	2	3
Farmland	6	7	10	11	9	10
1,000 acres or more						
Farms	3	3.5	2	3	2	3
Farmland	61	64	49	57	53	57
Average farm acreage	209	254	143	199	159	213

Sources: U.S.D.C. Bureau of the Census 1927;1946.

manager-operated farms were still few in 1945, yet they controlled a disproportionately large share of the land, especially in Kings County (table 14).

Clear distinctions between the eastern and western basin had persisted, had even grown stronger. The west side, occupied later and in larger units by fewer families, was much slower to intensify than the east side—yet it converted much more quickly to capital-intensive operations (especially corporate cotton farms) when conditions began to favor such enterprises. A look specifically at the east side reveals a great diversity in land-tenure patterns. The average farm in the Tulare, Lindsay-Strathmore, Terra Bella, Ivanhoe, and Alpaugh irrigation districts (I.D.'s) varied between twenty-five acres (Terra Bella) and fifty-one acres (Tulare). In both Terra Bella and Tulare, nearly all of the farms (99.6 percent) were operated by individuals rather than by corporations, yet family farms controlled more of the land in the Tulare I.D. (74,573 acres, or 91 percent) than in the Terra Bella I.D. (6,204 acres, or 46 percent): the owners of two corporate farms controlled 54 percent of the land in the Terra Bella I.D. (U.S.D.I. Bureau of Reclamation 1946–1948). The Tulare I.D., on the Kaweah Delta, experienced early and persistent small-farm settlement and rapid land-use intensification, while the Terra Bella I.D., on old valley fill in a remote corner of the basin, was initially settled in large parcels and was still (in 1945) used

TABLE 14
Farm Operation and Landholding by Farm Type, 1945

	Kings County	Tulare County	Lake Basin
Total number of farms	2,119	6,386	8,505
Operated by full owner			
Farms	63%	69%	67%
Farmland	25	42	37
Operated by part owner			
Farms	14	13	14
Farmland	47	38	41
Operated by tenant(s)			
Farms	21	12	14
Farmland	16	9	11
Operated by manager			
Farms	2	6	5
Farmland	12	10	11
Total vacant dwellings on farms	818	712	1,530
As % of all farm dwellings	21	7	9

SOURCE: U.S.D.C. Bureau of the Census 1946.

predominantly for the extensive cultivation of grain and field crops. Rural settlement patterns reflected these contrasts as well: there were fewer farmsteads per square mile in the Terra Bella I.D. than in the Tulare I.D. Other irrigation districts revealed similar interplay among land acquisition, settlement history, agronomic development, and the endowments of the natural environment (Goldschmidt 1947).

The conditions and patterns that surfaced after the depression were actually more typical of the long-term character of basin agriculture than those that had prevailed during the early years of the twentieth century. Large-scale operations were hardier and more flexible than the small farms that had flourished briefly, for any strain in market conditions or the environment could be weathered more easily by large farmers. They could absorb losses better, could buy up the land of their failed neighbors to increase their own holdings, could transform their capital into technological assets or new practices (including advertising) to relieve the strain. The decline of small farms in the basin was evident not only in basin landscapes but in the 1945 census of agriculture as well. Nearly 21 percent of all farm dwellings in Kings County (818) and 7 percent of those in Tulare County (712) stood vacant; 11 percent of farm owner-operators did not live on their farms, and an additional 5 percent left farm operations to hired managers (U.S.D.C. Bureau of the Census 1946). In Steinbeck's words, "they no longer worked on their farms. They farmed on paper, and they forgot the land, the smell, the feel of it, and remembered only that they gained and lost by it" (Steinbeck 1939, p. 317). As landholdings grew larger and landholders fewer, the relationships between farmers and their land became weaker and weaker.

Farm Organization and Regional Patterns of Land Use

The regional trend toward large, mechanized operations was evident in the evolution of dairies, orchards, and general farms. In preceding eras, each farm type had its own distinctive practices, yet all shared a similar arrangement of farmstead buildings and fields. Farmsteads became more specialized in the decades after 1925 as electrical and mechanical power replaced animals, human muscle, and wind power on farms and as the effects of specialization and government regulation became more apparent.

Orchards changed the least during this era, although barns gradually disappeared as tractors took over chores once performed by animals. The farm-worker population in orchard districts decreased, too (except at harvest time), as chemical herbicides began to replace hand weeding (Schoonover and Batchelor 1948, pp. 314–319). The influence of government regulation upon orchard farms was slight, for the U.S. Department of Agriculture regulated fruit grading and marketing rather than actual farm practices or farm structure. Although orchard operations remained small, the proportion of each orchard farm allocated to permanent plantings increased at the expense of field-crop cultivation; this was due in part to the conversion from work stock to tractors, which made pasturage and alfalfa fields unnecessary, and also to economic pressures to specialize in production of high-value crops. Truck transportation brought increased centralization of packinghouse operations in the larger basin towns, and abandoned community packinghouses and loading platforms were noted in small towns; truck transport also replaced rail transport to markets within California, but fruits were still taken to far-distant markets by rail or ship (Zimrick 1976, pp. 228–231).

Dairy farms came under heavy government regulation during this era. Some of the first voluntary local regulation of dairying in California occurred in the basin (Small 1926, p. 325); the Pure Milk Act of 1927 gave the state authority for sanitary control, and in 1937 additional requirements were established for designation as a grade-A dairy, a producer of milk fit for human consumption. These requirements affected both dairy procedures and dairy landscapes: they specified the location, construction, and use of corrals and milking barns, and made refrigeration facilities mandatory. Farmers who had kept a few milk cows as a sideline found that they needed to specialize in dairying or accept grade-B rating, for the costs and complexities of grade-A dairying made it a full-time occupation. Grade-B dairies, where food crops were still grown, remained numerous but generally kept only a few cows[3] (Rodner 1949, p. 184). Full-time Grade A dairies usually had forty cows or more, primarily Holsteins, and extensive acreages of irrigated pasture and alfalfa. On dairy farmsteads, old pump houses fell into disrepair or disuse; silos, special milking barns, refrigeration facilities, storage areas, and adjoining residences for hired milkers were added. As a result of improvements in refrigeration and transportation, basin dairies were able to specialize in the production of fresh, whole milk for Southern California markets; cream, cheese, butter, and dried milk were still produced as well.

On general farms, the depression era brought noteworthy increases in mechanization and in government regulation. Until 1935 cotton acreage varied widely because of an unstable market and problems with verticillium wilt. Price fluctuations and overproduction were

3. For instance, in 1949, 643 of the 1,604 farms in the Tulare Irrigation District had dairy cows; 244 kept them only for family milk needs, while 399 sold some milk (Rodner 1949, p. 184).

brought under control by the Cotton Acreage Adjustment Program (implemented in 1935), which imposed production quotas to raise the price of cotton, and new, wilt-resistant varieties of Acala cotton were developed. The great tensile strength and extreme whiteness of these varieties enhanced their market value, and they proved well suited to mechanized cultivation and harvesting as well (Gregor 1962*a*, p. 396). Rising land prices, cheap labor, and a wartime boom in cotton demand promoted an increase in cotton acreage in the basin, and general farming made inroads into regions of grazing and grain. Where grain farms remained, the landscapes were changing too, for as grain farmers adopted more intensive practices their farms became more like those of general farmers: irrigated, modern, mechanized, and planted to whatever promised to pay well that year. To wit, the following description of a 12,000-acre wheat ranch west of Corcoran: "His camp alone is a small town in itself. . . . He feeds 52 men at the camp. The water used in irrigating this enormous ranch comes from 9 deep wells. . . . Wolfsen does his work with 5 harvesters, which are able to cut and thresh 200 acres of grain in a day, or 6000 sacks of wheat" (*Fresno Republican* 1929). This scale of organization was increasingly characteristic; indeed, the mechanized grain farms of the prewar era were the direct antecedents of the great corporate cotton ranches of later years.

Despite the tremendous changes that came about during this era, it was largely a time of consolidation and simplification rather than of expansion. Agricultural acreage increased only gradually, actually declining during the war years (table 15), and the pace of intensification slowed as well. Districts that had once supported several kinds of farms became increasingly homogeneous; for instance, in the citrus district north of the Tule River, vast tracts of orange trees grew where grain and other crops had grown in 1916 (Meigs 1939, p. 258), and on the Kings Delta, apricots, plums, prunes, and grapes lost acreage to field crops

TABLE 15

Cropland Acreage, 1925–1945

Year	Cropland Acreage	Average Farm Acreage
1925	1,508,937	159
1930	1,767,858	190
1935	1,564,043	180
1940	1,977,947	232
1945	1,808,548	213

SOURCES: U.S.D.C. Bureau of the Census 1927; 1932, Agriculture, Vol. II; 1936, Vol. I; 1942 Agriculture, Vol. I; 1946.

and dairies (Storie and Weir 1940, pp. 12–13). A clear zonation of orchards began to emerge on the Kaweah and Tule deltas: walnuts were grown only on deep alluvial soils, while olives (which grow well in a wide range of soils) were planted in the transitional areas between the plains and the foothills; citrus fruits, more lucrative and more fragile, were grown only on the more elevated land within the thermal belt, and the hardier deciduous fruits fringed the western edge of the orchard belt. Regional specialization was even more prevalent in other districts: cotton fields stretched from the toe of the Kings Delta to Tipton, Woodville, Pixley, Earlimart, and Alpaugh and gradually advanced into the dairy lands on the eastern fans and the grain lands of the western and southwestern basin (fig. 54). Large tracts of wheat remained on the reclaimed lake bed and in the southeastern corner of the basin around Terra Bella, Ducor, and Richgrove, but as wheat farming merged with general farming, greater proportions of other grains, such as barley,

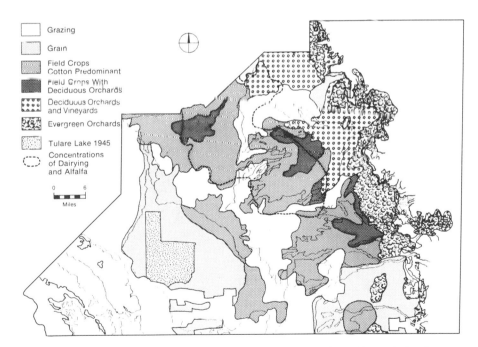

Figure 54. *Land Use, 1945.* The years between 1926 and 1945 brought land-use consolidation and simplification rather than expansion. Orchards and vineyards continued to expand on the Kaweah and Tule deltas, but on the Kings Delta orchards lost acreage to field cropping and dairying. Regional distinctions between the eastern and western sides of the basin grew stronger: Kings County became known for field crops, dairying, and livestock, Tulare County for its diversified farms. (Sources: Storie and Owen 1942; Storie and Weir 1940; Retzer 1946; U.S.D.A. Forest Service 1945; Crawford and Hard 1940.)

oats, and milo were planted. As cropping expanded slowly across the basin plains, livestock ranching was pushed still further westward from the basin trough and into the foothills.

As the differentiation of agricultural regions continued, the distinctions between Kings and Tulare counties grew stronger. Agricultural simplification on the Kings Delta and the rapid westward expansion of field cropping earned Kings County a reputation as a producer of field crops (including cotton), dairy products, and livestock: 91 percent of its land was planted to field crops in 1945, and field crops, livestock products, and dairy products led in value of agricultural production. Tulare County was still known for diversified farming: although 66 percent of its farmland was planted to field crops, fruits and nuts were its primary income-producing crops (Wilson and Clawson 1945; Kings County Agricultural Commissioner 1945; Tulare County Agricultural Commissioner 1945). Within each county, regional differences reflected distinctive settlement histories and environmental contexts. Table 16 and figure 55 illustrate typical cropping and tenure patterns of three distinctive types of basin districts in about 1946: an orchard district on old-valley-fill and residual soils near Lindsay, a dairy and cotton district on recent alluvial soils near Tulare, and a transitional dryland-wheat and citrus district on old-valley-fill soils near Terra Bella. Corporate farms already controlled a disproportionately large share of farmland in each area, but the degree of corporate expansion varied

TABLE 16

Crops and Land Tenure in Selected Irrigation Districts, 1946

	Lindsay-Strathmore	Tulare	Terra Bella
Land in field crops	1%	86%	80%
Alfalfa		20	14
Cereal grains		12	66
Cotton		31	
Land in orchards	86	14	18
Land in other uses (fallow, etc.)	13		2
Owned by individuals			
Farms	98.8	99.6	99.6
Farmland	66.4	90.6	46.4
Owned by corporations			
Farms	1.2	0.4	0.4
Farmland	33.6	9.4	53.6

SOURCE: U.S.D.I. Bureau of Land Management 1946.

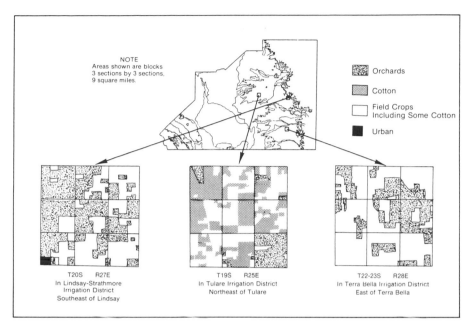

NOTE
Areas shown are blocks
3 sections by 3 sections,
9 square miles.

Orchards

Cotton

Field Crops
Including Some Cotton

Urban

T20S   R27E
In Lindsay-Strathmore
Irrigation District
Southeast of Lindsay

T19S   R25E
In Tulare Irrigation District
Northeast of Tulare

T22-23S   R28E
In Terra Bella Irrigation District
East of Terra Bella

Figure 55. *Regional Land Use Patterns, 1945.* Within a context of land-use consolidation and simplification throughout the basin as a whole, portions of Tulare County still were associated with diversified farming. Subregional differences on the east side reflected distinctive histories and environments. (Source: U.S.D.I. Bureau of Reclamation 1946–1948.)

significantly. The dense initial settlement of rich lands around Tulare hindered the development of large, corporate farms to some extent, whereas the belated settlement of the Terra Bella district and the massive grants to railroads in that vicinity made it quite easy for individuals to amass tremendous holdings there.

Environmental Alteration

Perhaps the most dramatic change to occur during this period was the widespread adoption of automobile transportation. The effects of automobiles were dramatically evident in rural and urban settlement patterns and land uses: the built environment changed to accommodate the new machines and reflected the new mobility of basin residents. In more subtle ways, automobiles began to alter the basin's atmosphere as well: engine exhaust diminished visibility and had adverse effects upon human health and agricultural productivity, although these ramifications were not clear until much later.

The cumulative effects of many years of agricultural use were also evident: soils and water resources were strained, in some cases to the point of affecting local productivity. Groundwater withdrawals increased thirtyfold between 1905 and 1955, and the water table fell beyond the reach of many basin farmers (Davis, Olmstead, and Brown 1959; Rodner 1949, p. 145). Rapid withdrawals also reduced the recharge capacities of basin aquifers through compaction, and caused gradual subsidence of lands in heavily pumped areas, especially terraces of old valley fill (fig. 56). The significance of groundwater over-draught became increasingly apparent as more and more people vied for the basin's hydrologic resources. On the other hand, seepage from irrigation canals had detrimental effects in some areas near the Kings River, where high groundwater and surface concentrations of alkali killed a number of apricot and peach trees in 1937 (Retzer 1946, p. 81), contributing to the process of agricultural simplification there.

Although agricultural expansion paused, the basin's vegetation included an ever-increasing number of introduced cultivates and ornamentals and accidentally introduced weeds. The new successional communities were less stable than the original stands, and their composition varied more directly with land use: grazed lands developed communities of winter annuals, while intermittently farmed lands developed communities of summer annuals. Pockets of original vegetation remained in pasture and cropland areas, especially in the western basin,

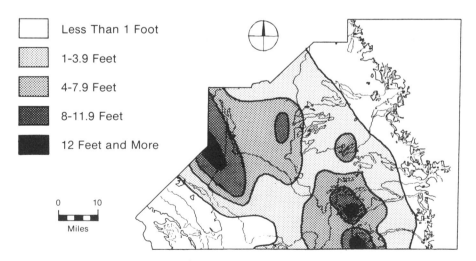

Less Than 1 Foot

1-3.9 Feet

4-7.9 Feet

8-11.9 Feet

12 Feet and More

0   10
Miles

Figure 56.   *Land Subsidence, 1975.* Rapid withdrawals of groundwater caused compaction, which severely reduced the recharge capacities of the underlying aquifers. Land subsidence began to be noted in the first decades of this century, but it grew more pronounced after the Second World War. (Source: Poland et al. 1975.)

but even these included large components of introduced species. The destruction of marshland communities continued as the lake and its marginal swamps were drained and reclaimed, though some marsh species flourished along ditch banks. Lowland communities persisted on abandoned lands near the basin trough where groundwater and salt concentrations were high, and in some areas lowland species invaded the ground quickly after plowing. Spiny saltbush communities survived nearly intact because of their tolerance to grazing and the inhospitability of alkali desert soils to cultivation, but desert saltbush was largely removed by plows and cattle and replaced by a simplified cover of winter annuals. The perennial bunchgrass prairies had long since been destroyed, and annual weeds grew in their place; some bunchgrasses still grew on protected slopes in the uplands, but always in association with a secondary growth of annuals or invasive perennials (Piemeisel and Lawson 1937; Talbot, Biswell, and Hormay 1939, pp. 398–402).[4] The oaks of the tree savanna were nearly gone as well, although some remained near farmsteads and streams. Despite the radical alteration of basin communities, species diversity still was greatest on the moist east side, and communities became simpler (though more pristine) westward toward the basin trough. The meager remnants of natural communities would be further altered with renewed agricultural expansion and the introduction of chemical herbicides after the Second World War.

Summary

From 1895 until 1925, conditions fostered the extension of small-farm settlement over the Tulare Lake Basin, but between 1926 and 1945 economic and social upheavals and a dwindling supply of irrigation water brought a return to normalcy: the reassertion of economies of scale. Small farms, unable to economize without sacrificing market flexibility or profits, gradually gave way to larger operations. The regional population continued to grow, but many of the newcomers were indigent farm workers rather than prospective farmers. Increased production of citrus fruits and cotton brought a dramatic rise in the regional labor demand, and still more farm workers were recruited from the ranks of agricultural peasants in Mexico, Asia, and the American South. Established attitudes and values supported social segregation, low

4. A 1939 study found that annuals comprised 94 percent of the herbaceous cover in San Joaquin Valley grasslands and that introduced plants—mostly annuals—constituted 63 percent of the grassland species (Talbot, Biswell, and Hormay 1939, pp. 398–402).

wages, and growers' irresponsibility toward their seasonal employees. When farm workers finally began to demand better social and economic conditions, they were met with organized opposition in the form of grower cooperatives and grower-generated antagonism.

With the onset of the depression, conditions became intolerable for most seasonal workers; many who were not repatriated worked their way back home or fled to larger California cities to seek employment or government relief. This situation was exacerbated by the arrival of thousands of families escaping the Dust Bowl, who sought not only farm employment but a permanent place in the basin communities. The geographical expressions of migrant labor included distinctive settlement forms and farmstead facilities. Near groves, vineyards, and cotton fields, rural towns acquired large Okie populations almost overnight, and densely clustered residential tracts appeared—legally and illegally—in scattered locales where existing housing was insufficient. On the larger fruit and cotton ranches, growers erected additional barracks or cabins for migrant families.

Contrasts between prosperous farm businesses and foundering family farms grew stronger as foreclosures and farm abandonment continued. Very large farms became especially common in the western basin, where many homes stood empty, and outbuildings gave way to equipment lots. With this reemergence of large-scale farming in the basin, as elsewhere throughout the Central Valley, came increased capitalization of farm enterprises and increasing alienation of people from the land. In some ways, government restrictions and regulations fostered these trends. As agricultural economies of scale grew and spread, regional patterns of land use became more sharply delineated, and by the end of the war—when substantial subsidies and government-funded irrigation projects became available to basin farmers—corporate farming had clearly begun to replace family farming in the Tulare Lake Basin.

9

Agribusiness and the Waning Regional Identity 1946 to the Present

In the name of progress and efficiency our countryside has been turned over to machines and technology and our population, in large part, has lost the beauty and the joys and the peace of the land. (Wollenberg 1977)

The Tulare Lake Basin, as it emerged from the Great Depression and the Second World War, was largely closed to new farmers. Farming continued to expand, but under the management of a dwindling number of farmers and businessmen. The requirements for agricultural success on the basin's varied lands had changed, and, more than ever before, survival demanded strict adherence to business principles and the ability to make the most of technology and labor. Farmers who understood business but lacked capital could still succeed, if they knew their land and knew how to translate that knowledge into financial power and economic planning. They learned to involve themselves more deeply with the business world and with the government to increase their access to technological innovations, to land, to water, and to capital. Successful farm businesses combined with other successful businesses—local canneries and shipping companies at first, but soon every manner of enterprises headquartered across the nation—to work the land in a corporate manner, to gain greater financial flexibility at the expense of further alienation from the land. Those who were neither good businessmen nor good farmers forfeited their land to those who could do better. Agriculture in the basin, as throughout the American West, had become an arena for business investment rather than a unique and special relationship between people and their land. The supports to agribusiness grew stronger in the decades after the war. Irrigation expanded with public financing; farm labor remained cheap and plentiful, in part because of government involvement; and a rash of innovations eased the lives of the remaining farmers and enhanced their profit margins. When and where economic or environmental problems caused these supports to falter, the state and federal governments intervened.

Basin agriculture received a new boost from the rapid urbanization of Southern California. The markets for basin products expanded tremendously, and highly capitalized farm enterprises fled the Los Angeles Basin for lands not yet urbanized. There were still opportunities in the Tulare Lake Basin for those who had sufficient capital, and the regional population continued to grow. The majority of the newcomers flocked to basin towns. Many of them were unfamiliar with the surrounding countryside and had few contacts with it, and so as the basin became urbanized, its character and its image changed. Towns became the prevailing concern, the focus of hopes and investments, for they had proved their ability to grow steadily and well on any kind of soil. Town growth was still supported by agriculture, but as the basin attracted service workers, realtors, and manufacturers, towns became increasingly self-sufficient. As regional landscapes and activities became more and more like those of other Central Valley places, more like those throughout the West, the distinction and identity of the Tulare Lake Basin was lost.

Homogenization and the World Farm

Ever since the beginning of American occupation in the mid—nineteenth century, farmers had tried to enhance the basin's agricultural potential by changing the land. They manipulated the terrain and water supply; they developed new crops to suit the land and changed the land to suit new crops; they changed land and crops to suit new techniques and new machinery; and they adapted machinery and techniques to suit local crops and terrain. Most of all, though, basin farmers adapted their land, their crops, and their techniques to suit the market. Agricultural innovations arose within the basin as farmers grew increasingly familiar with the capabilities of their land and increasingly confident of their own power to alter the conditions of their relationships to the land. Attitudes, values, and ideas from outside the basin guided local perceptions and innovations, as did the commercial market; yet until after the war, agricultural practices were almost always rooted in knowledge gained from working and living on the land. During periods of dramatic change in the conditions of farming and of the rampant speculation that was partner to it, practical experience with the land gave rise to more practical evaluations and more profitable techniques. As interest in exploiting the land's diverse capabilities became stronger, people's control over the land grew stronger still. Natural variations were overshadowed by new patterns of diversity imposed by artificial manipulation, yet agricultural changes were still locally conceived and locally implemented as the people of the basin attempted to make the land and landscapes better suit their own hopes and requirements.

This local relationship between land and life was enhanced by a natural environment that could absorb large numbers of people and could respond to their attentions and abuses without jeopardy to its own ecological stability. The basin's frontiers expanded, strong outside markets clamored for its products, yet the region's soils and terrain displayed remarkable tolerance for varied land uses. The land rewarded agricultural experimentation and environmental modification, and farmers prospered. This relationship changed rather suddenly just prior to the Second World War: the countryside lost its capacity to absorb newcomers, and the decisions of farmers came increasingly under the influence of outside regulation. Fewer people controlled the land, and the effects of each decision affected more of the land. Experimentation, innovation, and invention continued, affecting the land more dramatically than ever before, but they arose less and less often as outgrowths of local experience. The commercial desires and investment decisions of people who did not know the land, who had perhaps never seen it, became more and more influential. The basin's landscapes had long reflected the demands of distant urban markets, but now decisions as to how to translate those demands into action came increasingly from people of the markets, rather than from people of the land. Some of these decisions were passed along to managers to be implemented on factory farms—impersonal institutional manifestations of business and industry—rather than on family farms that, as institutions, called industry and business into being.

Broad distinctions in terms of location and land quality still influence agricultural decisions in the basin to some extent, but once water became available in sufficient quantities, the land's own character mattered little. Chemical fertilizers, hybrid crops, and expensive machinery can make almost any land perform according to the wishes of its managers, at least for a while. The basin's variability and its identity have been lost in the decision-making process: now the area is considered merely a small part of the world farm, an arbitrarily designated pair of production units (Tulare and Kings counties) within the increasingly homogenous agricultural realm known as the San Joaquin Valley. Family farms retain some control over the decision-making process, and some have prospered from their intimate relationships with the land, their application of local experience and knowledge. The proportion of basin land farmed by such enterprises, however, dwindles every year.

Change has been most drastic in the landscapes of the countryside, where intensification no longer brings the growth of rural population nor the spread of more settled landscapes. As parcels are consolidated into corporate operations, the identity of each piece of land— its fences, its farmstead, its trees and terrain—is lost or obliterated. New identities, expressed in modern buildings, machine lots, signs, and cyclone fences, are imprinted all at once; since fewer people are working the land, few new farmhouses are built. The working landscape of the countryside is simplified as the vestiges of its historical development are destroyed. Accompanying the loss of residual landscapes and places is a rapid erosion of the memories of the past, memories built by direct and intimate relationships with the land. It remains to be seen whether the lessons learned through such relationships will be lost as well, or whether lessons learned in other regions or in college classrooms can be applied effectively and safely to the land, yet local concern for the environmental consequences of new practices appears to be diminishing. Fewer people are directly affected by mistakes made in basin farming nowadays, and business or technology can rectify mistakes more quickly or hide them more thoroughly. Crop losses and soil depletion are no longer little deaths; in some cases they count only on paper in distant offices, and may even provide welcome tax write-offs for corporations. A generation from now, the landscape expressions of the basin's early agricultural history may be entirely gone, remembered only by a handful of people who grew up when those landscapes were still being formed and who are thus still able to associate landscape features with actions of people upon the land.

The rise of the world farm is clearly reflected in the changing patterns of land tenure and the basin. Between 1945 and 1974, 2,215 farms went out of business, and the average size of basin farms rose to 340 acres, still larger on the west side (table 17). The proportion of farms that are large, and the proportion of the basin's acres controlled by large farms, increased as well. While farm ownership increased, fewer farmers lived on their land. In 1945, only 14 percent of all farm operators in the basin had lived away from their farms; by 1974, 28 percent did so. Independent and family-operated farms still predominate, but corporations and partnerships are becoming increasingly important (table 18). Even these statistics do not fully reflect the situation, however, because separate farms owned by a single corporation are listed in the census as separate operations (McWilliams 1945, p. 5). It is clear, though, that basin agriculture is being guided by fewer people, and that fewer of these people have direct contact with the practice of farming. That this may be cause for alarm is evident: "By and large, where democratic conditions prevail, the man who tilled the soil was a free-holder and in control of his enterprise. Where, on the other hand,

TABLE 17

Farms by Size Category and Landholding by Farm Size, 1945 and 1969

| | Kings County | | Tulare County | | Lake Basin | |
	1945	1969	1945	1969	1945	1969
Farms (all sizes)	2,119	1,109	6,386	5,725	8,505	6,834
Under 100 acres						
Farms	70%	58%	75%	75%	73%	72%
Farmland	10	3	12	10	11	7
100–499 acres						
Farms	24	30.5	19	18	21	20
Farmland	19	11	20	17	20	15
500–999 acres						
Farms	2.5	5.5	3	3.5	3	4
Farmland	7	6	11	10	10	9
1,000 acres or more						
Farms	3.5	6	3	3.5	3	4
Farmland	64	80	57	63	59	69
2,000 acres or more						
Farms		3.4		1.8		2
Farmland		75		51		59
Average farm acreage	254	609	199	276	213	300

SOURCES: U.S.D.C. Bureau of the Census 1946;1972.

TABLE 18

Farm Ownership and Operation, 1974

	No. of Farms	% of Farms	% of Farmland
Ownership			
Individual/family	4,446	82	43.8
Partnership	697	13	23
Corporation	253	4.5	33
Other	29	0.5	0.2
Operation			
By full owner	3,958	73	30.5
By part owner	1,071	20	60
By tenant(s)	396	7	9.5
Operator residence			
On farm operated	3,607	70	
Not on farm operated	1,436	30	

SOURCE: U.S.D.C. Bureau of the Census 1977.

farming lands are owned and controlled in urban centers and the men engaged in farming are merely . . . hired laborers, democratic institutions do not prevail" (Goldschmidt 1975, p. 171).

The Foundations of Capital-Intensive Farming

The character of agriculture in the Tulare Lake Basin is changing rapidly. The decision-making process, the technological assets available to farmers, and the regulatory mechanisms that control farm practices have been radically altered. The technologies of mechanization, water manipulation, fertilization, and weed and pest control have grown tremendously since the war, and the conditions of labor recruitment and farm employment have also changed. Access to and use of innovations is regulated by public agencies, which have financed irrigation systems, technological research, labor relief, and price supports, and have regulated the growing, processing, and marketing of many crops.

New developments in irrigation have been particularly important, serving as a catalyst for the expansion of intensive practices into new areas of the basin and helping sustain intensive farming in areas with dwindling water resources. Although early irrigation projects were built primarily with local capital, all important post-war projects were proposed, planned, financed, and constructed by either the state or the federal government. The Friant-Kern Canal brought water from the San Joaquin River along the eastern flank of the basin by gravity flow in 1949 (fig. 57). The water was distributed primarily to lands already partially irrigated by other means. Rather than expanding the net acreage of intensive agriculture, the Central Valley Project thus helped sustain intensive cropping in areas where drought and a falling water table had threatened to cause a return to simpler land uses. Projects of the U.S. Army Corps of Engineers were valuable adjuncts to the Central Valley Project. Success Dam on the Tule River and Terminus Dam on the Kaweah River, both completed in 1962, provided flood control and irrigation-storage capacity. These dams also provided major recreation facilities, which gave Porterville and Three Rivers an economic and demographic boost. The federally supported Central Valley Project also helped irrigate new lands in the northwestern basin in association with California's State Water Project, which involved water transfer from Northern to Southern California through the Central Valley. A large area west of the Kings River was supplied with irrigation water by the San Luis Canal, and sound practices were facilitated by a publicly financed drainage system into which return flow is pumped to flush out excess salts brought by the water (Fellmeth 1973, p. 175).

The Central Valley Project was designated as a reclamation project of the U.S. government, and distribution of its water thus came under the jurisdiction of the U.S. Bureau of Reclamation. Bureau policies were designed to foster the occupation of frontier lands by family farmers and the distribution of water in an equitable fashion among the greatest possible number of users. Under the terms of the Reclamation Act of 1902 (and as revised in 1911, 1914, and 1926), no water in excess of that needed to irrigate 160 acres (or 320 acres held jointly by husband and wife) may be delivered to one farm operation. Lands in excess of the specified acreage which receive project water must be sold to small farmers within ten years of contracting for water deliveries, and the price of sale must not reflect the existence of the irrigation project itself (Fellmeth 1973, p. 177). Only bona fide resident farmers (those who live on or near their land) are to receive federal water. The overriding objective of the Reclamation Act was to increase the number of livelihoods gained from the land, not simply to irrigate more land, and in essence the limitations are upon water rather than upon land: any land in excess of the stipulated acreage may be retained so long as it does not receive federal water nor severely affect the underlying water table. Although the provisions of the act favor simple ownership and moderate farm size, they say little about actual farm operations. For example, an operator can lease tracts of land from project participants and still obtain project water under the terms of the

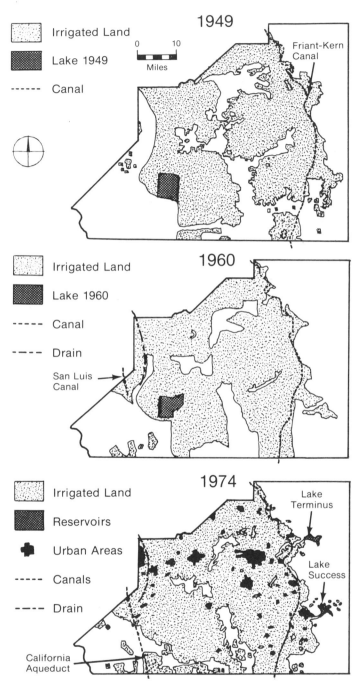

Figure 57. *Irrigated Land, 1949, 1960, 1974.* The Friant-Kern Canal of the Central Valley Project brought water from northern counties to the basin in 1949. The canal, and increased groundwater pumpage, caused slight increases in irrigated acreage in the basin. The completion of the California Aqueduct in 1971 brought a rapid increase of irrigated acreage on the west side; groundwater use increased further as well. (Source: State of California Department of Water Resources 1949; 1960; 1974.)

ownerships that are leased—that is, water rights accompany leased land (deRoos 1948, p. 88). The practicality of the Reclamation Act has never been tested in the Tulare Lake Basin, however, for wholehearted enforcement never materialized. If it were enforced, the act would have dramatic effects upon land tenure and the character of farming in the basin, and in altered form the Reclamation Act may yet temper the rapid advance of corporate farming in the basin and reshape the landscapes of major rural regions throughout the American West.

While the basin trough benefited little from the Central Valley Project, new acreage was irrigated there as a result of advances in pumping technology. During the late 1940s, large turbines that could tap groundwater to depths of 4,000 feet were developed (Lantis, Steiner, and Karinen 1963, p. 403), and hundreds of deep wells were drilled; by the early 1960s, the average depth of basin wells was 600 feet, over 80 percent of the groundwater being drawn from beneath the Corcoran clay (Poland 1958, p. 90). Groundwater became increasingly important, providing water for half of the basin's irrigated land as well as for most municipal and industrial uses (Davis et al. 1959, p. 9). Deep wells also spread intensive cropping over lands far from streams or canals, and served as an important hedge against fluctuations in surface-water availability due to drought, competition, or price restrictions. Drilling of new wells accelerated in the 1970s when the surface-water supply was sharply curtailed by statewide drought. Kings County wells have an average life span of only seven years, and wells in most parts of the basin must be renewed or replaced regularly. Because wells are so expensive to drill and to maintain, groundwater is in the long run accessible primarily to the larger and more highly capitalized farms (Cooper 1968, p. 165). Large operations have caught up with small farms in their ability to intensify production through irrigation, particularly in Kings County, where the vast majority of irrigated acreage is in very large farms (fig. 58). In Tulare County, small-farm settlement and local irrigation projects have a long history, and much more of the irrigated acreage is in smaller farms.

A recent development in basin irrigation, the California Aqueduct began to deliver water to the western flank of Kings County in 1971. Financed by the state, this project imposes few restrictions upon the use of its water by large landowners. California Aqueduct water is, however, relatively expensive, and its use for irrigation is economical only where high-value crops such as fruit and nuts are grown (Dean and King 1970, pp. 71–73). In conjunction with groundwater development and the nearly complete extinction of Tulare Lake, the California Aqueduct has revolutionized the character of west-side farming. Permanent cropping—especially the cultivation of almonds, pistachios,

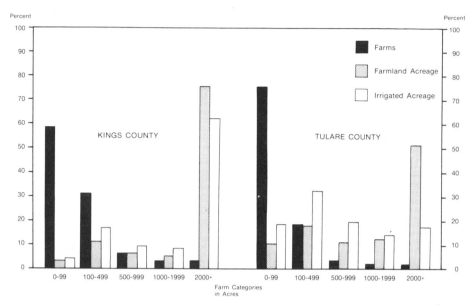

Figure 58. *Farms, Farmland Acreage, and Irrigated Acreage by Farm Size, 1969.* Large farms have rapidly caught up with small farms—and, indeed, surpassed them—in terms of their proportional share of irrigated and total farmland acreage. In both Kings and Tulare counties, most farms are under 100 acres, yet most acreage is contained in farms larger than 2,000 acres. In Kings County a disproportionately large share of the irrigated acreage is in large farms as well, while in Tulare County early intensification and cooperative extension of irrigation systems has led to a greater proportion of irrigated acreage in small farms. (Source: U.S.D.C. Bureau of the Census 1972.)

and other lucrative tree crops—has begun to spread west of the basin trough; most of the lake bed is under irrigated cultivation as well. Once described as "a country nearly bare of vegetation, without shade, where the blistering sun seems hot enough to set fire to the grass, if there was any grass" (Latta 1949b, p. 289), the west side is still the basin's agricultural frontier—it is, indeed, one of the liveliest farming frontiers of the state. Where dry but rich lands were until recently considered unfit for farming, investment and experimentation are now flourishing. The traditional isolation of the west side has declined with the growth of Kettleman City, Avenal, and Lemoore, the installation of Lemoore Naval Air Station, and the construction of a major freeway, Interstate 5.

The landscapes of irrigated farming have finally spread across the basin from east to west, breaking against the foothills of the Coast Range as a great wave of change. More than a century of local endeavors culminated in the development of distant water resources and an influx of additional capital from people outside the basin. By 1970,

1,035,254 acres in Kings and Tulare counties were irrigated, including nearly all of the agricultural land of the basin floor. Along the eastern, southern, and southwestern edges of the old lake bed, and north and south of the Kaweah Delta, some farmers still lack access to irrigation water, but these areas are slowly succumbing to irrigation as ways are found to deal with the high concentrations of alkali in their soils. The Kettleman Plain and McClure Valley are still dry, too, but intensive agriculture is slowly transforming these areas as well. The newly watered frontiers of the basin still reflect the varied interrelationships among land-alienation policies, land-use evolution, and the original natural environment, yet because these frontiers are so modern in appearance, people are seldom inclined to attribute their landscapes to century-old processes and patterns.

The Dynamic Roles of Technology, Labor, and Government

A wide array of technological innovations became available to basin farmers after the Second World War. As during World War I, high wartime prices and a seemingly unlimited demand for farm products encouraged rapid adoption of technological advances, but while a postwar slump in farm prices and the Great Depression delayed the adoption of innovations in the 1920s and 1930s, no such letdown came in the late 1940s or 1950s: wartime prosperity continued (Rasmussen 1962, p. 579). An ongoing, expanding foreign market and domestic price supports for many commodities enabled farmers to purchase massive new machinery and to employ the sophisticated techniques and products of a major new field of endeavor: agricultural chemistry. Local farming lost much of its distinction and grew more and more like farming elsewhere in the Central Valley and the West, as basin farms became interlinked with world industry in order to receive the benefits of innovations in mechanization, irrigation, frost prevention, plant science, fertilization, pest and weed control, and animal husbandry. Developments in laboratories around the world were eagerly applied to basin farming, and the effects were awesome. New systems of pipes, sprinklers, and drip hoses were tested for irrigation; helicopters and airplanes were integrated into farm operations, performing anything from seeding and spraying to frost prevention; huge, powerful tractors towed an array of ingenious implements across the fields, and an array of smaller engines were installed for other purposes ranging from pumping to frost prevention. Chemists produced new lines of potent chemicals to control weeds and insects, fertilize the soil, or accelerate plant growth and ripening. Plant-genetics research produced new crops that were better suited to basin conditions and that yielded better or commanded higher market prices, while artificial breeding produced new and more productive livestock.

The most significant trend of recent years has been the application of technology to meet the needs of technology, a dramatic reflection of the heavy dependence of basin farmers upon machines and chemicals as fewer and fewer people work the land. One example would be the cultivation of plants bred specifically to be harvested by machine, such as canning tomatoes (grown near Yettem) and some varieties of cotton and fruits. Such innovations have gradually reduced the seasonal demand for farm workers in some areas, most notably the basin's cotton regions, where machines have taken over not only harvesting but weed control as well. When basin farming is fully mechanized, the social and economic problems associated with agricultural labor may disappear; technology will once again have served to alleviate the symptoms of a problem without actually confronting its causes. For the time being, however, very large numbers of farm workers are still needed for the citrus and grape harvests and for other assorted activities. In 1977 a minimum of 26,570 people were employed in basin fields and orchards on a wage or piecework basis (in March), and farm employment rose to a high of 48,460 in July; the fluctuation in labor demand amounted to more than 20,000 jobs in just four months (State of California Employment Data Research Division 1977). The problems inherent to cyclical, large-scale employment and unemployment are clearly unresolved, although public assistance (unemployment benefits, welfare, and food stamps) has finally been made available to most farm workers and their families. The labor camps that were once scattered across the countryside have all but disappeared; basin farmers have responded to newly stringent government regulation of wages and living conditions by removing, rather than renovating, housing facilities for seasonal workers. A large proportion of the basin's farm workers now live in densely packed rural subdivisions, such as Plainview, or in segregated sections of rural towns. Others remain migratory, as was the rule prior to the depression, and many are still recruited illegally from Mexico to complement or compete with the local work force.

As farming grew more complex, local initiative and cooperative efforts were no longer able to confront all of the problems present. Government regulation of the quantity and quality of agricultural production increased, as did government's role as farm advisor and farm monitor. When prices fall, public subsidies now shore up the incomes of farmers and farm corporations by means of crop insurance and price supports. When foreign products threaten to steal national markets, embargoes are imposed to protect American farmers. Public money has been paid to basin farmers—including several very wealthy ones— *not* to grow certain crops, under the auspices of such programs as the 1959 Soil Bank and the 1970 Crop Set-Aside Program, which were designed to protect the soil and curtail excess production. Public funds have also been used to buy up certain surplus commodities (wheat, cotton) to guarantee profits in years of market glut. Much government intervention has come in response to the pleas of farmers, although certain government policies and regulations have been loudly condemned by farmers and may appear to be detrimental to the farming situation. In any case, the role of government has been extremely important in the maintenance of farming—and its continued transformation—in the Tulare Lake Basin, as throughout the entire nation. The regional dominance of large farms has been enhanced by state and federal "force-feeding" of large farmers and farm corporations: by the government's providing huge crop subsidies and abundant, cheap irrigation water; by its thwarting the operation of any processes (including those specified in the Reclamation Act) that might have eroded corporate profits or expansion—processes such as those that eventually supported the development and success of small farms in the basin after the wheat-boom era.

> Is this an inevitable development? Is it possible that there is no stemming the tide of an evolution toward corporate control of agriculture? There is no real evidence that this is the case; government policies with respect to tax laws, agricultural subsidies and farm labor have been potent forces affecting the growth of large-scale and corporate farming. This growth cannot therefore be said to be natural; it is the result of force-feeding, of the injection of fiscal hormones, if you will. If the growth of corporate farming can be force-fed, so too can the time-honored traditions of American life. (Goldschmidt 1975, p. 175)

Farm Organization and Farm Landscapes

Prior to the depression, the spread of intensified agriculture usually resulted in a net increase of settlement, a proliferation of farmsteads and of rural facilities. Since the depression, agricultural progress has usually involved the emergence of fewer and larger farms and the simplification of rural landscapes: the abandonment and gradual disintegration of farmsteads and packinghouses, the tearing up of old fences and ornamental plantings, windbreaks and the remaining vestiges of the natural flora. In part this has been due to the emergence of corporate farms, larger in their scale of operations than even the bonanza wheat farms of a century ago. The disappearance of rural farmsteads has been partly mitigated by a proliferation of rural nonfarm dwellings and by the arrival of family-scale dairy and citrus operations from the Los Angeles Basin, but the traditional correlation between irrigated agriculture and densely clustered farmsteads is no longer evident.

The same processes that worked to consolidate more farmland in the hands of each operator have severely affected the processing and marketing aspects of dairying, fruit raising, and general farming. Processing and marketing facilities are fewer and larger than in the past: for example, more than 75 percent of the basin's citrus crop is handled by a single marketing firm, Sunkist, and 80 percent of its cotton is ginned and sold by only four firms (Zimrick 1976, p. 241). Advances in mechanization and transportation have increased the service area of each processor, and rail transport to markets has been replaced by the more flexible use of trucks (Bennett 1964, pp. 21–36). The market for the basin's products is now worldwide, even for such perishable crops as table grapes, which are shipped or flown to buyers as far away as Europe and Southeast Asia.

Basin orchardists received an unexpected boon when their primary competitors in citrus production, Los Angeles and Orange County farmers, lost tremendous acreage to urban expansion. Innovations in irrigation and frost prevention facilitated the expansion of basin orchards, and soon the remainder of the thermal belt was planted to citrus groves. Some of the expansion was made by citrus growers from the Los Angeles Basin and some by agricultural businesses and financial corporations that merely saw Tulare County orange groves as a promising investment. In either case, managers were generally hired to operate the orchards, or neighboring farmers were paid to do so (Opitz 1966, p. 3). Deciduous orchard acreage also expanded, both on the Kings Delta and in new areas west of the basin trough, where stone fruits and nuts were planted in response to strong markets and abundant irrigation water from the new canal (table 19). The dramatic increase of orchard acreage on the eastern flank of the basin is evident on contemporary maps of the area as well as in the landscape; on the Kings fan, however, recent expansion has not yet caught up with the past extent of permanent plantings (fig. 59). The scale of orchard operations is much larger than it once was: a family may need 75 or 100 acres of citrus trees to survive financially, or much larger acreages of deciduous trees, depending upon the local prices of irrigation water and the varieties of fruits grown. The orchards themselves are larger, too, and typically include several parcels planted to different kinds of trees and vines. Farmsteads are still simple, even austere; sometimes a

TABLE 19

Acres in Orchards and Vineyards, 1945–1974

Year	Kings County	Tulare County
1945	16,477	131,342
1954	7,572	132,075
1964	10,043	194,719
1974	16,422	222,447

SOURCES: U.S.D.C. Bureau of the Census 1946; 1956; 1967; 1977.

pump house or barn remains, usually used for equipment storage although the equipment inventory is still relatively small because non-cultivation techniques and sprinkler irrigation have been adopted and hand labor is still relied upon at harvest time. Migrant-labor housing, once an important element of orchard landscapes, has nearly all been torn down in the past decade.

Automation, low milk prices, and consolidation brought a reduction in the number of dairies in the basin until the mid-1960s, when a number of Los Angeles dairy firms decided to relocate there, primarily within the established dairying districts. These new operations are striking in their modern appearance, their complete lack of such relict forms as wooden fences, tank houses, and barns. Most have walk-through milking barns and adjacent milk houses that enclose refrigerated bulk milk tanks. Beside the barn are metal bins that dispense feed concentrates to cattle during milking; baled hay and piles of feed concentrates are stored in the open under tarps or pole-barn shelters. The scale of dairying has grown tremendously, while the number and proportion of farms that engage in any form of dairying has declined sharply (table 20). Cows are kept on drylots, enclosures a few hundred feet across surrounded by metal fences and partly shaded by metal awnings. The bare lots, built of mounded earth to promote drainage, stand out above the flat terrain. Alfalfa and corn may be grown on surrounding fields, and some pasturage is usually maintained for dry cows and heifers. Many dairies buy all of their feed, however, sometimes from out of state. Housing on the new dairies resembles small suburban tracts: three or four identical ranch-style houses are usually provided for milkers and their families, and another, larger home for the owner or manager. The houses are arranged in a row facing the road, and equipment lots, sheds, and fuel-storage tanks are nearby. Older dairies still retain signs of their past: there are wooden fences, barns, and tank houses, and the homes of the owners and hired milkers are older, less uniform, less rigidly aligned. Even on older dairies, though, the milking barn has usually

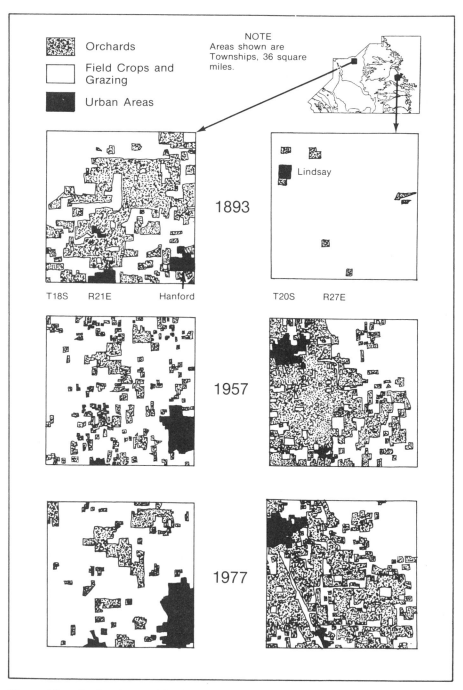

Figure 59. *Orchards near Hanford and near Lindsay, 1893, 1957, and 1977.* The increase of orchard acreage on the eastern flank of the Basin is vividly apparent in the Lindsay area, but contemporary orchard expansion has not yet caught up with the past extent of permanent plantings in the Hanford area. (Sources: U.S.D.I. Geological Survey, 7.5' series; Tulare County Agricultural Commissioner 1977; State of California Department of Water Resources 1974.)

TABLE 20

Characteristics and Production of Dairy Farms, 1945–1974

	Kings County	Tulare County
Farms reporting milk cows kept		
1945	68%	50%
1959	36	17
1974	18	6
Average number of cows per dairy farm		
1945	19	12
1959	53	117
1974	197	276
Value of dairy products sold, per dairy farm		
1945	$5,148	$6,383
1959	21,830	44,362
1974	264,354	346,617

SOURCES: U.S.D.C. Bureau of the Census 1946; 1961b; 1977.

been modified to meet new requirements and to accomodate new equipment. Both new and old dairies commonly have adjacent sump holes for the collection of wastes.

Cotton is still the mainstay of the general farm in the Tulare Lake Basin, but cotton acreage fluctuates greatly. Cultivation expanded rapidly after the war as restrictions on nonfood cropping were removed, but in 1954 an allotment program was reinstated (Gregor 1962a, p. 396). Allotments were based upon a complex formula that took into account nationwide cotton acreage, yields, and the previous crop history of each farmer. Its effect was to reduce the amount of cotton grown on each farm and to increase the cultivation of other field crops and row crops—alfalfa, sugar beets, vegetables, and grains. Wheat, barley, and sugar beets became especially widespread because their production was subsidized. In 1956 cotton was subsidized as well, as competition with synthetic fibers on the world market began to drive cotton prices down. In 1970 a voluntary Crop Set-Aside Program was instituted by the Agricultural Adjustment Act: cotton subsidies were limited, and most acreage limitations were dropped. A series of good market years has led to "wall-to-wall cotton" across the basin plains, despite the government's requests to limit cotton acreage in the interest of price stabilization (table 21), and cotton has replaced wheat as the primary pioneer crop on newly irrigated lands (Rodner 1949, p. 45).

The size of general farms has increased with consolidation and mechanization, especially in the western basin. Half of the cotton-based farms are between 100 and 500 acres in size, and nearly

TABLE 21

Harvested Cotton Acreage, 1940–1974

Year	Kings County	Tulare County
1940	31,856	74,868
1945	37,002	57,751
1950	115,568	179,678
1954	116,055	161,739
1959	101,135	156,840
1964	109,655	136,085
1969	80,300	109,511
1974	175,886	156,452

SOURCES: U.S.D.C. Bureau of the Census 1942, Agriculture, Vol. I; 1946; 1952b; 1956; 1961b; 1967; 1972; 1977.

one-fourth are larger than 1000 acres (Zimrick 1976, p. 182). A trait typical of general farms but rare on orchard or dairy farms is the control of several noncontiguous parcels of land: in the process of amalgamation and consolidation, many farmers have leased or purchased additional parcels of land some distance from their "home place." The feasibility of this sort of arrangement was enhanced by the public construction and maintenance of a dense network of rural roads. The larger the operation, the greater the spread of its land fragments (*California-Arizona Cotton* 1973). The landscape of the general farm has retained its traditional structure, except for the adoption of new building materials (stucco, aluminum) and the construction of larger facilities to store the great quantities of specialized machinery now needed (Tavernetti and Carter 1964, p. 4).

A more significant change in the general farm landscape and organization involved the evolution or implantation of the corporate farm. Corporate farming is associated with both orchards and general farms, but in the basin it more frequently represents an elaboration of the latter. The development of corporate farms in the Tulare Lake Basin is an outgrowth of the many forces that have favored large-scale, capital-intensive agriculture, including the historical development and success of land monopolies. The corporate farm is a point at which the industrial and business communities touch the land directly. There are no intermediaries, as represented by family farmers, local processors, or local marketing associations, between the industrial world and the land of the corporate farm. It is a self-contained and self-regulated institution. Very few mechanisms have developed in the basin to temper decisions or relay lessons of the past to corporations engaged in farming. It is as if factories have been set down, full grown, in the countryside and set in to maximize production without first building a relationship to the surrounding land and people. Land, labor, water, and energy are the raw materials; the world is the market. Corporate farms are often run by boards of directors, which may include as members "officials of banks, publishers of newspapers, and politicians; and . . . have interlocking associations with ship-owner associations, public utilities corporations, and transportation companies" (Steinbeck 1938, p. 10). The corporate farm is as tightly organized and centrally directed as the industries and institutions that support it. As such, it represents the ultimate product of the heritage of large-scale farming and the traditional association of farmers with bankers and commercial markets.

Wherever corporate farming exists, the old landscapes are wiped away, and the power of the corporation is expressed far beyond the boundaries of its fields. The most favorable region for the growth or implantation of corporate farms in the basin has been the west side, where large-scale agricultural endeavors and land monopolies have been characteristic from the beginning. South of the early-intensified Kings Delta and west of Tulare County's hearths of intensive farming, agriculture has traditionally been a more expensive and expansive undertaking, with larger acreages needed to offset the higher costs of water, mechanization, and transportation. Here the new corporate farms range in size from 3,000 to over 50,000 acres. Because their primary crop is cotton, grown in rotation with such winter crops as barley, flax, wheat, and alfalfa, they resemble huge plantations rather than traditional basin farms. The center of operations is more institutional in appearance than even the ranch headquarters of the bonanza-wheat era. It consists of office buildings, equipment sheds, garages, machine and repair shops built of corrugated metal or cinder block, and equipment lots surrounded by high cyclone fences that hold an enormous collection of expensive specialized machinery: combines, cotton pickers, earthmovers, planters, trucks, tractors, and an array of specialized tools. Private airstrips, hangars, and airplanes (both crop dusters and Lear jets) are found near the headquarters of the larger corporate farms, serving operational functions as well as the far-flung transportation needs of management. These headquarters rarely double as homesteads, for the corporate directors and their families live in far-distant cities, and the local managers, supervisors, and laborers live in west side towns, such as Corcoran, Alpaugh, Stratford, and Kettleman City. Additional installations in the surrounding countryside include subsidiary equipment yards complete with repair shops and storage facilities: new kinds of landscapes, and peculiar to corporate operations.

Every aspect of farming, from planting to marketing, is under the corporate roof. Huge corporate cotton gins, canneries, mills, packinghouses, and warehouses are attached to the small towns of the corporate farming regions, and the growth and expansion of corporate farms have had dramatic effects upon these towns. Corcoran, especially, functions almost as a company town: many of its services and functions are intertwined with the operations of adjacent corporate farms, and in turn the farm corporations provide for town improvements and basic economic sustenance. With the trend toward corporate and other large-scale farm enterprises, cultural and economic poverty and social isolation may become more pronounced in the rural regions of the Tulare Lake Basin:

> If the production of agricultural goods is to become increasingly large-scale and corporation-dominated, rural communities as we have known them will cease to exist. Instead, the landscapes will be dotted by . . . company towns, made up of workers and overseers, together with such service personnel as the company chooses not to provide itself. Lacking any orientation to community and other sense of social belonging, the farmworker will find his interests increasingly identified with his union. In fact, the absentee and corporate owners will favor unions, because they will find, as industrialists readily do, that this makes for easier management. (Goldschmidt 1975, p. 174)

Regional Land-Use Patterns

Large tracts of basin farmland have been taken out of agricultural production since the war as a result of urban and suburban expansion and the construction of canals, highways, airports, and a military base, yet in the 1970s agricultural expansion still produced a net increase in cultivated acreage. Kings County farm acreage declined 18 percent between 1964 and 1969 but thereafter, because of new supplies of irrigation water, began to increase dramatically (U.S.D.C. Bureau of the Census 1972). Areas of most rapid expansion and intensification include the old lake bed and other regions still, at the end of the war, used for grazing and dryland farming (fig. 60). Field cropping has expanded more than orchards and now constitutes the predominant form of basin farming in terms of both acreage and value of production (Kings County Agricultural Commissioner 1974; Tulare County Agricultural Commissioner 1974). Field cropping even increased in Kings County, where it already represented 91 percent of agricultural land use in 1945, to 97 percent in 1974. Orchards have spread on the Kings Delta and on the newly cultivated lands of the southwestern basin, but orchard expansion has not kept pace with the rapid expansion of field cropping on the old lake bed. The proportions of Tulare County cropland planted to orchards and to field crops have remained the same, but farm acreage

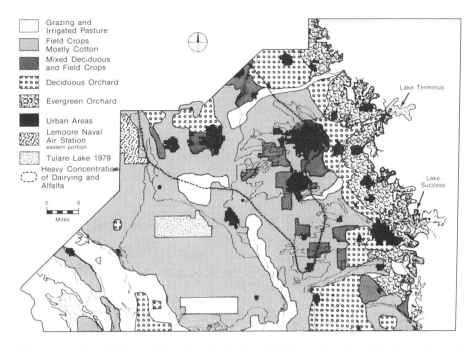

Figure 60. *Land Use, 1979.* In the 1970s the old lake bed has been the focus of most rapid agricultural expansion, due largely to new supplies of irrigation water. Field cropping has expanded more rapidly than orchards and now constitutes the primary agricultural land use in the basin. Urban and suburban expansion are proceeding even more swiftly, however, and these new uses have removed large tracts of the most productive basin land from farms. (Sources: Tulare County Agricultural Commissioner 1979; Kings County Agricultural Commissioner 1979; U.S.D.I. Geological Survey, 1:250,000 series.)

has declined slightly as a result of urban expansion: agricultural land was converted to other uses at a rate of 0.9 percent per year between 1964 and 1969, and the rate has certainly increased since then (Tulare County Planning Department 1975, p. 273).

Although areas identified as dairy districts, orchard districts, or general farming districts have become more internally homogenous in terms of land use and landscapes, some areas have continued to display a mixture of dairying, orchards, and general farming. Land-use diversity has remained most noticeable on the delta hearths of innovative farming: the Kings Delta north of Hanford, the Kaweah Delta north and east of Tulare, and along the fringes of the orchard district further north. In some instances the farms themselves are diversified, producing both deciduous orchard crops and row or field crops. Regional distinctions in land use are illustrated in table 22, a sampling of crop reports for ten irrigation districts located within townships selected to represent each major environmental and agricultural region of the basin. Figure 61a and b illustrates some typical cropping patterns of the

TABLE 22

Proportion of Land in Selected Crops, by Irrigation District

District	Year	Cereals	Feed and Forage	Cotton	Other Field	Fruits and Nuts	Vegetables
Alpaugh	1970	16%	28%	56%	2%		
Alta	1976	12	21	9	7	52%	4%
Corcoran	1962	42	18	34			
Empire—Westside	1975	74	1	22	3		
Ivanhoe	1976		0.2	0.2	0	99.4	0.2
Kings County Water District	1973		38	19	36	7	
Lindsay—Strathmore	1976	1	2	0.5		96	0.5
Pixley	1975		15	28	49	8	
Terra Bella	1976	7	3	1		88	1
Tulare	1976	39	22	31	2	5	1

SOURCE: U.S.D.I. Bureau of Reclamation 1976.

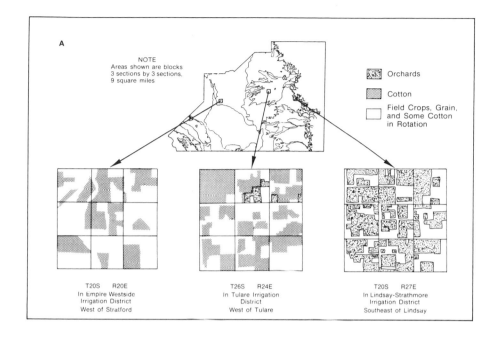

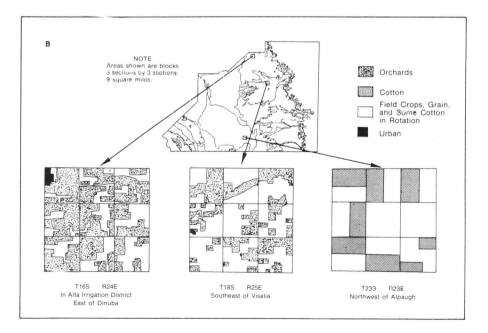

Figure 61a, b. *Regional Land-Use Patterns Today*. Distinctive regional landscapes are reflected in distinctive cropping patterns. The historical interplay between land and life in the distinctive subregions of the basin, the legacies of environmental variation and settlement history, are still apparent despite many years of homogenization and consolidation.

1970s for various regions of the basin. These maps reveal the distinctive contemporary landscape expressions of the historical interplay between natural environment, land-alienation policies and practices, technology, and settlement history in the diverse subregions of the Tulare Lake Basin.

Expanding Townscapes: A Changing Image and Identity

Tulare County is Big Country in Industry as well as Recreation and Agriculture. Located on the main line of two railroads and served by two major freeways, the urban areas of the county contain industrial parks which have expanded rapidly in the past decade. In addition to the many agriculturally-related industries, manufacturing in the county includes electronics, tools, printing, mobile homes, business forms, batteries, building materials, and consumer products. (Tulare County Chamber of Commerce 1977)

Many agricultural landscapes of the basin have been replaced by townscapes during the late 1960s and 1970s, signifying a dramatic change in the basin's settlement geography and regional character. The basin has prospered since the end of the war, and the regional population has nearly doubled. Nearly all of the growth has been in towns and cities that already had 2,500 inhabitants or more by 1950; smaller towns and rural settlements gained population as well, but their proportion of the basin's population declined. By 1970 more than half of the basin's people lived in urban areas, which have grown rapidly since 1960 (table 23). The main basin towns—Visalia, Tulare, Hanford, and Porterville—have become substantial communities; services employment has, indeed, surpassed agricultural employment in the basin since 1960 (Tulare County Planning Department 1975, p. 92). Urbanization has become the next step in the sequence of land uses, following the traditional succession of grazing, grain, and intensive cultivation (fig. 62). The spread of townscapes has replicated the spatial patterns of diffusion of previous land-use changes, expanding outward from the delta hearths where intensification, diversification, irrigation, and town founding originally began.

Concern for the dwindling agricultural space in the basin led to the institution of agricultural zoning under the Williamson Act of 1965, but attempts at urban restriction invariably fail in the face of economic pressure. The extension of pavement and buildings has done more than reshape the basin's landscape image: it has added heat, water vapor, and impurities to the regional atmosphere, altering local humidity, temperature and visibility (Hays 1974, pp. 59–60). Rural changes

TABLE 23

Differential Increase of Population, 1940–1975

	1940	1950	1960	1970	1975
Total population	142,320	196,032	218,357	252,932	280,516
Percent increase from					
preceding census	38	38	11	16	11
Urban:rural ratio	31:69	33:67	43:57	54:46	n.a.
Populations of major towns and cities:					
Corcoran	2,092	3,150	4,976	5,249	5,700
Dinuba	3,790	4,971	6,103	7,917	8,850
Exeter	3,883	4,078	4,264	4,475	4,970
Hanford	8,234	10,028	10,133	15,179	17,750
Lemoore	1,711	2,153	2,561	4,219	5,475
Lindsay	4,397	5,060	5,397	5,206	5,625
Porterville	6,270	6,904	7,991	12,602	14,350
Tulare	8,259	12,445	13,824	16,235	18,100
Visalia	8,904	11,749	15,791	24,268	34,750

SOURCES: U.S.D.C. Bureau of the Census 1942, Population, Vol. II; 1952a; 1961a; 1973; Tulare County Planning Department 1975, tables 3 6.

have promoted similar degradation of air quality, introducing dust, agricultural chemicals, and water vapor. Average dry-season humidity has increased markedly, and the winter fog blanket is thicker and more persistent than before (Vaudt 1972, pp. 4–8). Air pollution also has had noticeable effects upon crop productivity, both in terms of chemical actions upon plants and of reduced insolation (Coppock 1973). In the long run these changes may alter regional weather as well as the healthfulness of the regional climate.

Paralleling these changes in settlement patterns and environmental quality, there has been a significant change in the regional character of the Tulare Lake Basin. Fewer people than ever before are involved in agricultural relationships with the land: the proportion of the basin's work force employed as farmers and farm managers dropped to 5 percent by 1970, and the proportion employed as farm laborers fell from 17 percent in 1950 to 13 percent in 1970 in Kings County and from 23 percent to 17 percent in Tulare County (Tulare County Planning Department 1975, pp. 110–112). Few people are actively engaged in regional agriculture, and few are reaping the benefits of the accelerating transformation of rural landscapes and the rural economy. As the value of agricultural production climbs, proportionately less of the profits are reinvested in the basin. The greatest local investments have already been made: now, profits are funneled back into the global

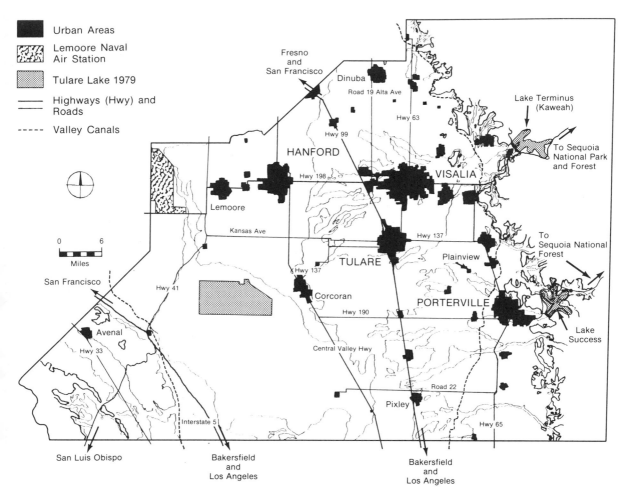

Figure 62. *Towns and Important Roads in the Basin Today.* Just as grain replaced grazing and, in turn, diversified farming displaced grain fields, urban areas are now expanding at the expense of farming on the Kings, Kaweah, and Tule fans. Similar processes of urban expansion and agricultural retreat occurred in the Santa Clara Valley and the Los Angeles Basin not so very long ago. Is it happening again? (Source; U.S.D.I. Geological Survey, 1:250,000 series.)

business and industrial system that supports basin farming and, increasingly, determines basin land uses.

In sharp contrast to the days of bonanza wheat farms, variations in the physical environment no longer figure strongly in descriptions of the basin: flat, hot, and monotonous, it is popularly said to benefit from its central location between the Pacific beaches and the lofty Sierra Nevada. Specific attitudes toward the countryside are influenced more by what crops are presently grown there than by soil quality, the availability of water, or the character of the rural landscape. With fertilizers, any soil can be made productive; with irrigation, there is plenty of water; with time the rural landscapes become more and more alike, throughout the basin as well as throughout the San Joaquin—or, indeed, the entire West. Most people garner these impressions from the window of a speeding automobile, which precludes detailed attention to the varied aspects of the basin's landscape. It is this general and ongoing alienation of people from the land which nourishes the pace of urbanization and corporate expansion.

Environmental Alteration

The native vegetation of the Tulare Lake Basin is almost completely gone now. Remnant species survive on the last remaining grazing lands at the basin's edge; along fence lines, canals, and streams; in abandoned farmsteads and fields; and intermingled with ornamental plantings in towns. The habitats of native animals have also been destroyed, and wildlife is scarce. Like native plants, a few wild creatures have found new niches in towns. Domesticated plants and animals have replaced the basin's native flora and fauna, but these depend upon the continued care of farmers for their survival. Many crop plants are completely cleared away at harvest, leaving the soil bare and exposed to the elements, interrupting the natural processes of soil formation and regeneration. Cropping practices and artificial irrigation have made the basin's soils—like its plants and animals—increasingly artificial. The soils retain their ability to respond well to cultivation, yet each year more irrigation water spreads more salts onto the basin soils. When standing water evaporates, the salts remain in the soil; they may eventually be leached into underground aquifers. Severe problems with soil salinization have not yet been experienced on a large scale, but salt accumulation continues.

Basin hydrology has suffered too. Since 1940 the water table has dropped rapidly. Until 1963 it fell about fifteen to twenty feet a year (Lantis, Steiner, and Karinen 1963, p. 403); this rate has since accelerated. Accompanying land subsidence has lowered parts of the basin twelve feet or more in elevation (Poland et al. 1975, pp. 11–32), and subsurface compaction has reduced the recharge capabilities of water-bearing layers. The introduction of large amounts of water from outside the basin, via the Friant-Kern Canal, has caused some rebound, but the effects of compaction are essentially irreversible (Lofgren and Klausing 1969, pp. 1–54).

10

Retrospect and Prospect

During the millennia preceding 1770, the people of the Tulare Lake Basin adjusted to the regional mosaic of land and life. Cultural processes that had evolved elsewhere either were adapted to fit the new environment or were replaced with processes and techniques developed at home in the basin. This regional adjustment to land and life did not prevent early inhabitants from causing considerable environmental change, yet because the people were relatively few in number and because they accepted the natural patterns of life in the basin, these changes were easily absorbed and did not weaken the basin's natural productivity.

About 200 years ago, however, the Tulare Lake Basin began to be subjected to a new sequence of alterations, as new ways of life and powerful technologies were imposed upon its richly diverse habitats. These new cultural processes had evolved in other lands and were

238

extremely disruptive to the human and natural environments upon which they encroached. In contrast to preceding occupation, the new dwellers began to alter forcefully the basin's natural patterns of land and life to fit imported economies and values. At first this new process of alteration proceeded with tremendous success. The basin's environments were modified by a technology that continued to grow in its capability to reshape the land according to the desires of people, and the results of this modification were rewarding to the human ingenuity that directed it. The basin's carrying capacity grew, and it proved itself well able to maintain the foreign ways of life that were imposed upon it and the foreign landscapes that rapidly spread across its lands. The initial relationship of people and their economy to the land—one of intimate and permanent attachment—has gradually been replaced by relationships of increasingly withdrawn detachment. Fewer and fewer people are concerned by the prospect that the basin's lands may not be able to continue to satisfy the desires and needs of all of its inhabitants, and fewer care that the basin's lands may one day finally give out, smothered by the intensive application of so many demands, technologies, and materials that had been imported from other environments.

The spatial dimensions of regional landscape evolution in the Tulare Lake Basin are summarized and recapitulated in a series of cartographic vignettes (fig. 63a–g).

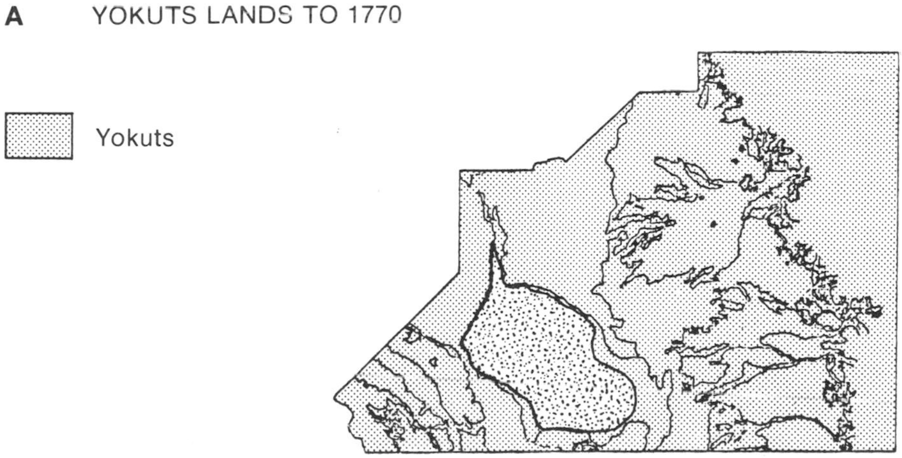

A   YOKUTS LANDS TO 1770

Yokuts

Figure 63.(a) *Yokuts Lands to 1770.* The Yokuts exploited the rich habitats of the basin fully, taking advantage of seasonal and regional variations in resources. By altering habitats, trading with distant groups, and carefully scheduling their seasonal migrations, the Yokuts established the densest nonagricultural populations in North America; still, they caused relatively minor changes in the natural environment.

B   INVASION, DEVASTATION, AND REORIENTATION
1770-1850

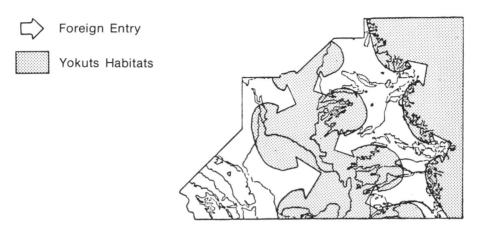

⟿ Foreign Entry

▨ Yokuts Habitats

(*b*) *Invasion, Devastation, and Reorientation, 1770–1850.* Spanish, Mexican, and American visitors from the 1770s onward not only killed or displaced Yokuts directly but also drastically altered the basin's plant and animal communities. Native communities were largely displaced by wild and domesticated exotic species introduced by foreigners, and the Yokuts were crowded out of the basin's richest habitats. Soon a rectangular survey was imposed, and the basin was ready for American settlement.

C   GRAZING AND AGRICULTURAL EXPERIMENTATION
1850-1870

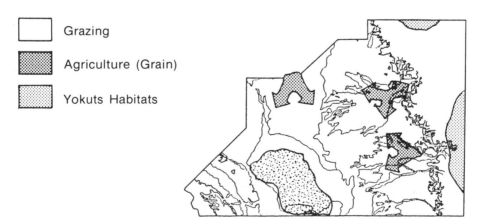

☐ Grazing

▨ Agriculture (Grain)

▨ Yokuts Habitats

(*c*) *Grazing and Agricultural Experimentation, 1850s–1870s.* Early American settlers let their herds of sheep and cattle and pigs roam across the entire basin, yet they preferred to live on alluvial fans and in the foothills. In the 1860s, farmers experimented with water diversion for irrigation and with a variety of new crops, including wheat. As the cattle economy weakened, small farms began to prosper; they spread onto the alluvial fans of the Kings, Kaweah, and Tule rivers.

D   RAILROADS AND WHEAT
               1870-1890

               Grain

               Diversified Farming
               (Irrigated)

               Grazing

               Railroads

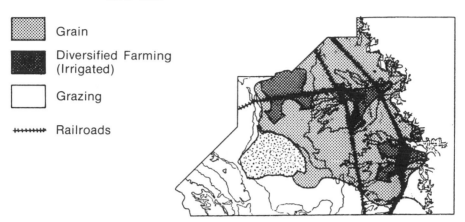

(*d*) *Railroads and Wheat, 1870s–1890s.* With the coming of the railroad in1872, the basin was firmly linked to the outside world; cheaply grown wheat could be shipped to world markets. Great bonanza wheat farms spread across the basin, even onto old alluvial lands at the basin's edge. As market demand and soils weakened, wheat was in turn displaced by diversified farming based upon intensive practices and dependent upon artificial irrigation, which spread across the recent alluvial lands of the Kings, Kaweah, and Tule fans, creating new landscapes characterized by smaller farms and permanent plantings.

E   IRRIGATION AND SMALL-FARM PROSPERITY
               1890-1920

               Intensive Agriculture
               Irrigated

               Grain

               Grazing

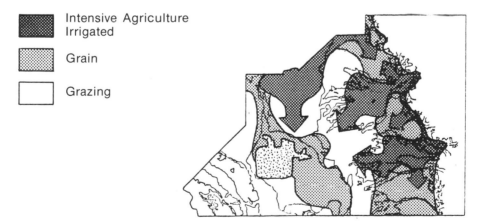

(*e*) *Irrigation and Small-Farm Prosperity, 1890s–1920s.* Increasing intensification of agriculture, involving locally based irrigation projects, dairying, and specialized cultivation of orchards and field crops, spread beyond the limits of the alluvial fans. A growing understanding of the natural potential of the basin and enhanced communications via new networks of roads and railroads symbolized this golden age of land and life in the Tulare Lake Basin.

F CONSOLIDATION AND REGIONAL SPECIALIZATION
1920-1940

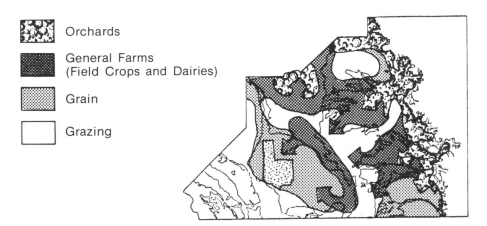

(*f*) *Consolidation and Regional Specialization, 1920s – 1940s.* With the depression and changing technologies, small family farms, especially those on the west side, found it increasingly difficult to compete against larger economies of scale. Regional simplification of cropping patterns accompanied the rise of agribusiness, bringing an areal specialization of production which was clearly evident in the subregional landscapes of the basin.

G URBANIZATION AND CORPORATE FARMS
1940-1980

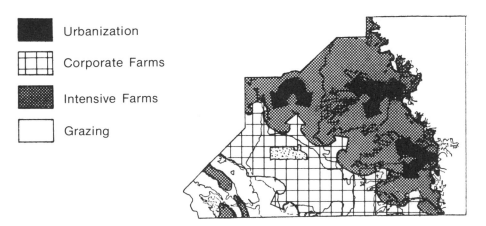

(*g*) *Urbanization and Corporate Farming, 1940s – 1980s.* Since World War II, the larger-scale agribusinesses have expanded at the expense of small farms. Intensive cultivation of the basin is complete as a result of new technologies, imported water, and imported investment. Urban land uses have begun to erode the agricultural base—especially upon the alluvial fans around Hanford, Visalia, Tulare, and Porterville—signaling the end of a regional identity.

Today, after fully two centuries of increasingly intensive exploitation by nonindigenous cultures and economies, the basin's most prominent landmarks are cultural creations or social traits rather than natural patterns. Towns have replaced Tulare Lake and the oak forests of the Kings and Kaweah deltas as regional symbols, but they are rather inferior substitutes. They have grown to be so very similar to small towns and cities throughout the American West that even local residents see very little that is distinctive about them: "He drove on, passing through the small towns, Fowler and Kingsburg, Goshen and Pixley, town after town, Famosa and Bakersfield, mixing them up, thinking one was the other" (Bezzerides 1938, p. 43). American occupation has served to homogenize the basin, to reshape it increasingly in the image of the rest of the San Joaquin Valley. The cultural and physical diversity and distinctiveness that once gave the Tulare Lake Basin an identity of its own have now been lost. The lake's waters have been stolen from it, and it is gone; the natural vegetation is all but gone as well. The countryside is no longer a refuge for wild things, for rural landscapes are as completely altered as townscapes. Landscapes created by centuries of close interrelationships between land and life have been cleared away, and new patterns have taken over—patterns distinguishable in degree, perhaps, but not in kind, from those of adjacent communities and regions.

To outsiders and residents alike, the regional identity of the Tulare Lake Basin has been severely diluted by this homogenization within the context of the world farm. People no longer speak of the Tulare Lake Basin or of the Tulare Valley, but rather the region must usually be described as "halfway between Fresno and Bakersfield." Even this may leave fellow Californians without a clear mental image of the region. The basin is now simply the southern end of a large whole, the San Joaquin Valley, which itself is only the southern end of the Great Central Valley—that vast flat area down the middle of the state, where there are very large farms and it gets far too hot in summer.

To those who take the time to look around them, however, the influences of history and distinctive local ecologies may still be detected in the landscapes of the Tulare Lake Basin.

APPENDIX I

Native Plants of the Tulare Lake Basin with Latin Binomials

From Philip A. Munz,
A California Flora (1963)

Tree Savanna

white oak	*Quercus lobata* Nee
blue oak	*Quercus douglasii* H. and A.
live oak	*Quercus wislizenia* A. D. C.

Riparian Forest

Arizona ash	*Fraxinus velatina* Torr.
California sycamore	*Platanus racemosa* Nutt.
Oregon ash	*Fraxinus latifolia* Benth.
walnut	*Juglandaceae californica* Wats.
	Juglandaceae hindsii (Jeps) Jeps
cottonwood	*Populus fremontii* Wats.
	Populus trichocapra T. and G.
willow	*Salix* spp. L.
California buckeye	*Aesculus californica* (Spach) Nutt.
white alder	*Alnus rhombifolia* Nutt.
California laurel	*Umbellularia californica* (H. and A.) Nutt.
tule	*Scirpus* spp. L.
nettle	*Utica* spp. L.

wild hemp   *Apocynum* spp. L.
wild blackberry   *Rubus* spp. L.
wild grape   *Vitis* spp. L.

Marsh

tule   *Scirpus acutus* Muhl.
bulrush   *Scirpus californicus* (C. A. Mey) Steud
cattail   *Typha latifolia* L.
                         Typha angustifolia L.
spike rush   *Heleocharis acicularis* (L.) R. and S.
sedges   *Carex* spp. L.

Prairie

purple needlegrass   *Stipa pulchra* Hitchc.
nodding needlegrass   *Stipa cernua* Steb. and Love
bluegrass   *Pea* spp. L.
California melic   *Melica imperfecta* Trin.
June grass   *Koeleria cristata* (L.) Pers.
foothill needlegrass   *Stipa lepida* Hitchc.
bromegrass   *Bromus* spp. L.
fescue   *Festuca* spp. L.
beardless wild rye   *Elymus triticoides* Buckl.
peppergrass   *Lepidum nitidum* Nutt.
plantain   *Plantago erecta* Morris
tarweeds   *Hemizonia* spp. DC.
matchweed   *Gutierrezia californica* (DC.) T. and G.
mariposa lily   *Calochortus* spp. Pursh
wild onion   *Allium* spp. L.
goldfield   *Baeria* spp. F. and M.
fiddle-neck   *Amsinckia* spp. Lehm.
California poppy   *Eschscholzia* spp. Cham.
buttercup   *Ranunculus* spp. L.
beardtongue   *Penstemon* spp. Mitch.
California sagebrush   *Artemesia californica* Less.
juniper   *Juniperus californica* Carr
wild buckwheat   *Eriogonium fasciculatum* Benth.
golden aster   *Chrysopsis villosa* (Pursch.) Nutt.
mule fat   *Baccharis viminea* DC.

Desert Saltbush

desert saltbush	*Artiplex polycarpa* (Torr.) Wats.
peppergrass	*Lepidum latipes* Hook
	Lepidum nitidum Nutt.

Spiny Saltbush

spiny saltbush	*Artiplex spinifera* Macbr.

Lowland Heath

seepweed	*Suaeda moquini* Green
alkali heath	*Frankenia grandifolia* Cham. and Schlect
pickleweed	*Allenrolfea occidentalis* (Wats.) Kuntze
salt grass	*Distichlis spicata* (L.) Greene

APPENDIX II

Native Animals of the Tulare Lake Basin with Latin Binomials

From Raymond E. Hall and Keith R. Kelson, *The Mammals of North America* (1959); Peter B. Moyle, *Inland Fishes of California* (1976); and Joseph Grinnell, *A Distributional List of the Birds of California* (1915)

Mammals

pronghorn antelope	*Antilocapra americana* Ord.
tule elk	*Cervus nannodes* Merriam
mule deer	*Damahemionus californicus odocoileus* Caton
grizzly bear	*Ursus horribilis californicus* Merriam
black bear	*Ursus americanus californiensis* J. Miller
grey wolf	*Canis lupis youngi* Goldman
valley coyote	*Canis latrans ochropus* Eschscholtz
mountain lion	*Felis concolor californica* May
bobcat	*Lynx rufus californicus* Mearns
gray fox	*Urocyon cinereoargenteus californicus* Mearns
kit fox	*Vulpes macrotis mutica* Merriam

raccoon	*Procyon lotor psora* Gray
badger	*Taxidea taxus neglecta* Mearns
blacktail hare	*Lepus californicus richardsonii* Bachman
Audubon cottontail	*Sylvilogus audobonii vallicola* Nelson
ground squirrel	*Citellus* spp.
chipmunk	*Eulamias* spp.
porcupine	*Erethizon dorsatum epixanthum* Brandt
skunk	*Spilogale phenax gracilis* Merriam
	Mephitis mephitis holznen Mearns
weasel	*Mustela frenata xanthogenys* Gray
gopher	*Thomomys* spp.
beaver	*Castor canadensis subauratus* Taylor
river otter	*Lutra canadensis brevipilosus* Grinnel
mink	*Mustela vison aestuarina* Grinnel

Fish

Sacramento perch	*Archoplites interruptus* Girard
Tule perch	*Hysterocarpus traski* Gibbons
Sacramento sucker	*Catostomus occidentalis* Ayres
hitch	*Lavinia exilicauda* Baird and Girard
thick-tailed chub	*Gila crassicauda* Baird and Girard
Sacramento blackfish	*Orthodon microlepidotus* Ayres
Sacramento splittail	*Pogonichthys macrolepidotus* Ayres
Sacramento squawfish	*Ptychocheilus grandis* Ayres
rainbow trout	*Salmo gairdneri* Richardson
white sturgeon	*Acipenser transmontanus* Richardson
steelhead rainbow	*Salmo gairdneri gairdneri* Richardson
Chinook salmon	*Oncorhynchus tshawytscha* Walbaum
prickly sculpin	*Cottus asper* Richardson
hardhead	*Mylopharodon Conocephalus* Baird and Girard
California roach	*Hesperoleucus symmetricus* Baird and Girard
speckled dace	*Phinichthys osculus* Girard

Birds

California roadrunner	*Geococcyx californianus* Lesson
Costa hummingbird	*Calypte costae* Bourcier
gilded flicker	*Colaptes chrysoides mearnsi* Ridgeway
quail	*Phainopopla nitens* Swainson

burrowing owl	*Speotyto cunicularia hypogaea* Bonaparte
California horned lark	*Otocoris alpestris actia* Oberholser
western meadowlark	*Sturnella neglecta* Audubon
western grasshopper sparrow	*Ammodramus savannarum bimaculatus* Swainson
turkey vulture	*Cathartes aura septentrionalis* Wied
American sparrow hawk	*Falco sparverius* Linnaeus
western mourning dove	*Zenaidura macroura marginella* Woodhouse
western kingbird	*Tyrannus verticalis* Say
western mockingbird	*Mimus ployglottos leucopterus* Vigors
band-tailed pigeon	*Columba fasciata fasciata* Say
screech owl	*Otus asio queicinus* Grinnel
nuttall woodpecker	*Dryobates nuttallii* Gambel
bushtit	*Psaltriparis minimus californicus* Ridgeway
valley quail	*Lophortyx californica vallicola* Ridgeway
long-eared owl	*Asio wilsonlanus* Lesson
willow woodpecker	*Dryobates pubescens turati* Malherbe
tree swallow	*Iridoprocne bicolor* Viellot
western crow	*Corvus brachyrhynchos hesperis* Ridgeway
California yellow warbler	*Dendroica aestiva brewsteri* Grinnel
great blue heron	*Ardeaherodias hyperonca* Oberholser
common egret	*Herodias egretta* Gmelin
Canadian goose	*Branta canadensis canadensis* Linnaeus
mallard	*Anas platyrhynchos* Linnaeus
marsh hawk	*Circus hudsonius* Linnaeus
sandhill crane	*Grus mexicana* Muller
redwing blackbird	*Agelarius phoeniceus neutralis* Ridgeway
common loon	*Gavia immer* Brunnich
white pelican	*Pelicanus erythrorhynchos* Gmelin
bald eagle	*Haliacetus leucocephalus leucocephalus* Linnaeus
American osprey	*Pahdionhaliaetus carolinensis* Gmelin
American coot	*Fulica americana* Gmelin
California gull	*Larus californicus* Lawrence
wood duck	*Aix sponsa* Linnaeus
belted kingfisher	*Ceryle alcyon caurina* Grinnel

BIBLIOGRAPHY

Aikens, C. Melvin. 1978. "The Far West." In *Ancient Native Americans*, edited by Jesse D. Jennings. San Francisco: W. H. Freeman.

Alexander, B. S., George Mendell, and George Davidson. 1874. *Irrigation of the San Joaquin, Tulare, and Sacramento Valleys, California*. House Executive Document no. 290, serial 1615, 43rd Cong., 1st sess.

Allen, W. W., and R. B. Avery. 1893. *California Gold Book: First Nugget, Its Discovery and Discoverers, and Some of the Results Proceeding Therefrom*. San Francisco: Donohue and Henneberry.

Anderson, Oscar E. 1953. *Refrigeration in America: A History of a New Technology and Its Impact*. Princeton: Princeton University Press.

Applegate, Richard B. 1978. *Atishwin: The Dream Helper in South-Central California*. Socorro, N.M.: Ballena.

Audubon, John James, and John Bachman. 1851. *The Viviparous Quadrupeds of North America*. Vol. III. New York: V. G. Audubon.

Audubon, John W. 1906. *Audubon's Western Journal, 1849–1950: Being the MS Record of a Trip from New York to Texas, and an Overland Journey through New Mexico and Arizona to the Gold-fields of California*. Cleveland: Arthur H. Clark.

Austin, Mary. 1903. *The Land of Little Rain*. Boston: Houghton, Mifflin.

———. 1906. *The Flock*. Boston: Houghton, Mifflin.

———. 1927. *The Lands of the Sun*. Cambridge, Mass.: Riverside.

———. 1932. *Earth Horizon*. Boston: Houghton, Mifflin.

Baker, Howard. 1931. *Orange Valley*. New York: Coward-McCann.

Balls, Edward K. 1962. *Early Uses of California Plants*. California Natural History Guide no. 10. Berkeley and Los Angeles: University of California Press.

Bancroft, H. H. 1888. *History of California*. Vol. 4. San Francisco: The History Co.

Bandini, Jose. 1951. *A Description of California in 1828 by Jose Bandini*, translated by Doris Marion Wright. Berkeley: Friends of the Bancroft Library.

Barker, John. 1955. *San Joaquin Vignettes: The Reminiscences of Captain John Barker*, edited by William H. Boyd and Glendon J. Rodgers. Bakersfield: Kern County Historical Society.

Barrett, S. A., and E. W. Gifford. 1900. "Miwok Material Culture." *Bulletin of the Public Museum of the City of Milwaukee* 2 (4).

Barton, Stephen. 1874. "Early History of Tulare." *Visalia Weekly Delta*, June–November.

Baumhoff, Martin A. 1963. "Ecological Determinants of Aboriginal California Populations." *University of California Publications in American Archaeology and Ethnology* 49 (2): 155–236.

Baur, John E. 1965. "Francis Ziba Branch." In *The Mountain Men and the Fur Trade of the Far West*, edited by LeRoy R. Hafen. Glendale: Arthur H. Clark.

Bean, Lowell J. 1973. "Social Organizations in Native California." In *Antap: California Indian Political and Economic Organization*, edited by Lowell J. Bean and Thomas F. King. Ramona, Calif.: Ballena.

Bean, Lowell J., and Thomas F. King, eds. 1974. *Antap: California Indian Political and Economic Organization*. Ramona, Calif.: Ballena.

Bean, Lowell J., and H. Lawton, 1976. "Some Explanations for the Rise of Cultural Complexity in Native California with Comments on Proto-Agriculture and Agriculture." In *Native Californians,* edited by Lowell J. Bean and Thomas C. Blackburn. Ramona, Calif.: Ballena.

Beck, Warren A., and Ynez Haase. 1974. *Historical Atlas of California.* Norman: University of Oklahoma Press.

Becker, Robert H. 1964. *Disenos of California Ranchos: Maps of Thirty-Seven Land Grants*. San Francisco: Book Club of California.

Bell, Horace. 1927. *Reminiscences of a Ranger on Early Times in Southern California*. Santa Barbara: Wallace Hebberd.

Bennett, Robert M. 1964. *Interstate Hauling of California-Arizona Fresh Fruits and Vegetables by Rail and Truck*. U.S.D.A. Marketing Research Report no. 673. Washington, D.C.: Government Printing Office.

Bezzerides, A. T. 1938. *Long Haul.* New York: Carrick and Evans.

Blake, William P. 1853. *Geological Report of Exploration and Surveys for a Railroad Route from the Mississippi River to the Pacific Ocean, under R. S. Williamson*. Washington, D.C.: U.S. Department of War.

Bolton, Herbert E. 1935. *In the South San Joaquin Ahead of Garces*. Bakersfield: Kern County Historical Society.

Bookman and Edmonston. 1972. *Report on Investigation of the Water Resources of the Kaweah Delta Water Conservation District, Visalia, California*. Glendale: Bookman and Edmonston.

Botsford and Hammond. 1885. *Tulare County California: A Truthful Description of Its Climate, Soil, Towns, and Vast Agricultural and Other Resources*. Visalia: Botsford and Hammond.

Bower, C. A., and Milton Freeman. 1957. "Saline and Alkaline Soils." In *Soils: U.S.D.A. Yearbook of Agriculture*. Washington, D.C.: Government Printing Office.

Bowles, Samuel. 1869. *Our New West: Records of Travel between the Mississippi River and the Pacific Ocean*. Hartford: Hartford Publishing.

Bowman, J. N. 1958. "Index of the Spanish-Mexican Private Land Grant Records and Cases of California." Bancroft Library, University of California, Berkeley.

Brewer, William H. 1949. *Up and Down California in 1860–1864: The Journal of William H. Brewer, Professor of Agriculture in the Sheffield Scientific School from 1864 to 1903.* Edited by Francis P. Farquhar. Berkeley and Los Angeles: University of California Press.

Bright, John. 1856. In *Los Angeles Star*, May 10.

"Britton and Rey's 1857 Map of California." Drawn by George H. Goddard. Bancroft Library, University of California, Berkeley.

Brown, J. L. 1941. *The Story of Kings County, California.* Berkeley: Lederer, Street and Zeus.

Brown, Robert R. 1940. *History of Kings County; Narrative and Biographical.* Hanford: A. H. Cawston.

Browne, J. Ross. 1869. *Resources of the Pacific Slope: A Statistical and Descriptive Summary.* New York: D. Appleton.

———. 1872. *Reclamation of Marsh and Swamp Lands and Projected Canals for Irrigation in California.* San Francisco: Alta California.

———. 1873. "Agricultural Capacity of California." *Overland Monthly* 10 (4): 297–314.

Bryant, Edwin. 1967. *What I Saw in California: Being the Journal of a Tour in the Years 1846, 1847.* Minneapolis: Ross and Haines.

Burcham, Levi T. 1957. *California Range Land: An Historical-Ecological Study of the Range Resources of California.* Sacramento: State Department of Natural Resources.

California-Arizona Cotton. 1973. "Expansion through Dispersed Cotton Fields." July, 1973, pp. 8–10.

California Immigrant Union. 1875. *All about California and the Inducements to Settle There.* San Francisco: Bancroft.

California State Agricultural Society. 1869. *Transactions of the California State Agricultural Society during the Year 1868.* Sacramento: State Printing Office.

———. 1875. *Transactions of the California State Agricultural Society during the Year 1874.* Sacramento: State Printing Office.

Camp, Walter. 1921. *Cotton Culture in the San Joaquin Valley, California.* U.S.D.A. Department Circular no. 164. Washington, D.C.: Government Printing Office.

Capp, Charles S. 1873. "Cotton Culture." *Transactions of the California State Agricultural Society during the Year 1872.* Sacramento: State Printing Office.

Carson, James H. 1852. *Recollections of the California Mines and a Description of the Great Tulare Valley: Account of the Early Discoveries of Gold, with Anecdotes and Sketches of California.* Reprint. Oakland: Biobooks, 1950.

Carson, Kit. 1851. "Copy of a Letter By Kit Carson." *Los Tulares: Quarterly Bulletin of the Tulare County Historical Society* 1960 (1): 3.

Centennial Home Tour Committee. 1972. *Tulare's Heritage of Homes: A Guide for the Conducted Tour of These Historic Homes.* Tulare: Advance Register.

Central Pacific Railroad Company. 1876. *Annual Report of the Board of Directors.* Sacramento: Central Pacific Railroad Company.

———. 1885. *Annual Report of the Board of Directors*. Sacramento: Central Pacific Railroad Company.

Chapman, H., and J. A. Gordon. 1867. *Map of Tulare County, California*. San Francisco: Britton and Rey.

Cleland, Robert Glass. 1951. *The Cattle on a Thousand Hills: Southern California, 1850–1880*. San Marino, Calif.: Huntington Library.

Cogswell, Howard L. 1977. *Water Birds of California*. Berkeley, Los Angeles, and London: University of California Press.

Coit, J. E. 1927. *Citrus Fruits*. New York: Macmillan.

Cone, Mary. 1876. *Two Years in California*. Chicago: S. C. Griggs.

Conkling, Roscoe P., and Margaret B. Conkling. 1947. *The Butterfield Overland Mail, 1857–1869*. Glendale: Arthur H. Clark.

Cook, A. J. 1913. *California Citrus Culture*. Sacramento: State Department of Agriculture.

Cook, O. F. 1925. "Cotton Improvement Laws in California." *Journal of Heredity* 16 (Sept.): 335–338.

Cook, S. F. 1955*a*. "The Aboriginal Population of the San Joaquin Valley, California." *University of California Anthropological Records* 16 (2): 31–80.

———. 1955*b*. "The Epidemics of 1830–1833 in California and Oregon." *University of California Publications in American Archaeology and Ethnology* 43:303–326.

———. 1960. "Colonial Expeditions to the Interior of California: Central Valley, 1800–1820." *University of California Anthropological Records* 16 (6): 238–292.

———. 1962. "Expeditions to the Interior of California: Central Valley, 1820–1840." *University of California Anthropological Records* 20 (5): 151–214.

———. 1976. *The Conflict between the California Indian and White Civilization*. Berkeley, Los Angeles, and London: University of California Press.

Cooper, Erwin. 1968. *Aqueduct Empire: A Guide to Water in California, Its Turbulent History, and Its Management Today*. Glendale: A. H. Clarke.

Coppock, Raymond H. 1973. *Air Pollution: A Pamphlet on Environmental Concerns*. Berkeley: University of California Division of Agricultural Sciences.

Coy, O. C. 1973. *California County Boundaries*. Rev. ed. Fresno: Valley Publishers.

Crawford, L. A., and E. Hard. 1940. *Types of Farming in California*. University of California Agricultural Experiment Station Bulletin no. 654.

Crofutt, G. A. 1879. *New Overland Tourist and Pacific Coast Guide*. Vol. II. Chicago: Overland.

Cronise, Titus Fey. 1868. *The Natural Wealth of California*. San Francisco: H. H. Bancroft.

Curtis, Edward S. 1907–1930. *The North American Indian: Being a Series of Volumes Picturing and Describing the Indians of the United States and Alaska*. Reprint. New York: Jonson, 1970.

Cutter, Donald C. 1950. "Spanish Explorations of California's Central Valley." Ph.D. dissertation, University of California, Berkeley.

Daggett, Stuart. 1922. *Chapters on the History of the Southern Pacific*. New York: Ronald Press.

Dana, C. W. 1861. *The Great West; or, The Garden of the World*. Boston: Thayer and Eldridge.

Dana, Samuel, and Myron Kruger. 1958. *California Lands*. Washington, D.C.: American Forestry Association.

Davis, G. H., J. H. Green, F. H. Olmstead, and D. W. Brown. 1959. *Groundwater Conditions and Storage Capacity in the San Joaquin Valley, California*. U.S.G.S. Water Supply Paper no. 1469. Washington, D.C.: Government Printing Office.

Davis, James T. 1961. *Trade Routes and Economic Exchange among the Indians of California*. University of California Archaeological Survey Report no. 54.

Dean, Gerald, and Gordon King. 1970. *Projection of California Agriculture to 1980 and 2000: Potential Impact of San Joaquin Valley West Side Development*. University of California Agricultural Experiment Station Giannini Research Report no. 312.

Derby, George H. 1852. *Report to the Secretary of War, Communications in Compliance with a Resolution of the Senate: A Report on the Tulare Valley*. Senate Executive Document no. 110, 32nd Cong., 1st sess.

DeRoos, Robert. 1948. *The Thirsty Land: The Story of the Central Valley Project*. Stanford: Stanford University Press.

Doyle, C. B. 1942. "Climate and Cotton." In *Climate and Man: U.S.D.A. Yearbook of Agriculture*. Washington, D.C.: Government Printing Office.

Drury, Aubrey. 1935. *California: An Intimate Guide*. New York: Harper and Brothers.

Ducor Chamber of Commerce. 1915. "Ducor, Tulare County, California: Coming City of the Early Orange Belt." Historical Clippings File, Tulare County Library, Visalia.

Eaton, Frank M. 1935. *Boron in Soils and Irrigation Waters and Its Effects on Plants*. U.S.D.A. Technical Bulletin no. 448. Washington, D.C.: Government Printing Office.

Eigenheer, Richard A. 1976. "Early Perceptions of Agricultural Resources in the Central Valley of California." Ph.D. dissertation, University of California, Davis.

Eilsen, Elisebeth. 1947. "The Central Valley Project: 1947." *Economic Geography* 23 (1): 23–31.

Elliott, Wallace W. 1883. *History of Tulare County, California, with Illustrations*. San Francisco: Wallace W. Elliott.

Elsasscr, A. B. 1960. *The Archaeology of the Sierra Nevada in California and Nevada*. University of California Archaeological Survey Report no. 51, pp. 1–93.

Engelhardt, Zephyrin. 1912. *The Missions and Missionaries of California*.

Vol. II and III; *Upper California*. San Francisco: James H. Barry.

Estudillo, Jose Maria. 1819. "Vista de la Sierra que llaman Nevada de los Tulares . . . y . . . rancherias de indios gentiles y tierras reconocidas." Bancroft Library, University of California, Berkeley.

Fabian, Bentham. 1869. *The Agricultural Lands of California*. San Francisco: H. H. Bancroft.

Farnham, B. J. 1851. *Life, Adventures, and Travels in California*. New York: Cornish, Lamport.

Farquhar, Francis P., ed. 1930. *Up and Down California in 1860–1864: The Journal of William H. Brewer, Professor of Agriculture in the Sheffield School from 1864 to 1903*. New Haven: Yale University Press.

Fellmeth, Robert. 1973. *Politics of Land*. New York: Grossman.

Flynn, P. J. 1890. *Reports on the Projected Works of the Tulare Irrigation District, Tulare County, California*. Tulare: Daily Evening Register Steam Print.

Fremont, John Charles. 1845. *Report of the Exploring Expedition to the Rocky Mountains in the Year 1842 and to Oregon and North California in the Years 1843–44*. Washington, D.C.: Blair and Rives.

———. 1848. *Geographical Memoir upon Upper California*. Reprint. San Francisco: Book Club of California, 1964.

———. 1887. *Memoirs of My Life*. Chicago: Belford, Clarke.

Fresno Republican. July 27, 1929.

Garner, William Robert. 1970. *Letter from California 1846–1847*, edited by Donald Munro Craig, Berkeley, Los Angeles, London: University of California Press.

Gates, Paul Wallace. 1961. "California's Agricultural College Lands." *Pacific Historical Review* 30:103–122.

Gayton, Anna H. 1936. "Estudillo among the Yokuts, 1819." In *Essays in Anthropology in Honor of Alfred Louis Kroeber*. Berkeley and Los Angeles: University of California Press.

———. 1946. "Culture-Environment Integration: External References in Yokuts Life." *Southwestern Journal of Anthropology* 2.

———. 1948. "Yokuts and Western Mono Ethnography." *University of California Anthropological Records* 10:1–290.

George, Henry. 1868. "What the Railroad Will Bring Us." *Overland Monthly* 1 (10): 303.

Gifford, E. W., and W. E. Schenck. 1926. "Archaeology of the Southern San Joaquin Valley, California." *University of California Publications in American Archaeology and Ethnology* 23:1–122.

Gist, Brooks D. 1952. *The Years Between*. Tulare: Advance Register.

———. 1974. *Tales by the Campfire*. Tulare: Advance Register.

Goldschmidt, Walter. 1947. *As You Sow*. New York: Harcourt, Brace.

———. 1975. "A Tale of Two Towns." In *The People's Land: A Reader on Land Reform in the United States*, edited by Peter Barnes. Emmaus, Pa.: Rodale Press.

Grayson, A. J. 1920. "Game in the San Joaquin Valley in 1853." *California Fish and Game* 6 (3): 104–107.

Gregor, Howard. 1962*a*. "The Regional Primacy of San Joaquin Valley Agriculture." *Journal of Geography* 61 (8): 394–399.

———. 1962*b*. "The Plantation in California." *Professional Geographer* 14 (2): 1–15.

———. 1970. "The Industrial Farm as a Western Institution." *Journal of the West* 9 (1): 78–92.

Griffin, James R., and William B. Critchfield. 1972. *The Distribution of Forest Trees in California*. U.S.D.A. Forest Service Research Paper no. PSW-82.

Grinnell, Joseph. 1915. *A Distributional List of the Birds of California*. Hollywood, Calif.: Cooper Ornithological Club.

Grunsky, Carl E. 1898*a*. *Irrigation near Bakersfield, California* U.S.G.S. Water Supply Paper no. 17. Washington, D.C.: Government Printing Office.

———. 1898*b*. *Irrigation near Fresno, California*. U.S.G.S. Water Supply Paper no. 18. Washington, D.C.: Government Printing Office.

Gudde, Erwin G. 1965. *California Place Names: The Origin and Etymology of Current Geographical Names*. Berkeley and Los Angeles: University of California Press.

Hall, Raymond E., and Keith R. Kelson. 1959. *The Mammals of North America*. New York: Ronald Press.

Hall, William H. 1886. *Topographical and Irrigation Map of the San Joaquin Valley*. Sheets 3 and 4. Sacramento: State Engineering Department.

———. 1886–1888. *Report of the State Engineer of California on Irrigation and the Irrigation Question*. Sacramento: Office of the State Engineer.

Hardy, Osgood. 1929. "Agricultural Changes in California, 1860–1900." *Proceedings of the American Historical Association, Pacific Coast Branch*, pp. 216–230.

Hayes, John. 1872. "Wants and Advantages of California." *Overland Monthly* 8 (4): 338–347.

Hays, Michael. 1974. "Visibility Changes in Fresno, California, from 1939 to 1971." *The Professional Geographer* 26 (1): 59–60.

Heermans, Edward McGrew. 1915. *Kings County, California: The Little Kingdom of Kings*. Hanford: Kings County Exposition Commission.

Heizer, R. F. 1974. *The Destruction of the California Indians*. Santa Barbara: Peregrine, Smith.

Hicks, Frederic N. 1963. "Ecological Aspects of Aboriginal Culture in the Western Yuman Area." Ph.D. dissertation, University of California, Los Angeles.

Higgins, C. A. 1895. *New Guide to the Pacific Coast: Santa Fe Route*. Chicago: Rand McNally.

Hilgard, Eugene W., T. C. Jones, and R. W. Furnas. 1882. *Report on the Climatic Features and the Agricultural Practices and Needs of the Arid Regions of the Pacific Slope, Made under the Direction of the Commissioner of Agriculture*. Washington, D.C.: Government Printing Office.

Hittell, John S. 1866. *The Resources of California: Comprising Agriculture, Mining, Geography, Climate, Commerce, and the Past Agricultural*

Development of the State. San Francisco: A. Roman.

Hittell, Theodore H. 1911. *The Adventures of James Capen Adams: Mountaineer and Grizzly Bear Hunter of California*. New York: Charles Scribner's Sons.

Hodges, R. E., and E. J. Wickson. 1923. *Farming in California*. San Francisco: Californians Inc.

Holmes, L. C., and E. C. Eckmann. 1916. *Reconnaissance Soil Survey of the Middle San Joaquin Valley, California*. U.S.D.A. Bureau of Soils Field Operations Report no. 18. Washington, D.C.: Government Printing Office.

Hutchinson, W. H. 1969. *California: Two Centuries of Man, Land, and Growth in the Golden State*. Palo Alto: American West.

Hyatt, T. Hart. 1867. *Hyatt's Handbook of Grape Culture*. San Francisco: H. H. Bancroft.

Ingles, Lloyd Glenn. 1954. *Mammals of California and Its Coastal Waters*. Stanford: Stanford University Press.

Irrigation Districts of Kings and Tulare Counties. N.d. *General Records, District Maps*, and other pertinent materials from the following: Alpaugh, Alta, Corcoran, Empire Westside, Ivanhoe, Lindmore, Lindsay-Strathmore, Pixley, Terra Bella, and Tulare irrigation districts and from Kings County Water District.

Jackson, Donald, and Mary Lee Spence, eds. 1970. *The Expeditions of John Charles Fremont*. Vol. I, *Travels from 1838 to 1844*. Urbana: University of Illinois Press.

Jackson, John Brinckerhoff. 1972. *American Space: The Centennial Years, 1865–1876*. New York: W. W. Norton.

Jennings, C. W. 1953. "Mines and Mineral Resources of Kings County, California." *California Journal of Mines and Geology* 49 (3): 273–296.

Jenny, Hans. 1948. "Exploring the Soils of California." In *California Agriculture*, edited by Claude Hutchinson. Berkeley and Los Angeles: University of California Press.

Jepson, W. L. 1923. *The Trees of California*. 2nd ed. Berkeley: Sather Gate Bookshop.

Judge, Elliott W. 1914. *Wagon Roads of California: County Wagon and Automobile Roads*. San Francisco: Complete Map Works.

Kern County Weekly Courier (Bakersfield). October 24, 1874.

King, T. Butler. 1850. *Report of the Honorable T. Butler King on California*. Washington, D.C.: Gideon.

King, Thomas F. 1974. "The Evolution of Status Ascription around San Francisco Bay." In *Antap: California Indian Political and Economic Organization*, edited by Lowell J. Bean and Thomas F. King. Ramona, Calif.: Ballena.

Kings County Agricultural Commissioner. 1945. *Crop Report*. Hanford: County Agricultural Commissioner's Office.

———. 1974. *Crop Report*. Hanford: County Agricultural Commissioner's Office.

————. 1979. *Crop Report*. Hanford: County Agricultural Commissioner's Office.

Kings County Planning Department. 1972. "The Environmental Resources Management Element, Phase I." In *Kings County General Plan*. Hanford: Kings County Planning Department.

Kip, Ingraham. 1892. *The Early Days of My Episcopate*. New York: Ingraham Kip.

Kitchener and Baker. 1884. *The 76 Land and Water Company's Lands: Geography, Topography, Soil, Climate, and Productions of Fresno and Tulare Counties, California*. Traver, Calif.: Kitchener and Baker.

Kroeber, Alfred L. 1904. "The Yokuts Language of South Central California." *University of California Publications in American Archaeology and Ethnology* 2 (5): 169–377.

————. 1906. "Indian Myths of South Central California." *University of California Publications in American Archaeology and Ethnology* 4 (4): 169–245.

————. 1925. *Handbook of the Indians of California*. Berkeley: California Books.

————. 1939. "Cultural and Natural Areas of Native North America." *University of California Publications in American Archaeology and Ethnology* 38 (1).

————. 1941. "Culture Element Distributions, Part XV: Salt, Dogs, Tobacco." *University of California Anthropological Records* 6 (1): 1–20.

————. 1961. "The Nature of Landholding Groups in Aboriginal California." In *Aboriginal California: Three Studies in Culture History*. Berkeley: University of California Archaeological Research Facility.

————. 1971. "The Food Problem in California." In *The California Indians*, edited by R. F. Heizer and M. A. Whipple. Berkeley, Los Angeles, and London: University of California Press.

Lantis, D. W., R. Steiner, and A. E. Karinen. 1963. *California: Land of Contrast*. Belmont, Calif.: Wadsworth.

Lapham, Macy, and W. H. Heileman. 1901. *Soil Survey of the Hanford Area, California*, U.S.D.A. Bureau of Soils Field Operations. House Document no. 655, 57th Cong., 1 sess.

Larkin, Thomas Oliver. 1953. *The Larkin Papers: Personal, Business and Official Correspondence of Thomas Oliver Larkin, Merchant and United States Consul in California*, edited by George P. Hammond. Berkeley and Los Angeles: University of California Press.

LaRue, R. G., and M. B. Rounds. 1948. "Planning and Planting the Orchard." In *The Citrus Industry*, Vol. II, *Production of the Crop*, edited by Herbert J. Webber and Leon A. Batchelor. Berkeley and Los Angeles: University of California Press.

Latta, Frank F. 1929. *Uncle Jeff's Story: A Tale of a San Joaquin Valley Pioneer and His Life with the Yokuts Indians*. Tulare: Tulare Times.

————. 1933. *El Camino Viejo*. Bakersfield: Kern County Historical Society.

————. 1937. *Little Journeys in the San Joaquin*. Tulare: Frank F. Latta.

————. 1949*a*. *Handbook of Yokuts Indians*. Oildale, Calif.: Bear State Books.

————. 1949*b*. *Black Gold in the San Joaquin*. Caldwell, Idaho: Caxton Printers.

————. 1976. *Tailholt Tales*. Santa Cruz, Calif.: Bear State Books.

Leighly, John. 1937. "Some Comments on Contemporary Geographic Method." *Annals of the Association of American Geographers* 27 (3): 125–141.

Leonard, Zenas. 1904. *Leonard's Narrative: Adventures of Zenas Leonard, Fur Trader and Trapper, 1831–1836*. W. F. Wagner, editor. Cleveland: Burrows Brothers.

Leopold, A. Starker. 1950. "Deer in Relation to Plant Succession." *Transactions of the 15th North American Wildlife Conference*, pp. 571–580.

Levick, M. B. 1912. *Tulare County, California*. Visalia: Tulare County Board of Trade.

Lewis, Henry T. 1973. "Patterns of Indian Burning in California: Ecology and Ethnohistory." In *Native Californians*, edited by Lowell J. Bean and Thomas C. Blackburn. Ramona, Calif.: Ballena.

Lofgren, B. E., and R. L. Klausing. 1969. *Land Subsidence due to Groundwater Withdrawal, Tulare-Wasco Area, California: Studies of Land Subsidence*. U.S.G.S. Professional Paper no. 437-B. Washington, D.C.: Government Printing Office.

Los Tulares. 1978. "Fishing in Tulare Lake." No. 118.

Ludeke, John. 1980. "The No Fence Law of 1874: Victory for San Joaquin Valley Farmers." *California History* 59 (2): 98–115.

Lufkin, Elwyn W. 1952. "From Boom Town to Bust in Four Short Years." *Tulare Advance Register*, May 31, 1952.

Lyman, George D. 1931. *John Marsh, Pioneer*. New York: Chautauqua.

Magee, Thomas, 1868. "Overworked Soils." *Overland Monthly* 1 (10): 327–331.

Mainwaring, Daniel. 1932. *One against the Earth*. New York: Ray Long and Richard R. Smith.

Manly, Lewis W. 1929. *Death Valley In '49*. New York: Wallace Hebberd.

Manning, John C. 1972. *Resume of Ground Water Hydrology in the Southern San Joaquin Valley*. San Joaquin Geological Society Publications 4:26–32.

Martin, John H., and Warren Leonard. 1949. *Principles of Field Crop Production*. New York: Macmillan.

McAllister, Walter A. 1939. "A Study of Railroad Land-Grant Disposal in California with Reference to the Western Pacific, the Central Pacific, and the Southern Pacific Railroad Companies." Ph.D. dissertation, University of Southern California.

McCullough, D. R. 1969. *The Tule Elk: Its History, Behavior, and Ecology*. University of California Publications in Zoology no. 88.

McIntosh, Barron C. 1976. "Patterns of Land Alienation." *Annals of the Association of American Geographers* 66 (4): 570–582.

McWilliams, Carey. 1939. *Factories in the Field: The Story of Migratory Farm Labor in California*. Reprint. Santa Barbara: Peregrine, 1971.

———. 1942. *Ill Fares the Land: Migrants and Migratory Labor in the United States*. Boston: Little, Brown.

———. 1945. *Small Farm and Big Farm*. Public Affairs Pamphlet no. 100. New York: Public Affairs Committee.

Meigs, Peveril, III. 1939. "Water Planning in the Great Central Valley, California." *Geographical Review* 29 (4): 252–573.

Meinig, Donald W. 1968. *The Great Columbia Plain: A Historical Geography, 1805–1910*. Seattle: University of Washington Press.

———. 1971. *Southwest: Three Peoples in Geographical Change, 1600–1970*. New York: Oxford University Press.

Mendenhall, W. C. 1908. *Preliminary Report on the Groundwaters of the San Joaquin Valley, California*. U.S.G.S. Water Supply Paper no. 222. Washington, D.C.: Government Printing Office.

Mendenhall, W. C., R. B. Dole, and Herman Stabler. 1916. *Groundwater in the San Joaquin Valley, California*. U.S.G.S. Water Supply Paper no. 398. Washington, D.C.: Government Printing Office.

Menefee, Eugene L., and Fred A. Dodge. 1913. *History of Tulare and Kings Counties, California*. Los Angeles: Historic Record Co.

Merriam, C. Hart. 1923. "First Crossing of the Sierra Nevada: Jedediah Smith's Trip from California to Salt Lake in 1827." *Sierra Club Bulletin* 11 (4): 375–379.

———. 1955. *Studies of California Indians*. Berkeley and Los Angeles: University of California Press.

Miller, Alden H. 1951. "An Analysis of the Distribution of the Birds of California." *University of California Publications in Zoology* 50 (6): 531–644.

Miller, Gorden R. 1973. "Shaping California Water Law, 1781–1928." *Southern California Quarterly* 55 (1): 9–42.

Miller, May Merril. 1938. *First the Blade*. New York: Alfred A. Knopf.

———. 1944. *House of Cedar*. London: Jarrold's Publishers.

Miller, William J. 1957. *California through the Ages*. Los Angeles: Western Press.

Miot, A. E. 1915. *Tulare County: The Key to Success*. Visalia: Tulare County Board of Trade.

Mitchell, Annie R. 1941. *King of the Tulares*. Visalia: Times-Delta.

———. 1974. *A Modern History of Tulare County*. Visalia: Limited Editions of Visalia.

———. 1976. *The Way It Was*. Fresno: Valley Publishers.

Morgan, Dale L. 1953. *Jedediah Smith and the Opening of the West*. Indianapolis: Bobbs-Merrill.

Morgan, Wallace M. 1914. *History of Kern County*. Los Angeles: Historic Record Co.

Morse, Hermann N. 1915. *A Rural Survey of Tulare County, California*. New York: Presbyterian Church Board of Home Missions.

Moye, Lawrence A. 1920. *Official Map of Tulare County*. San Francisco: Lawrence A. Moye.

Moyle, Peter B. 1976. *Inland Fishes of California*. Berkeley, Los Angeles, and London: University of California Press.

Muir, John. 1874. "Letter from Grangeville." *Los Tulares: Quarterly Bulletin of the Tulare County Historical Society* no. 80, Jan. 1971.

Munz, Philip A. 1963. *A California Flora*. Berkeley and Los Angeles: University of California Press.

Murphy, Thomas D. 1915. *On Sunset Highways: A Book of Motor Rambles in California*. Boston: Page.

Narvaez, Jose Maria. 1830. "Plano del territorio de la Alta California construido por las mejores noticias y observaciones propias del capitan de Progata." Bancroft Library, University of California, Berkeley.

Nelson, J. W. 1917. *Reconnaissance Soil Survey of the Upper San Joaquin Valley, California*. U.S.D.A. Bureau of Soils Field Operations Report no. 19. Washington, D.C.: Government Printing Office.

Nevins, Allen, and Dale L. Morgan, eds. 1964. *Geographical Memoirs of John Charles Fremont upon Upper California, in Illustration of His Map of Oregon and California*. San Francisco: Book Club of California.

Nikiforoff, C. C. 1941. *Hardpan and Microrelief in Certain Soil Complexes of California*. U.S.D.A. Technical Bulletin no. 745. Washington, D.C.: Government Printing Office.

Nordhoff, Charles. 1872. *California for Health, Pleasure, and Residence: A Book for Travelers and Settlers*. New York: Harper and Brothers.

———. 1882. *California For Health, Pleasure, and Residence*. Reprint. New York: Harper and Brothers.

Norris, Frank. 1903. *The Octopus: A Story of California*. New York: Doubleday, Page.

———. 1928. *The Octopus*. Reprint. New York: Doubleday, Doran.

Norris, Robert M., and Robert W. Nebb. 1976. *Geology of California*. New York: John Wiley and Sons.

Nougaret, R. L., and M. H. Lapham. 1928. *A Study of Phylloxera Infestation in California as Related to Types of Soils*. U.S.D.A. Technical Bulletin no. 20. Washington, D.C.: Government Printing Office.

Nugen, John A. 1853. "Topographical Sketch of the Tulare Valley." Bancroft Library, University of California, Berkeley.

Oakeshott, Gordon B. 1971. *California's Changing Landscapes: A Guide to the Geology of the State*. New York: McGraw Hill.

———. 1978. *California's Changing Landscapes: A Guide to the Geology of the State*. Reprint. New York: McGraw Hill.

Odum, Howard T. 1971. *Environment, Power, and Society*. New York: John Wiley.

Opitz, Karl. 1966. "Echoes of the Boom." *Western Fruit Grower* 20.

Palmer, Sutton, and Mary Austin. 1914. *California: The Land of the Sun*. New York: Macmillan.

Paul, Rodman W. 1958. "The Wheat Trade between California and the United

Kingdom." *Mississippi Valley Historical Review* 45:391–412.

Petersen, W. E. 1939. *Dairy Science*. Chicago: J. B. Lippincott.

Peterson, George W. 1933. "American Colonization of the Upper San Joaquin Valley, California, to 1860." Master's thesis, University of Southern California.

Piemeisel, R. L., and F. R. Lawson. 1937. *Types of Vegetation in the San Joaquin Valley of California and Their Relation to the Beet Leafhopper*. U.S.D.A. Technical Bulletin no. 557. Washington, D.C.: Government Printing Office.

Poland, J. F. 1958. *Progress Report on Land Subsidence Investigations in the San Joaquin Valley, California, through 1957*. Sacramento: Inter-Agency Committee on Land Subsidence in the San Joaquin Valley.

Poland, J. F., B. E. Lofgren, R. L. Ireland, and R. G. Pugh. 1975. *Land Subsidence in the San Joaquin Valley, California, as of 1972*. U.S.G.S. Professional Paper no. 437-H. Washington, D.C.: Government Printing Office.

Pomeroy, Earl. 1965. *The Pacific Slope: A History of California, Oregon, Washington, Idaho, Utah, and Nevada*. New York: Alfred A. Knopf.

Powell, John J. 1874. *The Golden State and Its Resources*. San Francisco: Bacon.

Powell, L. C. 1948. "San Joaquin Vision." *Wilson Library Bulletin* 23 (2): 161–164.

Powers, Stephen. 1877. "The Tribes of California." *Contributions to North American Ethnology*, Vol. III. Washington, D.C.: Government Printing Office.

Prokopovich, Nikolaf, and Richard L. Bateman. 1975. "Calcareous Concretions in the Corcoran Clay: Western Merced County, California." *California Geology* 28 (4): 75–81.

Putnam, Royal Porter. 1857–1860. *Journal of Royal Porter Putnam, September 1857 to July 1860*. Reprint. Porterville, Calif.: The Farm Tribune, n.d.

Ragir, Sonia. 1972. *The Early Horizon in Central California Prehistory*. University of California Archaeological Research Facility Contribution no. 15. Berkeley: University of California Department of Anthropology.

Raney, W. A., and A. W. Cooper. 1968. "Soil Adaptation and Tillage." In *Advances in Production and Utilization of Quality Cotton*, edited by Fred C. Elliott, Marvin Hoover, and Walter K. Porter. Ames: Iowa State University.

Rasmussen, Wayne D. 1962. "The Impact of Technological Change on American Agriculture, 1862–1962." *Journal of Economic History* 22 (4): 578–591.

Rawls, James. 1975. "Images of the California Indians: American Attitudes towards the Indians of California, 1808–1873." Ph.D. dissertation, University of California, Berkeley.

Reading, Alice. 1844. Manuscript of a Letter Dated February 7, 1844. Alice

Reading Papers, Bancroft Library, University of California, Berkeley.

Retzer, John L. 1946. *Kings County, California.* U.S.D.A. Agricultural Research Administration Soil Survey no. 9, series 1938. Washington, D.C.: Government Printing Office.

Rice, John G. 1978. "The Effect of Land Alienation on Settlement." *Annals of the Association of American Geographers* 68 (1): 61–72.

Riddell, Francis A., and William H. Olsen. 1969. "An Early Man Site in the San Joaquin." *American Antiquity* 34 (2): 121–130.

Robinson, William Wilcox. 1948. *Land in California.* Berkeley and Los Angeles: University of California Press.

———. 1955. *The Story of Tulare County and Visalia.* Los Angeles: Title Insurance and Trust.

Rodner, J. W. 1949. *Technical Studies in Support of Factual Report: Tulare Irrigation District, Tulare, California.* Fresno: U.S.D.I. Bureau of Reclamation, Region II.

Root, Riley. 1955. *Journal of Travels from St. Joseph to Oregon, with Observations of That Country, Together with a Description of California, Its Agricultural Interests, and a Full Description of Its Gold Mines.* Oakland: Biobooks.

Rush, Philip S. 1964. *A History of the Californias.* San Diego: Neyenesch Press.

Saroyan, William. 1937. *My Name Is Aram.* New York: Harcourt, Brace.

Sauer, Carl O. 1941. "Foreword to Historical Geography." In *Land and Life*, edited by John Leighly. Berkeley and Los Angeles: University of California Press.

———. 1952. "Folkways of Social Science." In *Land and Life*, edited by John Leighly. Berkeley and Los Angeles: University of California Press.

Saunders, Margery H. 1960. "California Wheat, 1867–1910: Influences of Transportation on the Export Trade and the Location of Producing Areas." Master's thesis, University of California, Berkeley.

Schoonover, Warren R., and Leon A. Batchelor. 1948. "Cultivation or Tillage?" In *The Citrus Industry*, Vol. II, *Production of the Crop*, edited by Herbert J. Webber and Leon A. Batchelor. Berkeley and Los Angeles: University of California Press.

Scofield, James T. 1967. "Physical Geography: A Study of Tulare County, California." Master's thesis, California State University, Fresno.

Shideler, James H. 1957. *Farm Crises 1919–1923.* Berkeley and Los Angeles: University of California Press.

Shuck, Oscar T. 1869. *The California Scrap-Book: A Repository of Useful Information and Select Reading.* San Francisco: H. H. Bancroft.

Silver, J. S. 1868. "Farming Facts for California Immigrants." *Overland Monthly* 1 (18): 176–183.

Small, Kathleen. 1926. *History of Tulare County.* Chicago: S. J. Clarke.

Smith, Richard H. 1976. "Towns along the Tracks: Railroad Strategy and Town Promotion in the San Joaquin Valley, California." Ph.D. dissertation, University of California, Los Angeles.

Smith, Wallace. 1925. "Spanish Exploration of the San Joaquin Valley."

Fresno Republican, November 29, 1925.

————. 1939. *Garden of the Sun: A History of the San Joaquin Valley, 1772–1939*. Reprint. Fresno: California History Books, 1976.

Smith, W. P. V. 1932. "The Development of the San Joaquin Valley, 1772–1882." Ph.D. dissertation, University of California, Berkeley.

Southern Pacific Company. 1888. *Official List of Offices, Stations, Agents; Table of Distances*. San Francisco: Southern Pacific Company.

State of California Advisory Commission on Indian Affairs. 1966. *Progress Report to the Governor and the Legislature on Indians in Rural and Reservation Areas*. Sacramento: State Printing Office.

State of California Department of Natural Resources. 1959. *Geological Maps of California*. Santa Cruz and San Luis Obispo sheets. San Francisco: Division of Mines and Geology, Ferry Building.

————. 1965. *Geological Maps of California*. Bakersfield sheet. San Francisco: Division of Mines and Geology, Ferry Building.

————. 1966. *Geological Maps of California*. Fresno sheet. San Francisco: Division of Mines and Geology, Ferry Building.

State of California Department of Public Works. 1922. *Water Resources of Tulare County and Their Utilization*. Sacramento: State Printing Office.

State of California Department of Water Resources. 1949. *Irrigation Map of California*. Sacramento: State Printing Office.

————. 1958. *The Southern San Joaquin Valley*. Sacramento: Division of Resources Planning, Meteorological Unit.

————. 1960. *Irrigation Map of California*. Sacramento: State Printing Office.

————. 1974. *Irrigated, Irrigable, and Urban Lands*. Sacramento: State Printing Office.

————. 1978. *Boundaries of Public Water Agencies, San Joaquin District*. Sacramento: State Department of Water Resources.

State of California Employment Data Research Division. 1977. *Farm Labor Report: Employment By County*. Sacramento: State of California Employment Development Division.

State of California Engineer. 1880. *Report of the State Engineer to the Legislature of the State of California, Session of 1880*. Sacramento: State Printing Office.

State of California Surveyor General. 1854. *Annual Report of the Surveyor General*. Sacramento: State Printing Office.

————. 1855. *Annual Report of the Surveyor General*. Sacramento: State Printing Office.

————. 1863. *Annual Report of the Surveyor General*. Sacramento: State Printing Office.

Stein, Walter J. 1973. *California and the Dust Bowl Migrants*. Contributions in American History, no. 21. Westport, Conn.: Greenwood.

Steinbeck, John. 1938. *Their Blood Is Strong*. San Francisco: Simon J. Labin Society of California.

————. 1939. *The Grapes of Wrath*. New York: Viking.

Steward, Julian H. 1955. *Theory of Culture Change: The Methodology of*

Multilinear Evolution. Urbana: University of Illinois Press.

Stewart, George W. 1885. *Resources of the Southern San Joaquin Valley, California: Fresno, Tulare, and Kern Counties*. San Francisco: Immigration Association of California.

Storie, R. Earl, and Bruce Owen. 1942. *The Pixley Area, California*. U.S.D.A. Bureau of Plant Industry Soil Survey no. 23, series 1935. Washington, D.C.: Superintendent of Documents.

Storie, R. Earl, and Walter W. Weir. 1940. *The Visalia Area, California*. U.S.D.A. Bureau of Plant Industry Soil Survey no. 16, series 1935. Washington, D.C.: Superintendent of Documents.

Strahorn, A. T., L. C. Holmes and C. W. Mann. 1908. *Soil Survey of the Porterville Area, California*. U.S.D.A. Bureau of Soils Field Operations Report no. 10. Washington, D.C.: Government Printing Office.

Talbot, M. W., H. H. Biswell, and A. L. Hormay. 1939. "Fluctuations in the Annual Vegetation of California." *Ecology* 20 (3): 394–402.

Tavernetti, James R., and Lyle M. Carter. 1964. *Mechanization of Cotton Production*. University of California Agricultural Experiment Station Bulletin no. 804.

Taylor, Carl C. 1952. *Rural Life in the United States*. New York: Alfred A. Knopf.

Taylor, Walter W. 1961. "Archaeology and Language in Western North America." *American Antiquity* 27 (1): 71–81.

Taylor, William A. 1900. "The Influence of Refrigeration on the Fruit Industry." In *U.S.D.A. Yearbook 1900*. Washington, D.C.: Government Printing Office.

Teilman, I., and W. H. Shafer. 1943. *The Historical Story of Irrigation in Fresno and Kings Counties in Central California*. Fresno: Williams and Son.

Thompson, Kenneth. 1969. "Irrigation as a Menace to Health." *Geographical Review* 59 (2): 195–214.

Thompson, Thomas H. 1892. *Official Historical Atlas Map of Tulare County*. Reprint. Visalia: Limited Editions of Visalia, 1973.

Thompson, William. 1857. "Essay on the Alkaline Soils, Tule Lands, and Salt Marshes of California." In *Official Report of the California State Agricultural Society's Annual Fair, Cattle Show, and Industrial Exhibition*. Sacramento: California State Agricultural Society.

Thompson and Warren. 1888. *Business Directory and Historical and Descriptive Hand-Book of Tulare County, California*. Tulare: Pillsbury and Ellsworth.

Tinley, J. M. 1936. "Price Factors in the Los Angeles Milk Market." Mimeographed. Berkeley: Giannini Foundation of Agricultural Economics, University of California, report no. 48.

True, D. L. 1957. "Fired Clay Figurines from San Diego County, California." *American Antiquity* 22 (3): 296–391.

Tulare Advance Register. May 4, 1931.

Tulare County Agricultural Commissioner. 1945. *Crop Report*. Visalia: Tulare County Agricultural Commissioner's Office.

————. 1974. *Crop Report*. Visalia: Tulare County Agricultural Commissioner's Office.

————. 1977. *Land Use Map*. Visalia: Tulare County Agricultural Commissioner's Office.

————. 1979. *Crop Report*. Visalia: Tulare County Agricultural Commissioner's Office.

Tulare County Chamber of Commerce. 1977. *Tulare County, California*. Visalia: Tulare County Chamber of Commerce.

Tulare County Planning Department. 1975. *Bi-County Economic Base Study, Kings and Tulare Counties*. Visalia: Tulare County Association of Governments and Tulare County Planning Department.

Tulare County Times (Visalia). August 15, 1874.

U.S. Army Corps of Engineers. 1966. "Terminus Reservoir: Report of the Inter-Agency Archaeologic Salvage Program." Woodward Library, California State University, Fresno.

U.S.D.A. Forest Service. 1945. *Map of Vegetation Types of California*. Berkeley: California Forest and Range Experiment Station.

U.S.D.A. Office of Experiment Stations. 1912. *Irrigation Map of Central California to Accompany Report on the Irrigation Resources of Central California*. Washington, D.C.: Government Printing Office.

U.S.D.C. Bureau of the Census. 1913. *Thirteenth Census, 1910*. Vol. II and VI. Washington, D.C.: Government Printing Office.

————. 1922. *Fourteenth Census, 1920*. Vol. III and VI (3). Washington, D.C.: Government Printing Office.

————. 1927. *Census of Agriculture, 1925*. Reports for States, pt. III. Washington, D.C.: Government Printing Office.

————. 1932. *Fifteenth Census, 1930*. Population, Vol. III (1); Agriculture, Vols. II (3) and III (3). Washington, D.C.: Government Printing Office.

————. 1936. *Census of Agriculture, 1935*. Vols. I (3) and II (3). Washington, D.C.: Government Printing Office.

————. 1942. *Sixteenth Census, 1940*. Population, Vol. II (1); Agriculture, Vols. I (6) and II (3). Washington, D.C.: Government Printing Office.

————. 1946. *Census of Agriculture, 1945*. Vol. I (33). Washington, D.C.: Government Printing Office.

————. 1952a. *Seventeenth Census, 1950*. Census of Population, Vol. II (5). Washington, D.C.: Government Printing Office.

————. 1952b. *Census of Agriculture, 1950*. Vol. I (33). Washington, D.C.: Government Printing Office.

————. 1956. *Census of Agriculture, 1954*. Vol. I (33). Washington, D.C.: Government Printing Office.

————. 1961a. *Eighteenth Census, 1960*. Census of Population, Vol. I (6). Washington, D.C.: Government Printing Office.

————. 1961b. *Census of Agriculture, 1959*. Vol. I (48). Washington, D.C.: Government Printing Office.

————. 1967. *Census of Agriculture, 1964*. Vol. I (48). Washington, D.C.: Government Printing Office.

————. 1972. *Census of Agriculture, 1969*. Vol. I (48–2). Washington, D.C.: Government Printing Office.

————. 1973. *Nineteenth Census, 1970*. Census of Population, Vol. I (6). Washington, D.C.: Government Printing Office.

————. 1977. *Census of Agriculture, 1974*. Vol. I (5). Washington, D.C.: Government Printing Office.

U.S.D.I. Bureau of Land Management. N.d. *The New Public Land Records for California*. Historical Indices and Land Status Records. Microfilm. Sacramento: District Office, U.S.D.I. Bureau of Land Management.

U.S.D.I. Bureau of Reclamation. 1939. *Depth to Groundwater, 1939; Groundwater Lowering 1921–1939*. Fresno: Regional Office, U.S.D.I. Bureau of Reclamation.

————. 1946–1948. *Irrigation District Crop Reports*. Manuscript forms and summaries. Fresno: Regional Office, U.S.D.I. Bureau of Reclamation.

————. 1976. *Irrigation District Crop Reports*. Manuscript forms and summaries. Fresno: Regional Office, U.S.D.I. Bureau of Reclamation.

U.S.D.I. Census Office. 1864. *Eighth Census, 1860*. Vols. I and III. Washington, D.C.: A. O. P. Nicholson.

————. 1872. *Ninth Census, 1870*. Vols. I, II, and III. Washington, D.C.: Government Printing Office.

————. 1883. *Tenth Census, 1880*. Vols. I and III. Washington, D.C.: Government Printing Office.

————. 1896. *Eleventh Census, 1890*. Vols. I (1) and V. Washington, D.C.: Government Printing Office.

————. 1901. *Twelfth Census, 1900*. Vols. I (1), V (1), and VI (2). Washington, D.C.: Government Printing Office.

U.S.D.I. General Land Office. 1853–1856. *Survey Plats and Surveyors' Notes, Original Survey*. Visalia: Tulare County Recorder's Office.

————. 1855. *Instructions to Surveyors General of the Public Lands of the United States, for Those Surveying Districts Established in and since the Year 1850, Containing Also a Manual of Instructions to Regulate the Field Operations of Deputy Surveyors*. Washington, D.C.: A. O. P. Nicholson.

————. 1866. *Map of Public Surveys in California and Nevada to Accompany the Report of the Commissioner of the General Land Office*. Washington, D.C.: Government Printing Office.

————. N.d. (manuscript). *Visalia Land Office District Entry Tract Books 1–15; Plat Books 1–13; Patent Books A–Z; Indices 1–5*. Visalia: Tulare County Recorder's Office.

————. 1908. "Statement Showing Land Grants Made by Congress to Aid in the Construction of Railroads, Wagon Roads, Canals, and Internal Improvements, with Data Relative Thereto." *Statutes at Large*, vol. 14, p. 392. Washington, D.C.: Government Printing Office.

U.S.D.I. Geological Survey. *Topographic Quadrangle Maps*. 7.5′, 15′, and 1:250,000 series, Southern San Joaquin Valley sheets; most recent editions.

————. 1966. *Water Resources Data for California*. Menlo Park: U.S.D.I. Geological Survey, Water Resources Division.

Vaudt, John. 1972. "Humidity Changes in the San Joaquin Valley Attributed to Man's Activities." Paper submitted to Dr. Charles Markham, Department of Geography, California State University, Fresno.

Visalia Weekly Delta. October 26, 1876.

Visalia Weekly News. June 5, 1873.

Wallace, William J. 1978. "Southern Valley Yokuts." In *Handbook of North American Indians*, vol. 8, edited by William C. Sturtevant. Washington, D.C.: Smithsonian Institution.

Webber, Herbert J. 1948. "Cultivated Varieties of Citrus." In *Citrus Industry*, Vol. I, edited by Herbert J. Webber and Leon A. Batchelor. Berkeley and Los Angeles: University of California Press.

Wells, Andrew J. 1908. *The San Joaquin Valley of California: Resources, Industries, and Advantages*. San Francisco: Southern Pacific Railroad, Passenger Department.

Wester, Lyndon L. 1975. "Changing Patterns of Vegetation on the West Side and South End of the San Joaquin Valley during Historic Times." Ph.D. dissertation, University of California, Berkeley.

White, Chris. 1974. "Lower Colorado River Area Aboriginal Warfare and Alliance Dynamics." In *Antap: California Indian Political and Economic Organization*, edited by Lowell J. Bean and Thomas King. Ramona, Calif.: Ballena.

White, Raymond C. 1963. "Luiseno Social Organization." *University of California Publications in American Archaeology and Ethnology* 48 (2): 99 194.

Whitney, J. D. 1865. *Geological Survey of California*. Sacramento: Legislature of California.

Wik, Raymond. 1967. "Mechanization on the American Farm." In *Technology in the Twentieth Century*, Vol. II, edited by Melvin Kranzberg and Carroll W. Purshell, Jr. New York: Oxford University Press.

Wilkes, Charles. 1845. *Narrative of the United States Exploring Expedition during the Years 1838–1842*, in Five Volumes, and an Atlas. Philadelphia: Lea and Blanchard.

————. 1849. *Western America, Including California and Oregon, with Maps of Those Regions and of the Sacramento Valley*. Philadelphia: Lea and Blanchard.

Williamson, R. S. 1853. *Report of a Reconnaissance and Survey in California, in Connection with Explorations for a Practicable Railway Route from the Mississippi River to the Pacific Ocean, in 1853*. House Document no. 129.

Wilson, E. E., and Marion Clawson. 1945. *Agricultural Land Ownership and Operation in the Southern San Joaquin Valley*. Berkeley and Los Angeles: University of California Press.

Wolf, Carl B. 1945. *California Wild Tree Crops*. Santa Ana. Rancho Santa Ana Botanic Garden of the Native Plants of California.

Wollenberg, Charles. 1977. "Farming, California-Style." *San Francisco Sunday Examiner and Chronicle*, "California Living," March 20, 1977.

W.P.A., Federal Writers' Project. 1939. *California: A Guide to the Golden State*. New York: Hastings House.

Zimrick, Steven J. 1976. "The Changing Organization of Agriculture in the Southern San Joaquin Valley, California." Ph.D. dissertation, Louisiana State University and Agricultural and Mechanical College.

Index

Acala cotton, 182, 204
Acorns, 33, 34−35, 74, 82
Adams, James "Grizzly," 27, 36, 62
Agribusiness, 79, 171, 212, 224. *See also* Corporate farms; Farmers, business orientation of,
Agricultural: chemicals, 202, 209, 221−222, 235; colonies, 149−154, 165, 186; experimentation, 93−94; 135, 142, 145; perceptions, 49−53, 56, 68−69, 71, 154−156; societies, 92. *See also* Land classification; Land-use patterns; Soil fertility, assessments of
Agricultural Adjustment Act (1970), 227
Airplanes, use of, in farming, 221, 229
Air quality, urbanization and, 234−235
Aiticha, 41, 42
Alfalfa, 180, 181, 225. *See also* Field crops; Land-use patterns
Alila. *See* Earlimart
Alkali, 12. *See also* Soil, alkalinity; Soils, alkali
Allensworth, 165
Alluvial fans, 10, 15, 16−17, 183. *See also* Kaweah Delta; Kings Delta; Recent alluvium; Soils, recent alluvial; Tule River fan
Alpaugh, 165, 186, 192, 229
Alpaugh Irrigation District, 201
Alta Irrigation District, 138, 146
Angiola, 165, 186
Animals, native. *See* Fauna, native
Antelope, 26−27, 36, 69, 117
Aquatic habitats, 28, 29, 161
Aquifers. *See* Groundwater
Armenians, 167, 173
Armona, 123, 125, 186
Arrillagas, Governor Jose, 49
Artesian flow, 141, 161. *See also* Groundwater
Associated Farmers of California, 196
Atchison, Topeka and Santa Fe Railroad, 165

Atwell's Island, 18, 165
Audubon, John, 26, 28, 62, 69
Aukland, 149
Austin, Mary, 22−23, 27, 142
Automobiles, 168−169, 207, 237. *See also* Tractors; Trucks
Avenal, 192, 220

Bakersfield, 129
Bandini, Jose, 37, 46, 52
Barbed wire, 90, 130
Barley. *See* Grain crops
Barton, Orlando, 134
Barton, Stephen, 75
Basques, 91n
Battle Mountain, 82
Bellville, 149
Big Four, 122, 123, 129
Birds, 28−29. *See also* Waterfowl
Bison, 32
Blacks, 173, 196
Blake, William, 62, 65, 68, 69
Blanco, 166
Bokninuwiad, 41
Bonanza wheat farms, 121, 130, 132, 135. *See also* Wheat boom
Boosterism, 92−93, 139, 149−150, 154−157, 171−172, 175. *See also* Towns, promotion of
Braceros, 197. *See also* Farm labor; Mexican, farm workers
Brewer, William, 44
Bryant, Edwin, 59
Bubal, 39, 42, 43, 44, 54
Buckeyes, 22, 35
Buena Vista Lake, 18, 32
Buena Vista Slough, 18
Bunchgrasses, native, 23, 56, 59, 209
Butterfield Overland Mail, 114

Cabot, Fray Juan, 52, 58
California Aqueduct, 219–220
California Fruit Exchange. *See* Sunkist
California Immigrants Union, 156
California State Agricultural Society, 92, 101
California State Water Project, 217
California Water Plan, 193
Callisan's Slough, 96
Camp Badger, 149
Canals, 136, 137–138, 139, 217, 219. *See also* Irrigation, development and spread of
Carson, James, 62, 69, 71
Cash entry (direct purchase), 98, 104, 106
Castro, Manuel, 55, 100
Cattle: feral, origins and effects of, 58, 59–60; round-ups of, 73–74; Yokuts and, 49, 59, 82
Cattle ranching: beginnings of, 56, 59, 72, 73–75, 79; heyday of, 86–91; legacy of, 88–89, 117; persistence of, 90, 135, 139, 144, 150, 184–185, 206, 230
Central Pacific Railroad, 122, 123
Central Valley Project, 217, 219
Chapman, William, 104
Chi, 44
Chinese: farm workers, 133, 173; railroad labor, 128–129, 129n
Chischa, 44
Choinok, 41
Chukamina, 41
Chunut, 39, 40–41, 42
Citrus orchards. *See* Orchards, citrus
Clams and mussels, 27–28, 36
Climate, 4–8; perceptions of, 68, 95, 155
Coast Range, 2, 3, 4, 5, 10
College scrip, 101–102. *See also* Morrill Act
Communications, improvements in, 112–114. *See also* Railroads; Roads
Cone, Mary, 156
Consolidated Peoples Ditch, 138
Cooperative associations, 175, 181, 200
Corcoran, 165–166, 167, 186, 229, 230
Corcoran clay, 3, 19, 141
Corcoran cotton strike, 196
Corn. *See* Field crops
Corporate farms, 201, 204, 206–207, 212, 223, 228–230
Cottage, 149
Cotton, 93, 182–183, 203–204, 227; labor demand and, 196, 222
Cotton Acreage Adjustment Program, 204
Cotton gins, 183, 224, 229–230
Cramer, 149
Creameries, 180, 181
Cream separator, 181
Crocker, Charles, 122. *See also* Big Four
Crofutt, G. A., 156
Crop: experimentation, 94, 136, 145, 155–156, 199; rotation, 118, 135, 136, 145, 180, 181–182, 229; subsidization, 222–223, 227. *See also* Land-use patterns
Crop Set-Aside Program (1970), 223, 227
Cross Creek (town), 115, 129, 146

Cultivated acreage, 85, 94, 150, 193, 204, 230–231
Cutler, 167

Dairy: farms, 180–181, 203, 225–227; regions, 144, 146, 181, 184, 185, 204–205, 206, 231
Dairy Union, 181
Deciduous orchards. *See* Orchards, deciduous
Deep Creek, 96
Deer, 27, 36
Deer Creek, 17, 70, 95, 139
Delano, 123
Depots, *See* Railroad, stations
Derby, George H., 15–16, 17, 62, 64, 70, 71, 80
Desert Lands Act (1877), 99; entries under, 106
Desert saltbush community, 24, 209
Devil's Den, 149
Dinuba, 146, 147, 149, 150, 181, 185
Dog Camp. *See* Tailholt
Droughts, agriculture and, 89, 94, 95, 107, 139–141, 155
Dryland cultivation, 95, 130. *See also* Grain farming
Ducor, 149, 185
Dudley, 149
Dudley Ridge, 18, 32, 192
Dust Bowl. *See* Okies

Earlimart, 125, 186, 198
El Camino Viejo, 72
Elk, 27, 36, 69, 117
Environmental alteration, summaries of: to 1843, 59–60; 1844 to 1856, 83–84; 1857 to 1871, 117–118; 1872 to 1894, 157–158, 160–161; 1895 to 1925, 187–188; 1926 to 1945, 207–209; 1946 to present, 237
Erosion, acceleration of, 60, 91, 117
Estudillo, Jose Maria, 51, 52
Esperanza, 149
Evergreen orchards. *See* Orchards, citrus; Orchards, olive
Excess lands. *See* Reclamation Act
Exeter, 146–147, 185

Family farms, 199, 201–202, 210, 214, 215, 217
Famosa, 146
Farm: abandonment, 193, 200, 202, 210; equipment and machinery, 130, 131, 169, 177, 183, 199, 221, 225, 229; ownership and operation, 171–172, 200–201, 202, 215, 228–229; specialization, 79, 133–134, 135, 189, 190, 199, 203, 231; tenancy, 130, 150, 171, 201, 228
Farmers: arrival of, 75, 89–90; attitudes of, 145–146, 161–162, 170, 191, 214, 223; business orientation of, 119, 133–134, 171, 176, 199, 211–212, 228–229; gambler mentality of, 80, 86, 95, 134–135, 146, 189

Farmersville, 115, 129, 198

Farming, changes in nature of, 212–214, 238–243

Farm labor: conditions of, 133, 173–175, 176, 178–179, 194–199, 209–210, 222, 230; housing of, 190, 194, 197–199, 222, 225; supply of, 83, 132–133, 169, 173, 178–179, 182, 196, 202–203, 209, 222, 225

Farm size: agricultural colonies and, 149, 150, 154, 156–157, 170; increases in, 95, 107, 112, 131–132, 150, 191, 199–202, 215, 224, 227–228; irrigation and, 96–97, 156–157, 199–200, 217–219; land alienation policies and, 100–104, 106–112, 166, 201–202; mechanization and, 103, 106, 199; regional patterns of, 107–112, 185–186, 229. See also Agribusiness; Corporate farms; Small farms

Farms, number of, 87, 107, 132, 150, 170, 200, 215

Farmsteads: abandoned, 169, 223–224, 237; corporate, 214, 223–224, 228, 229; dairy, 181, 203, 225–227; distribution of, 106–109; early, 91, 132, 159; general, 183, 204, 228–229; number of, 106–109, 202, 223–224; orchard, 171, 178–179, 202–203, 224–225

Farm workers. See Farm labor

Farnham, B. J. 62, 68

Fauna, native, 26–29, 59, 84, 117, 237. See also Fish; Game animals; Waterfowl

Fences and fencelines, 86, 90, 130, 155, 223, 229, 237

Ferries, 72

Field crops, 181–182, 199, 206, 227, 230. See also Alfalfa; Cotton

Figueroa, Governor Jose, 56

Filaree, 35, 118

Filipinos, 173, 194–195, 197, 199

Fire, use of, by Yokuts, 36–37

Fish, 28, 36, 161

Fish Slough, 15, 144

Floods, 15, 89

Flora. See Vegetation; Wildflowers

Fogs, 8, 235

Fort Babbot, 87

Fort Miller, 81, 82

Fountain Springs, 115

Four Creeks country, 82, 146

Frazier, 149

Frazier Valley, 91

Fremont, John C., 27, 34, 62, 63, 68, 69, 80, 156

Fresno, 122, 196

Fresno County, 86, 87, 94, 97, 107, 142, 143

Fresno Slough, 15

Friant-Kern Canal, 193, 217, 237

Fur trappers, 55, 56

Gambler mentality. See Farmers, gambler mentality of; Land, speculation

Game animals, 32, 34, 35–36, 117

Garcia, Felipe Santiago, 27

Gawia, 41, 43

General farms, 181–183, 203–204, 227–228

Geological history, 2–4

Gold rushes, 72, 75, 114; legacies of, 95, 141

Golon, 44

Goshen, 123, 125, 129

Grain crops, 69, 79, 84, 89, 93, 94, 130, 133, 135, 205–206, 227, 229

Grain farming: beginnings of, 89–90, 130; effects of, on soils, 118, 134; heyday of, 93–95; persistence of, 103, 139, 144, 146, 150, 182, 183–184, 201–202, 204, 205; regions, 131–132, 146, 183–184, 185, 204, 205–206

Grandview. See Cross Creek

Grangeville, 115, 129

Grapes. See Vineyards

Grasslands: description and extent of, 23–24; disturbance of, 36, 37, 59, 60, 83; expansion of cultivation onto, 69, 79, 89, 92, 95, 106, 131–132

Grayson, Col. Andrew J., 28, 62

Grazing. See Cattle; Cattle ranching; Sheep ranching

Great Basin cultures, 33, 39

Groundwater: availability of, 3–4, 8, 19, 96, 141; development of, 141–142, 192–193, 219; influence of, on native flora, 21–22; overdraught of, 141, 187, 192–193, 195, 199, 208, 237

Guernsey, 166

Haas, S., 104

Hanford, 123, 125; county seat at, 142; functions of, 186, 197, 234; Portuguese in, 173

Hardwick, 125

Hatch Experiment Station Act (1887), 145

Health, 69, 155, 158. See also Malaria; Yokuts, epidemics among

Heinlein, 125

Hicks, Frederic, 35

Hilgard, Eugene W., 156

Hired labor, 132–133, 178–179, 181, 182. See also Farm labor

Hogs, 74

Hog wallows, 12, 13; agriculture and, 79, 130, 131, 154, 156; distinctive flora of, 23

Hokaltekans, 32–33

Homestead Act (1862), 98–99, 103–104

Homesteading, 100, 103–104, 106

Hopkins, Mark, 122. See also Big Four

Horses: feral, 59, 69; theft of, by bandits, 89n; theft of, by Yokuts, 49, 56, 82

Houses: Appalachian dogtrot, 116; early, shabbiness of, 115–116, 132; of farm laborers, 173, 198; Victorian-style, 159; of Yokuts, 44

Hudson's Bay Company, 55

Hunsaker, 149

Huntington, Collis P., 122. See also Big Four

Hutchinson, H. L., 102

Improvement Act (1841), 99
Indemnity lands, 99
Indian reservations, 83
Indians. *See* Native peoples; Yokuts
Industrial Workers of the World (IWW), 195
Initial survey. *See* Public Land Survey
Insects, 27
Irrigated acreage, 97, 138, 150, 217, 220–221
Irrigation: districts, 137, 138–139, 140, 201–202; development and spread of, 75, 95–97, 103–104, 136–144, 149–150, 156–157, 199–200, 216, 221; early proposals for, 52, 69, 71, 91; effects of, 158–159, 161, 187–188, 230; legal considerations in, 136–137, 217–219; water for, 136–137, 139, 144, 177, 192–193, 209, 217, 219, 237. *See also* Groundwater
Ivanhoe, 167
Ivanhoe Irrigation District, 201

Japanese, 173, 197, 199
Johnson, E., 102

Kaweah Cooperative Colony, 149
Kaweah Delta: agriculture on, 75, 94, 119, 167, 184, 186, 205, 231; alkali on, 161; descriptions of, 17, 22, 52, 68, 70; early settlement on, 92, 93, 106, 129; irrigation on, 95–96, 97, 138, 139, 142; land acquisition on, 100, 101, 102, 104–106; proposed mission on, 49, 52; Yokuts on, 39–40, 42, 58
Kaweah River, 16–17, 28, 142, 217
Kaweah Station, 146–147
Kern County, 94, 97, 107, 143
Kern Lake, 18
Kern River, 75, 86
Kettleman City, 192, 220, 229
Kettleman Dome, 192
Kettleman Hills, 10, 14, 146
Kettleman Plain, 14, 221
Kings County, 86, 142; agriculture in, 200, 206, 219, 230; land rush in, 187; oil boom in, 192. *See also* Kings Delta; Mussel Slough district; West side
Kings Delta: agriculture on, 142, 204–205, 224, 230, 231; descriptions of, 15–16, 52, 69–70; early settlement on, 92, 106, 129; irrigation on, 95, 137–138, 139, 142; Yokuts on, 39–40. *See also* Mussel Slough district.
Kings River, 14–16, 95, 142
Kingston, 113–114, 115, 129
Koyeti, 41, 42, 43
Kreyenhagen Hills, 14
Ku Klux Klan, 196
Kumachisi, 41

Lacustrine, deposits, 11, 18. *See also* Soils, lacustrine
Laguna de Tache, Rancho, 55, 76, 100
Lake bed. *See* Reclaimed land; Tulare Lake
Lakelanders, 187

Lakeshore: agricultural appraisals of, 49–50, 70, 71; land use on, 89, 101; Yokuts on, 32, 37, 40, 44–46, 58. *See also* Lowland heath community; Marshland, communities; Reclaimed land; Tulare Lake
Lakeside district, 146
Lake soils. *See* Soils, lacustrine
Land: acquisition, process of, 99–100, 101, 104, 107; alienation policies, 97–100, 104, 119, 234; classification (federal), 76–79; grants, federal, 76, 99, 102–103, 106, 107, 123, 165; grants, Mexican, 54–55, 98, 100; monopoly, 100–104, 228, 229; prices, 101, 102, 130, 131, 135, 136, 157, 171–172, 204; selection, patterns of, 104–106; speculation, 79–80, 86, 92, 95, 96–97, 100, 101–104, 115–116, 149–150, 154, 171–172, 187; subsidence, 208, 237; use, determinants of, 79, 119, 121, 130, 145, 146, 155, 212–214. *See also* Public Land Survey
Landforms, 8–19
Landholding patterns, 107–112, 201–202, 215. *See also* Farm size
Land-use patterns, changes in, 76, 85, 91, 119, 131–132, 135, 142–144, 145–146, 183–186, 204–207, 230–234, 239–243
Last Chance Ditch, 137–138
Latache, 115, 129
Law of Colonization (1840), 54–55, 79
Lemon Cove, 149, 167
Lemoore, 91, 125, 186, 220
Lemoore Canal, 137
Lemoore Naval Air Station, 220
Level Orchard Land Colony, 150, 151
Limekiln, 149
Lindsay, 146–147, 148, 185
Lindsay-Strathmore Irrigation District, 201
Livestock. *See* Cattle; Cattle ranching; Hogs; Horses; Sheep ranching
Lone Tree District, 146
Los Angeles: farms from, relocate in basin, 212, 224, 225; as market, 181, 212; as port, 113, 183; railroad to, 123; roads to, 72, 168
Los Angeles Trail, 54. *See also* El Camino Viejo
Los Gatos Creek, 15
Lower Kings River Ditch, 137
Lowland heath community, 24–25, 209
Lucerne Colony, 150, 153
Lucerne district, 146

McClure Valley, 149, 221
Magee, Thomas, 118
Malaria, 57, 69, 95, 158
Marginal lands, definition of, 91n
Markets: for cotton, 182, 183, 203–204; for dairy products, 181; expansion of, 73, 169, 212, 221, 224; for fruits, 176, 224; regulation of, 175, 182–183, 203–204, 222–223; for wheat, 130, 135

Marshland: communities, 22, 24, 29, 69, 209; reclamation, 71, 92, 93, 106, 156. *See also* Reclaimed lands; Reclamation; Tulares
Martin, Fray Juan, 49
Martinez, Fray Luis Antonio, 49–52
Mechanization, 103, 106, 131, 169, 183, 196, 199, 221–222
Merced, 122
Mexican: exploration, 54; farmworkers, 173, 194–195, 196, 197, 222; land grants, 54–55, 98, 100
Migrant labor. *See* Farm labor
Military Bounty Act (1847), 98
Military scrip, 102
Milking machines, 181
Mill Creek, 96
Miller, May, 25
Miller and Lux, 102
Milo (settlement), 149
Milo (sorghum). *See* Field crops; Grain crops
Mima mounds. *See* Hog wallows
Modesto, 122
Monson, 146, 147
Moraga, Gabriel, 27
Morrill Act (1862), 99, 101. *See also* College scrip
Muir, John, 136, 159
Mussel Slough, 96
Mussel Slough district: agriculture in, 131, 136, 145, 146, 158–159, 182, 188; alkalization in, 161; irrigation in, 136, 142, 158–159; land acquisition in, 101, 123, 131; soil depletion in, 135. *See also* Kings Delta
Mussel Slough incident, 131

Narvaez, Jose Maria, 50
Native animals. *See* Fauna, native
Native peoples, 32–33. *See also* Yokuts
Native plants. *See* Vegetation, natural
New alluvial soils. *See* Soils, recent alluvial
New alluvium. *See* Recent alluvium
No Fence Law, 90
Nordhoff, Charles, 90, 93, 132, 134, 156
Norris, Frank, 131, 132
Nutunutu, 41

Oakland (port of), 183
Oaks, 21–22, 34, 35, 36–37, 157
Oats. *See* Grain crops
Oats, wild, 35, 56, 118
Octol, 125
Octopus, The, 131
Oil and gas production, 167, 192
Okies, 196–198, 210. *See also* Farm labor
Old valley fill, 11. *See also* Soils, old valley fill
Orchards, 176–180, 183–184, 185–186, 199, 202–203, 224–225, 230; citrus, 94, 145, 146, 176–177, 179, 185, 204, 205, 224–225; deciduous, 145, 146, 155, 176–177, 184, 186, 200, 204, 205, 219–220, 224; expansion of, 142, 144, 145, 171, 176, 183–

184, 203, 224, 230; frost prevention in, 177, 221, 224; nut, 94, 155, 177, 205, 219; olive, 94, 145, 176–177, 186, 205; zonation of, 205
Original survey. *See* Public Land Survey
Orosi, 149, 185
Orris, 146–147, 148
Ortega, Juan, 58
Outside Creek, 96
Owen, W. R., 101
Owens Valley, 86

Pacific Improvement Company, 125, 147–148
Packinghouses, 203, 223, 229–230
Packwood, 115
Packwood, S. J., 102
Packwood Creek, 123
Panama Canal, 178
Patent acquisition. *See* Land, acquisition
Payeras, Fray Mariano, 53
Pelican Island, 18
Penutians, 33
Peoples Ditch, 137
Peoples Road. *See* San Joaquin Valley Railway
Pico, Jose Dolores, 53, 57
Pikes, 87–89, 90, 116
Pixley, 125, 146, 186
Plainview, 222
Plano, 115, 129, 146–147, 148
Plants, native. *See* Vegetation
Poplar, 149, 181, 186
Population: density, 33, 160; ethnicity, 75, 87, 128–129, 129n, 173, 174, 196 197; statistics, 80, 101, 107, 234, 235
Porter Slough, 96
Porterville, 115; functions of, 181, 185, 217, 234; railroad and, 147, 148
Portuguese, 173
Powers, Stephen, 58
Prairies. *See* Grasslands
Precipitation, 4–5, 7, 8. *See also* Droughts
Pre-Emption Act (1841), 98
Price supports. *See* Crop, subsidization
Prior appropriation, 136, 137
Property values. *See* Land, prices
Public Domain, 74, 97–112
Public Land Survey, 76–80
Pumps, 141–142, 177. *See also* Groundwater, development of
Pure Milk Act (1927), 203
Pyramid Hills, 14, 192

Quail, 125

Railroad: lands, 99, 102–103, 106–107, 123–124, 131; stations, 123, 125, 146–147, 165–166; towns, 123, 124–125, 128, 129, 147–148, 149
Railroads: construction of, 122–124, 146–148, 165–166, 168; decline of, 167, 168–

169, 203; effects and influences of, 90, 94, 121–163, 167; surveys for, 62, 68
Rainfall. *See* Droughts; Precipitation
Raisins. *See* Vineyards
Ranching. *See* Cattle ranching; Sheep ranching
Ranchos, Mexican, *See* Laguna de Tache; Law of Colonization
Recent alluvial soils. *See* Soils, recent alluvial
Recent alluvium, 10, 11, *See also* Alluvial fans
Reclaimed land: early crop suggestions for, 71, 93; fertility of, 156; field crops on, 230; grain on, 135, 184, 187, 205; irrigation of, 143, 144
Reclamation, progress of, 92, 93, 101, 143, 160, 187, 209. *See also* Tulare Lake, decline of
Reclamation Act (1902), 137, 217–219, 223
Rectangular Survey. *See* Public Land Survey
Redlands, 12, 142, 154, 161. *See also* Soils, old valley fill
Reed, Charles, 101
Reef Ridge, 14
Refrigeration, innovations in, 177–178, 203
Remnoy, 125
Reservoirs, 139
Residual slopes, 10–11, 14. *See also* Soils, residual
Richgrove, 167
Riparian forests, 22, 118, 157. *See also* Oaks
Riparian rights, doctrine of, 136–137
Roads, 72, 113–114, 150, 167–168, 169, 228
Rodeos, Act to Regulate (1851), 74
Rodeos, sites of, 75n
Rough stony ground, 12–14
Rural landscapes, 185–186, 214–215, 223–224, 243. *See also* Farm labor, housing of; Farmsteads; Seasonal landscapes

Sacramento, 73, 116, 194
Salinization of soils. *See* Soil, alkalinity
Salt grass, 24, 35, 180, 186
Sand Creek, 95
Sand dunes, 12, 18
"Sandlappers," 90, 146
S and O Lands. *See* Swamp and Overflowed Lands
San Francisco, 73, 88, 113, 116, 130, 183
San Joaquin Labor Bureau, 194
San Joaquin River, 15, 18
San Joaquin Valley Agricultural Society, 92
San Joaquin Valley Railway, 165
San Luis Canal, 217
Santa Fe Railroad. *See* Atchison, Topeka and Santa Fe Railroad
Santa Rosa Indian Reservation, 83
Saroyan, William, 24, 27
Savanna. *See* Tree savanna
School lands, 106
Scrip, use of, 101–102, 106
Seasonal landscapes, 25–26, 159, 179–180. *See also* Wildflowers

Sequoia National Park, 91
'76 Canal, 139
Seville, 167
Shacktowns, 197. *See also* Farm labor, housing of
Sheep ranching, 90–91, 117, 186
Sierra Nevada, 2, 4, 8, 10, 14
Skull Island, 18
"Sky farmers," 90
Sloughs, 95, 131
Small farms, era of, 169–171, 199–202. *See also* Family farms; Farm size
Smith, Peg-Leg, 56
Smith Lever Act (1914), 169
Smudge pots, 177
Soil: alkalinity, 49, 52, 158, 161, 208, 237; compaction, 117; depletion, 118, 134, 214; enrichment, 178; fertility, 49, 52, 68–69, 70, 92–93, 155–156; surveys. 68. *See also* Alkali; Land classification; Soils, alkali
Soil Bank, 223
Soils, 11–14, 17–19, 237; alkali, 12, 49, 77, 79, 92–93; alkali, uses of, 156, 158, 177, 180, 182, 184; lacustrine, 18, 79, 119, 156, 184; old valley fill, 12, 79, 92–93; old valley fill, uses of, 91, 94, 104, 119, 141, 156, 183; recent alluvial, 17–18, 78–79; recent alluvial, uses of, 104, 139, 140, 141, 156, 184; residual, 12, 14, 156, 183. *See also* Kaweah Delta; Kings Delta; Reclaimed lands; Redlands; Terraces; Tule River fan
Southerners, 75, 87–89. *See also* Okies; Pikes
Southern Pacific Railroad, 102–103, 106, 122–124; 129, 131, 146–148, 165
Spa, 166
Spanish: exploration, 48–53; impact, 48, 55
Speculation. *See* Land, speculation
Speer, Riddell, 101
Spiny saltbush community, 24, 209
Springville, 149, 185
Stage routes, 114, 115
Standard Oil Company, 192
Stanford, Leland, 122. *See also* Big Four
State Bounty Act (1862), 94
Steinbeck, John, 5, 200
Stock culture, 86–91
Stock raising. *See* Cattle ranching; Hogs; Sheep ranching
Stockton, 73, 75, 112, 116, 122
Stockton, Albuquerque and Kansas City Mail, 114
Stockton-Los Angeles Road, 72, 113, 114, 122, 146
Stoil, 166
Stratford, 123, 165–166, 229
Strathmore, 167, 185
Stream regimes, 8, 14–17
Subsidence, *See* Land, subsidence
Subsidies. *See* Crop, subsidization
Success Dam, 217

Sugar beets. *See* Field crops
Sultana, 167
Sunflower Valley, 149. *See also* McClure Valley
Sunkist, 175, 224
Surveys: American, 62–71; soil, 68; Spanish, 48–53
Sutherland, John, 86
Swamp and Overflowed Lands, 76, 78, 100, 101, 106, 166. *See also* Marshland, reclamation; Reclaimed land; Reclamation
Swamp and Overflowed Lands Act (1850), 99, 101

Tachi, 36, 40–41, 42, 43, 57; annual round of, 44–46
Tachi Lake, 19
Tagus, 149
Tailholt, 75, 115
Tanai, 44
Taurusa, 146–147, 148
Telamne, 54
Telamni, 41, 42, 43, 44, 58
Telegraph connections, 114
Terminus Dam, 217
Terra Bella, 135, 146–147, 148, 167, 185
Terra Bella Irrigation District, 201–202
Terraces, irrigation on, 142, 143. *See also* Redlands; Soils, old valley fill, uses of
Terrain modification, 60, 131. *See also* Erosion
"Thermal belt," 176–177, 205
Three Rivers, 149, 167, 185, 217
Timber Culture Bill (1873), 99
Tipton, 125, 129, 146, 181, 186
Tobacco, 37, 93
Tokay, 149
Ton Tachi Lake, 19
Town-and-country regions, 185–186. *See also* Land-use patterns
Towns: founding of, 72–73, 113–114, 123, 125, 146–149, 165–166, 167, 192; growth and functions of, 88, 114–115, 167, 176, 197, 212, 229, 230, 234; plats of, 124–125, 159; promotion of, 122, 123–129, 146–148, 160, 167
Townsend, 149
Tractors, 131, 183, 202, 221, 229. *See also* Farm, equipment and machinery; Mechanization
Transcontinental Railroad, 62, 68, 122. *See also* Southern Pacific Railroad
Traver, 125, 128, 132, 149, 157, 181
Traver Colony, 144, 150, 157, 161, 187–188
Trees, 22, 92, 118, 156, 157–158, 178. *See also* Oaks
Tree savanna, 21–22, 23, 37, 156, 209
Trespass Act, 90
Tribelets, Yokuts, *See* Yokuts, tribelets
Trucks, 181, 203, 224
Tulare (city): founding of, 123, 125; growth and

functions of, 129, 181, 186, 197, 234; new rail lines to, 147, 165
Tulare County, 86–87; agricultural characteristics of, 94, 107–112, 170–171, 206, 219, 230–231; livestock in, 86, 90–91; population of, 86, 87, 89, 129
Tulare County Co-operative Creamery, 181
Tulare County Cow Testing Association, 181
Tulare Irrigation District, 138, 193, 201–202
Tulare Lake, 3, 4, 15, 17, 18; decline of, 139, 144, 158, 161, 187, 219
Tularenos, 33, 53. *See also* Yokuts
Tulares, 22–23, 53, 74. *See also* Marshland, communities
Tule fog. *See* Fogs
Tule River, 17, 95, 142, 217
Tule River fan, 17; irrigation on, 95–96, 97, 139, 142, 161; land use and settlement on, 75, 92, 129, 184, 205
Tule River Indian Reservation, 83
Tule River Station, 114
Tules, 22. *See also* Marshland, communities; Tulares
Turnbull, 166
Twin Buttes, 14

Udjiu, 44
U.S. Army Corps of Engineers, 217
U.S. Bureau of Reclamation, 193, 217
U.S. Department of Agriculture, 131, 203
U.S. General Land Office, 98. *See also* Land, alienation policies
Urbanization, 212, 234. *See also* Towns, functions of

Vandalia, 115
Vegetables. *See* Field crops
Vegetation, natural, 19–26, 187, 208–209, 237
Venice, 115
Venice Hills, 14
Vineyards, 93, 144, 155, 176, 177, 178, 181, 183, 185, 186, 199–200
Visalia, 73; county seat at, 73, 123, 129; functions of, 75, 99, 114, 115, 116–117, 181, 186, 234; population of, 87, 117, 122, 197; railroads and, 122–123, 129, 147, 165
Visalia and Goshen Railroad, 123, 124
Visalia Electric Railway, 167
Vise, Nathan, 73

Waiu, 44
Walna, 44
Walnuts. *See* Orchards, nut
Water: quality, 161, 166–167; rights, 136–137, 217–219
Water companies, 137–138, 139. *See also* Irrigation, districts
Water diversion. *See* Irrigation; Tulare Lake, decline of
Waterfowl, 29, 36, 187

Waukena, 149, 150, 165–166
Wells, 141, 158, 192, 219. *See also* Ground-
    water; Oil and gas production
Western Specialty Crop Regions, 175–176
West side, 154, 166–167, 201, 215, 219–220,
    229
Wheat. *See* Grain crops
Wheat boom, 94–95, 130–135, 159. *See also*
    Grain farming
White River, 17, 58, 75, 114
White River (town). *See* Tailholt
Whitney, J. D., 93
Wildflowers, 23–34, 26, 44
Wilkes, Charles, 62
Williams, J., 104
Williamson, R. S., 62, 70, 73, 122
Williamson Act (1965) 234
Wimilchi, 41
Wind machines, 177
Wolasi, 41
Wood, John, 72
Woodlake, 167
Woodsville, 72, 73
Woodville, 115, 129, 181, 186
World farm, 214–215, 243

Wowol, 40–41, 42. *See also* Bubal
Wright, 146
Wright Irrigation Act (1887), 137, 238
Wukchumni, 41, 44
Wutchumna Canal Company, 138
Wutchumna Point, 16

Yaudanchi, 31–32, 41, 43, 44
Yettem, 167, 173
Yokod, 41
Yokohl, 149
Yokohl Valley, 91
Yokuts, 32–33; epidemics among, 57–58, 82;
    fire use by, 36–37; foreigners' attitudes to-
    ward, 49, 53–54, 80–83; horse-stealing by,
    56, 58–59, 82; impact of foreigners upon,
    55, 56–59, 74, 80–83
Yokuts: demography, 33–34, 39–46, 54, 57,
    58, 82, 83; subsistence, 33–39; trade, 38–
    39, 46, 59; tribelets, 38, 40–42, 46; villages,
    42–44, 53–54; warfare and raiding, 37–38,
    53–54, 57, 82. *See also* Bubal

Zalvidea, Fray Jose Maria de, 52